Qualified Lawyers Transfer Test
Head I – Property

Study Manual

For Tests in 2010

QLTT Civil Litigation Study Manual

ISBN: 9780 7517 7272 2
(previous edition 9780 7517 7268 5)

e-book ISBN 9780 7517 8019 2

Third edition December 2009
First edition January 2008

British Library Cataloguing-in-Publication Data
A catalogue record for this book has been applied for from the British Library

Printed in the United Kingdom

Your learning materials, published by BPP Learning Media Ltd, are printed on paper sourced from sustainable, managed forests.

A note about copyright

Dear Customer

What does the little © mean and why does it matter?

Your market-leading BPP books, course materials and elearning materials do not write and update themselves. People write them: on their own behalf or as employees of an organisation that invests in this activity. Copyright law protects their livelihoods. It does so by creating rights over the use of the content.

Breach of copyright is a form of theft – as well being a criminal offence in some jurisdictions, it is potentially a serious breach of professional ethics.

With current technology, things might seem a bit hazy but, basically, without the express permission of BPP Learning Media:

- Photocopying our materials is a breach of copyright
- Scanning, ripcasting or conversion of our digital materials into different file formats, uploading them to facebook or emailing them to your friends is a breach of copyright

You can, of course, sell your books, in the form in which you have bought them – once you have finished with them. (Is this fair to your fellow students? We update for a reason.) But the ilearns are sold on a single user license basis: we do not supply 'unlock' codes to people who have bought them second hand.

And what about outside the UK? BPP Learning Media strives to make our materials available at prices students can afford by local printing arrangements, pricing policies and partnerships which are clearly listed on our website. A tiny minority ignore this and indulge in criminal activity by illegally photocopying our material or supporting organisations that do. If they act illegally and unethically in one area, can you really trust them?

Contents

BPP
LEARNING MEDIA

Introduction

This Study Manual has been specially written to assist candidates in their preparation for Head I: Property of the Qualified Lawyers Transfer Test (QLTT). It comprehensively covers the syllabus, namely Land Law and Conveyancing (Section 1) and Wills, Probate and Administration (Section 2).

Features include:

- Comprehensive syllabus coverage
- A user friendly style for easy navigation
- Chapter introductions to put the topic into context and explain its significance in the Test
- Section overviews and chapter summaries
- Self test questions and answers to assess understanding

Notes

- The Civil Partnership Act 2004 came into force on 5 December 2005. It enables same sex couples (who are not closely related to each other) to obtain legal recognition of their relationship. Couples who form a civil partnership will have a new legal status, that of 'civil partner'. Persons who have registered a civil partnership will, as a result, be treated as spouses for all legal and tax purposes. Please, therefore, assume that all references in this Study Manual to 'spouse', 'marriage' and 'divorce' could equally refer to 'civil partner', 'formation of a civil partnership' and 'dissolution of a civil partnership'.

- In the interests of brevity, the male gender has been used in this Study Manual. Students are requested to assume that, where applicable, the masculine references refer to both the male and female genders.

As the QLTT is an 'open book' test, candidates may refer to this Study Manual and to any other written materials during the assessment (but please see the note about BPP Learning Media copyright on the next page).

Updates

It is important that you remain up to date as you study for the Property QLTT Test . This book is fully up to date at 31 December 2009 but there may be further legal developments before you take the Test. Essential updates are provided to students who have purchased this edition of this book. Go to **www.bpp.com/qltt** where you will find an updates section.

For further information on BPP Learning Media Products, or to order, call 0845 0751 100 (within the UK) or +44 (0)20 8740 2211 (from overseas) or order online at www.bpp.com/learningmedia

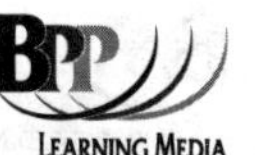

QLTT Test Procedure: BPP Learning Media Copyright

The published QLTT materials within this Study Manual are the copyright of BPP Learning Media, and purchasers of this material have no right to reproduce it for any purpose. Copying material in any way without the express permission of the copyright holder is a breach of copyright and candidates hoping to qualify to practise as solicitors in England and Wales, which carries with it an expectation of adherence to rigorous professional standards, should not consider doing it under any circumstances.

The QLTT Tests are conducted 'open book', in that you may take your study manuals into the examination room.

You should be aware that candidates will only be permitted to take **original copies of the BPP Learning Media study manuals into the exam room.** Photocopies or other reproduced forms of the BPP Learning Media materials are not acceptable.

It is likely that BPP Learning Media staff will attend the QLTT examination centres to check the provenance of the materials that candidates intend to bring into the examination room. If your study manual is anything other than an original edition, BPP Learning Media staff (or their representatives) may confiscate such materials.

List of annexures

Section 1

Land Law and Conveyancing

Part A

Principles of Land Law

Part A: Principles of land law

Overview

Part A of the Study Manual aims to cover the basic principles of land law. How these are applied in practice is covered in Parts B and C. In this section we look at:

- Land ownership
- Registration
- Interests in land
- Mortgages
- Tax

The whole concept of 'land ownership' is not straightforward. It is essential that the exact extent and type of the person's claim to, or interest in, a piece of land is identified, as it will have significant consequences in law. Even the word 'land' needs careful definition.

Part A will then go on to describe the different types of ownership in more detail, beginning with the two most significant: 'freehold' and 'leasehold' estates. You will learn about various rights being 'legal' or 'equitable' and this distinction will be explained. Easements, covenants, trusts and mortgages are all explained. Some of these terms will be new to you as they are not commonly used but are legal terms that require explanation. Taxation issues relevant to land law are also discussed.

There will be some overlap between the concepts as they are introduced to you, for example with reference to law and equity and to registration. This is unavoidable. It means that a first read-through of Part A may be difficult and a second reading should make a lot more sense. Do take time to understand these concepts and principles that are being described in Part A before you go on to Part B, as they are the necessary ingredients for a successful understanding and application of the conveyancing procedures in that section.

Test requirements

The QLTT Test Specification, insofar as it relates to this Part A, requires that you should be able to demonstrate an understanding of the basic principles of land law and the manner in which they apply to conveyancing transactions. This may be tested by questions on:

(a) The nature of third parties' interests, the rights they generate and the steps that need to be taken to protect purchasers

(b) The distinction between joint tenancies and tenancies in common and the manner in which co-ownership can be implied

(c) Mortgages

(d) Leases

(e) Easements and restrictive covenants

(Bear in mind that leases will be covered in much more detail in Part C.)

1

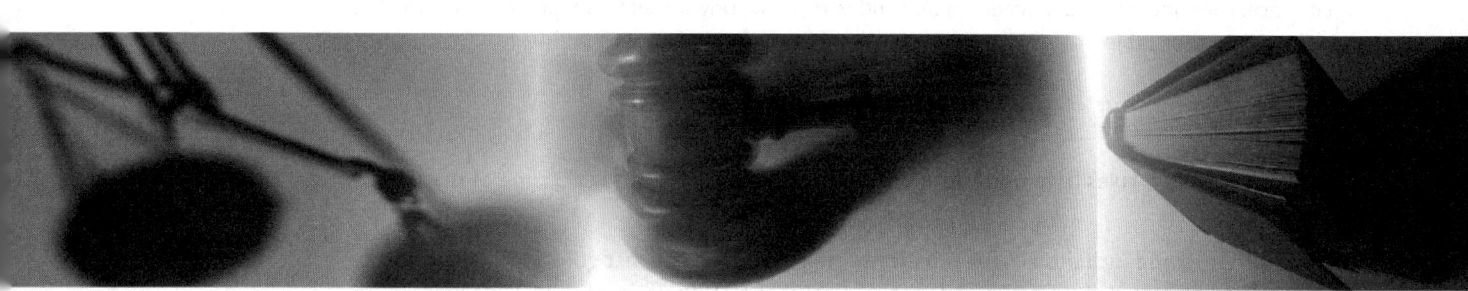

Land ownership

Topic List

Chapter overview

This chapter will:

- Define the term 'land', explaining its physical extent and also how 'fixtures' are included but 'fittings' are not included
- Explain the concept of 'ownership', introducing the freehold and leasehold estates, both of which entitle the owner to a proprietary right to possess the land
- Explain the concept of an interest in land being 'legal' or 'equitable'
- Explain the basic principles relating to trusts, where an estate in land is held for the benefit of another person
- Introduce the system of registration of title

1 Land

In considering estates and interests in land, how they are created, protected and transferred, it is obviously important to understand what constitutes 'land'. Essentially 'land' includes:-

- The physical land and any buildings or other fixtures attached to it (sometimes referred to as 'corporeal hereditaments'); and
- Intangible property rights and benefits, such as rights of way and grazing rights ('incorporeal hereditaments').

(You may see land and interests in land loosely referred to as 'realty'. Realty comprises both corporeal and incorporeal hereditaments and is to be distinguished from 'personalty', which is personal or moveable property.)

1.1 The extent of the physical land

A number of legal rules have been developed that determine the physical scope of the term 'land':

Subsoil Land includes all that is beneath the surface except that gold and silver 'treasure' vests in the Crown under the Treasure Act 1996 (as that term is defined in the 1996 Act). Note that certain minerals, for example unworked coal, are excluded from private ownership by legislation.

Airspace Land includes only that part of the airspace above it that is necessary for the ordinary use and enjoyment of it (including any structures on it).

Lakes The subsoil under the water of a lake belongs to the owner of the land in which a lake stands.

Rivers The bed of a river belongs to the owner of the land through which the river passes. Where the river forms a boundary between two plots, there is a presumption that each owner is the owner of the bed up to the middle line.

Roads Where a property is bounded by a non-adopted roadway, it is presumed that the adjacent landowner, or 'frontager', owns the roadway up to the middle line and has responsibility for its upkeep. If the road is 'adopted' by the local authority, the authority is responsible for its upkeep, but it only owns the surface of the road itself. The subsoil remains within the ownership of the frontager and the surface reverts to him should the road be closed. If an upadopted road is adopted, the frontager may be required to contribute towards the costs of such adoption.

Sea If the land is bounded by the sea, the boundary is the high water mark. The foreshore, ie. the land between the high and low water mark, belongs to the Crown.

1.2 Fixtures

A fixture is a thing which is attached physically to the land, thereby becoming a part of the land. Identifying which items constitute fixtures is important because fixtures are deemed to be included in the sale of the land unless the seller specifically excludes them from sale. However, a chattel that remains *unattached* (sometimes referred to as a 'fitting', somewhat confusingly!) does not form part of the land and does not form part of the sale unless it is specifically included in the sale to the buyer.

There are two tests as to whether an item is a fixture or a chattel:

- The *degree* of annexation, ie the more firmly and permanently an item is affixed to the property, the more likely it is to be a fixture, whereas if it rests on the land by its own weight (even if it is connected to electrical supplies for example) it is a fitting or chattel only

- The *purpose* of annexation, ie whether the item was fixed in order to make it part of the parcel of land for all time or just as a matter of temporary enjoyment

The purpose of the annexation is generally considered to be the more significant test.

You should be aware that there is extensive case law concerning the issue of whether an item is a fixture or a fitting, that you may need to consult if the issue arises in practice (see for example *TSB Bank plc v Botham 1996*, where the Court of Appeal held that carpets and curtains were fittings and could be retained by the borrower in a mortgage repossession). For the purposes of this Study Manual, it is sufficient that you recognise the essential distinction and understand its significance.

In residential transactions, the seller will usually complete a standard form specifying which items are included in, or excluded from, the sale to the buyer. Likewise, the matter should be expressly addressed in any commercial transaction prior to exchange of contracts.

2 Ownership: estates in land

When we talk about 'owning land', we are really talking about owning an '**estate**' in land. The Crown owns all the land in England and Wales (although this is little more than a theoretical technicality). The most any other person may own is a proprietary right of temporary possession or use of land, known as an 'estate' in land.

There are two main legal estates in land. They are the:

- **Freehold** estate
- **Leasehold** estate

Estates in land must be created by, or transferred by deed, to be legal. There are also registration requirements, which will be covered later. Freehold and leasehold estate owners may choose to grant (or may acquire land that is already subject to) rights to others which do not confer possession, but rather some lesser form of use of the land, for example, a right of access or a charge on the land to be held as security for a loan.

These proprietary rights are known as **'interests in land'** and, depending on the nature and type of the right, they may bind the land and be enforceable against subsequent owners of the land. Interests in land may be legal or equitable.

2.1 The freehold estate

The most valuable estate in land is a **freehold** estate, sometimes (for historical reasons) called a **'fee simple absolute in possession'**. (By way of explanation, 'fee' indicates that the land is capable of being inherited; 'simple' indicates that there are no restrictions on to whom it may be passed; and 'absolute' indicates that it is freely alienable.) The freehold estate lasts indefinitely until such time as the owner dies without heirs.

The owner of a freehold estate, or 'freeholder', is free to sell it or give it away. A freehold should be transferred by deed and the transferee becomes the new legal owner upon registration (see later). If the freeholder dies intestate (without a valid will) and without next of kin, the land automatically reverts to the Crown. The owner may grant a lesser estate for a certain duration (that is shorter than his own period of possession). Such a lesser estate is called a leasehold estate (see 2.2 below). In such circumstances, the residue of the freeholder's estate after the expiry of such lease is known as the '**freehold reversion**'. At the termination of the lease, possession of the land will automatically revert back to the freeholder.

2.2 The leasehold estate

As we have seen, a leasehold estate is one carved out of the freehold (or a longer leasehold). It is a right to possession for a certain duration, or 'term of years'. Equally, a leaseholder may himself grant a lease (of a lesser duration) out of his own, whilst still retaining his own original lease (albeit now subject to the 'sublease' or 'underlease'). For the duration of the sublease, the original leaseholder holds a **'leasehold reversion'**.

This process may continue with subleases for shorter and shorter periods of possession being granted by the successive 'subtenants'.

It follows that any piece of land may be subject to a hierarchy of rights of possession. The same piece of land may simultaneously support a freehold, a lease and one or more subleases, with the holder of each right owning not the land itself, but rather the right to possession of the land in reversion, ie following the expiry of the lesser rights he has granted.

Example

A is the freeholder of a three-storey office building. A grants a lease of the whole building to B for a term of 99 years. B in turns grants three leases of one floor to each of X, Y and Z. The leases are each for a term of 10 years. B owns a leasehold estate. He is both tenant (under the 99 year lease) and landlord (of the 10 year leases). X, Y and Z also own leasehold estates and are subtenants. They are in actual occupation of the property, paying rent to B and B is, in turn, paying rent to A. Each owner, A, B, X, Y and Z, has an interest in the property (more accurately, a freehold or leasehold estate as the case may be) which he will be able to sell.

Note

The sale or other dealing with a leasehold interest may be restricted under the terms of the lease itself (see further chapter 16)

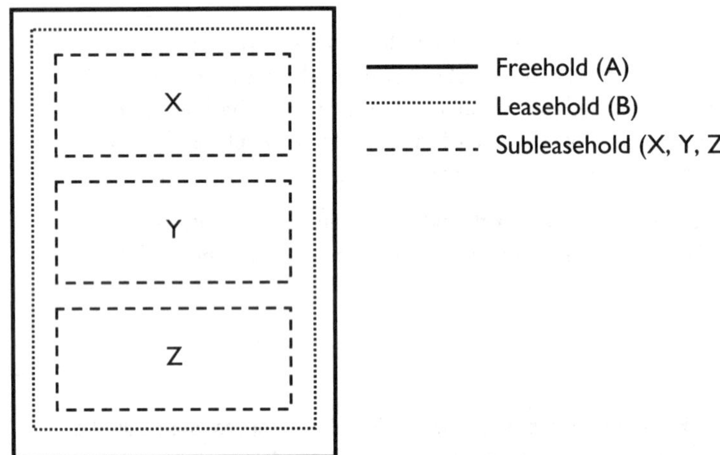

Terminology can be confusing. You should be aware that 'lessor', 'landlord' and 'reversioner' all refer to the person granting the lease or sublease. The terms 'leaseholder' 'lessee' and 'tenant' all refer to the person in whom the lease is vested. A freeholder may obtain value from his interest by 'transferring' or 'conveying' his freehold or by granting a lease. A leaseholder may do so by either granting a sublease or by 'assigning' (ie transferring) his own leasehold.

This terminology will be explained again when we examine leases in Section C of this Study Manual. Section B will focus on freeholds.

2.3 Commonhold

Flats and other interdependent properties (for example, units in a retail or industrial site) have traditionally been sold and managed as leaseholds, with the freeholder retaining ownership and management of the 'common parts', ie those areas used by all the tenants, such as staircases, access routes and the structure of the building.

The Commonhold and Leasehold Reform Act 2002 introduced a new concept of land ownership. Commonhold is created out of freehold land. Essentially, it allows for the freehold

estate to be divided into units, each of which is owned freehold by the individual unit-holders and the common parts are owned by a 'commonhold association'. This association is a limited company and the unit holders are entitled to membership of it. Commonholds are outside the scope of this Study Manual.

3 Legal and equitable interests

You will soon learn about **interests** in land being either legal or equitable. Some interests are *capable* of being legal and may be either legal or equitable. Others are not capable of existing in law and, therefore, can be equitable only.

3.1 The historical distinction between law and equity

This distinction has arisen because English law has developed in the courts according to two systems: common law and equity.

Historically, the common law system was administered by the courts according to a body of law based on the precedents of previous cases. However, the common law was rigid and often unjust and, as a result of this, those who could not obtain justice in the courts petitioned the Crown via the Lord Chancellor. As a result of this, a new and fairer body of law arose, administered by the Court of Chancery, which corrected individual injustices. This body of law became known as '**equity**'.

For example, in unregistered land (we will consider unregistered and registered land, or rather title, later) whoever is shown on the title deeds to the property has a legal estate in the property and is free to sell the land as they wish. However, there are circumstances where equity will intervene to protect the interests of a third party, for example where the owner of the legal estate actually holds the property for the benefit of another person. In such circumstances, he is said to hold property 'on trust' for that other person. Equity will ensure that the legal owner cannot sell the property without accounting to the third party for the proceeds of sale. The third party has an **equitable interest** (or '**beneficial interest**') in the property, which equity will protect. The concept of the trust is equally relevant in registered land. Even though the systems of common law courts and courts of equity were merged by legislation in 1875, the distinction between legal and equitable interests is still relevant.

3.2 The practical distinction between law and equity

As mentioned above, the common law was only concerned with the *legal* ownership of interests in land. If an interest existed at law, it was said to be good against the whole world, ie everyone was bound by it, whether or not they knew about it. The same is true of legal estates.

If the interest was equitable only, however, its effectiveness against a third party depended on whether or not that third party was aware of it. In fact the so-called 'doctrine of notice' provided that an equitable interest would **not** bind a 'bona fide purchaser of the legal estate for value without notice' of it. This includes any person who buys the legal estate in good faith (without fraud), without notice. If a purchaser satisfied that definition, the equitable interest would not bind him and he would take free of it.

When registration was introduced (which you will learn more about shortly), most estates and interests were able to be registered and registration constituted notice.

4 Trusts

Trusts concern a division between the ownership of land in law and in equity. For that reason they will be dealt with here, even though the interests in land created by the trust might seem to fall more squarely into Chapter 3.

4.1 Types of trust

Basically, a trust of land exists where the legal estate is held for the benefit of one or more persons other than, or including, the owner.

A trust may be expressly created, either during a lifetime or by a will, or it may arise by operation of law.

Whether the trust is created expressly or by implication, the legal estate is held by the owner, ie the person(s) entitled to it. The owner(s) is also called the 'trustee(s)'. The equitable interest, often called a 'beneficial interest', is held for a beneficiary or beneficiaries. These principles can be explained by the following illustration:

Property is owned by Oscar who holds the legal estate for the benefit of Ben, Boris and Beryl.	Oscar (trustee)	Legal estate
	.... holds on trust for ...	
	Ben, Boris, Beryl (beneficiaries)	Equitable interest

4.2 TLATA

Prior to 1997, all trusts were regulated either by the Law of Property Act 1925 ('LPA 1925') or by the Settled Land Act 1925. Whether expressly created or arising by implication (in the ways that we have seen) all such interests were termed 'trusts for sale' and governed by the LPA 1925.

With effect from 1 January 1997, the Trusts of Land and the Appointment of Trustees Act 1996 ('TLATA') introduced the 'trust of land', which is very similar to the trust for sale but differs from it in some respects.

Under TLATA, a statutory trust of land arises, inter alia, where:

- There is more than one owner of the legal estate (co-ownership)
- A resulting trust arises, for example where property is purchased by A with B paying some or all of the purchase price

In most cases, as will be seen two or more trustees are needed in order to give a valid receipt for the sale proceeds (s.27 LPA 1925). Exceptions include where the trustee is a trust corporation or a personal representative of a deceased owner.

4.3 Co ownership

Quite often, a legal estate is acquired by two or more people, for example where a married couple or civil partners purchase property or where partners in a business jointly own the firm's property. In such cases, they are referred to as 'co-owners' of the legal estate and will hold that legal estate on trust for themselves as beneficial owners.

Remember

The legal estate can only be co-owned as joint tenants

4.3.1 The legal estate

The legal estate can only be held as **'joint tenants'** (s.1(6) LPA 1925). Each joint tenant is deemed to own the whole, together with the other joint tenant(s), rather than a share in, or proportion of, the interest.

Alert

The terms 'joint tenants' and 'tenants in common' have nothing to do with the terms 'tenant' or 'tenancy' in leasehold matters

Being held as joint tenants means that if one co-owner dies, the legal estate automatically 'passes' to the survivor. This is known as the 'right of survivorship'. (A buyer of the property will simply need proof that the deceased has died.)

Not more than four persons can hold the legal estate, so if a conveyance or transfer names more than four, only the first four will be registered as proprietors and they will hold on trust for all those named. (There is no limit on the number of owners of the beneficial interest). In anticipation of future dealings with the land, the legal estate should normally be held by at least two trustees.

4.3.2 The equitable interest

However, as far as the equitable (or beneficial) interest is concerned, the co-owners have a choice: they may hold the beneficial interest either as:

- Joint tenants, or
- '**Tenants in common**'.

Holding the equitable interest as tenants in common means that each person has a distinct share in the whole (for example A and B own equal shares or A owns 75% and B 25%).

Whichever way they choose to hold the equitable interest will be stated in the purchase deed and will be significant in practice in determining what happens when one of the co-owners dies.

Example

Carl and David purchase property in their joint names. Therefore, they own the legal estate jointly and they would also be said to have a beneficial interest in the property, as follows:

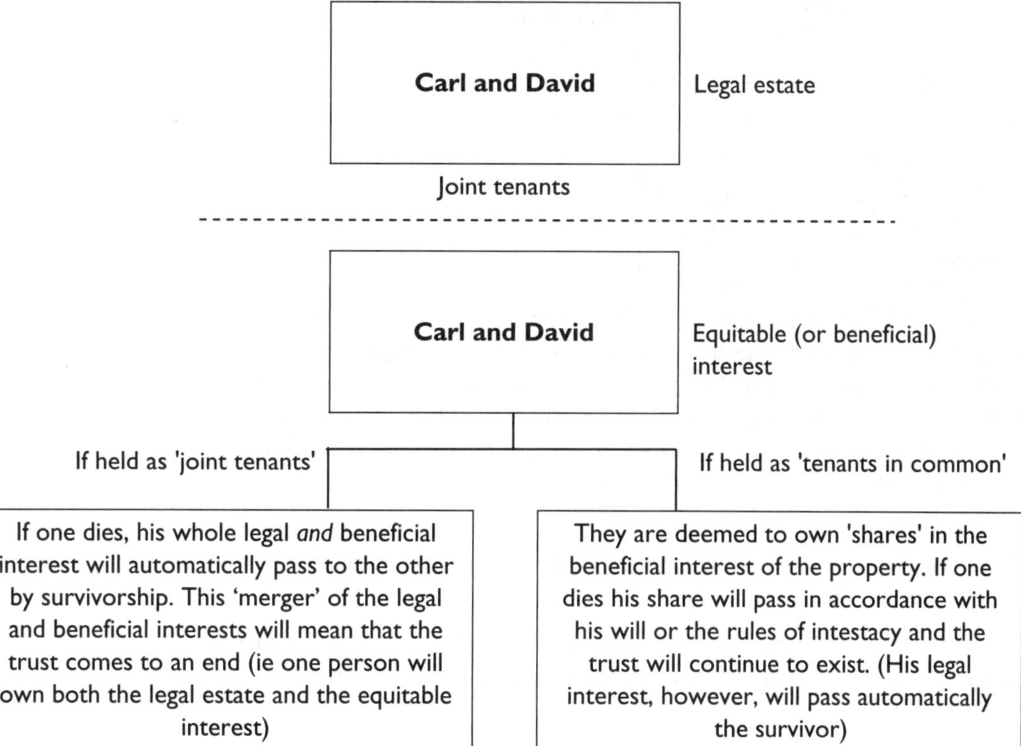

Carl and David are said to be holding the property on trust for themselves: they both own the legal estate and they both have a beneficial interest in the property. They are both trustees.

4.3.3 The distinction in practice

As noted above, the legal estate will always be held as joint tenants but the equitable estate may be held as joint tenants or tenants in common. How co-owners wish to own the beneficial interest will depend on their circumstances. If they wish the right of survivorship to apply, they may prefer to hold as beneficial joint tenants (eg married couples). If they have contributed unequally and/or wish to leave their beneficial share by will, they may prefer to hold as beneficial tenants in common.

The conveyancing aspects and consequences of selecting to own property as beneficial joint tenants or beneficial tenants in common will be addressed more fully in Section B. An understanding of the legal principles is sufficient at this stage.

4.4 Third party contributes to purchase price

Where someone other than the named purchaser pays all or part of the purchase price, a statutory trust of land arises.

Example

Adam purchases the freehold of a property for £100,000, to which Ben contributes £40,000. The property is purchased in the sole name of Adam. As far as the common law is concerned, Adam is the sole owner of the property and is entitled to sell or dispose of the property as he wishes and keep the proceeds. This is clearly unfair and it is in this situation that equity intervenes.

Equity looks behind the 'legal' position and provides that Adam holds the property 'on trust' for Adam and Ben, as beneficial tenants in common, with Adam owning 60% of the beneficial interest in the property and Ben 40%:

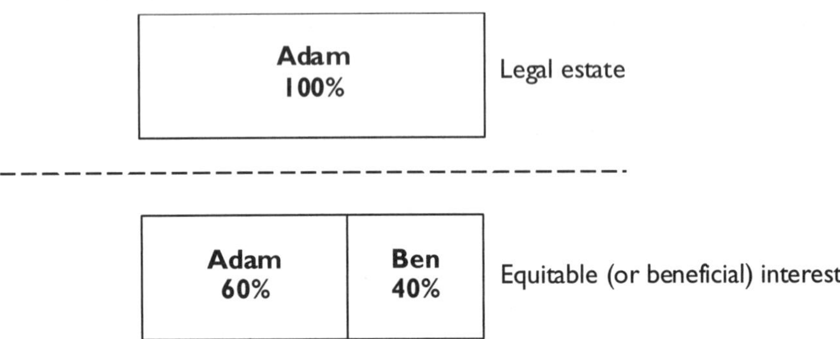

Therefore, as far as the outside world is concerned, Adam is the sole legal owner of the property and the legal interest may be transferred by him alone. However, because of the rules of equity, even though third parties may be unaware of the existence of Ben's interest, Ben is said to have an 'equitable' or 'beneficial' interest in the property. A trust (often called a 'resulting trust') is said to arise, under which Adam is the 'trustee' and Adam and Ben the 'beneficiaries'. Such a resulting trust is now a trust of land under the TLATA.

Had Ben paid 100% of the purchase price, a resulting trust would still have arisen in favour of Ben. Adam, as in the example above, would hold the legal estate on a trust in which Ben would be presumed to have the absolute beneficial ownership.

(Any resulting trust is a matter of presumption, based on the presumed intention of the parties, and evidence of a contrary intention can be effective to deny the existence of a trust.)

4.5 Severance

As you have learned, the equitable interest may be held as joint tenants or as tenants in common. A joint tenancy of the equitable interest may be 'severed' and, effectively, converted into a tenancy in common. Severance may be brought about by a number of circumstances, including:

- By written notice (s.36 (2) LPA 1925) from one co-owner
- By mutual agreement
- By homicide
- By bankruptcy of one co-owner

It should be noted that a beneficial joint tenancy cannot be severed by will.

Note

Severance of a joint tenancy only applies to the equitable interest. The legal joint tenancy cannot be severed

4.6 Protection of beneficial interests

4.6.1 Overreaching

Overreaching is the process by which equitable interests under a trust are said to become detached from the land and transferred to the money paid by the buyer, thus enabling a buyer of a legal estate to take the land free from those interests. Thus, if a beneficiary has a 75% share in the property, he will be entitled to 75% of the proceeds of sale and the seller holds the proceeds 'on trust' for the beneficiary.

Note
Overreaching applies to equitable interests under a trust but not to all equitable interests

4.6.2 The two-trustee rule

In order for the interests to be overreached, the purchase price must be paid to at least two trustees or to a trust corporation or to a sole personal representative.

Where the seller is a sole trustee, therefore, the purchaser should insist on the appointment of a **second trustee** (or trust corporation) to receive the purchase money. The trustees would then have a duty to account to the beneficiaries for the proceeds of sale and the buyer will purchase the land free from their interests.

If payment has not been made to two trustees, overreaching will not have occurred.

5 Registration

In England and Wales, we have both 'registered land' and 'unregistered land'.

Even though 'registration' is a word used in relation to unregistered land, for example regarding the registration of land charges, when we talk about 'registered land' we mean the system of registering the **title** (ownership) to land that was introduced by the Land Registration Act 1925 ('LRA 1925').

LRA 1925 introduced a framework for registration of title to each parcel of land in England and Wales. LRA 1925 has now been repealed by the Land Registration Act 2002 ('LRA 2002'). LRA 2002 has maintained the basic structure of registered land. It has always been the intention that all land in England and Wales becomes registered land and since the introduction of compulsory registration in 1990 (see Chapter 2), which has been extended by LRA 2002, most titles are now registered. However, there are still titles which remain unregistered, which is why you need to be familiar with both systems. Freeholds and certain leasehold estates are registered under separate and distinct titles, each with its own registration number.

The essential features of the system of registration (ie 'registered land') are:

- A register of title, which names the proprietor (owner) of that title and contains an almost **complete record** of all matters relating to the title, including the interests affecting the land. However, there are some interests which do not have to be registered, known as 'unregistered interests which override registered dispositions' (more commonly known as **'overriding interests'**)
- The **provision of an easy mode of transfer** by eliminating lengthy investigation of title and a simplified document of transfer. The LRA 2002 also provides the framework for electronic conveyancing to come into effect within the next few years
- The **introduction of a state indemnity scheme** under which compensation is paid to a registered proprietor who is deprived of his title or to any person who suffers loss as a result of an official search of the register not revealing the true state of the register in some way

Registration of title and the registration of land charges in unregistered land is discussed more fully in the next chapter.

Summary

- 'Land' means the extent of the physical land (according to certain principles) and fixtures attached to it.
- A freehold is an estate entitling the owner of it to exclusive possession of land for an open-ended duration. It is capable of being a legal estate.
- A leasehold is an estate carved out of the freehold, entitling the owner of it to exclusive possession of land for a certain term of years. It is capable of being a legal estate.
- A subleasehold is an estate carved out of, and shorter in duration than, an existing (and 'superior') leasehold.
- A legal estate may be held on trust for one or more beneficiaries who are said to have equitable interests (or 'beneficial interests') in the land.
- Equitable interests arising under a trust may be 'overreached' and, effectively, transferred into interests in the sale proceeds.
- Although title to most land is registered, the principles of unregistered land still need to be understood.

Self-test questions

1. Where a river runs between two plots of land, who owns the riverbed?
2. What is the principal test for determining whether something is a fixture or a fitting?
3. Fixtures are included in a sale of land unless they are specifically excluded. True or false?
4. What are the two estates in land that are capable of existing in law?
5. What is the name given to the freeholder's interest when he grants a leasehold estate?
6. State the equitable doctrine of notice.
7. Where two or more persons hold the legal estate, they must specify whether they hold it as joint tenants or as tenants in common. True or false?
8. How many persons can own the (a) legal estate? (b) beneficial interests?
9. What is a statutory trust?
10. What is the consequence of one co-owner dying where the beneficial interest is held (a) as joint tenants? (b) as tenants in common
11. What is the effect of a purchase price of £250,000 being paid by A (£200,000) and B (£50,000), where A is the sole named buyer?
12. How many trustees are required to overreach beneficial interests under a trust?
13. What is the term used to describe a joint tenancy being converted into a tenancy in common?

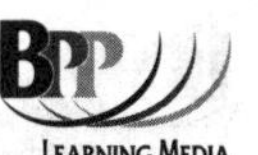

Answers to self-test questions

1 In the absence of evidence to the contrary, it is presumed that each landowner owns up to the middle line of the riverbed.

2 The purpose of annexation

3 True.

4 Freehold and leasehold estates.

5 The freehold reversion

6 Equitable interests do not bind a bona fide purchaser of the legal estate for value without notice of them.

7 False. The legal estate can only be held as joint tenants. The beneficial interest can be held in either way.

8 (a) Up to four persons (b) there is no maximum number

9 A statutory and trust is a trust of land that arises under TLATA, for example in cases of co-ownership and resulting trusts.

10 (a) his interest automatically passes to the surviving joint tenant(s)
(b) his interest passes under his will or the rules on intestacy

11 A resulting trust of land arises, under which A holds the legal estate on trust for A and B in respective shares of 80% and 20%.

12 Two (save in the case of a trust corporation or sole personal representative).

13 Severance

2

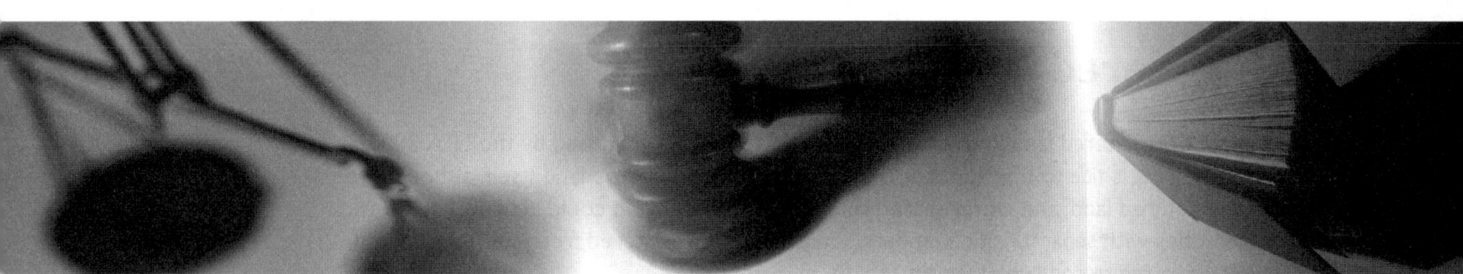

Registration

Topic List

Chapter overview

This chapter will:

- Describe the two systems of land that apply in England and Wales: registered and unregistered
- Describe the various parts of a register of title
- Identify those transactions which need to be substantively registered
- Explain how interests are protected by registration
- Identify interests which are not registered but which override dispositions
- Explain how interests are protected in unregistered land
- Describe the consequences of failing to register land charges

Chapter overview continued

Registration was briefly introduced in Chapter 1, where you learned about the two estates in land: freehold and leasehold. Any dealing with a freehold estate and any dealing with a leasehold estate of seven years or more will need to be registered, even if the land has not previously been registered. Such registration is called 'substantive' registration, meaning that the title to the estate is registered with its own register and title number. You have also learned about interests in land. Those interests are not substantively registrable, but there are nevertheless registration requirements to consider. Before going on to learn about other interests in land, that either should be registered or that cannot be registered, we will consider in more detail what is meant by substantive registration (and 'registered land' and 'unregistered land'), how registration takes place and the consequences of both registration and failing to register.

1 Registered land

The system of registered land, introduced by LRA 1925, is now governed by the LRA 2002. Remember that it is *title* to the land that is registered, rather than the land itself, although we still refer to 'registered land' and 'unregistered land'. One parcel of land could actually have several registered titles with separate title numbers, for example, a registered freehold, a registered leasehold and a registered subleasehold.

1.1 The register

For each freehold estate and each leasehold estate for more than seven years, there is a register. Each register comprises three parts: a property register, a proprietorship register and a charges register. The contents of the register are as follows:

A The property register	B The proprietorship register	C The charges register
Includes: ▸ Whether the property is freehold or leasehold ▸ The address of the property (with reference to a plan) ▸ Any interests/rights benefiting the property *Examples of benefits entered:* ▸ Easements	Includes: ▸ Details of the owner of the property ▸ The class of the title registered (see below) ▸ Any restriction affecting the owner's ability to deal with the property *Examples of restrictions:* ▸ Beneficial interests arising under a trust ▸ requirement for a mortgagee's consent	Includes: ▸ Notice of third party interests/rights burdening the property *Examples of notices:* ▸ Charges ▸ Express legal easements ▸ Restrictive covenants

We will be considering the register in more detail in Chapter 8. There you will learn how to read and interpret the various entries that appear on each of the three registers, so that you are in a position to advise a client regarding any issues that arise from them.

1.2 When land must be registered

1.2.1 First registration

Where the title to land in England and Wales is presently unregistered, most dealings with it will give rise to **compulsory first registration**. Previously, it was only in designated 'areas of compulsory registration' that the specified dealings would need to be registered, but on 1 December 1990, the whole of England and Wales became an area of compulsory registration. The dealings which trigger compulsory first registration (s.4 LRA 2002) include:

(a) a transfer of the freehold estate or leasehold estate with more than seven years to run, by sale.

(b) a grant (out of such an estate) of a lease of more than seven years for valuable consideration

(c) an assent following death, which is a disposition of the freehold or a leasehold with more than seven years to run

(d) a first legal mortgage of the freehold, or of a leasehold with more than seven years to run, protected by the deposit of documents with the lender.

Where one of these dealings with unregistered land arises, the land must be registered, by the (new) owner, within **two months** of the disposition (s.6 LRA 2002).

If application for registration is not made within two months, the disposition becomes void (s.7 LRA 2002). (The consequences depend upon the transaction involved, but the transfer will either revert to the seller who will hold it on a bare trust for the buyer or the disposition takes effect as a contract to grant or create the legal estate concerned.)

1.2.2 Subsequent registration

Where title to the land is already registered, all dealings with land that are capable of registration must be registered.

These dealings are called 'registrable dispositions' and are set out in s.27 LRA 2002. **The disposition will not operate at law (that is to say the legal estate will not be transferred) until the relevant registration requirements have been met.** The registrable dispositions include:

- A transfer
- The grant of a lease for more than seven years.
- The express grant or reservation of an easement
- A legal charge

1.3 The consequences of registration

1.3.1 State guarantee of title

Once registered as a proprietor of a legal estate, that registration is **conclusive**. This amounts to a **state guarantee of title** and compensation may be payable where a defect in a registered title is found. The extent of the guarantee depends on the class of title registered. The proprietor's title may be absolute, qualified or possessory (freehold or leasehold) or good leasehold.

Absolute title This is given where the Registrar is of the opinion that the applicant's **title** to the estate is such as 'a willing buyer could properly **be advised** by a competent professional adviser to accept'. This is **the best class** of title and the most commonly encountered. It indicates that there were no defects in title when application for first registration was made, other than defects that would 'not cause the holding under the title to be distorted', which defects the Registrar is entitled to disregard (s.9(3) LRA 2002).

Qualified title This is given where title has been established only for a limited period, or subject to reservations which cannot be disregarded, for example where certain title documents were missing when the land was registered.

Possessory title This is given where the Registrar is satisfied that the applicant is in actual possession of the land or in receipt of the rents and profits from it, but has no further evidence of title that would justify qualified or absolute title.

Good leasehold title This is given where the Registrar considers that the lessee's title is such as a willing buyer could properly be advised to accept. It does not, however, make any guarantee as to the reversionary title.

Note that a title may be **upgraded** by the Registrar at his discretion or on application by a registered proprietor. Thus, if a proprietor can later produce a document which was missing when he applied to register his title, the registrar will upgrade qualified title to absolute title. Also, if the registrar can be satisfied that the proprietor is in possession of land that has been registered as possessory for at least twelve years, he may upgrade the class of title to absolute title.

Note that a buyer for value of an estate registered with absolute title takes the land subject only to entries appearing on the register and unregistered interests that override dispositions (see below). Consequently, with the exception of overriding interests, if an interest is not correctly protected on the register, a buyer for value takes free from it. The fact that the buyer may be aware, for independent reasons, of the existence of the unprotected interest would not make any difference.

1.3.2 Title information document

Prior to 13 October 2003, a 'land certificate' would be issued to the registered proprietor or (if the land were mortgaged) a 'charge certificate' would be issued to the registered chargeholder. Either certificate would have to be produced to the Land Registry in order to register a subsequent disposition.

However, land and charge certificates were abolished by LRA 2002 and certificates issued before that date no longer need to be produced.

Now, a **'title information document'** is issued to a registered proprietor. This contains an official copy of the entries on the register and title plan. It does not need to be produced on a subsequent dealing. Only the register itself constitutes proof of ownership and **'official copies of the register'** are admissible as proof of ownership. Official copies can be obtained by anyone who submits an application (and payment of a small fee) for them.

1.4 Registration of interests

Essentially, a prospective buyer of land needs to know that the seller is entitled to sell the property to him. He will therefore need to see the seller named as the registered proprietor and take note of any restrictions on the proprietor's ability to deal with the property. Both matters are addressed on the proprietorship register.

The buyer will also want details of any **third party interests** to which he may take subject and of interests over the land which will be beneficial to his ownership. Similarly the third party with the benefit of interests over the land needs to be satisfied that they will endure after a transfer of that land and so he will wish to ensure that his rights are noted against the register of title to that land.

Interests are either:

- Registered charges
- Interests which must be protected by an entry on the register or
- Unregistered interests which override dispositions

1.4.1 Registered charges

A legal charge of registered land is a registrable disposition (s.27 LRA 2002). Details of the charge are entered on the charges register of the registered title of the borrower's title. (Failure to register means that the charge only has an equitable charge as the disposition takes effect to create a contract to create a mortgage only). A corresponding restriction is also usually entered in the proprietorship register, preventing the borrower from selling without the consent of the lender.

1.4.2 Interests which must be protected by an entry on the register

Interests other than registered charges and interests overriding a registered disposition (see below) have to be protected by an entry on the register in order to bind a successor.

Sometimes an interest may fall into two categories, that is it may be capable of being protected by an entry on the register or it may be capable of overriding a registered disposition even if unregistered. However, it is best practice to ensure that an entry is made, since there may always be a risk that no overriding will occur. For example, where someone who occupies the land has a beneficial interest in the land, a notice should be entered on the register because his occupation may not be 'obvious' on a 'reasonably careful inspection' sufficiently to make it an overriding interest (see below).

Prior to 2002, interests could be protected by entry of:

- Restrictions
- Notices
- Cautions
- Inhibitions

The LRA 2002 put an end to cautions and inhibitions (although existing ones remain valid). Notices (now in two forms: 'agreed' and 'unilateral') and restrictions can still be entered and examples of both have already been given (see 1.1).

Registrable interests are usually interests in land. However, a notice may be entered on the charges register to protect the statutory right of occupation of the legal owner's spouse or civil partner (who is not also an owner). The right is neither an interest on land nor a right to the sale proceeds, but it does need to be cancelled before the owner can give vacant possession.

1.4.3 Unregistered interests which override the disposition

There are some interests that bind a buyer whether they are capable of registration or not and whether or not they have been registered. (Of course, if they are capable of registration and have been registered, they bind under the principles we have discussed.) These are set out in Schedules 1 and 3 of LRA 2002 and are similar to 'overriding interests' under LRA 1925. Although the term 'overriding interests' is no longer used in the statutory provisions, it is often still used (and will be used in this Study Manual) to describe 'unregistered interests which override registered dispositions' and 'unregistered interests which override first registration'.

The position following LRA 2002

Unregistered interests that override a *first registration* (sch.1 LRA 2002)	Unregistered interests that override *registered dispositions* (sch. 3 LRA 2002)
These include: Legal leases for a term not exceeding seven years	These include: Legal leases for a term not exceeding seven years
An interest belonging to a person in actual occupation	Any interest held by a person in actual occupation An interest will *not* be overriding if either it: ▸ Is not disclosed on reasonable inquiry ▸ Belongs to a person whose occupation would not have been obvious on a reasonable inspection of the land and the buyer is not actually aware of it Such an interest is only binding to the extent that it relates to land that is actually occupied. (Not surprisingly, these interests tend to be a particular concern for a buyer and, in Section B, you will see the steps that are advisable for a buyer's solicitor in relation to these.)
Legal easements	Legal easements acquired by implied grant or reservation or by prescription, *provided that* the right: ▸ was within the actual knowledge of the buyer of the burdened land or ▸ would have been obvious on a reasonable inspection of the land or ▸ had been exercised within one year prior to the disposition or ▸ was registered under the Commons Registration Act 1965 or Commons Act 2006 (An *express* legal easement over registered land should be registered)
Local land charges	Local land charges
Customary and public rights	Customary and public rights
Rights to mines and minerals (in certain cases)	Rights to mines and minerals (in certain cases)

Legal leases for a term exceeding seven years are 'registrable dispositions' and must be registered separately

1.5 Summary of registration in registered land

The protection of proprietary interests by registration in registered land will be addressed again in Chapters 3 and 4 dealing with easements, restrictive covenants and mortgages. In addition, you will be revisiting this subject in Chapter 8 when you look at title in more detail. However, the following summary may be useful in beginning to put the principles of land law into a practical context.

Estate or interest	Registration
Freehold estate	Separate title number
Leasehold estate over seven years	Separate title number Notice on charges register of superior title
Legal leasehold interest not exceeding seven years	Overriding interest (although a lease of more than three years can be noted on the charges register of the superior title)
Beneficial interests arising under a trust	Indicated by a restriction on the proprietorship register Overreachable
Contracts for sale, option agreements, agreements for lease and other estate contracts	Notice on charges register
Express legal easement	The benefit is noted on the property register of the dominant land The burden is noted on the charges register of the servient land
Other legal easements	Capable of being overriding interests
Equitable easement	Notice on the charges register of the servient land
Restrictive covenants	The benefit is noted on the property register of the dominant land The burden is noted on the charges register of the servient land
Legal charge	Notice on the charges register of the land charged Lender named as proprietor of that charge Restriction often entered

Important

If there is more than one registered proprietor (co-ownership), this indicates the existence of a trust

dominant land

The land with the benefit

servient land

The land with the burden

2 Unregistered land

Unregistered land is land to which title has not yet been registered. This probably means that there has been no registrable disposition of it since 1990 (when compulsory registration was extended to cover the whole of England and Wales) and the last disposition of it prior to 1990 was at a time when compulsory registration did not apply to the location of the land in question.

2.1 Title to unregistered land

As you will see in Chapter 8, title to unregistered land is evidenced not by a register pertaining to the land, but by former conveyances and other legal documents affecting it (the title deeds). The seller must show an unbroken chain of ownership of at least 15 years.

2.2 Protection of interests

How interests are protected in unregistered land depends on whether they are legal or equitable interests. You have already learned that estates and interests may be classified as legal or equitable. Freehold and leasehold estates can be legal and charges and easements can be legal. Restrictive covenants and beneficial interests will always be equitable.

2.2.1 Legal interests

Where a person owns a legal interest in land, generally speaking, he will be able to enforce that interest automatically against any owner of that land, on the basis that a legal interest binds the whole world and does not need to be registered.

There is only one exception to this rule and that is the '***puisne* mortgage**.' A puisne mortgage is a legal mortgage over a legal estate that is not protected by the deposit of title deeds. This is usually because the land is subject to a prior legal mortgage and that first mortgagee is holding the title deeds to the property for security. Such mortgages are subject to registration as a land charge (see below).

2.2.2 Equitable interests

Equitable interests can be subdivided into three categories:

- Equitable interests that are subject to overreaching (predominantly beneficial interests under a trust)
- Equitable interests subject to registration under the Land Charges Act 1972 (predominantly commercial interests)
- Equitable interests which fall into neither of the above and thus are subject to the equitable doctrine of notice

You should also keep in mind that there are unregistered interests which override first registration (see above).

Interests subject to overreaching

You have already seen in Chapter 1 that where land is subject to a trust (for example, in cases of co-ownership) the device of overreaching is used in order to enable the buyer to take the land free from the equitable interests of the beneficiaries, whilst still protecting those interests. Overreaching applies equally to unregistered and registered land.

Remember that to overreach beneficial interests under a trust, the purchase monies must be paid to at least two trustees or a trust corporation or a sole personal representative. Where this is done, the buyer takes free from the equitable interests of the beneficiaries, which are said to have been overreached and, in effect, transferred away from the land and into the purchase monies.

Obviously, if overreaching has not been successful, because purchase monies were not paid over to at least two trustees for example, the equitable doctrine of notice will apply, which means that only a buyer who is a bona fide buyer for value of the legal estate without notice will take the land free from the beneficial interests.

Interests subject to registration under the Land Charges Act 1972

Most equitable interests that cannot be overreached (and the *puisne* mortgage) should be protected by registration on the Register of Land Charges (sometimes referred to as the Central Land Charges Register) in order to bind a buyer, in accordance with the Land Charges Act 1972.

Alert

Do not confuse registration of land charges with the system of registration of title.

The registration of land charges in unregistered land will be addressed again, in the context of conveyancing, in Chapter 8. However, it should be noted that the following interests should be protected in this way:

- Restrictive covenants
- Equitable easements

In addition, the statutory right of occupation for a non-owning spouse under the Family Law Act 1996 can be protected in this way.

Unregistrable interests subject to the doctrine of notice

The two principal categories of unregistrable equitable interests to note are:

- Beneficial interests arising under a trust that are not overreached
- Pre-1926 restrictive covenants

The enforceability of such interests as against successors in title depends on the equitable doctrine of notice, ie they are void against a bona fide purchaser for value of the legal estate without notice of them.

2.3 The effect of registration of land charges

Registration of an interest which is registrable as a land charge constitutes actual notice of the interest to all persons and for all purposes. Once registered, therefore, it will be binding on a buyer and it is immaterial whether a person is actually aware of the registered interest. Thus the old doctrine of notice is rendered redundant in respect of those interests which are registrable, provided they are actually registered. Registration does not guarantee the validity of the interest in question, however, so that if something is registered which is not actually an interest in land, registration will not make it an interest in land.

As you will see later, an official search of the register is deemed to be conclusive. As a result, if a search incorrectly fails to reveal a registered land charge, the land charge is effectively destroyed and the person with the benefit of it loses that benefit but may proceed against the registry in negligence.

2.4 The effect of failure to register a land charge

The consequence of failing to register a land charge before completion of the purchase will depend upon the category of land charge concerned, but broadly speaking they will be void against a purchaser.

Summary

- Title to most land in England and Wales is now registered and subject to the 'registered land' system of conveyancing.

In registered land:

- A registered title is evidenced by a register in three parts, namely a property register, a proprietorship register and a charges register.
- Most dealings in land are registrable dispositions or trigger compulsory first registration, including transfers, leases of over seven years and the creation of legal mortgages.
- There are four classes of registered title.
- Freehold and leasehold estates (of over seven years) are substantively registered with their own title number.
- Beneficial interests, to which the registered title is subject, are protected by entry of a restriction on the proprietorship register.
- Restrictive covenants, easements and charges may be protected by entry of a notice on the charges register.
- Certain interests override registered dispositions and first registration, including legal leases for seven years or less, interests of persons in occupation and some legal easements.

In unregistered land:

- Legal interests (except puisne mortgages) bind the world.
- Some equitable interests are overreachable, some are registrable as land charges and some are subject to the equitable doctrine of notice.
- Restrictive covenants and equitable easements can and should be registered as land charges
- Failure to register a land charge will, broadly speaking, render it void against a buyer.

Self-test questions

1 Name the three parts of the register of title in registered land.

2 Give two examples of interests that may be protected by a notice on the charges register.

3 Within what timescale must first registration be effected?

4 What is meant by 'substantive registration'?

5 What class of title is appropriate where title appears sound but can only be evidenced for a short period?

6 What are the two types of entry that may appear on a register of title but which can no longer be entered?

7 Is a legal lease for five years registrable?

8 In unregistered land, do legal interests need to be registered?

9 Where beneficial interests under a trust are not overreached, does a purchaser take free from them?

10 Name two categories of equitable interest that are subject to the doctrine of notice in considering whether or not they bind successors in title?

Answers to self-test questions

1. Property register, proprietorship register and charges register
2. Restrictive covenants, charges and easements
3. Within two months of completion
4. Registration with a separate title number (principally freeholds and leases over seven years).
5. Qualified title
6. Cautions and inhibitions
7. It is not a registrable disposition requiring substantive registration but, being over three years, it can be noted on the charges register of the superior title. It is an overriding interest.
8. Normally no. The exception is the puisne mortgage, which is registrable as a land charge.
9. The answer depends on the equitable doctrine of notice. If he is a bona fide purchaser for value of the legal estate without notice of them, he will take free of them. Otherwise he will take subject to them.
10. Beneficial interests arising under a trust that are not overreached and pre-1926 restrictive covenants.

3

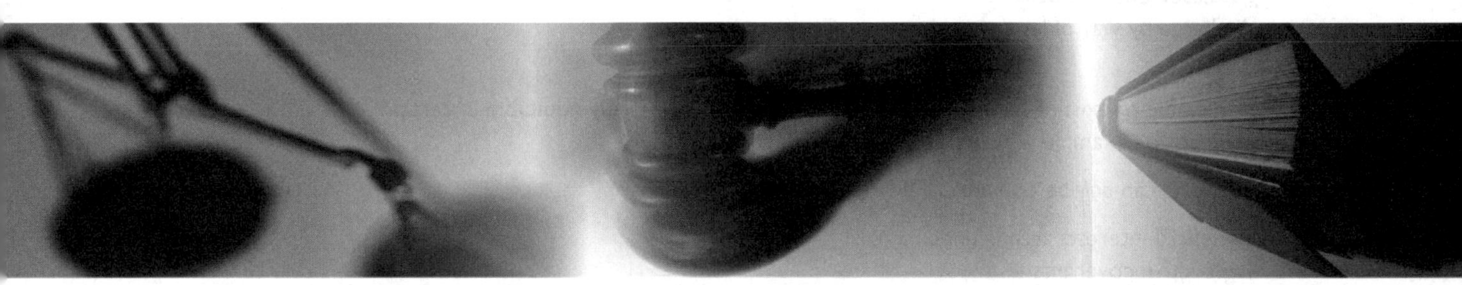

Interests in land, including easements and covenants

Chapter overview

This chapter will

- Identify interests are capable of existing in law and which can only be equitable
- Explain what constitutes an easement
- Describe freehold covenants and explain the rules governing their enforceability

1 The nature of interests in land

Interests in land are rights that affect land and which may be transferred either with or independently of a transfer of an estate in land. Interests in land may also be referred to as 'proprietary rights' or 'encumbrances' or 'incumbrances'. The person who enjoys the right may be able to enforce it against a new owner of the estate over which the right exists.

In order to be a 'legal' interest, the interest must be one of those specified in s.1(2) LPA 1925 and must be created by deed. S.1(2) includes:

- An easement (see below)
- A charge by way of legal mortgage (see Chapter 4)

Although capable of existing in law, these interests may also be merely equitable in certain circumstances, for example where not created by deed.

Other interests can *only* be equitable. They include:

- Beneficial interests arising under a trust
- Restrictive covenants

In registered land, an interest must be protected by registration in order to be legal.

2 Easements

2.1 What is an easement?

An easement may be a *positive* right to use another's land, such as a right of way or a right of drainage. It may also be a *negative* right to restrict the use of another person's land, such as a right of light. Easements do not give the right to occupation or possession, other than for the limited purposes of enjoying the easement.

A right must satisfy the following four tests in order to be an easement:

Dominant and servient tenements	There must be a dominant tenement and a servient tenement, ie two pieces of land, one with the benefit of the right (the dominant tenement) and the other with the burden (the servient tenement).
Benefit the dominant tenement	The easement must have some form of direct beneficial impact on the dominant tenement ie it must be connected with the enjoyment of the land. A personal benefit will not suffice. The test is likely to be satisfied if it can be shown that the right makes the dominant tenement a better and more convenient tenement.
Diversity of ownership or occupation	The dominant and servient plots of land must be owned or occupied by different persons. (Note that if a person exercises rights over one part of his land for the benefit of another part of his land, these are simply the natural incidents of ownership. Such rights are known as 'quasi-easements' and are capable of becoming easements on a subsequent division of his ownership.)

Note

Statutory easements, eg in favour of gas and electricity suppliers, do not require a dominant tenement

Grant	The right must be capable of 'lying in grant' ie forming the subject matter of a deed. This requires that the following be satisfied: ▸ There must be a **capable grantor and grantee** (with separate legal personality); ▸ The rights must be **capable of reasonably exact description** and not vague (for example, there can be no 'right to a scenic view'); and ▸ The right must be within the general nature of rights traditionally recognised as easements. These include: – **Rights of way** – Rights of light through defined windows – Rights to water in a defined channel – Rights to air in a defined channel – Rights of support – Rights of drainage through a defined channel and other rights of 'pipeline', for example gas, electricity etc

2.2 Creation of easements

An easement is usually, but not necessarily, created on the sale of part of a plot of land.

An easement may be acquired in three ways:

- By express provision
- By implication (ie implied into a document dealing with the property)
- By presumption (ie by long uninterrupted use)

A '**grant**' is the bestowing of certain right(s) on the dominant owner for the benefit of his land.

A '**reservation**' is relevant on a sale of part and is the retention of rights by a landowner over the land he is selling, for the benefit of the land he retains.

Example

Sayed is selling part of his land to Brian and each party requires rights over the other's land. Brian requires a right of way and this will be expressly **granted** to him in the transfer of the land. Sayed will need to retain the right of drainage over Brian's land and this will be expressly **reserved** out of the transfer to Brian:

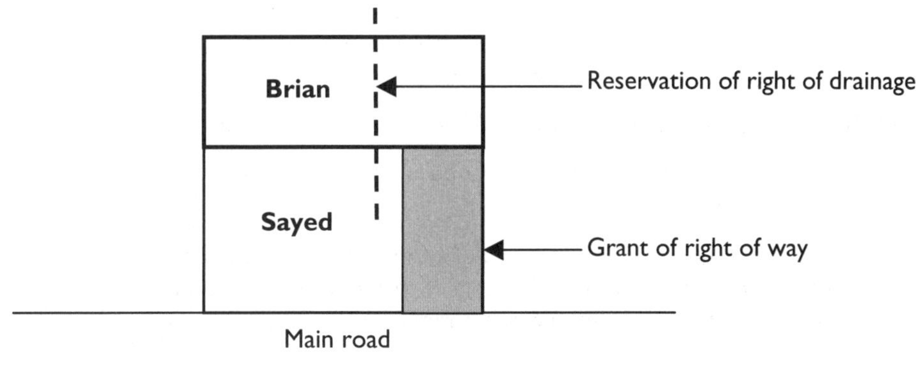

2.2.1 Express grant or reservation

An express grant or reservation must be made by deed if it is to create a legal easement and must be registered if it is over registered land. The grantor of the easement must also hold a legal estate in the servient land. If he only has an equitable estate, the easement can only be equitable. Similarly, the easement must be created on either a freehold or leasehold basis, ie without time limit or for a certain term. If it is created for an indeterminate period, it can only be equitable.

2.2.2 Implied grant or reservation

Where land has been transferred and the owner has failed to expressly grant or reserve easements, there are four sets of circumstances where the law may **imply** that such easements have been granted (to the buyer) or reserved (to the seller). Such implied easements will always be legal since the law deems them to be incorporated in a deed of transfer. These are:

- Easements of necessity
- Intended easements
- Easements under the rule in *Wheeldon v Burrows*
- Easements under s.62 LPA 1925

Easements of necessity	An easement of necessity is one which is **absolutely essential** to the use of the property. It can be implied *in favour of either party*. The principal example is a right of way to a piece of land which would otherwise be landlocked. If not expressly granted, it would be acquired by him as an easement of necessity. It would be implied as it is presumed that the parties did not intend to make the land inaccessible. No easement of necessity will be inferred if there is some other means of access, even if that other means is difficult or inconvenient. Rights that are desirable or even highly advantageous, such as drainage, sewerage and the supply of electricity, are not considered 'essential', since it cannot be alleged that without the rights the land cannot be used at all.
Intended easements	An intended easement is one that is needed in order to carry out the common intention of the grantor and grantee that the property is to be used in some definite and particular manner. In practice, an easement is only likely to be implied as one of common intention *in favour of the transferee*.
Under the rule in Wheeldon v Burrows (1879)	Under this rule, an easement may be implied on a sale of part *in favour of the buyer only*. Effectively the rule elevates quasi-easements into full easements. The easement must be: ▸ **Continuous and apparent**, ie it must have been used by the seller and must be discoverable or detectable from careful inspection of the land. (For example, a worn pathway would be evidence of a right of way.) ▸ **Reasonably necessary**, ie it must enhance the enjoyment of the land. ▸ **In use at the time of transfer**, ie there must be an element of use in existence at around that time.
Under s.62 LPA 1925	Under s.62 an easement may be implied on a sale of a freehold or leasehold, *in favour of the buyer only*. It does not apply on of a sale of part where, prior to the sale, the land was in common ownership and occupation. S.62(1) LPA 1925: 'A conveyance of land shall be deemed to include and shall convey with the land, all buildings, fixtures...... easements...appertaining or reputed to appertain to the land or any part thereof, or, at the time of the conveyance, demised, occupied or enjoyed with, or reputed or known as part or parcel of or appurtenant to the land or any part thereof.'

2.2.3 Presumed grant (easements by prescription)

An easement may also be created or acquired by way of presumption, after use for a sufficiently long period of time. Such easements are always legal as the presumption is made by the common law. They are frequently called '**easements by prescription**'.

In every case the use must be as of right and never by force, stealth or permission.

The use must be continuous until established (subject to permitted interruptions where a claim is made under the Prescription Act 1832).

An easement by prescription can only be claimed for the benefit of a freeholder against another freeholder who knows of the use and is able to resist it.

Easements by prescription may be acquired:

- By common law
- Under the doctrine of lost modern grant
- Under the Prescription Act 1832

Common law prescription	The law will presume the grant of an easement if it has been enjoyed since time immemorial (since 1189). If it can be shown that the use has lasted for at least **twenty years**, it will be **presumed** that it commenced in 1189, unless it can be shown that at some time since 1189 the right could not or did not exist. This might be shown, for example, where an easement of light is claimed for a building which was clearly erected after 1189 or where it can be shown that at some stage in the past the land was in common ownership (a person cannot have an easement over his own land).
Lost modern grant	This is a complete fiction introduced to avoid the difficulties which may arise under common law prescription (which must be applied first). If continuous user for at least twenty years can be shown, there is a presumption that at one stage there was a valid deed of grant of an easement which has since been lost.
Prescription Act 1832	The Act draws a basic distinction between easements of light and other types of easement. We will consider easement other than light here. The Act provides that an easement (other than light for which slightly different rules apply) can be claimed where it was actually enjoyed without interruption for 20 years. It cannot be defeated by showing that the user began after 1189. The law changes as regards uninterrupted actual enjoyment for 40 years: this extended user makes the right absolute and indefeasible unless enjoyed by express consent given by deed or in writing.

3 Covenants

Restrictive covenants (negative covenants) are proprietary interests in land. They can be equitable interests only. We shall, however, consider the nature of all freehold covenants (restrictive and positive) and how they are treated. You will see how the enforcement of *positive* covenants is generally a matter of contract law, whereas the enforcement of *negative* covenants is a matter of property law.

Leasehold covenants made between a landlord and a tenant are quite different and will be discussed in Section C of this Study Manual.

3.1 What is a covenant?

 **Covenantor**

the person who gives the promise, and thus undertakes the burden of it.

 **Covenantee**

the person who receives the benefit of the promise

A covenant is a promise contained in a deed. It is made by a 'covenantor' in favour of a 'covenantee'. It is enforceable without the need for consideration. The land owned by the covenantor, which suffers the **burden** of the covenant, is called the servient land and the covenantee's land, which enjoys the **benefit** of the covenant, is called the dominant land.

A covenant can be positive or negative in nature. A **positive covenant** requires the covenantor to do something positive, for example, a promise to maintain a boundary fence. A **negative covenant** is one that can be satisfied by mere inaction on the part of the covenantor and typically involves a promise to refrain from doing something, for example a promise not to build. It is the *effect* of the covenant, rather than its wording, which determines whether it is negative or positive. The usual test is to ask whether performance involves the expenditure of money. If so, it is positive. Care needs to be taken. For example, a covenant 'not to allow a wall to fall into a state of disrepair' may sound like a negative covenant but is, in fact, a positive covenant, since expenditure and positive action are required to comply with it.

A covenant can also be classified as either one that is purely *personal* to the covenantee, ie entered into simply for that person's benefit, or as one that 'touches and concerns the land', ie made for the benefit of the covenantee in his capacity as owner of that particular property. It is only covenants that touch and concern the land that are capable of binding or benefiting successors in title. (Personal covenants will only ever be enforceable as between the original covenanting parties as a matter of contract law.)

3.2 Covenants as interests in land

Where covenants are not merely personal they may be said to attach to the land. At this point, the party with the benefit of the covenant has a proprietary interest. As already mentioned, and for reasons you will see below, it is only **restrictive covenants** that are capable of being **proprietary equitable interests in land**. Enforcement of such covenants may then extend beyond the original parties and contract law and be enforced by and against successors in title to the dominant and servient lands.

The questions arise on a transfer of either the dominant or servient land, or both, as to whether the covenant entered into by the original owners of those lands can be enforced against either or both transferees. This is a matter of whether the benefit passes on a transfer of the dominant land and whether the burden passes on a transfer of the servient land. Whilst legislation assists in a number of areas, still the questions fall to be answered largely from a complex mass of case law. Equity has played a major role.

3.2.1 The burden of a restrictive covenant: the rule in *Tulk v Moxhay 1848*

Following *Tulk v Moxhay*, **all** the following conditions must be satisfied for a successor in title to the servient land to be subject to the burden of a restrictive covenant.

- **The covenant must be negative.** Remember that this is a matter of substance not form.
- **Notice.** The buyer of the servient land must have notice of the covenant in order to be bound by it.

Registered land	The entry of a notice in the charges register of the servient property constitutes notice.
Unregistered land	A registered land charge constitutes notice.

- **The covenant must accommodate a dominant tenement.** This means that the covenant must 'touch and concern' the land, (ie the dominant land must benefit from the covenant).

- **The original parties must have intended the burden to run.** Covenants relating to the covenantor's land are deemed to be made by the covenantor on behalf of himself and his successors in title, unless a contrary intention appears.

3.2.2 The burden of a positive covenant: indemnity covenants

The burden of a positive covenant does not run and bind a successor in title to the servient land. However, since the covenantor remains liable under the general principles of contract law, in practice he will require his successor to enter into an indemnity covenant.

An **indemnity covenant** is simply a promise, given by a buyer to a seller, to ensure the future observance of the covenants burdening the land and to pay to the seller any losses the seller incurs as a result of the breach by the buyer or a subsequent owner.

Where a covenantor is found liable for damages as a result of his successor's breach, he can enforce such an indemnity covenant against his successor and recover from him the damages that he was liable to pay to the covenantee for his successor's breach.

When a succession of owners gives such covenants, this is known as a **chain of indemnity covenants**. Thus, when the convenantor's successor sells the land, he too will extract an indemnity covenant from his buyer. As will be seen, SCS 4.6.4 (Chapter 10) requires a buyer to enter into an indemnity in similar form as given by the buyer, if the indemnity is still enforceable.

In practical terms, chains of indemnity covenant may 'break' because of the death or insolvency of one of those in the chain. In such a case, the indemnity will stop with the previous person who gave the indemnity, who would have no further rights to enforce against later owners.

3.3 Transmission of the benefit and burden of freehold covenants

Let us imagine that Dom and Serv enter into a number of covenants on a sale of part of Dom's land to Serv. These covenants include a positive covenant to build and maintain a boundary fence between the two plots. They also include a negative, or restrictive, covenant not to use the property except for residential purposes. Dom later sells his estate to Ben and Serv sells his estate to Burd.

Dom (covenantee) ----------------- Ben
+
–
Serv (covenantor) ----------------- Burd

We shall now consider the various questions arising from these scenarios.

3.3.1 Dom and Serv still own their respective freehold interests

Both positive and negative covenants are enforceable between the parties, as a matter of contract law, given the privity of contract that exists between them.

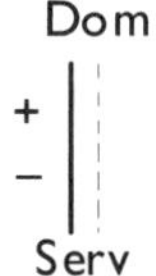

3.3.2 Serv sells his freehold to Burd who commits a breach of both covenants

- **Can Dom still enforce the covenants against Serv?**

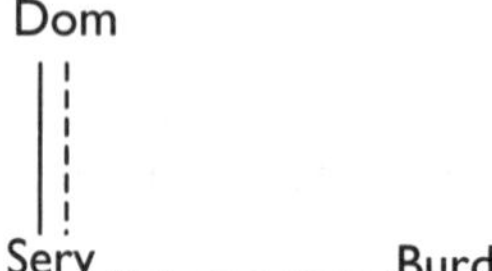

Yes. He can enforce both positive and negative covenants as a matter of contract law. Serv will have probably obtained an indemnity covenant from Burd in respect of his potential liability under the covenants.

- **Can Dom enforce the covenants against Burd?**

  – **Positive covenant**: No. The burden of a positive covenant does not bind the servient landowner's successor either at law or in equity, but remains personal to the covenantor only. Dom's course of action is therefore to proceed against Serv, as above (and Serv would then enforce his indemnity covenant against Burd).

  – **Restrictive covenant**: Yes. The burden of a negative covenant will not run in law but may run in equity under the rule in *Tulk v Moxhay 1848* if the four conditions (see above) are satisfied.

3.3.3 Serv retains his land but Dom transfers his freehold title to Ben. Serv commits a breach of the covenants

- **Can Dom still enforce the covenants against Serv?**

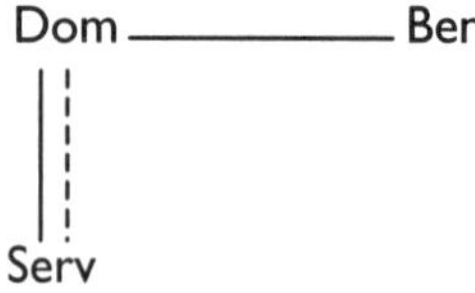

In theory, yes, as a matter of contract law, unless he has expressly assigned the benefit of the covenant or unless the covenant was drafted so as to apply only whilst the covenantee owned the dominant land. However, Dom is quite unlikely to have any interest in doing so, having parted with the land, nor is he likely to be able to demonstrate any loss.

- **Can Ben enforce the covenants against Serv?**

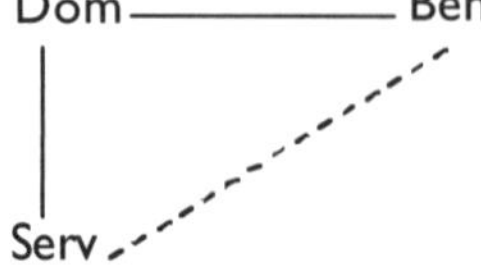

It is possible (and likely) that the benefit of the covenants will pass from Dom to Ben when the freehold interest is transferred, both at common law and in equity and so Ben will most likely be able to enforce against Serv. The rules for each are slightly different although you will see their similarities.

Passing of the benefit at common law

The benefit of a covenant may always be expressly assigned unless it is personal only. In the absence of an express assignment, the benefit may pass nonetheless, provided:

- The covenant can be said to 'touch and concern' the dominant land (which really means that it must benefit the dominant land in some way);
- The transferee is taking a legal interest in the land benefited; and
- It was intended that the benefit should pass with the land owned by the covenantee at the time of the covenant.

In fact, statute has also intervened to echo the common law approach, namely s.78 LPA 1925.

S.78 LPA 1925: 'a covenant relating to any land of the covenantee shall be deemed to be made with the covenantee and his successors in title...and shall have effect as if such successors...were expressed...'

Furthermore, under the **Contracts (Rights of Third Parties) Act 1999**, in respect of covenants entered into after 10 May 2000, a person who is not a party to the contract may 'in his own right' enforce the terms of the contract provided, either the:

- Contract expressly provides that he may
- Term purports to confer a benefit on him and it is not apparent that the parties did not intend the term to be enforceable by a third party

Successors in title are therefore likely to be entitled to enforce covenants under this Act.

Passing of the benefit in equity (which, essentially, is concerned with restrictive covenants only)

The benefit must 'touch and concern' the land and may be transmitted to a successor in the following ways:

Annexation	Annexation may be express or implied or (more likely) will be deemed to occur by virtue of s.78 LPA 1925 (see above). The Court of Appeal recently said in *Federated Homes Ltd v Mill Lodge Properties Ltd 1980*, that provided a covenant touches and concerns the land of the covenantee, s78 will operate to make it pass to his successor, unless there is some clear intention to the contrary (for example a stipulation that the covenant is personal or that transmission is only possible by express assignment). The effect of s.78 as it is now interpreted, means that there is little need for express assignments, although they are likely still to be considered good practice.
Assignment	The benefit can be expressly **assigned** at the time of transfer of the dominant land.

3.3.4 Ben acquires Dom's freehold and Burd acquires Serv's freehold

Can Ben enforce the covenants against Burd?

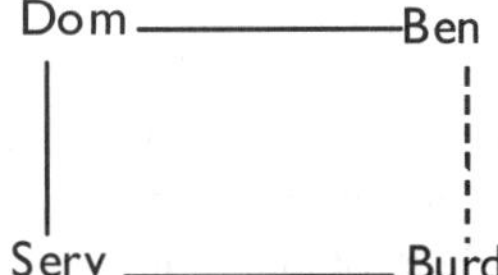

The answer simply depends on whether the benefit has passed to Ben (likely) and the burden has passed to Serv, according to the rules mentioned above. Provided both have passed, Ben will be able to enforce the covenants against Burd. **It follows that Ben is likely to be able to enforce the negative covenant but not the positive covenant.**

3.4 Discharge or modification of a restrictive covenant

Under s.84(1) LPA 1925, the Lands Tribunal has the power to discharge or modify a restrictive covenant on specified grounds. These are that the:

- Covenant ought to be deemed **obsolete**
- Covenant **impedes some reasonable user** of the land where the restriction does not offer substantial benefit or is contrary to public policy
- Person entitled to the benefit of the restriction has **agreed**, expressly or by implication, to the covenant being discharged or modified
- Proposed discharge or modification of the covenant **will not injure** the persons entitled to the benefit of it

Any person interested in the freehold land affected by the restrictive covenant can apply for relief under this provision. In addition to ordering any discharge or modification, the Lands Tribunal may also order the payment of compensation to any person entitled to the benefit of the covenant.

3.5 Breach of covenant

Breach of a restrictive covenant may entitle a covenantee to damages or an injunction. A covenantor, being sued for breach of covenant, may request leave to apply to the Lands Tribunal for discharge or modification of the covenant.

3.5.1 Breach of restrictive covenant

Where the **seller** or his predecessor is in breach of a restrictive covenant, the buyer should consider:

- Insurance against any claim by the person with the benefit of the covenant
- Retrospective consent from the person with the benefit of the covenant
- Application to the Lands Tribunal for discharge or modification of the covenant

Where the **buyer** himself intends to act in breach of the restrictive covenant, he should consider:

- Insurance against any claim by the person with the benefit of the covenant (although this is likely to be expensive)
- Obtaining the consent of the person with the benefit of the covenant
- Application to the Lands Tribunal for discharge or modification of the covenant

3.5.2 Breach of positive covenant

Where the **seller** or his predecessor is in breach of a **positive** covenant, the buyer should require him to make good the breach (for example to erect the fence that he should have erected or to put it into a state of good repair) or ensure that he will not be bound by an indemnity.

Where the **buyer** proposes to be in breach of a positive covenant, he might resist the requirement to enter into an indemnity covenant but is unlikely to succeed. Otherwise he will be bound by the covenant unless there is a break in the chain of indemnity.

Summary

- Interests in land are proprietary rights.
- All interests may be equitable. Only specified interests may be legal (including easements and mortgages) and then only if certain criteria are met.
- Beneficial interests arising under a trust of land are equitable interests in land.
- An easement is a positive or negative right that satisfies four conditions (dominant and servient tenements, dominant tenement benefits, diversity of ownership and occupation and capable of lying in grant).
- Easements may arise by express grant or reservation or they may be implied or presumed.
- Implied and presumed easements are legal. Express easements may be legal
- Easements may be implied in cases of necessity or intention or under the rule in *Wheeldon v Burrows* or under s.62 LPA 1925.
- Easements by prescription may be acquired under common law or the doctrine of lost modern grant or under the Prescription Act 1832.
- Freehold covenants can be positive or negative. Only restrictive covenants are equitable interests in land.
- Both positive and negative covenants are enforceable as between the original parties.
- A covenantor's successor is generally bound by restrictive covenants under the rule in *Tulk v Moxhay 1848*. He may be liable for breach of a positive covenant under an indemnity covenant in favour of the original covenantor or an earlier successor.
- A covenantee's successor generally takes the benefit of covenants.

Self-test questions

1. Can the following exist in law? (a) easements (b) restrictive covenants (c) beneficial interests arising under a trust.
2. Is an easement a positive right or a negative right?
3. What is a quasi-easement?
4. What does 'lying in grant' mean?
5. What conditions must be satisfied in order for an easement to be legal?
6. In favour of which party might (a) an easement of necessity and (b) an easement under the rule in *Wheeldon v Burrows* be implied?
7. An easement by prescription must always be as of right? What does that mean?
8. What occurrence might break a chain of indemnity covenants?
9. Is a covenant 'not to allow a fence to fall into a state of disrepair' a positive covenant or a negative covenant?
10. How is notice of a restrictive covenant given in (a) registered land and (b) unregistered land?

Answers to self-test questions

1 (a) Yes
(b) No
(c) No

2 It may be either.

3 It is a right exercised over one part of land for the benefit of another part of land owned by the same person. It may be converted into an easement on a subsequent division of that ownership.

4 It means capable of being granted or reserved in a deed, ie in the nature of an easement recognised by law.

5 It must be created by deed, the servient landowner must own a legal interest, the easement must be granted on a freehold or leasehold basis (ie not for an indeterminate length of time) and (in registered land) it must be registered.

6 (a) In favour of either party.
(b) In favour of the buyer

7 That it must never be enjoyed by force, stealth or permission.

8 The death or insolvency of a person in the chain.

9 A positive covenant.

10 (a) by a notice on the charges register of the servient land (b) by registration of land charge.

4

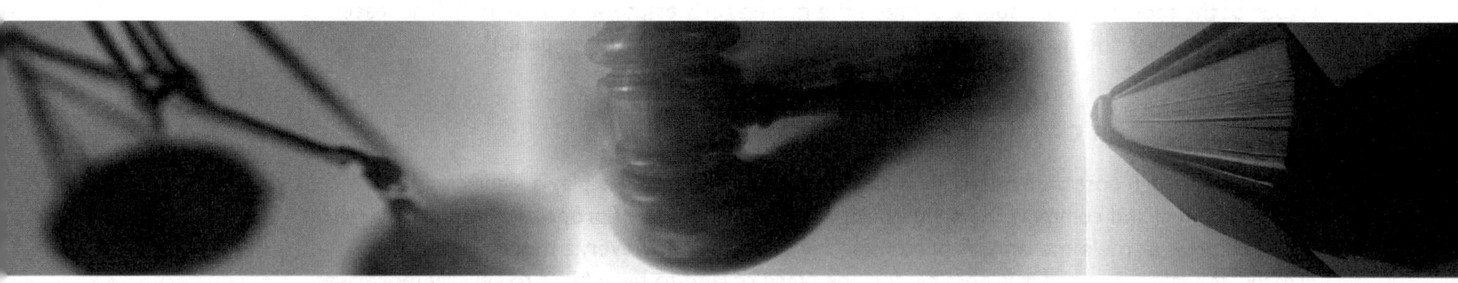

Mortgages

Topic List

Chapter overview

This chapter will:

- Explain that a mortgage is a charge on property given by way of security for a loan
- Briefly explain the different types of mortgage
- Explain the significance of the date for redemption
- Describe the various remedies available to a mortgagee
- Set out the rules governing the priority of legal mortgages
- Explain what is meant by the term 'tacking'
- Identify when and how mortgages need to be protected by registration and how they are discharged

1 What is a mortgage?

A mortgage is a form of security over land which is created by a **mortgagor** (the borrower) in favour of the **mortgagee** (the lender).

A charge by way of legal mortgage is the most common form of mortgage and is what we will consider in this Chapter.

(Historically, a mortgage was created by conveying the legal estate to the mortgagee, with a reconveyance back to the mortgagor on payment of the debt secured. This was no longer possible after 1925. Another form of mortgage, generally considered as archaic and no longer available in respect of registered land (s.23(1) LRA 2002), was the creation of a long lease in favour of the mortgagee (or sublease where the mortgagor's estate was leasehold). The lease would provide for automatic termination on repayment of the mortgage debt.)

1.1 The types of mortgage

Owing to the high cost of property in England and Wales, mortgages play a significant part in both residential and commercial conveyancing. Typically, a buyer of property creates a charge by legal mortgage at the same time as purchasing the property. However, a mortgage can be created at a later date and it is possible for one piece of land to be subject to several mortgages simultaneously.

At least in residential transactions, the mortgagee is usually a bank or building society and the loan will normally be over a 20 or 25 year period. The amount of the loan available is usually limited by reference to:

- Borrower's earnings (for example, three times his salary)
- Lender's valuation of the property (for example, a maximum loan of 90% of the value of the property)

There are many different types of mortgage. Perhaps the two most common are:

- Repayment mortgage
- An endowment mortgage

1.1.1 Repayment mortgages

During the term of the loan, the borrower makes monthly payments to the lender which are part-capital and part-interest. At the end of the loan period, the sum borrowed has been completely repaid and the mortgage is discharged.

If the borrower **sells** the property during the mortgage term, he will repay the mortgage debt out of the proceeds of sale. Depending on the terms of the mortgage, particularly if the sale is very early in the term, he may incur charges or penalties for redeeming the mortgage while it is still running.

If the borrower **dies** during the mortgage term, the whole amount of the mortgage debt is payable from his estate. To cover this eventuality, therefore, the borrower will usually obtain life insurance in the form of a 'mortgage protection policy' that guarantees to pay the amount outstanding on the loan in the event of his death (or permanent disability). Co-owners often take out a policy written in trust on their joint lives so that the balance of the debt can be discharged by the survivor when if either of them dies before the mortgage has been repaid. .

1.1.2 Endowment mortgages

During the term of the loan, the borrower makes monthly payments to the lender which represent interest only. He also takes out a life policy of insurance in the same sum as the amount borrowed. At the end of the loan period, the policy matures and, it is hoped, repays the capital. However, most policies do not guarantee to do so and where the fund has not grown sufficiently, the borrower is liable to pay any shortfall in the amount borrowed. For this reason

endowment mortgages have become increasingly unpopular and there have been various reports of endowment policies not being adequate to discharge the mortgage as they were designed to do. On the other hand, where a policy yields an excess (most are 'with profits' which means that the borrower shares in profits made by the insurance company during the term), this excess is paid to the borrower.

If the borrower **sells** the property during the mortgage term, he will repay the mortgage debt out of the proceeds of sale. Depending on its terms, the endowment policy may be terminated or transferred as security for another loan. The mortgagor may surrender the policy but its surrender value is likely to be very low, especially during the early part of the term.

If the borrower **dies** during the mortgage term, the endowment policy will pay the amount outstanding on the loan.

1.2 A mortgage as an interest in land

A mortgage can be a legal interest but may also be equitable. As mentioned in the previous chapter, a mortgage is capable of being a legal interest since it is one of those specified in s.1(2) LPA 1925. In order to be legal the charge must be by deed. Where it is in respect of registered land or where it is in respect of unregistered land but creation of the mortgage triggers compulsory first registration, it must also be registered in order to take effect as a legal charge.

2 The date for redemption

It is important to understand that the legal, or contractual, date for redemption specified in a mortgage is very early (usually a matter of months after creation of the charge), not because that is when repayment is intended to take place, but for two reasons:

- The date for redemption is when the mortgagor becomes entitled to redeem (although typically the mortgage will lay down redemption fees, or 'penalties', for such early redemption); and
- It is when the mortgagee's power of sale **arises** (see below).

3 Leases

Although a mortgagor is given the right to grant leases (albeit subject to a maximum term of 50 years in the case of residential leases) by s.99 LPA 1925, this right is usually excluded in the mortgage deed. The mortgagor is therefore required to obtain the mortgagee's consent to any lease. If he does not obtain consent, the lease will not bind the mortgagee since the mortgagee has an unqualified right to possession. The tenant under any such unauthorised lease has a contractual cause of action against his landlord.

4 Remedies of the mortgagee

A first legal mortgagee is protected by virtue of the lender having the title deeds (unregistered land, although creation of a legal mortgage will trigger first registration and so the registered proprietor will instead register a legal charge) or (in the case of registered land) by being the registered proprietor of a legal charge. In addition, a mortgagee generally has a number of rights during the mortgage term, including the following:

- A right to possession
- A right to sue on the debt
- A right to appoint a receiver
- A power of sale
- A right to foreclose

4.1 Right to possession

The right to possession is normally limited to situations where the borrower is in default of one or more of the terms of the mortgage, typically where the borrower is in default of repayments.

In taking possession, a mortgagee should take care to avoid potential liability under the Criminal Law Act 1977.

In the case of **residential property**, the mortgagee would also need to obtain a court order before exercising this right.

Under s.36 Administration of Justice Act 1970, (applicable to dwelling houses) the court has power to adjourn or suspend court proceedings brought by a mortgagee claiming possession of the mortgaged property for a reasonable period, if it seems likely that the mortgagor is likely to be able to pay any sums due under the mortgage within a reasonable period. 'Any sums due' means arrears which have so far accrued, not the whole amount of the loan, notwithstanding any clause in the mortgage to the effect that in the event of default the whole amount outstanding forthwith becomes due and payable (s.8 Administration of Justice Act 1973).

4.2 To sue on the debt

The mortgagee has a contractual right to take action for breach of the obligation to make payments under the mortgage, under the law of contract. This right continues notwithstanding any exercise of his power of sale (see below) or where the mortgagor 'throws the keys back'.

Of course, the remedy might not be suitable. If the mortgagor is in default because he has no financial resources, there may be little benefit in suing him.

4.3 To appoint a receiver

A mortgagee has a statutory power to appoint a receiver in the event of default once the legal date for redemption has passed and the mortgagor is in breach. The mortgage deed will almost certainly contain an express right also. This is an attractive alternative to taking possession where the property is income-producing, as the mortgagee avoids the risk of personal liability in taking possession. Briefly, the role of the receiver is to collect any income due, to make payments owed and to pass any remaining surplus to the mortgagor.

4.4 Power of sale

This is the most likely remedy to be pursued by a mortgagee.

A power of sale exists where the mortgage is made by deed (s101 LPA 192S), unless it has been expressly excluded.

4.4.1 When the power can be used

It is important to distinguish between when a power of sale **arises** and when it becomes **exercisable**.

A buyer from a mortgagee needs only be concerned with whether the power of sale has **arisen** and does not need to check that it has become **exercisable**. A mortgagee, on the other hand, will be liable in damages if he sells before the power has both arisen **and** become exercisable, even though he can pass title to a purchaser once the power has arisen.

A statutory power of sale **arises** once all or part of the debt has become due (once the legal date for redemption has passed).

The power of sale becomes **exercisable** if:

- The mortgagor has been in default for three months following service of a demand for payment

- Interest remains outstanding for two months after becoming due, or
- The mortgagor is in breach of a mortgage term other than the covenant for repayment of capital or interest

This power of sale can be exercised without any further court order, although if the property is a **dwelling house**, the mortgagee will need to obtain an order for possession, in order to sell with **vacant possession**.

A selling mortgagee can sell when and to whom he likes so long as he does not sell to himself or his nominee. However, he does owe a duty of care to the mortgagor when selling the property. This is generally taken to include a duty to obtain the true market value of the property at the time of the sale.

4.4.2 Effect of the sale

The mortgagee is able to vest the mortgagor's full legal title in a purchaser, subject to any rights ranking in priority to the mortgage. The purchaser takes free from any subsequent mortgage. A sale by a mortgagee is capable of overreaching beneficial interests that are capable of being overreached.

The mortgagee must apply the proceeds of any sale in the following order:

(1) In satisfaction of all costs and expenses properly incurred by him
(2) In satisfaction of sums due under the mortgage
(3) In payment of any subsequent mortgage
(4) In passing any surplus to the mortgagor

(Where a second mortgagee exercises its power of sale, the property will be sold subject to the first mortgage. In practice, of course, any sale will be on the basis that the first mortgage is also satisfied out of the sale proceeds, so that the buyer acquires the property free from all mortgages.)

4.4.3 Application to court for sale

If the property has '**negative equity**', (ie the mortgage debt exceeds the current market value) the mortgagee may choose to take possession and rent it out in the hope that property prices will improve, and then sell it at a later date. If the rent is not enough to cover the current interest, the borrower will fall deeper into debt. In this situation the borrower can apply for an order for sale under s.91(1) LPA which gives the court discretion to order a sale on the application of anyone entitled to redeem the mortgage. The court will make the order if it is just and equitable, striking a balance between the parties (see *Palk v Mortgage Services Funding plc 1993*, where the court ordered a sale as the likely rent was not enough to meet current interest and there was no realistic prospect of house prices recovering sufficiently to pay off ever-increasing arrears).

4.5 Foreclosure

Foreclosure enables the mortgagee to retain the whole title and benefit of the mortgaged property and the mortgagor's rights are extinguished, regardless of the amount of the outstanding debt. The mortgagee's right to foreclose exists, but is hardly ever exercised. It can only be exercised where the court allows an application for foreclosure and, in practice, the court will almost certainly exercise its power to order a sale instead.

Under s.91 LPA 1925, any 'person interested' may request the court to direct a sale of the mortgaged property instead of foreclosure. Thus a second mortgagee, who otherwise would receive nothing, may request a sale so that his debt, or at least part of it, may be satisfied from the sale proceeds.

Example

Gregor buys a house for £150,000. He has a mortgage with A for £105,000. Two years later he takes out a second mortgage with B for £30,000, also secured on the property. He defaults and A attempts to foreclose.

If A were to be successful, A would become the owner of the property and B would receive nothing. However, B applies for the court to direct a sale instead and the court does so. The property sells for £200,000, A receives satisfaction of its debt together with interest and costs and B also receives payment of its debt together with interest and costs. Gregor receives the balance.

These remedies are cumulative and, with the exception of foreclosure (that terminates all other remedies), can be pursued together where appropriate. Thus, for example, where a sale does not raise sufficient monies to discharge the mortgage debt, the mortgagee may also sue for the balance.

5 Registration

5.1 Registered land

A charge by way of legal mortgage must be registered (s.27(2) LRA 2002) in order to be legal. The mortgage is entered on the charges register of the mortgagor's title and the mortgagee is named as proprietor of that charge.

Priority as between registered charges over the same registered estate is determined by the date of registration and not the date of creation.

Pending registration, the legal mortgage takes effect as an equitable charge only.

5.2 Unregistered land

To be legal, the charge must be created by deed. Provided it is to be protected by deposit of the title deeds, the charge triggers compulsory first registration if it is in respect of a freehold estate or a leasehold estate with more than seven years to run. Following registration, the charge is then a registered charge.

Without requirement for deposit of title deeds, a legal mortgage does not trigger compulsory first registration and should be registered as a puisne mortgage land charge.

6 Priority between legal mortgages

Whether one mortgagee has priority over another can be crucial where the security turns out to be insufficient to satisfy all mortgage debts and other claims.

6.1 Registered land

Basically, in registered land, charges rank according to their date of registration (not creation).

If the mortgagee has a **legal** charge over a legal estate in registered land that has been duly registered, he takes priority over legal charges registered subsequently (even if created previously).

6.2 Unregistered land

If the mortgagee has a **legal** charge over a legal estate in unregistered land, if he has the title deeds, this triggers compulsory registration which will give him priority over all subsequent legal charges.

7 Tacking

Tacking is adding to or making a further advance under a mortgage so as to rank in priority with the initial advance ie it takes priority over any second or subsequent mortgage created since the first mortgage.

Example

ABC Bank lends £100,000 to Mena who then borrows a further £50,000 from XYZ Bank, secured over the same property. ABC Bank subsequently advances an additional £20,000, again on the same security. Under the normal rules of priority, the £20,000 advance would rank behind the second mortgage in favour of XYZ Bank. However, where tacking applies, ABC Bank will be entitled to claim its whole £120,000 before XYZ can demand repayment of its £50,000 loan.

Since the provisions of LRA 2002 came into force, tacking in both registered and unregistered land is permitted in the following three circumstances:

- Where there is **agreement** with the subsequent mortgagee
- Where the mortgagee has **no notice** of the subsequent mortgage when making the further advance (in registered land this means notice given by the subsequent mortgagee)
- Where, regardless of notice, the mortgage imposes an **obligation** to make such further advances. (An obligation to make a further advance should be noted on the register in registered land.)

In addition, S.49 LRA 2002 introduces a fourth method of tacking relevant to **registered land only**:

- Where the borrower and lender have agreed a maximum sum for which the charge is security and that agreement is entered on the register of title. A maximum sum mortgage could be used to secure an agreed overdraft limit where the amount outstanding fluctuates, or a flexi-mortgage (or off-set mortgage) where the borrower can reduce the debt and reborrow up to the original sum lent.

8 Discharge of a mortgage

A mortgage is discharged when the debt secured is paid in full. This often happens where the mortgagor sells his estate and uses the proceeds to pay off his mortgage. A mortgage is also terminated where the property is sold under the lender's power of sale, or in the event of foreclosure.

- In registered land, the mortgagor can apply to the Land Registry for cancellation of the relevant entries in the charges register if he is retaining the property. On a sale, the entry is cancelled.
- In unregistered land, a receipt is usually endorsed on the mortgage deed (s.115 LPA 1925).

(The methods for discharging mortgages will be addressed in more detail in Part B.)

Summary

- A charge by way of legal mortgage is the most common form of security over land.
- A charge that is not by deed or is not registered when it should be will be equitable only.
- A mortgagee has a number of remedies available in the event of the borrower's default. The remedy that is most commonly exercised is the **power of sale**.
- Registered legal mortgages rank in priority according to their date of registration.
- In registered land, a charge should be registered by notice on the charges register of the mortgagor's title.
- In unregistered land, a legal charge triggers compulsory first registration. A legal charge without deposit of title deeds should be registered as a land charge.
- Where tacking is allowed, a subsequent advance by a mortgagee may rank in priority to a second mortgage created or registered before that advance where certain criteria are met.

Self-test questions

1 What effect does a borrower's death have on an ordinary repayment mortgage?

2 Is a mortgage a legal or equitable interest in land?

3 Why is the 'date of redemption' important?

4 If a mortgagor has been in default for three months following service of a demand for payment of sums due under the mortgage, what is the most likely remedy the mortgagee will exercise?

5 Which of the following statements is correct:

(a) The borrower must repay the mortgage after the date of redemption has passed.

(b) A purchaser will need to check that the legal date for redemption has passed if he is buying from a mortgagee.

(c) The date for redemption of a mortgage is usually 20 or 25 years after the date the mortgage was executed.

6 Which of the following statements is most correct:

(a) A mortgagee can sell the charged property provided that the mortgage was created by deed, provided that all or part of the debt has become due and provided that there is no contrary intention expressed in the mortgage.

(b) It is likely that a mortgagee will need to obtain a court order for possession when exercising his power of sale.

(c) A purchaser buying from a mortgagee exercising his power of sale must check that the mortgagor has been in default for three months following service of a demand for payment; or that interest remains outstanding for two months after becoming due; or the mortgagor is in breach of a mortgage term other than the covenant for repayment of capital or interest.

7 Is a mortgagee entitled to pursue more than one remedy?

8 Ulrika is buying an unregistered property with the assistance of a mortgage from Westminster Bank, the terms of which are that it is to be protected by deposit of the title deeds. You are acting for Ulrika and Westminster Bank (which is likely). How will you ensure that Westminster Bank's interest is protected?

9 In the above example, the property is already subject to a legal mortgage, protected by deposit of the title deeds. Why is it important that this mortgage is discharged on the sale to Ulrika and how is it done?

10 What is tacking?

Answers to self-test questions

1. The whole amount of the mortgage debt becomes payable from his estate. He may have in place a mortgage protection policy to cover this eventuality.
2. It can be either, but a legal mortgages (created by deed and registered if necessary) are more common.
3. Primarily because it is when the mortgagee's power of sale arises.
4. Power of sale.
5. (b)
6. (b) Because the purchaser is likely to require vacant possession.
7. Yes, the remedies are cumulative (save that foreclosure terminates all other remedies).
8. The purchase will trigger first registration and so the mortgage will be protected as a charge on the charges register and this is likely to be one of Westminster Bank's requirements in their instructions to you.
9. Otherwise, Ulrika will take subject to it! In unregistered land, a receipt is usually endorsed on the mortgage deed by the lender once the mortgage has been discharged.
10. The making of a further advance under a mortgage with the result that it ranks in priority to subsequent mortgages.

5

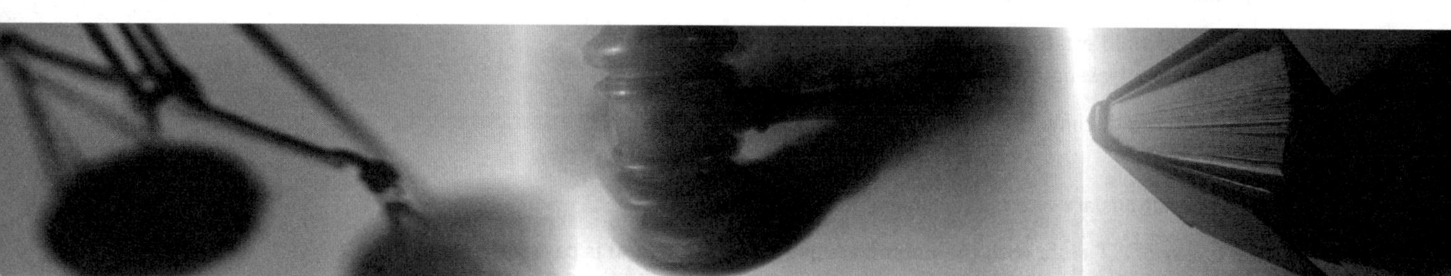

Tax

Topic List

Chapter overview

This chapter will:

- Explain when SDLT is payable and at what rate
- Give an outline introduction to VAT and its applicability to dealings in land
- Explain how CGT works and how relief may be available for the disposal of a principal private residence

1 Stamp Duty Land Tax (SDLT)

SDLT was introduced by the **Finance Act 2003** and came into force on 1 December 2003. It replaced 'stamp duty' which, although payable in much the same circumstances, was paid by affixing stamps to the document itself. SDLT is paid to HM Revenue and Customs (HMRC) and the documents are not stamped.

1.1 When is SDLT payable?

SDLT is a tax on '**chargeable transactions**' involving land in the UK. Chargeable transactions include, but are not limited to the acquisition:

- Of a freehold estate or
- Grant of a leasehold estate

The nature of the document is immaterial: the tax is charged on the transaction, not the document.

Certain transactions are exempt, including mortgages.

Liability to pay SDLT rests with the person acquiring the estate and is payable within **30 calendar days of completion** of the acquisition. It is payable to HMRC.

1.2 How much is payable?

SDLT is payable at a rate of between 1% and 4% of the whole purchase price. If any part of the purchase price is attributable to chattels, this is excluded for the purposes of calculating SDLT. The thresholds and rates are

Purchase price (excluding chattels)	*% of purchase price payable as SDLT*
Up to £125,000 (residential) *	0%
Up to £150,000 (mixed or non-residential)	0%
Over £125,000 and up to £250,000 (residential)*	1%
Over £150,000 and up to £250,000 (mixed or non-residential)	1%
Over £250,000 and up to £500,000	3%
Over £500,000	4%

* There are certain reliefs available, including where the acquisition is of residential land in an area designated as 'disadvantaged'.

New thresholds introduced from 3 September 2008 mean that if a person buys wholly residential property and the purchase price is £175,000 or less no SDLT is payable. This 'stamp duty holiday' is due to expire on 31 December 2009 although may be extended beyond this date.

If the purchase price is more than £175,000, SDLT is paid at between 1% and 4% (as above) on the whole purchase price.

The 'purchase price' is usually cash but may also be other consideration valued as at market value, including other property, works and services and the release of debt. The 'whole purchase price' for SDLT purposes means the price for the property including any VAT (see below) that is payable, whether or not that VAT is recoverable.

(There are rules on 'linked transactions', designed to prevent the minimising of SDLT by fragmenting a single transaction into a series of smaller transactions. For example, where the seller and buyer are the same or where the smaller transactions can be said to form a 'scheme' of transactions, these rules would apply and SDLT would be payable on the aggregate value of each transaction.)

As mentioned, SDLT is not payable on chattels and so the purchase price may be expressed to exclude payment for chattels. An apportionment of part of the overall cost of the property in

respect of chattels, will, therefore reduce the amount of SDLT payable. This is particularly advantageous where the agreed price is just above an SDLT threshold.

2 Value Added Tax (VAT)

VAT is a notoriously complex tax, not least in relation to land and buildings. It is governed by the **Value Added Tax Act 1994.** Although, as a basic rule, supplies of land are 'exempt', there are some exceptions.

For the purposes of this Study Manual, however, only an introduction to the general principles will be given.

2.1 What is VAT?

Generally speaking, VAT is payable on '**taxable supplies**' made in the UK by a taxable person in the course of a business, which are not exempted or zero-rated.

Some businesses are required to register for VAT purposes (for example if the value of their supplies is over a certain limit), others may choose to do so in specified circumstances. If registered, a person must account for 'output tax', ie VAT chargeable on standard-rate and reduced-rate supplies made by him. He will pay the amount of output tax minus input tax (ie VAT incurred by him on expenditure relating to standard or reduced rate supplies). If the amount of his input tax exceeds his output tax, generally speaking he may reclaim the amount of that excess from HMRC.

2.2 How much VAT is payable?

There are currently three rates of VAT:

	%
Standard rate	17.5
Reduced rate	5
Zero rate	0

In 2001, the reduced rate of VAT was introduced. This is applicable to certain conversions and renovations of properties that have been empty for more than three years or conversions of non-residential properties for private use, among other things.

2.3 When is VAT payable?

A supply of land includes a sale of the freehold or leasehold or other interest and the grant of a lease.

As noted above, a supply of land is normally exempt. Exclusions from this usual exemption are the:

▸ Sale of the freehold or long lease in **'qualifying buildings'**, ie new dwellings and relevant residential or charitable buildings by the person constructing them.	These supplies are zero-rated.
▸ Sale of the freehold of new or partly completed **'non-qualifying buildings'**, ie commercial premises (including office, retail, factory and warehouse buildings) during the first three years following completion.	These supplies are standard-rated.
▸ Grant of facilities for parking or holiday accommodation.	These supplies are standard-rated.

You will see from these exclusions that VAT is primarily of concern in relation to commercial clients and commercial transactions.

The creation of a **mortgage** is not a taxable supply of land for VAT purposes.

There are special rules for the transfer of land and buildings as part of the transfer of a business as a going concern.

Charities are not automatically exempt from VAT but certain supplies to charities are relieved from VAT.

3 Capital Gains Tax (CGT)

CGT is a tax payable on disposals if there is a capital gain within the asset which is being disposed. It is primarily governed by the **Taxation of Chargeable Gains Act 1992** (TCGA 1992).

3.1 When does CGT arise?

Typically, CGT arises when a person disposes of a '**chargeable asset**', including property, and makes a profit in doing so, ie he sells it for more than he bought it. CGT also arises when he makes a gift of an asset (ie sales and gifts are disposals for CGT purposes). In this case, the sale price is replaced with a market value. If he was given the asset (or inherited it) then, likewise, the acquisition cost is replaced with the market value at that time.

Some disposals do not give rise to CGT, principally:

- Transfers to a spouse/civil partner - there is no CGT payable on the disposal, but the receiving spouse/civil partner is deemed to take the acquisition cost of the disposing spouse/civil partner for later disposals - the gain is effectively deferred.
- Transfers to a registered charity.
- Transfers on death. On death, all earlier gains are effectively 'wiped out' and the beneficiaries of the estate take the assets at an uplifted base cost (the market value at the date of death) which is deemed to be their acquisition cost on later disposals. This will be relevant in Section 2 of the of the Study Manual (Wills, Probate and Administration).

3.2 Private residence relief

Chargeable assets for CGT purposes include land and buildings. However, there is one very important exception. Under s.222 TCGA 1992, the disposal of a dwelling house or part of it, or all or part of the garden attached to it, may attract **private residence relief** with the result that no CGT is payable. 'Dwelling house' may include a house, flat, houseboat or fixed caravan. Generally speaking, however, it must be the person's 'home' or principal dwelling. The principal features of this relief are set out below.

3.2.1 Who qualifies for relief?

The relief is only available to an **individual** owning (or co-owning) a freehold or leasehold estate in the property or beneficial interest in such estate. Companies are not entitled to this relief.

Note that relief is **not** available where property is acquired wholly or partly for the purpose of making a profit from selling it.

3.2.2 Full relief

There is no CGT charge (ie there is total relief) where the following four conditions are met:

- The dwelling house has been the only or main residence throughout the period of ownership.

- The dwelling house has been occupied throughout the period of ownership except for allowed periods of absence or because of having to live in job-related accommodation.
- The garden or grounds do not exceed 0.5 hectares (approximately 1 $^{1}/_{4}$ acres), including the site of the dwelling house.
- No part of the dwelling house has been used exclusively for business purposes during the period of ownership.

Failure to meet all these conditions may result in partial relief.

3.2.3 'Only or main residence'

If a person owns two or more houses, only one can qualify for private residence relief. It is open to the owner to **nominate** which residence is to be treated as his 'only or main residence' within two years of owning two or more. Each time his combination of residences changes, he has a new two year period in which to make the nomination. If no nomination is made, which house is to be treated as the only or main residence will be determined as a matter of fact, having regard to all the circumstances.

A married couple/ couple in a civil partnership may have only one main residence between them. If each spouse/civil partner owned one property before the marriage, the two year nomination period begins on the date of the marriage (or registration as civil partners). If the couple are separated, each person may have a different main residence and be entitled to relief.

3.3 Calculation of CGT

CGT is payable on the total amount of the chargeable gain less any reliefs and allowable losses (for example costs of acquiring, selling or improving the asset), ie the 'net gain'. The chargeable gain is the sale price (or value less acquisition cost or value or base value in 1982 if it was acquired earlier).

If the net gain is over the annual exemption then CGT is payable on that excess. CGT is now charged at a flat rate of 18%. If the net gain is below the annual exemption, no CGT is payable. The annual exempt amount for tax year April 2009 – April 2010 is £10,000 for an individual.

Summary

- SDLT is payable on all chargeable transactions involving land within 30 days of completion.
- SDLT is assessed at between 0% and 4% on the purchase price.
- SDLT is not payable on chattels.
- Supplies of land are generally exempt for VAT purposes. Exceptions include freehold sales of new or partly completed commercial premises within the first three years (that are standard-rated) and freehold sales and long leases in new dwellings by the developer (that are zero-rated)
- CGT is payable on the net gain arising from a disposal of a chargeable asset (including land) after an annual exemption allowance. It is charged at a flat rate of 18%.
- Private residence relief of up to 100% is available for a sole or main residence.

Self-test questions

1. Is the acquisition of an equitable interest in land a 'chargeable transaction' for SDLT purposes?
2. Within what timescale must SDLT be paid?
3. What rate of SDLT is payable on a purchase price of £550,000 where it is (a) residential property (b) commercial property?
4. At what point (in terms of purchase price) does SDLT become payable at 3% in the case of a purchase of non-residential property?
5. What is the (a) standard rate and (b) reduced rate for VAT?
6. To what types of transaction is the VAT reduced rate applicable?
7. Does the creation of a mortgage attract VAT?
8. Is CGT payable when a person gives away a chargeable asset?
9. Name two types of disposal that do not attract CGT
10. What is the effect of a private residence being used partly for business use, in relation to the CGT private residence relief?
11. If Peter sells his home (he only has one house) will CGT be payable?

Answers to self-test questions

1 Yes

2 Within 30 days following completion

3 4% in both cases

4 On a purchase price of more than £250,000.

5 (a) 17.5%
(b) 5%

6 Certain conversions and renovations of properties that have been empty for more than three years and conversions of non-residential properties for private use.

7 No.

8 Yes. The sale price is replaced with a market value in calculating the gain.

9 Transfers to a spouse/civil partner, transfers to a registered charity; transfers on death.

10 Full relief is not available.

11 No – principal private residence relief will apply.

Part B
Freehold Conveyancing

Part B: Freehold conveyancing

Overview

Now that you have learned the fundamental principles of land law, we turn to the practical application of those principles in conveyancing.

'Conveyancing' is the term used to describe the buying and selling of title to land. The word derives from 'conveyance' which is the name given to a deed of transfer in unregistered land. The word is still used, however, in relation to the newer system of registered land (even though the deed by which title passes is not called a conveyance, but a transfer).

Part B begins by giving an overview of conveyancing, setting out the structure of a conveyancing transaction (Chapter 6). After considering some aspects of professional practice that are of particular relevance to conveyancing transactions (Chapter 7), the subsequent chapters (Chapters 8–14) describe and explain each of the steps undertaken by the seller's and buyer's solicitor.

Part B addresses both registered land and unregistered land. The steps are similar in each. Some differences are explained.

Part B is based on a sale of a **freehold** estate. Much of the material in this section is also applicable to a sale (assignment) of an existing leasehold estate and even to the grant of a new leasehold estate. However, there are some differences and additional considerations. These are addressed in Part C.

Test requirements

The QLTT Test Specification stipulates that candidates should be able to demonstrate:

- An understanding of the basic principles of land law and the manner in which they apply to conveyancing transactions
- An understanding of the basic principles of contract law and the manner in which they apply to conveyancing transactions and
- A broad knowledge of conveyancing procedures

Section A has taught you the basic principles of land law. Have those in mind as you see them placed in the practical context of conveyancing in this Section.

The basic principles of contract law, as applicable to conveyancing, will be covered in this section, as they are relevant. Your knowledge in this area may be tested by questions on the:

- Impact of the Law of Property (Miscellaneous Provisions) Act 1989
- Characteristics of the contract required to effect a change of ownership
- Nature of remedies available for breach of contract in the context of a conveyancing transaction

Your knowledge of conveyancing procedures may be tested by questions that require you to demonstrate that you can:

- Given a typical range of conveyancing transactions, identify from the documentation:
  - The extent of the property
  - In whom the property will vest and in what capacity
  - The encumbrances which will subsist
  - Any unremedied defects in title or matters affecting enjoyment of the property

- Identify the steps needed to conduct pre-contract and pre-completion searches, identify difficulties arising from the searches and inquiries, including relevant planning considerations, and explain the legal effects of issues identified in the searches and inquiries
- Recognise implications of the Land Registry Rules and taxation of transactions including VAT, stamp duty land tax and capital gains tax

6

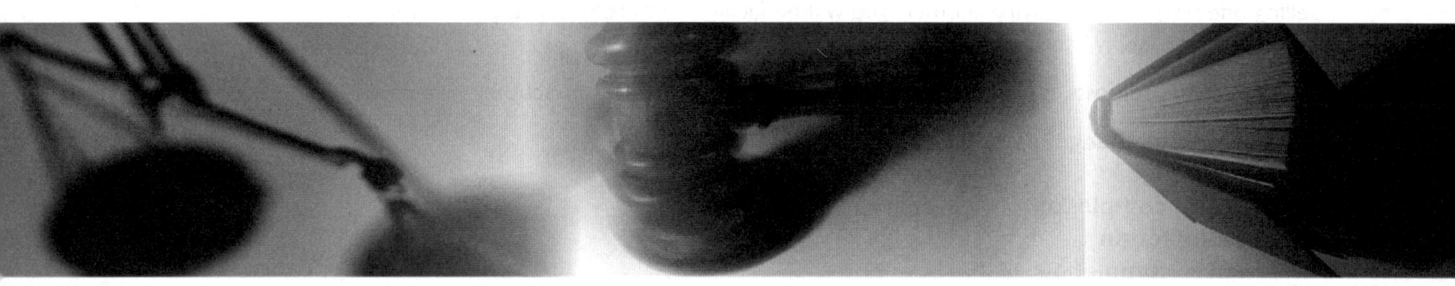

Freehold conveyancing: an overview

Topic List

Chapter overview

This chapter will:

- Illustrate the structure of a typical sale and purchase of a freehold estate in land, indicating the steps that need to be taken up to exchange of contracts, up to completion and after completion
- List the types of questions that need to be asked when taking instructions from either a buyer or a seller
- Consider certain topics that are particularly relevant to residential conveyancing, including Home Information Packs and surveys

1 The structure of a conveyancing transaction

There is an established formula to conveyancing, involving a number of steps undertaken by the solicitor acting for the seller and the solicitor acting for the buyer (and their respective mortgagees, if applicable). It is very important that you understand the structure of a conveyancing transaction, from taking initial instructions to closing your file, and that you know at which point the various steps are taken.

You should find the following flowchart of assistance in helping you to understand the conveyancing process.

It is the solicitor acting for the buyer who has the most to do. Needless to say, if your client is selling one property and buying another, you will be fulfilling both roles (in respect of the appropriate property in each case).

As the diagram suggests, it is convenient to think of a conveyancing transaction in five parts:

- **Up to exchange of contracts**
- **Exchange**
- **Up to completion**
- **Completion**
- **After completion**

Part	Broadly, what it covers	Refer to chapter
Up to exchange (note the parties are **not** contractually bound until contracts are exchanged)	Taking instructions	6
	Professional conduct matters	7
	Buyer's solicitor investigates what his client is buying:	
	▶ Title	8
	▶ Enquiries	9
	▶ Searches etc	9
	▶ Drafting the contract	10
Exchange	▶ Deposit paid ▶ Completion date fixed ▶ Parties contractually bound	11
Up to completion	▶ Searches ▶ Drafting the transfer	12
Completion	▶ Balance paid	12
	▶ Transfer and mortgage dated	12
After completion	Post-completion steps, including: ▶ Discharge of seller's mortgage ▶ Payment of SDLT ▶ Registration	13

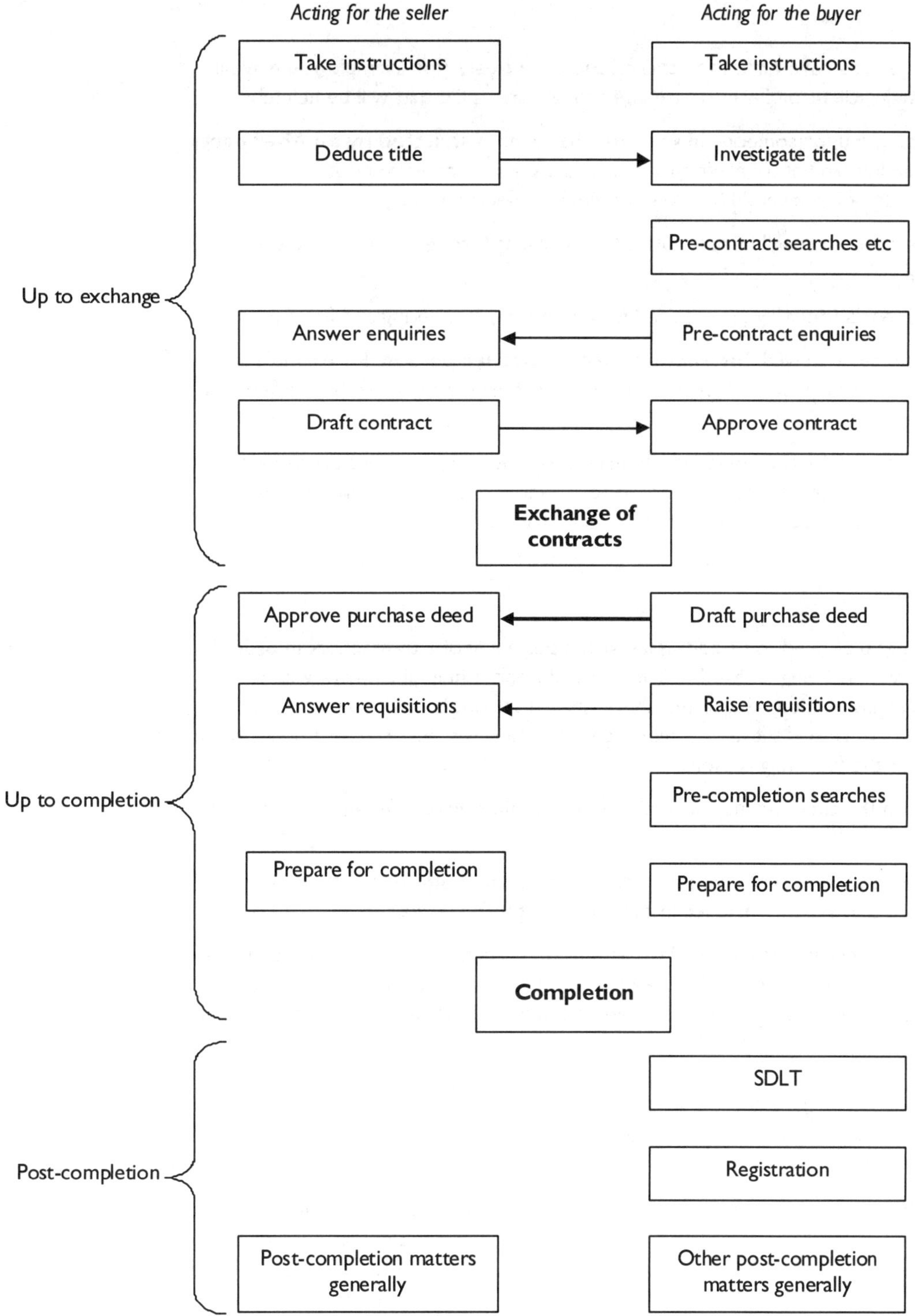

2 Taking instructions

At the outset of the conveyancing transaction, you will need to obtain full instructions from your client. This is obviously to enable you to select and carry out the appropriate steps needed in the transaction to reflect what he has agreed with the other party prior to instructing you. However, it is also so that you can give legal advice on all relevant matters arising from your client's proposed transaction, both at the outset and as and when they arise. Obtaining instructions efficiently and comprehensively will save time in the long run and help to avoid problems or oversights later on.

2.1 Good practice

- Check whether you have **acted for the client previously** (for example you may have acted for a seller-client on his purchase and so may have a file that will be helpful)
- Check whether you, or someone in your firm, has been **instructed by another party** to the transaction (and, if so, make sure that you are not in contravention of the Solicitors' Code of Conduct 2007 - you may need to decline to act) *
- Satisfy yourself that you will be able to act for the client throughout the **entire transaction***
- Check the **client's identity** (as required for anti-money laundering and fraud purposes)
- If you have already received **'instructions' from another person**, for example an estate agent or a prospective co-owner or co-seller, these will need to be verified with your client

* There are rules of professional conduct which dictate whether or not a solicitor can act for both buyer and seller or lessor and lessee (and/or borrower and lender) in conveyancing transactions. These are considered in detail in the next Chapter.

2.2 Checklists

There are many things that need to be addressed at the beginning of a transaction. In order to reduce the risk of anything being omitted, solicitors usually find it helpful to work with a 'checklist' in obtaining instructions. Suggested checklists are set out below. However, it is essential that you do not regard these as comprehensive in all cases. Any checklist needs to be used with caution for the following reasons:

- Some items on the checklist may be irrelevant in certain transactions and should not be mentioned
- Some transactions may require you to address additional or alternative special considerations that are not included in this (or any other) checklist

You will see from the checklists below that instructions on certain matters need to be obtained regardless of whether you are acting for the seller or the buyer, for example, details of the terms already agreed between the parties. However, for the purpose of completeness, these are included in each case.

2.2.1 Acting for the seller: checklist

Topics to address	The types of questions	Notes
1 **The transaction**		You will be responsible for drafting the contract where many of these details will be set out and you may be instructed to prepare searches and other relevant contents of a Home Information Pack (HIP) (see below), either before or at the same time as drafting the contract.
The property	What is the address? Is the seller's title freehold?	Consider any rights that need to be granted and/or retained

Topics to address	The types of questions	Notes
The price	What does it include?	What fixtures and fittings are included? Arrange for your client to complete the Seller's Property Information Form and Property Information Questionnaire and Fixtures, Fittings and Contents Form (if these have not already been provided in a HIP)
The deposit		Consider any related purchase and advise on the consequences in the event of failure to complete
The timetable	Are there any expectations/requirements as to exchange and/or completion? Is the sale linked to a purchase?	
The parties		Ensure that you have full details for all parties and contact details of their solicitors
Present use	Is the seller in breach of any relevant planning permission and/or covenants?	You may need to consider obtaining retrospective consents/insurance
Special provisions	Are there any particular terms that have been negotiated?	
2 **Existing mortgage(s)**	How much is outstanding? Will the proceeds be sufficient to repay it/them? Who is the mortgagee?	If there is to be a related purchase, you may need to consider this in conjunction with transfer of endowment policies etc Obtain full details of the mortgagee.
3 **Title deeds**	Does the client and/or existing mortgagee possess any relevant title documents?	If you need to request these from the mortgagee, you will need to provide an undertaking to either repay the loan or return the title deeds on request
4 **HIP**	Has a HIP already been produced?	See below If so, you need to obtain a copy from your client or the estate agent
5 **Persons in occupation**	Are there any? Who are they?	Obtain full details of tenancies and persons in occupation
6 **Tax**	Is VAT relevant? Is CGT relevant?	For example is your client VAT registered? Is it a sale of a second home? See Chapter 5

2.2.2 Acting for the buyer: checklist

Topics to address	The types of questions	Notes
1 **The transaction**		You will need to ensure that the draft contract and other documents and responses from the seller's solicitors are in line with your client's instructions
The property	What is the address?	Consider whether the location makes additional searches or enquiries necessary
	How old is the property?	This may be relevant for advising on surveys.
The price	What does it include? Is part of it attributable to chattels only (on which SDLT is not payable)?	Consider apportioning a part of the purchase price to chattels in order to reduce liability to SDLT
The deposit	Has this been addressed?	Does your client have funds available for a deposit? Consider the effect of a related sale
The timetable	Does your client have any expectations/ requirements as to time of exchange and/or completion? Is the purchase dependent on a sale?	
The parties		Make sure you have full contact details for the seller's solicitor
Intended use	What does your client intend to use the property for?	If your client proposes a change of use or physical alterations, planning consents may need to be obtained and/or binding covenants addressed
Special provisions	Are there any particular terms that have been negotiated?	

Topics to address	The types of questions	Notes
2 **Mortgage**	Does your client require a mortgage? Has he already obtained a mortgage offer?	If so, make sure your client understands his liabilities, including monthly commitments, and mortgagee's remedies Be aware that whilst *generic* advice about types of mortgage is usual advice, specialist advice regarding particular mortgage products and policies may require authorisation from the Financial Services Authority
3 **Finance**	Do the sums add up?	Run through the costs in outline. You should be able to advise the client of the costs of the transaction. Take any related sale into account
4 **Tax**	Is VAT relevant?	See Chapter 5
5 **Survey**	What type of survey and/or valuation is most appropriate?	See below
6 **HIP**	Has your client received a HIP?	Obtain a copy – see below.
7 **Co-ownership**	Is your client buying with another person(s)? Is someone else contributing to the purchase price?	You will need to advise on how the legal estate and beneficial estate are to be held (see Chapter 1)
8 **Insurance**		Ensure that your client understands his obligations as to insurance following exchange (see Chapter 11)

2.2.3 Action immediately following instructions

Having obtained instructions, you should now attend to the following:

- Attendance note for the file
- Confirm your instructions to your client and detail action to be taken by you and your client (for example, he might have agreed to provide you with relevant documents)
- Make contact with the other party's or parties' solicitor

3 Residential conveyancing

3.1 Home Information Packs (HIPs)

Under the Housing Act 2004, a seller may be required to produce a HIP and provide copies to prospective buyers within 14 days of any request.

3.1.1 When is a HIP needed?

The obligation applies to **residential properties** placed on the open market with vacant possession.

HIPs are now mandatory for all properties marketed in England and Wales, regardless of their size or number of bedrooms.

3.1.2 What does a HIP contain?

Some contents are compulsory and some optional. Broadly, the contents are as follows:

Compulsory	Optional
HIP index (list of contents)	**Home Condition Report** (HCR). This is essentially a report of the condition of the property carried out by a qualified home inspector. (Note that whilst a HCR remains optional at present, it is possible that the government will revert to its original plan to make HCRs compulsory.)
Property Information Questionnaire which is completed by the seller and is intended to provide useful information about the property, eg council tax band, information on parking etc.	**Guarantees, warranties and insurance policies** relating to any defects in the property
Energy Performance Certificate (EPC), which gives the home an energy efficiency rating and an environmental impact rating (both on a scale of A to G) and gives recommendations for improvement	Additional information such as plans, translations of HIP documents, extra title documents or ones relevant to leasehold or commonhold and additional searches
Sale statement, setting out the terms of sale (ie the property address and tenure, the seller and the capacity in which he sells and whether vacant possession is being given)	A Home Use Form and/or a Home Contents Form (published for use in a HIP) or the **Seller's Property Information Form and Fixtures Fittings and Contents Form** commonly used.
Evidence of title	
Additional information where the property is commonhold	
Additional information where the property is leasehold (eg copy of the lease and details of service charge and insurance)	
Local land charges search and standard **enquiries of the local authority**	
Drainage and water searches	

3.2 The National Protocol

In 1990, the Law Society introduced the first edition of the National Protocol. This was designed to standardise and simplify the conveyancing process in residential transactions. It is identified by the logo 'TransAction'.

Basically, the solicitors acting for both parties determine whether they intend to use the Protocol. If so, they will follow its prescribed procedures. For the most part, these simply reflect traditional conveyancing practice, but at times it means that they will use particular documents (and must use the Protocol form of contract). In this Study Manual we will assume the Protocol is being used.

3.3 Surveys

The seller is not under a legal obligation to disclose physical defects in the property. The legal principle of '*caveat emptor*' (or 'let the buyer beware') applies. In addition to his own physical inspection of the property, the buyer is therefore well advised to obtain a surveyor's report regarding the physical condition of the property, prior to exchange of contracts. However, usually for reasons of cost, in many cases he will choose to rely on an alternative.

There are four courses of action that a buyer will usually select from and cost and the age of the property will usually determine which course he chooses.

To rely on his lender's valuation	It is important that your client understands that this is not a survey at all. A valuation is only designed to satisfy the lender that the sums being advanced are not irresponsibly high.
To obtain a Homebuyer's Valuation and survey	This is something of a compromise between relying on just the lender's valuation and obtaining a full structural survey. It is often criticised for being somewhat superficial. If your client has concerns about the structural soundness, he should consider paying for a full structural survey.
To obtain a full structural survey	This is usually the most expensive option, but may be advisable, especially where the property is old, unusual, causing concern or not detached. In such cases, the cost of a full structural survey can be a lot less than the cost of actually carrying out works that may be needed at a later date. In addition, the results of a survey can often be used by the buyer to negotiate a reduction in the purchase price. In the event of negligence, the buyer also has a direct contractual relationship with the surveyor and does not need to establish a duty of care in tort, as he would where he relies on a report prepared for the lender.
To rely on a HCR contained in a HIP	This is prepared by a Home Inspector in a standard format. It does report on the condition of the property but does not contain a valuation and is not as detailed as a full structural survey.

Summary

- 'Conveyancing' describes the process of buying or selling title to land (registered or unregistered).
- A conveyancing transaction follows a standard procedure.
- The seller's solicitor deduces (proves) title and usually drafts the contract. He also answers enquiries and requisitions and prepares a completion statement.
- The buyer's solicitor investigates title and raises enquiries and requisitions, carries out searches prior to exchange and completion and drafts the purchase deed.
- The buyer's solicitor also attends to payment of SDLT and registration.
- A HIP is required for a residential property placed on the open market.
- Solicitors usually choose to adopt the National Protocol in a conveyancing transaction
- A buyer may need to be advised with regard to obtaining a survey of the property.

Self-test questions

1. Which solicitor drafts the contract for approval?
2. Which solicitor drafts the purchase deed for approval?
3. Which solicitor attends to registration following completion?
4. On taking instructions from a seller, why would you be concerned to enquire about his use of the property?
5. On taking instructions, why might the age of the property be relevant?
6. What size of property currently requires a HIP to be prepared?
7. What does the logo 'TransAction' signify?
8. Is a seller legally bound to disclose physical defects in the property?

Answers to self-test questions

1 The seller's solicitor

2 The buyer's solicitor.

3 The buyer's solicitor.

4 You may need to consider obtaining retrospective planning consents if his use has been in breach of any planning conditions. Also check for restrictive covenants.

5 If it is old, it is likely to make a full structural survey more advisable. If it is new, it may give rise to issues concerning VAT.

6 A residential property of any size needs a HIP when it is offered for sale on the open market.

7 TransAction signifies the Law Society's National Protocol that will usually be adopted by solicitors to a residential conveyancing transaction.

8 No. The principle 'caveat emptor' ('let the buyer beware') applies.

7

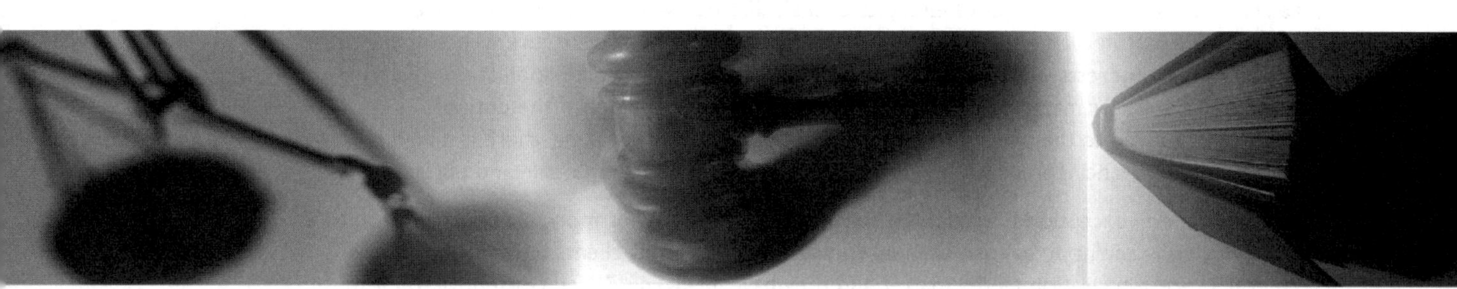

Professional conduct in conveyancing transactions

Topic List

Chapter overview

This Chapter will:

- Describe when a solicitor may act for both buyer and seller
- Describe when a solicitor may act for both buyer and lender
- Set out the rules regarding contract races
- Discuss the professional conduct rules relating to a solicitor engaged in 'property selling'
- Describe the rules to be followed when dealing with non-solicitors
- Address the duty of confidentiality in conveyancing transactions
- Consider solicitors' undertakings and the professional conduct aspects relevant to money laundering

Chapter overview continued

Aspects of professional conduct that are relevant to conveyancing will be addressed here.

Reference is made to the Solicitors Regulation Authority Code of Conduct 2007. As in that document, 'you' is used to refer to the solicitor concerned and here includes a solicitor in your firm or an associated firm.

1 Duty not to act (rule 3.01)

There is a general duty not to act for two or more clients in relation to any matter (or related matter) where there is a conflict of interests or a significant risk of a conflict arising from the duties owed to act in each of their best interests. Essentially, a conflict occurs where acting in one party's best interests would result in prejudice to another client. If a conflict arises during a transaction, a solicitor may only continue to act for one client and only if the duty of confidentiality owed to the other client is not breached. Broadly speaking, there is a high risk of conflict in a conveyancing transaction, just as there is in any contract for sale and purchase.

There is a general exception that allows a solicitor to act for two or more clients in relation to a matter, notwithstanding actual or potential conflict, if the different clients have a substantially common interest in relation to the matter and they have all given written consent (3.02) It must be reasonable in all the circumstances to do so and you must be satisfied that you have explained the issues in a way that the clients have understood. Thus it may be permissible to act for joint buyers or joint sellers for example.

There are also certain specific exceptions to this rule that may enable a solicitor to act for both buyer and seller or both borrower and lender.

2 Acting for both buyer and seller (or lessor and lessee)

Subrules 3.07–3.15 apply to transfers of land or the grant or assignment of a lease or other interest in land, for value. They apply to residential and commercial conveyancing.

2.1 The general rule (3.07)

The basic rule is that you cannot act for more than one party in any conveyancing, property selling or mortgage related services, except in accordance with 3.08-3.15. However, there are exceptions, namely where:

Property selling
Negotiating the sale for the seller.

- The transaction is not at arm's length
- The transaction is at arm's length but certain criteria apply
- You are providing only mortgage related services for the buyer or property selling services for the seller

Mortgage related services:
Advising on or arranging a mortgage or providing mortgage related financial services for a buyer. 'Mortgage' includes a remortgage.

2.1.1 Transactions not at arm's length (3.08)

You may act for a seller and buyer where the transaction is *not* at arm's length, provided there is no conflict or significant risk of conflict.

Whether or not a transaction is considered to be at **arm's length** is a question of fact in all the circumstances. The fact that the transaction is at full market value does not necessarily mean that it is at arm's length, nor does the fact that it is described as such. However, a transaction will usually be considered *not* to be at arm's length where the buyer and seller are:

- Related by blood, adoption or marriage, or living together
- Trustees or personal representatives and a beneficiary
- Associated companies

This exception does not apply where there is more than one prospective buyer. In these cases, you cannot act for both seller and buyer (10.06).

2.1.2 Transactions at arm's length (3.09)

Even where the transaction is at arm's length, you may still be able to act for both seller and buyer where one of the following applies:

- Both parties are **established clients** (see below)
- The transaction is for **£10,000 or less** (and is not the grant of a lease)
- Seller and buyer are represented by **two separate offices** in different localities (provided different individuals conduct the transaction for each party and neither client was referred to the office by another office of the same firm)

Whichever of the above applies, you can still only act for both parties if the following requirements are satisfied:

- Both parties must provide written consent
- There must be no conflict of interest
- The seller must not be selling or leasing as a builder or developer

Note that in determining whether a client is an **'established client'**, some degree of permanence in the solicitor-client relationship is needed. A former client is not necessarily an established client. However, someone related to or living with an established client is deemed to be one, as is someone who buys or sells jointly with an established client.

Again, this exception does not apply where there is more than one prospective buyer. In these cases, you cannot act for both seller and buyer (10.06).

2.1.3 Property selling and mortgage related services (3.11)

You may act for both seller and buyer, subject to the conditions below, where either you are only acting for the:

- Buyer in providing mortgage related services
- Seller in providing property selling services through a Solicitors' Estate Agency Limited ('SEAL')

The following conditions must also be satisfied:

- Both parties must provide written consent
- There must be no conflict of interest
- The seller must not be selling or leasing as a builder or developer
- Different individuals must conduct the transaction for the seller and for the buyer
- Before accepting instructions to deal with property selling, you must inform the seller of any services which might be offered to a buyer
- You must explain to the buyer (before he gives consent)
  - The implications of a conflict of interest arising
  - Your financial interest in the sale and
  - If you propose to provide mortgage related services to the buyer through a SEAL which is also acting for the seller, that you cannot advise the buyer on the merits of the purchase.

2.2 Is it advisable to act for both seller and buyer?

There may well be cases where it is convenient, or even sensible, to accept instructions from both seller and buyer, within one of the exceptions above. However, this choice must be exercised carefully. Generally speaking, it is not regarded as best practice to act for both, even where it is permitted by the Code of Conduct. Should a conflict arise once the transaction has commenced, you may only go on acting for one of the parties if the duty of confidentiality to the other client(s) is not put at risk (3.15). Any such necessary change in instructions is likely to cause delay and inconvenience to all concerned.

3 Acting for both borrower and lender (3.16)

Subrules 3.16–3.22 cover grants of mortgages and remortgages in residential and commercial conveyancing. It is common practice, in residential conveyancing, for a solicitor to act for both the buyer and his lender or the seller and his lender.

3.1 The basic rule (3.16)

The basic rule is that you *cannot* act for both borrower and lender on the grant of a mortgage of land in the following circumstances:

Individual mortgage
Any mortgage that is not a standard mortgage

- If a conflict of interest exists or arises
- On the grant of an 'individual mortgage' at arm's length
- If the matter involves a standard mortgage of property to be used as the borrower's private residence only and the lender's mortgage instructions extend beyond certain specified limitations or do not permit the use of a prescribed certificate of title
- If the matter involves any other standard mortgage and the lender's mortgage instructions extend beyond the specified limitations

Standard mortgage
A mortgage on standard terms, provided in the normal course of the lender's activities, where lending comprises a significant part of the lender's activities

The specified limitations are complex and long (3.19) but, broadly, cover standard conveyancing procedures, such as searches and enquiries, investigation of title and reporting on lease provisions.

It is normal practice either to obtain confirmation from the lender that its mortgage instructions and documents sent pursuant to those instructions are within the scope of the specified limitations set out in 3.19 or, perhaps more commonly, for the lender to give instructions according to a standardised set of instructions prescribed by the Council of Mortgage Lenders' Handbook (with individual variations as appropriate).

3.2 Acting for both parties on a standard mortgage

It follows that you may act for both borrower and lender in the case of a standard mortgage, provided:

- There is no conflict
- The mortgage instructions are within the specified limitations, and
- Where it is for a private residence, the approved certificate of title is used

Note that a conflict may arise where a buyer is unable to comply with one or more terms of a mortgage offer, for example a prohibition on letting or requiring that the balance of the purchase monies is provided from his own funds.

You must notify the lender (3.18) if you propose to act for seller, buyer and lender in the same transaction.

The prescribed form of certificate of title is included as an annex at the end of rule 3. Note that a lender may, alternatively, use a short form certificate of title which incorporates the approved certificate by reference.

Further Reference
Visit www.sra.org.uk/code-of-conduct for more detailed discussion of these rules

3.3 Acting for both lender and buyer on an individual mortgage

It also follows that you may only act for both lender and buyer on an individual mortgage if:

- No conflict arises and
- The mortgage is not at arm's length (3.16).

3.4 Acting for joint borrowers

Special care needs to be taken where you are instructed by a husband and wife who plan to mortgage their home, that is in their joint names, in order to secure a loan to a business owned by one of them. This is not an uncommon situation. The problem comes when the spouse with the business defaults and the other claims that he or she only entered into the mortgage as a result of undue influence.

In *Royal Bank of Scotland v Etridge (No 2) 2001*, the House of Lords held that the landowner who alleges undue influence in such circumstances has the burden of proving it. It may be presumed in the case of a special relationship, such as a parent and child or solicitor and client, although that presumption is rebuttable. No such presumption is made, however, in the case of a husband and wife.

Nonetheless great care must be exercised when acting for a lender in such a situation as, on the face of it, there is no obvious advantage to the spouse executing in the mortgage and hence a real prospect that he or she may be able to show undue influence and have the charge set aside. The lender is likely to seek your confirmation that you have fully and properly advised the spouse on the legal and practical issues involved and that he or she has, on that basis, agreed to your acting for both. If, at any point, you consider that the transaction is absolutely not in the spouse's best interests, you should decline to act. However, the fact that the transaction involves risks on his or her part is not a reason in itself to decline to act.

4 Contract races (10.06)

You cannot act for both seller and buyer, nor for more than one buyer, where there are two or more prospective buyers, ie where there is a 'contract race'.

Note that where the seller ceases to deal with one buyer in favour of another, this is not a contract race and the following provisions do not apply. However, if the first buyer had reached the stage of considering a draft contract, he should be asked to return it so that the situation is clear.

As soon as the seller gives an instruction to deal with more than one buyer, or indicates to you that he is dealing with more than one prospective buyer, you are under an obligation to disclose that fact to each prospective buyer or his solicitor (10.06). You must also make clear upon what terms the contract race is being conducted. Normally it will be a case of stipulating that the first buyer to produce a signed contract and deposit will secure the property.

If the seller refuses to agree to such disclosure, you must stop acting for him immediately.

Contract races are generally regarded as inadvisable and you might consider advising the seller-client that beginning a contract race can often lead prospective buyers to walk away from the intended purchase.

5 Property selling

You are permitted to engage in selling property on behalf of your client, ie to negotiate with a third party for its purchase. You are permitted to carry out a valuation of the property in order to advise on the selling price and to prepare the sales particulars. You may do so as part of your practice, from your normal office or from a separate location, or you may run (or be involved in) a separate estate agency business. Note that, in this latter case, you are also bound by rule 21 of the Code of Conduct, that deals with the conduct of separate businesses and is designed to ensure that members of the public are not confused into thinking that the separate business is regulated by the Solicitors Regulation Authority.

In fulfilling this role, however, you should remember that you are still a solicitor and bound by all the normal rules governing solicitors' professional conduct. You will also be subject to the Property Misdescriptions Act 1991, which makes it an offence to attach a misleading description to the property being sold (but not to the Estate Agents Act 1979).

6 Dealing with non-solicitors

The preparation of a contract or transfer for the sale of land for gain or reward can only be done legally by a qualified person, or 'authorised practitioner', including solicitors and licensed conveyancers (s.22 Solicitors Act 1974 as amended by the Courts and Legal Services Act 1990). Where an unqualified person appears to be acting for the other party, you should draw this law to their attention and suggest that a qualified person is instructed. An 'undertaking' (in the form of a solicitor's undertaking) from an unqualified person is not enforceable and should not be accepted.

If acting for a lender, where the borrower is represented by an unqualified person, you should ensure that the mortgage advance is only paid to a solicitor, licensed conveyancer or person properly authorised to receive the monies on the borrower's behalf.

If acting for a seller or buyer, where the other party is not represented by a qualified person, you should not advise that other party as you would your own client but you should suggest that he seek legal advice. In the meantime, you should ensure that you conduct the matter in a way that does not seek to take advantage of the fact that he is not legally represented (especially, perhaps, in relation to drafting the contract).

7 Other matters of professional conduct not exclusive to conveyancing

You should have regard to all professional conduct rules and guidance at all times. In particular, the following matters may be relevant:

- Confidentiality
- Undertakings
- Money laundering

7.1 Confidentiality

Under rule 4, you are required to keep all your client's affairs confidential, except where disclosure is required or permitted by law or by your client. This duty continues once the file is closed.

As mentioned above, if a conflict of interest arises between two clients, you may only continue to act for one provided that you do not breach the duty of confidentiality owed to the other.

7.2 Undertakings

There are several instances of where an undertaking might be given in a conveyancing transaction, for example:

- An undertaking by a seller's solicitor to discharge his client's mortgage immediately following completion
- An undertaking to forward a duly executed and dated contract or purchase deed

As with all undertakings, they should be given in writing and set out very clearly the precise scope of the promise. Remember that any breach of an undertaking amounts to professional misconduct.

Summary

- There is a general duty not to act for two or more parties where a conflict of interests exists or may arise
- A solicitor may only continue to act for one party provided there is no breach of the duty of confidentiality
- A solicitor can act for both buyer and seller where the transaction is either not at arm's length or where one of certain exceptions apply (established clients, £10,000 or less, separate offices) and certain criteria are met
- If one party is only receiving property selling services or mortgaged related services, a solicitor might act for both, subject to conditions
- You should think twice before acting for both parties, even if it is not prohibited by the rules
- A solicitor may act for both borrower and lender in most cases (but not if, for example, a conflict of interest arises or if it is for an individual mortgage at arm's length), provided the lender's instructions are within certain limitations
- Exercise extreme caution where acting for married joint borrowers where the mortgage is to secure a loan to a business of one spouse only
- A solicitor cannot act for buyer and seller nor for more than one buyer in the case of a contract race
- Appropriate steps need to be taken where the other party is not represented by a solicitor or licensed conveyancer

Self-test questions

1. What is a conflict of interest?
2. Do the rules on acting for both buyer and seller apply to commercial conveyancing in the same way as to residential conveyancing?
3. Is a sale by a husband to a wife necessarily 'not at arm's length'?
4. Can you act for both buyer and seller provided the purchase price is less than £10,000?
5. What is a SEAL?
6. Can you act for both borrower and lender on the grant of an individual mortgage?
7. What is a contract race?
8. Can you act for both buyer and seller in a contract race provided certain conditions are met?

Answers to self-test questions

1 A conflict of interest occurs where to act in one party's best interests would result in prejudice to another client

2 Yes

3 No, although this will often be the case. Relevant facts may suggest otherwise

4 *Prima facie* yes, but certain conditions must be satisfied (for example, written consent must be provided and there must be no conflict of interest)

5 A Solicitors' Estate Agency Limited which is a recognised body that does not undertake conveyancing, is owned by at least four participating firms and is based in separate accommodation

6 Yes, provided the mortgage is not at arm's length and no conflict arises

7 A contract race exists where a seller is dealing with more than one prospective buyer

8 No. You can never act for both buyer and seller (nor for more than one buyer) where there is a contract race

8

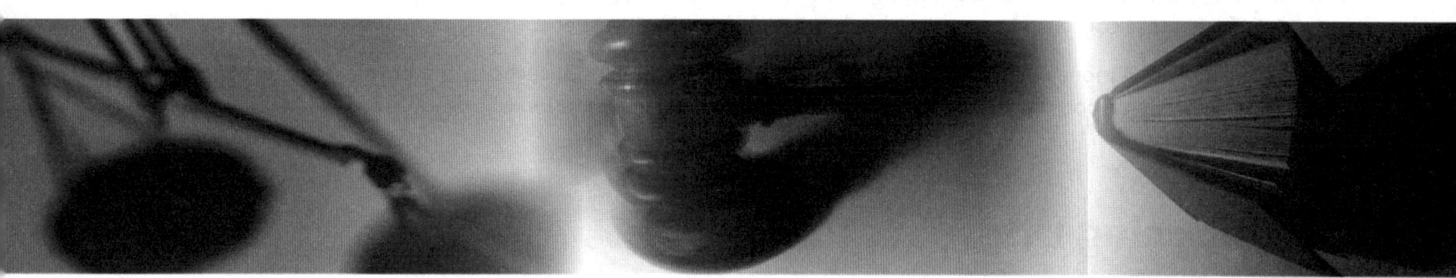

Deducing and investigating title

Topic List

Chapter overview

This Chapter will, in relation to both registered land and unregistered land:

- Describe the steps taken by the seller's solicitor in deducing title
- Describe the steps taken by the buyer's solicitor in investigating title
- Explain the meaning and significance of entries appearing on registers and title documents

1 Introduction

'**Deducing title**' is done by the seller's solicitor. It is the process of providing evidence of his client's ownership of the property to the buyer's solicitor.

'**Investigating title**' refers to the investigation carried out by the buyer's solicitor. It is the process of examining the title documents provided by the seller's solicitor, ascertaining the extent and quality of the title that will be acquired by his client and identifying any defects in that title. However, it is important that the *seller* also investigates his client's title before deducing it to the buyer's solicitor and drafting the contract. Therefore, the method of investigating title described in this Chapter applies to the task undertaken by each solicitor, although the emphasis is on the buyer's solicitor, since it is the buyer who is about to acquire title to the property and is, therefore, most concerned to ensure that it is satisfactory in all respects.

A lender advancing money on the security of the property has similar concerns to the buyer. If a solicitor is acting for both buyer and lender (which is likely), his investigation of title will serve both clients.

Alert

Note that where Protocol is used, title **must** be deduced prior to exchange

2 Deducing title

The seller's solicitor should not simply obtain and blindly send title documents to the buyer's solicitor. He too should examine them in order to:

- Identify any particular matters that need to be addressed in the contract for sale
- Resolve, as quickly as possible, any unsatisfactory aspects of his client's title

Epitome of title

A chronological list of the documents proving the seller's title, together with copies (or abstracts) of those documents

Where the seller is a mortgagee exercising its power of sale, the seller's solicitor needs to ensure that the power has arisen and has become exercisable (see Chapter 4).

The method of deducing title will depend on whether the land is registered or unregistered:

Abstract of title

A document that extracts the material information from a title document

Registered land	The seller's solicitor must send: ▸ Official copies of the register ▸ Title plan ▸ Copies of any documents referred to on the register
Unregistered land	The seller's solicitor must send either an epitome of title, together with copy or abstracted title deeds, or an abstract of title

The evidence of title to unregistered land is contained in the title deeds. The seller's solicitor will therefore deduce title by supplying the buyer's solicitor with particulars of the deeds. The seller's solicitor should deduce title from at least 15 years before the date of the contract and the chain of title must commence with a good root of title. There are two methods of deducing unregistered title – by preparing an abstract of title or by an epitome of title.

An epitome of title is usually used these days. As abstract is a summary of the material deeds, documents and events. An epitome is a list of the material deeds, documents and events, accompanied by photocopies of the material deeds and documents.

All documents dealing with the legal and equitable estate during this period should be deduced, together with any material pre-root documents.

3 Investigating title to registered land

When investigating title to registered land you should consider each part of the register and advise on it, identifying any issues which may need to be resolved on behalf of the buyer. You should of course, also consider overriding interests.

3.1 The official copies of the register

The official copies are exactly that, copies of the registered title provided by the Land Registry. In Chapter 2, you learned that the register is divided into three parts, each called a register. By way of reminder, these are:

A **Property Register**: describes property and rights benefiting the property

B **Proprietorship Register**: gives class of title, owner's name and entries affecting owner's rights of disposal

C **Charges Register**: lists charges affecting property and third party rights over the property

The following is an example of the register relating to a freehold property:

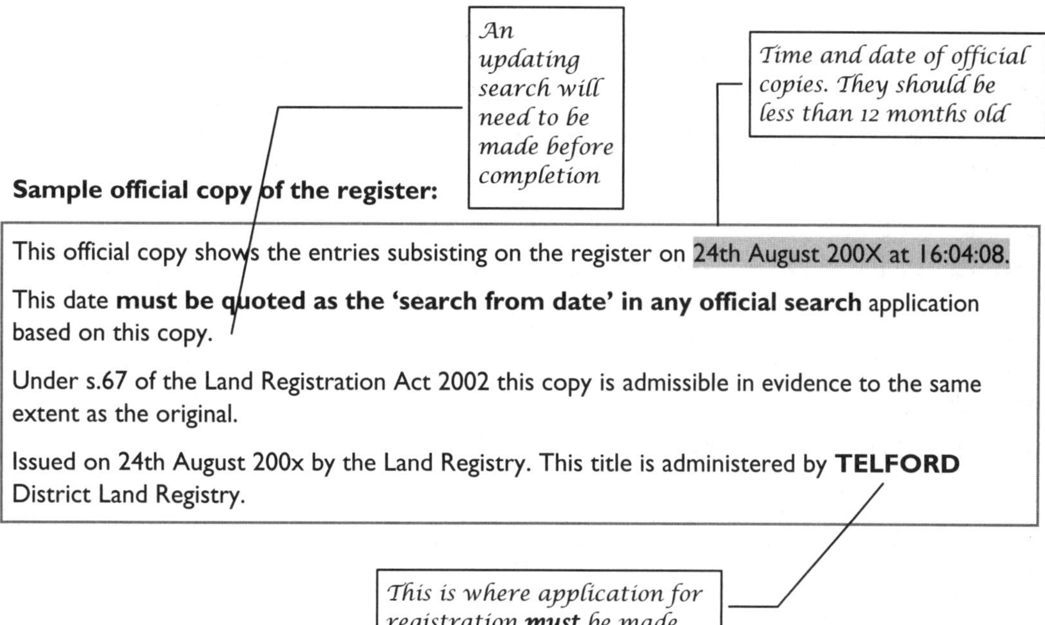

This is the all-important and unique number allocated to this title

Land Registry

Title Number: RDM86105

Edition Date: 1st September 1969

Date of first registration

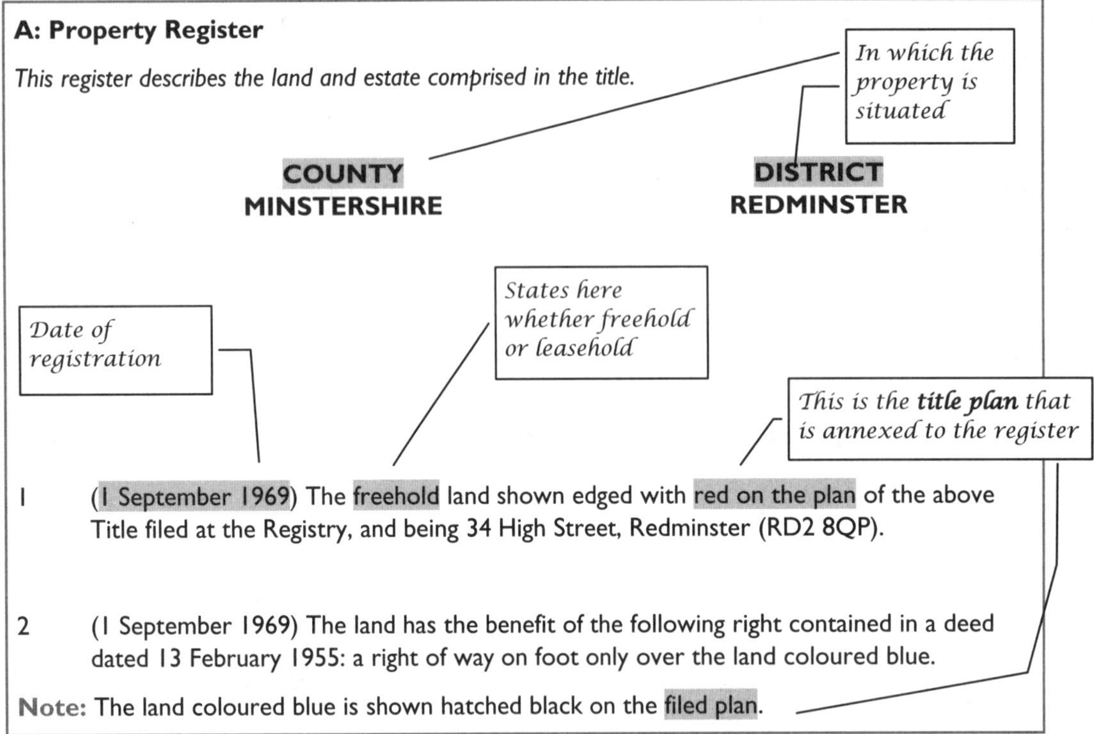

A: Property Register

This register describes the land and estate comprised in the title.

1 (1 September 1969) The freehold land shown edged with red on the plan of the above Title filed at the Registry, and being 34 High Street, Redminster (RD2 8QP).

2 (1 September 1969) The land has the benefit of the following right contained in a deed dated 13 February 1955: a right of way on foot only over the land coloured blue.

Note: The land coloured blue is shown hatched black on the filed plan.

Here, the rights have been fully set out in register. Alternatively, the rights may be referred to as contained in a document referred to on the register (in which case the sellers' solicitor must provide a copy), or set out in an annexed schedule.

B: Proprietorship Register

This register specifies the class of title and identifies the owner. It contains any entries that affect the right of disposal.

This shows the class of title (see Chapter 2)

Title Absolute

This is the current proprietor, registered on this date

1 (1 July 2006) Proprietor(s): FRANCIS PEARCE and ANNA PEARCE both of 34 High Street, Redminster, RD2 8QP.

2 (1 July 2006) RESTRICTION: except under an order of the Registrar no disposition by the proprietor(s) of the land is to be registered without the consent of the proprietor(s) of the charge dated the 17 June 2006 in favour of Franklyn Building Society as referred to in the Charges Register.

3 The price stated to have been paid on 17 June 2006 was £499,500.

Note: The Transfer to the Proprietors contains a covenant to observe and perform the covenants referred to in the Charges Register and of indemnity in respect thereof.

This indicates that there is a chain of indemnity covenants in place in respect of covenants

Shows mortgagee's consent needed. The absence of a further restriction shows that Francis and Anna Pearce hold the beneficial interest as joint tenants

C: Charges Register

This register contains any charges and other matters that affect the land.

Notice of restrictive covenants

1 (1 September 1969) A Conveyance of the land in this title dated 13 February 1936 made by Redminster Builders Limited ('Vendor') to James Smith ('Purchaser') contains covenants details of which are set out in the schedule of restrictive covenants hereto.

2 (1 July 2006) REGISTERED CHARGE dated 17 June 2006 registered on 1 July 2006 to secure the monies including the further advances therein mentioned.

Buyer will need to ensure this will be discharged on completion

3 (1 July 2006) Proprietor: Franklyn Building Society of 28 Market Street, Redminster RD6 9AR.

There is no need to obtain a copy of the whole conveyance

Schedule of covenants

The following is a copy of the covenants contained in the conveyance dated 13 February 1936 referred to in the Charges Register:

'And the Purchaser for himself his heirs, executors, administrators and assigns hereby covenants with the Vendor its heirs and assigns that he will perform and observe the stipulations set out in the first schedule hereto so far as they relate to the hereditaments hereby assured.'

(a) **The Purchaser shall within 3 months from the date of his purchase erect (if not already erected) and afterwards maintain in good condition a good and sufficient open pale or other approved fence or hedge on the side or sides of the plot marked 'T' on the plan within the boundary.**

Positive covenant

(b) No external alterations whatsoever shall be made to the premises without the written consent of the Vendor.

Restrictive covenant

The 'T' mark affects the northern and western boundaries of the land in this title.

**** **END OF REGISTER** ****

Note. A date at the beginning of an entry is the date on which the entry was made in the Register.

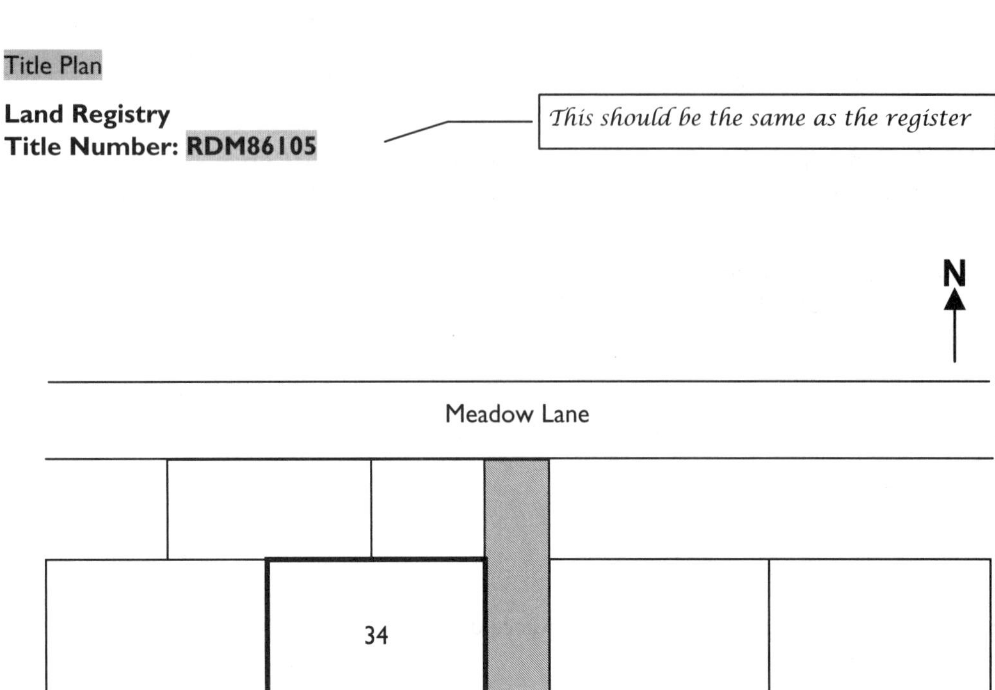

3.2 The Property Register

You should check that the description of the property corresponds with what your client believes he is buying. You should also refer to the filed plan. If there are any express easements benefitting the property they will be detailed in the Property Register. You will need to ascertain the extent of such easements (consider the wording and the filed plan) and check that they are adequate for your client. The benefit of any covenants will also be noted here (and as you now know it is likely that the benefit will pass to your client) and these should be brought to the attention of your client.

3.3 The Proprietorship Register

There are various things to note on the proprietorship register, in particular:

- The class of title
- The registered proprietor(s)
- Restrictions
- Cautions
- Inhibitions
- Notes

3.3.1 Class of title

The class of title assigned to each title is the **Land Registry's guarantee** of the title to the property. Any person who suffers loss as a result of a mistake in the register or rectification of it, is entitled to be indemnified by the register (s9 LRA 2002).

There are three possible classes of freehold title (and four in the case of leasehold title): absolute, qualified and possessory. These were explained in Chapter 2. By way of reminder, in relation to freehold titles only, the classes of title signify the following:

Absolute title – the best class of title, indicating that there were no material defects in title when application for registration was made

Qualified title – where title has been established only for a limited period or is subject to reservations that cannot be disregarded

Possessory – where the registrar is satisfied that the applicant is in actual possession or receipt of rents and profits but has no further evidence of title that would justify qualified or absolute title

3.3.2 The proprietor

The seller is likely to be the registered proprietor and may be:

- An individual
- A company
- Co-owners

On the death of one co-owner, it is unlikely that the survivor(s) would update the register; there is no requirement that they do and there is a fee for doing so. It is therefore quite possible that you will be acting for a buyer who is buying from the survivor(s) of a deceased co-owner.

However, it may be that the seller is someone *other than* the registered proprietor, in which case special considerations will apply. The seller could be:

- Personal representatives of a registered proprietor or
- An attorney acting under a power of attorney given by the registered proprietor or
- A mortgagee exercising its power of sale where the mortgagor is the registered proprietor

You should have regard to the following:

Seller	
Individual (and registered proprietor)	The seller must be the named party in and sign/execute the contract and transfer
Company (and registered proprietor)	The company must be the named party in and execute the contract and transfer. A company search must be carried out to confirm that the company: ▸ Still exists as a registered company ▸ Does not have fixed or floating charges registered that may affect the property. (If there is a relevant charge, you will need to ensure that it is to be discharged on completion.) (A company search is made at Companies House, see Chapter 9.)

Seller	
Co-owners (and registered proprietors)	You may wish to refresh your memory on co-ownership (see Chapter 1). Remember that the legal estate is always held as joint tenants so that the principle of survivorship applies and a survivor can deal with the legal estate. It is how the beneficial interest is held that is important and you will be able to ascertain this by looking at the proprietorship register. If there is a restriction entered, they are beneficial tenants in common. If none is entered, you may assume that they are beneficial joint tenants. The restriction would look like this: The Restriction you will see if there are two registered proprietors and they hold the beneficial interest as beneficial tenants in common is: **Restriction**: except under an order of the Registrar no disposition by the proprietor(s) being the survivor of joint proprietors (and not being a trust corporation) under which capital money arises is to be registered except by order of the registrar of the court The Restriction you will see if there are more than two registered proprietors and they hold the beneficial interest as beneficial tenants in common is: **Restriction**: No disposition by a sole proprietor of the registered estate (except a trust corporation) under which capital money arises is to be registered unless authorised by an order of the court.
As beneficial joint tenants	All joint tenants should be named in and sign/execute the contract and transfer. If one co-owner has died, the remaining owner(s) must sign/execute as the legal and beneficial title vests in him/ them. An official copy of the death certificate of the deceased co-owner is sufficient for registration purposes. Since the register is treated as conclusive, there is no need to ask whether the joint tenancy has been severed at any point.
As beneficial tenants in common	All co-owners should be named in and sign/execute the contract and transfer. Two trustees of the legal estate (or a trust corporation) will be needed to overreach the beneficial interests. If one of two co-owners has died, you will require an official copy of the death certificate of the deceased and appointment of a second trustee (whose name will also appear on the transfer deed along with that of the survivor) in order to be satisfied that overreaching has taken place.

Seller	
Personal representatives (PRs) of the registered proprietor	All PRs must execute the contract and transfer. The buyer's solicitor and Land Registry will require an official copy of the grant of representation to check that the PRs have been appointed as PRs for the registered proprietor. Remember that payment of monies to a sole PR overreaches all beneficial interests – this is an exception to the general rule that to overreach beneficial interests, the purchase monies must be paid to two trustees. If the seller is the personal representative or personal representatives of X (X and Y both shown as Registered Proprietors), it follows that Y must have predeceased X – the legal estate will have passed automatically by survivorship to X on Y's death. As regards the beneficial interest, it will either have been held as joint tenants or tenants in common. This will be clear from the proprietorship register. If they held the beneficial interest as tenants in common, payment to a sole PR is sufficient to overreach the beneficial interests. An official copy of Y's death certificate should be requested to prove Y is dead. An official copy of the grant of representation to X's estate should be requested to prove X is dead and that the personal representative has authority.
An attorney acting under a power of attorney	An **attorney** is a person authorised by another person (the donor) to act on that other person's behalf in dealing with his property. This authority is conferred by a deed called a **power of attorney**. In all cases, more than one attorney can be appointed. There are various categories of power, the most common of which is the general power. **General powers of attorney** A general power grants an attorney authority under s 10 of the Powers of Attorney Act 1971 to deal with all the donor's assets. It can be granted as follows: ***I appoint Q to be my attorney in accordance with s10 of the Powers of Attorney Act 1971*** It must be signed as a deed to be valid. **Limited powers of attorney** The donor can decide to limit the attorney's powers so that the attorney can deal with only limited assets or deal with a particular transaction. It must be signed as a deed to be valid. Both of the above types of power are revoked upon the donor's death, mental incapacity or bankruptcy. Express revocation is also possible. **Trustees** Trustees may use a general power only if they have a beneficial interest in the property (s.1 Trustee Delegation Act 1999). If the trustee uses a general power then the *attorney* must record that the trustee has a beneficial interest in the property. This is normally done in the transfer deed. A buyer may rely on such a statement. An example of such a statement is:

Seller

John Smith confirms that Adam Jones has a beneficial interest in the Property as the date of this Transfer

Alternatively, a trustee may use a trustee power under s25 Trustee Act 1925, as amended by s 5 Trustee Delegation Act 1999. This can be used whether or not the trustee has a beneficial interest in the property, but the power cannot last for more than 12 months from the date of the power

Co-owners

Under the Trustee Delegation Act 1999, a sole co-trustee cannot be appointed as an attorney. This is because s.7 of the Trustee Delegation Act 1999 provides that a receipt for capital money will only overreach beneficial interests if the attorney acts with at least one other person. This reinforces the two trustee overreaching principle.

See also the notes relating to trustees above.

Enduring powers of attorney

Under the Enduring Powers of Attorney Act 1985, it was possible for a person to make an enduring power of attorney (EPA) whilst they had the required level of mental capacity. It is no longer possible to make and EPA, but those that were made before 1 October 2007 are still valid. An EPA can operate as an ordinary power of attorney whilst the donor has capacity (unless there is any restriction within the power that it can only be used once the donor has lost capacity), but at the onset of mental incapacity the EPA must be registered at the Court of Protection, after which it is normally incapable of revocation. In such circumstances, until registration has taken place, the attorney has no authority to act. Once an application has been made, but before registration is complete (this can take a number of weeks) the attorney can only exercise his powers (during this period) in a very limited set of circumstances set out in the Enduring Powers of Attorney Act 1985.

Lasting powers of attorney

The Mental Capacity Act 2005 (which came into force on 1 October 2007) introduced two new kinds of lasting powers of attorney (LPAs) (to replace enduring powers of attorney). One LPA covers property and financial affairs. (The other covers the donor's welfare).

Unlike an EPA, an attorney under an LPA will only be able to act once the donor has lost capacity. All LPAs must be registered at the Court of Protection to be valid.

EPAs and LPAs must be executed in accordance with the provisions of their governing legislation.

Acting for a buyer from an attorney

There are two main concerns for the buyer:

- Does the attorney have authority to act?
- Has the power been revoked?

Seller

Does the attorney have authority to act?

- Examine a certified copy of the power and check that they were duly authorised
- Check whether the power is limited in some way.
- Has the power been executed correctly?

Has the power been revoked?

General and limited powers

The Powers of Attorney Act 1971 provides that, even if the power was revoked, the transaction by the attorney is still valid providing the buyer did not know it was revoked.

There is presumption that the buyer did not know of the revocation if the disposition occurred within 12 months of the power. If the disposition occurred later than 12 months from the power the buyer must (within 3 months after completion) make a statutory declaration that he was unaware of any revocation.

EPAs and LPAs

There is a presumption that the transaction is valid if it took place within one year of the power being registered or the person dealing with the attorney makes a statutory declaration that he had no reason to doubt the existence of authority. Such protection depends upon the ignorance of the buyer of any material facts.

A mortgagee exercising its power of sale

You will remember that a buyer is concerned only with whether the power of sale has **arisen** and not whether it has become **exercisable** (see Chapter 4). A power of sale belongs to every mortgagee where the mortgage is by deed. The power arises once the legal date for redemption passes. A buyer's solicitor's main concern is to ensure that the mortgage can be removed from the register following completion.

Where there is only one mortgage on the register, the Land Registry will see that the seller is the mortgagee on the register, deduce that it must be exercising its power of sale and will remove the mortgage on registration of the purchase.

Where there is more than one mortgage on the register, a mortgagee can (without providing any further documentation) sell free of interests registered after its own interest has been registered, but not free of those interests registered before it. The owner of a second registered charge who is exercising its power of sale will need to apply the proceeds of sale to discharge the first mortgage and provide evidence of that having been done, in order that the buyer can be registered as proprietor free of the charges.

Seller

Example

C: Charges Register

Containing charges, incumbrances etc. adversely affecting the land

1 (12 April 2002) REGISTERED CHARGE dated 2 April 2002 registered on 12 April 2002 to secure the monies including the further advances therein mentioned

2 PROPRIETOR: City & County Building Society of 10 Commercial Street, Halifax, West Yorkshire HX1 1HL registered on 12 April 2002

3 (2 June 2006) REGISTERED CHARGE dated 22 May 2006 registered on 2 June 2006 to secure the monies including the further advances therein mentioned.

4 PROPRIETOR: Chancer Finance Limited of 106 Chancery Lane, London WC2A 5BG registered on 2 June 2006.

If City & County Building Society is exercising its power of sale, it must apply the proceeds of sale to

- Paying all costs and expenses of the sale
- Repaying its own mortgage
- Paying any residue first to Chancer Finance Limited and, thereafter, to the registered proprietor

If Chancer Finance Limited is exercising its power of sale, it will need to provide a evidence of the discharge of City & County Building Society's mortgage. Under s.105 LPA 1925, Chancer Finance Limited would need to apply the proceeds of sale to:

- discharging City & County Building Society's outstanding mortgage
- paying all costs and expenses of the sale
- repaying its own mortgage and interest
- returning any surplus to the registered proprietor

3.3.3 Restrictions on the proprietorship register

The two most likely types of restriction have already been mentioned. They are restrictions on the registered proprietor's ability to deal with the property, because either:

- The consent of a mortgagee is required
- (Where there are co-owners) the beneficial interests are co-owned as tenants in common

If a person has a interest under a resulting trust, they can protect this by way of a restriction. They may feel that the standard restriction set out below (which you have already seen) is sufficient.

Restriction: No disposition by a sole proprietor of the registered estate (except a trust corporation) under which capital money arises is to be registered unless authorised by an order of the court.

Alternatively they may make an application to the Land Registry that notice is given to them before registration. This is preferable and likely if the registered proprietor agrees that there is such a resulting trust.

In the absence of such a restriction, a buyer takes free from the beneficial interest, unless of course the person with the beneficial interest is an occupier, in which case it may be an overriding interest (which is overreachable).

3.3.4 Cautions on the proprietorship register

Since 13 October 2003 a caution can no longer be entered, but you may need to understand and advise on any caution entered prior to that date.

A caution prevents any dealing with the land from being registered until the cautioner has been given the opportunity to show cause why the dealing should not take place. A buyer should not proceed until the caution has been removed.

3.3.5 Inhibitions on the proprietorship register

Like cautions, inhibitions can no longer be entered on the register but you may need to advise on one that still appears on the register.

An inhibition prevents any disposition of the land until it is removed and is normally related to the bankruptcy of the registered proprietor.

3.3.6 Notes on the Proprietorship Register: positive covenants

You will remember that positive covenants **do not** run with the land and bind successors to the servient land, because it is deemed inequitable to require someone to incur expense in complying with a covenant to which he was not originally a party.

However, in practice, the Land Registry will include an entry regarding positive covenants either:

- Where a buyer is entering into a new positive covenant with a seller
- Where the seller gave an indemnity covenant to the person it bought from to comply with a former positive covenant and has obtained an identical covenant from its buyer

The Land Registry will note this on the Proprietorship Register, by means of a 'NOTE' under the names of the registered proprietors. This Note confirms that there is a chain of indemnity covenants in place.

Example

Note: *The Transfer to the Proprietors contains a covenant to observe and perform the covenants referred to in the Charges Register and of indemnity in respect thereof.*

Of course, although the chain of indemnity covenants is in place, the question of whether or not the covenant is actually enforceable will depend upon many factors. But the prudent, conservative advice to a client who is required to give an indemnity covenant is that they should assume that the covenant is enforceable if the person who gave it is alive (ie the registered proprietor).

You will recall the SCS 4.6.4 (see Chapters 3 and 10) requires the buyer to enter into an indemnity in similar form if the indemnity is still enforceable.

3.4 The charges register

You will recall that a **notice** may be entered on the charges register to protect certain third party interests, so that a buyer takes subject to them (unless they are removed), in particular:

- Charges
- Restrictive covenants

3.4.1 Charges

Mortgages are protected by **two entries in** the charges register, one describing the charge and the other naming the chargee. For example:

> **C: Charges Register**
>
> This register contains any charges and other matters that affect the land.
>
> 1 (1 July 2006) REGISTERED CHARGE dated 17 June 2006 registered on 1 July 2006.
>
> 2 (1 July 2006) Proprietor: Chancer Finance Limited of 106 Chancery Lane, London WC2A 5BG
>
> ****** END OF REGISTER ******

The buyer's solicitor must ensure the procedures are in place for its removal on completion. This is dealt with in Chapter 12.

The various methods of discharging a mortgage on a sale are described in Chapter 13.

3.4.2 Restrictive covenants

Provided certain criteria are met (including the need for registration) restrictive covenants will bind successive owners of the land burdened by the covenant. A notice on the charges register can protect restrictive covenants in one of three ways:

- fully set out in the charges register or
- within a schedule of covenants annexed to the charges register or
- by reference to a document annexed to the register (in which case a copy must be provided when deducing title)

Example

> **C: Charges Register**
>
> *This register contains any charges and other matters that affect the land.*
>
> (1 September 1969) A Conveyance of the land in this title dated 13 February 1936 made by Redminster Builders Limited ("Vendor") to James Smith ("Purchaser") contains covenants details of which are set out in the schedule of restrictive covenants hereto.
>
> **Schedule of covenants**
>
> The following is a copy of the covenants contained in the conveyance dated 13 February 1936 referred to in the Charges Register:
>
> 'And the Purchaser for himself his heirs, executors, administrators and assigns hereby covenants with the Vendor its heirs and assigns that he will perform and observe the stipulations set out in the first schedule hereto so far as they relate to the hereditaments hereby assured.'
>
> (a) The Purchaser shall within 3 months from the date of his purchase erect (if not already erected) and afterwards maintain in good condition a good and sufficient open pale or other approved fence or hedge on the side or sides of the plot marked 'T' on the plan within the boundary.
>
> (b) No external alterations whatsoever shall be made to the premises without the written consent of the Vendor.
>
> The 'T' mark affects the northern and western boundaries of the land in this title.

The covenant at (b) above is a restrictive covenant. Because it is registered, negative in nature and fulfils the other requirements of *Tulk v Moxhay*, this covenant will bind the buyer.

Note that 'the Vendor' referred to within the terms of the covenant may not be the person from whom consent is obtained: because the benefit of the covenant will run with the dominant land, the person from whom consent must be obtained in (b) above is the person who *now* owns the land with the benefit.

(This may of course be Redminster Builders Limited if they have not sold the land, but in order to demonstrate that you understand that the benefit of the covenant may run with the land, you will be expected to state that the person from whom consent is required is the person who now owns the land with the benefit.)

3.5 Interests that override registered dispositions

In addition to any matters discovered on an investigation of the title deduced by the seller's solicitors, you should remember that a buyer will also take subject to interests that will override the purchase once registered, even where absolute title is registered. These have been covered in Chapter 2. By way of reminder, these include:

- Legal leases for terms not exceeding seven years
- Interests of persons in actual occupation unless they failed to disclose their interest when enquiry was made of them or unless the interest would not have been obvious on a reasonably careful inspection of the property (and the buyer did not have actual knowledge of the interest)
- Certain legal easements
- Local land charges

As you will see in the next Chapter, the searches and enquiries provided in a HIP or made by a buyer's solicitor prior to exchange will aim to discover any such overriding interests.

4 Investigating title to unregistered land

The aim of investigating title to unregistered land is to ascertain ownership and all third party interests affecting the land, with a view to securing registration with absolute title following completion.

As regards interests in unregistered land, as you have learnt, they can be legal or equitable.

In registered land, unless an interest is overriding, it must be shown on the register (whether legal or equitable) in order to bind a buyer.

With unregistered land, there is no register of title. A buyer will be bound by all legal interests (except puisne mortgages) and any equitable interests of which they have notice. They will also be bound by overriding interests. This will be explained in more detail later in this chapter.

4.1 The epitome of title

As already mentioned, the epitome of title supplied by the seller's solicitor is essentially a list of documents pertaining to the title of the property to be sold.

Further Reference
An example epitome of title is included at the end of the Chapter.

S.45 LPA 1925 provides that the buyer is only entitled to see title deeds and abstracts dating back to the '**root of title**' (see below), together with any:

- Power of attorney under which a document in the epitome has been executed
- Pre-root document referred to by a document in the epitome (eg where a document refers to restrictive covenants imposed by a pre-root conveyance, or describes the property by reference to pre-root document).

4.2 The root of title

In order to give the buyer a good title, the seller must deduce a "good root of title". A buyer's solicitor must check that it is a good root of title and then trace chronologically from the root document a chain of ownership to the current seller. The chain must be complete and without missing links. A 'good root' is not defined by statute, but common law has deemed it to be a conveyance which:

- Is at least **15 years old** at exchange of contracts. This means that the conveyance to the current seller is likely to be the root of title. It should be dated on or before 30 November 1990 (when compulsory registration was extended to the whole of England and Wales), otherwise the property should have been registered at the Land Registry already. If the root of title is an earlier conveyance, you need to ensure that there is an unbroken chain of ownership from the root to the current seller and that the property transferred is consistent throughout.
- Contains a **description** by which the property can be identified (a plan is desirable but not essential) or refers to an earlier conveyance (which must also be deduced) which contains a good description.
- Deals with both the **legal and beneficial** interest in the property being conveyed. To ensure that the legal interest has been validly dealt with, you must ensure that the conveyance was by deed and has been validly executed and stamped (see below). Provided proper conveyancing procedures were followed, all equitable interests will have been overreached and will not bind the buyer.
- Casts no doubt on the seller's title. A document will cast doubt if it depends on its effect on an earlier document, such as a power of attorney or a grant of representation. Such doubt can be removed if the seller can produce the earlier document.

4.2.1 Correct execution of documents

As indicated above, a conveyance will not be a good root of title if it is improperly executed. You therefore need to know how to ensure that a conveyance has been properly executed. Remember that a conveyance of a legal estate must be executed as a deed. The formalities of execution will vary depending on the capacity of the legal person executing it.

Person executing deed	Form of execution	Example
An individual pre 31 July 1990	The deed had to be signed, sealed and delivered. The seal was usually a red circular piece of adhesive paper or wax. Delivery could be inferred from the signature and the seal.	SIGNED, SEALED and DELIVERED as a deed by Lawrence Harrison the said Lawrence Harrison
An individual post 31 July 1990	The deed has to be signed in the presence of a witness (who attests to the signature) and delivered.	Signed as a deed by Lawrence Harrison Lawrence Harrison in the presence of: G Carmine of 34 Temple Lane, London, EC4Y 8HT

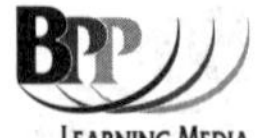

Person executing deed	Form of execution	Example
A company (with a company seal)	Proper execution could be assumed if the company seal was affixed in the presence of the company secretary and a director (s.74 LPA 1925) or (after 15 September 2005) by two directors	SIGNED SEALED AND DELIVERED AS A DEED BY REDWINGS LIMITED In the presence of: Director Director/Secretary
A company (without a company seal)	Alternatively (after 31 July 1990) execution could be by signature of a company secretary and a director (or two directors), provided it is expressed to be executed by the company. (s.130 Companies Act 1989)	**SIGNED** as a **DEED** and delivered by **ABC LIMITED** acting by: Director Director/Secretary
An attorney	Signed by the attorney in the presence of a witness In the examples, AB is the donor and XY is the donee of the power of attorney	**SIGNED** as a **DEED** by XY as attorney for AB *Signature – 'XY as attorney for AB'* In the presence of *(Signature, name & address of witness)* **OR** **SIGNED** as a **DEED** by AB Acting by his/her attorney XY *Signature – 'AB by his/her attorney XY'* In the presence of *(Signature, name & address of witness)*

4.2.2 Correct stamping of documents

Prior to the introduction of SDLT on 1 December 2003, 'stamp duty' was the tax payable upon the documentation involved in a transaction. The operation of stamp duty is similar to SDLT but under the system of stamp duty, stamps were actually affixed to the conveyance.

Stamp duty comprised two elements:

- Ad valorem duty, based on the value of the transaction
- |A 'produced stamp', also known as a Particulars Delivered, or PD, stamp

Ad valorem duty

Ad valorem duty was based on the value of the transaction, exactly as SDLT is today. Stamps were affixed to the conveyance, confirming the amount of stamp duty paid, *unless* the conveyance contained a **certificate of value**, confirming that the transaction fell below the threshold for payment of stamp duty, in which case no ad valorem duty was payable.

Example

Example of a certificate of value

'IT IS HEREBY CERTIFIED that the transaction hereby effected does not form part of a larger transaction or of a series of transactions in respect of which the amount or value or the aggregate amount or value of the consideration exceeds [sixty thousand] pounds'

It follows that a conveyance should have **either** an ad valorem stamp **or** a certificate of value.

Alert

An unstamped conveyance does not form a good root of title and will not be accepted by the Land Registry

If ad valorem stamps are not shown on a conveyance, you must check to ensure that there is a certificate of value. If there is not, then the conveyance has not been properly stamped and this must be rectified (and any penalty or interest paid) by the seller prior to completion. It might be advisable to insert a special condition into the contract to this effect. Note that any contractual provision purporting to make the buyer liable to pay the late stamp duty will be void (s.117 Stamp Act 1891).

The PD Stamp

All conveyances should have a 'Particulars Delivered' or 'PD' stamp. This shows that the conveyance has been submitted to the district valuer (a department of the Revenue) within 30 days of completion. Note that the 'Inland Revenue' dealt with stamp duty before HMRC.

INLAND REVENUE

19 SEPTEMBER 1987
FINANCE ACT 1931

Note that the following do *not* require to be stamped:

- Mortgages executed after 1971
- Powers of attorney
- A conveyance or transfer by way of gift, executed after 30 April 1987, provided a 'certificate of exemption' is included in the document.

4.2.3 Capacity of seller

If the seller is an individual proprietor, a company proprietor or co-owners (who are all alive), the considerations are the same as for registered land.

A purchase from the survivor of beneficial joint tenants

Where a beneficial joint tenant dies the doctrine of survivorship applies so his beneficial interest passes to the surviving joint tenant. The seller must produce an official copy of the death certificate of the deceased owner.

However, the buyer needs to ensure that the joint tenancy has not been **'severed'** prior to the co-owner's death. If it has been, the seller cannot convey the whole legal and beneficial interest to the buyer because the deceased's beneficial interest will have passed via his will or the rules of intestacy to a third party.

Therefore, in order to protect the buyer of unregistered land, the Law of Property (Joint Tenants) Act 1964 sets out three steps that a buyer from an apparent surviving joint tenant must take to ensure that there has been no severance of the joint tenancy:

Alert

These three steps only apply to unregistered land

(1) There must be a clear bankruptcy search (on form K16) against all joint tenants for the period of ownership (because bankruptcy severs a joint tenancy).

(2) There must be no 'memorandum of severance' on the conveyance to the joint tenants.

Example

Example of memorandum of severance

'**Memorandum**: From and including 5.12.1987 Thom Reese and Nelly Reese hereby declare that they hold the Property on trust for themselves as beneficial tenants in common.'

(3) In the conveyance to the buyer, the seller must state that he is solely and beneficially entitled to the property.

Note. The 1964 only applies to **unregistered** land. (In registered land, remember that provided there is no relevant restriction in the proprietorship register, the buyer is entitled to assume that there has been no severance of the joint tenancy.)

A purchase from the survivor of beneficial tenants in common	Where one tenant in common dies, survivorship does not apply so his beneficial interest passes with his estate. As in registered land, therefore, in order to overreach any beneficial interests, the buyer must: ▶ Insist on the seller appointing a second trustee ▶ Obtain from the seller an official copy of the death certificate of the deceased co-owner
A purchase from PRs	When the sole owner of unregistered land has died and his PRs are selling the land, the buyer must obtain a an official copy of the grant of representation, as this is the source of the PRs' authority to sell the land and proves that the owner is dead. If the sale is by the PR of the now deceased survivor of co-owners, then payment to a sole PR overreaches beneficial interests. The buyer's solicitor must also ensure that the PRs have not already (either inadvertently or knowingly) sold the land to another person. To do this he should check that: ▶ No memorandum of disposal of property appears on the grant of representation ▶ The PRs state in the conveyance to the buyer that there has been no previous disposal of the property (s.36(6) Administration of Estates Act 1925). The buyer should also insist that the PRs endorse a memorandum of the sale to the buyer on the grant of representation. Note. This is only necessary in **unregistered** land. (In registered land, the buyer can rely on the registered title as proof that the land has not previously been sold to another person.)

Alert
These steps only apply to unregistered land

With regards to a purchase from an attorney or a mortgagee, the position is the same as for registered land transactions, although the procedure for discharging mortgages is different with unregistered land.

Examining the chain from the root

It is quite likely that the root will be the conveyance to the current seller. However, events may have occurred which mean a chain needs to be followed from the root to the current seller. You should consider the following matters:

- Ensure that you see evidence of any change of name. For example, if the owner has, since the conveyance, changed her name following marriage, you should ask to see an official copy of the marriage certificate. The seller is not required to deduce this, as it is matter of public record, but likely will, as a matter of courtesy.

- Examine each deed in the chain for possible defects. You should check that the deed was executed correctly and stamped correctly.
- Check that the description of the property in root of title accords with what your client thinks they are buying. Check that there is consistency throughout the Epitome. Insist of seeing all plans.
- Ensure that you see evidence of death of any estate owner since the root and, if applicable a PR's authority to act.

4.3 Interests in land

In unregistered land, a buyer will be bound by legal interests (except puisne mortgages), equitable interests of which he has notice and overriding interests.

The existence of legal interest, such as express easements and legal mortgages will be revealed in the title deeds and by enquiries of the seller. Procedures will need to be put in place to ensure that existing mortgages are discharged on completion.

Certain equitable interests, notably the burden of post-1926 restrictive covenants can be protected as land charges (Chapter 2). If such interests have been registered as land charges then a buyer will be bound by them and, if not, broadly speaking will take free from them. It is therefore necessary to carry out a land charges search (see below).

Other equitable interests (for example, interests under trusts) are subject to the doctrine of notice. Suffice it to say that where two or more people own a legal estate there notice of an implied trust. You should refer to the notes above with regard to overreaching.

4.3.1 Searches of the register of land charges

As mentioned, certain third party rights are protected by registration on the Register of Land Charges. The rights are registered against the name of the person whose land is subject to the third party right (the 'estate owner').

 **Alert**

Note that where the Protocol is used, the seller should supply land charges search results against all previous owners and the seller. He may already have some with the title deeds which were carried out in relation to previous transactions.

The buyer's solicitor must ensure that he has land charges searches in the name of *each* estate owner disclosed by the epitome of title for that estate owner's period of ownership.

It is good practice to ensure that land charge searches were carried out against all **pre-root** estate owners of which the buyer has notice (ie those owners whose names are revealed by any pre-root documents disclosed by the seller either unnecessarily or because they reveal matters which affect title). However, there is a system of state compensation if an incumbrance registered before the root of title comes to light after completion (s.25 LPA 1969).

It is essential that the name of the estate owner is correctly spelt, because the search is carried out electronically against the name as it appears on the application. If there is any discrepancy in the title documents deduced, searches should be obtained against each version of the spelling.

Certified copies of marriage certificates (and searches against maiden and married names) should be present where an estate owner's name changed on marriage during her period of ownership.

An official certificate of search is conclusive in favour of a buyer if it gives no reasonable cause for misunderstanding.

An official certificate of search gives 15 working days protection against charges registered between the date of the search and completion. If the buyer completes the transaction before this period expires, he takes free from any entries made after the date of the certificate. If not, he should carry out fresh land charge searches on form K15 to check whether or not any third party rights were registered after the priority period expired. If it is not possible to establish the year in which they acquired the property, the search should be made to and from the dates before which and after which it was not possible to register a land charge The search periods given should be in whole years. The earliest year in which a land charge could have been entered was 1926.

If any land charges affecting the land are revealed, the buyer's solicitor should obtain an official copy of each land charge (using form K19), which will reveal the subject matter of the charge and the name and address of the person who applied to register it (and who therefore has the benefit of the charge).

The example below shows you should help bring these ideas together.

Example

You are acting for the buyer of an unregistered property from Timothy James Calder.

You have received the epitome of title. The notes are added in the sixth column for the purposes of this exercise only.

No of document	Date	Description	Evidence now supplied	Whether original to be handed over on completion	Notes
1	1980	Conveyance by Sarah Stokes and Brian stokes to Timothy James Calder	Photocopy	Yes	
2	1972	Conveyance from John Paul Foy to Sarah Hargreaves and Brian Stokes	Photocopy	Yes	This conveyance refers to an earlier conveyance by Arnold Peters to Mildred Kitson and Arthur Kitson dated 1961
3	1955	Conveyance by Halifax Mills Company to Edna Marjorie Robinson	Photocopy	Yes	

As a buyer's solicitor you would expect to see land charge search results against the following names for the periods shown.

Timothy James Calder	1980 – 2010
Sarah Stokes	1972 – 1980
Brian Stokes	1972 – 1980
Sarah Hargreaves	1972 – 1980
John Paul Foy	1961 – 1972
Mildred Kitson	1961 – 1972
Arthur Kitson	1961 – 1972
Arnold Peters	1955 – 1961
Edna Marjorie Robinson	1955 – 1961
Halifax Mills Company	1926 – 1955

4.3.2 The land charges

Under s1 LCA 1972, the Registrar is required to keep five registers, one of which is the land charges register. This register is divided into six classes; A, B, C, D, E and F, all of which deal with charges or obligations affecting land.

The *classes* of land charge that are likely to be revealed by your searches and on which you may need to advise are as follows:

Class C	**C (i) – Puisne Mortgage**, ie a legal mortgage not protected by a deposit of title deeds (s.2(4) LCA 1972). This is a legal interest in land that must be registered in order to be enforceable against buyers of the estate affected. (This is an exception to the rule that 'legal rights bind the whole world' and is based purely upon pragmatism. The first mortgagee (lender) is entitled to take possession of the title deeds. This will inform subsequent lenders of the fact that the land is subject to a mortgage (since the title deeds will not be available). But if a subsequent mortgage was not registered, how could one know if the land was subject to more than one mortgage? Without such knowledge, it would be unsafe to lend money against the security of the land. It is for this reason that a mortgage not secured by the deposit of title deeds is registrable.) **C (iv) – Estate Contract**, an estate contract is any contract dealing with land, for example a sale contract and, provided it is valid and enforceable (ie in writing and incorporating all the terms agreed between the parties), it constitutes an equitable interest in land.
Class D	**D (ii) – Restrictive Covenant**, ie a negative covenant affecting the land entered into on or after 1 January1926 **D(iii) – Equitable easement**, ie an easement which is not created by deed or which is over an equitable interest, created or arising on or after 1 January 1926. (Whether a pre-1926 restrictive covenant or equitable easement will bind successors in title or not is determined by the equitable doctrine of notice.)
Class F	This is a charge under the Family Law Act 1996 and gives a spouse, whose name does not appear on the legal title, the right, as against the owning spouse, to occupy the matrimonial home. Such a charge does not give the spouse an interest in land, or any right to the proceeds of sale, merely a statutory right of occupation. If a charge is registered, it will be impossible on a sale for the legally owning spouse to give vacant possession until such time as the charge is cancelled.

4.3.3 Interests that override first registration

In addition to any matters discovered on an investigation of the abstract of title and land charges searches, you should remember that a buyer will also take subject to interests that override first registration. These were set out in Chapter 2, but are summarised here, by way of reminder:

- Leases not exceeding seven years
- Interests of persons in actual occupation
- Legal easements
- Local land charges

4.4 Public index map search

Where land is unregistered, a **search of the index map** that is held by the Land Registry and shows each registered title in England and Wales. This search is more normally dealt with as one of the relevant searches described in Chapter 9, but is mentioned here as it relates to title in particular.

This search of the index map will confirm that the property has not already been registered and it will also reveal any registration of a caution against first registration which might protect, for example, a right of way over the property. Under the Protocol, the seller's solicitor carries out this search and provides the result to the buyer's solicitor.

5 Post-investigation

5.1 Requisitions

Having investigated title (whether registered or unregistered land), a buyer's solicitor may need to raise enquiries, or 'requisitions' of the seller's solicitors in order to obtain further information where something is unsatisfactory or unclear on the face of it. Although the contract is likely to restrict or exclude the right to raise requisitions on title, there is nothing to prevent the solicitor raising requisitions before exchange.

5.2 Report on title

Once the investigation is complete and requisitions have been dealt with, a buyer's solicitor should report to his client:

- the exact extent and tenure of the property to be acquired (ie whether it is freehold or leasehold)
- any third party interests to which he will take subject
- any unsatisfactory matters that have been revealed by the investigation
- any other significant points of interest

In each case, the report should include advice on the consequences of the matter revealed and any solution that can be sought.

If the seller has been unable to prove good title, the buyer may be best advised not to proceed. However, depending on the seriousness of the defect, it may be appropriate to consider whether the defect can be remedied or, if not, obtaining defective title indemnity insurance, if available, possibly to be paid for by the seller.

5.3 Verification of title

On completion in **unregistered land**, the buyer's solicitor will only have seen copy or abstracted documents and will usually verify these against the original deeds when he takes possession of them at completion.

A standard contract will normally oblige the seller to produce the original of every document or a certified copy where the original is not available.

Of course in **registered land**, official copies are sufficient evidence of the register and, together with an updating pre-completion search (see Chapter 12), mean that a buyer can be satisfied as to the true state of the register and hence the seller's title.

Summary

- The seller's solicitor deduces title to the buyer's solicitor prior to exchange
- The nature of investigation of title depends on whether land is registered or unregistered
- The property register describes the property and any rights benefiting it and refers to a title plan
- The proprietorship register names the registered proprietor and may contain restrictions on the owner's ability to deal with the property
- The charges register contains charges, covenants and other matters that burden the land
- Cautions and inhibitions can no longer be entered (but cautions against first registration can be entered in limited circumstances)
- The capacity of the seller may dictate that certain procedures need to be followed
- Always remember that there are some entries that may not appear on the register or deduced title documents but which override registration
- In unregistered land, a seller must deduce a good root of title, ie a conveyance at least 15 years old that identifies the property, deals with both the legal and beneficial ownership and casts no doubt on the seller's title
- Conveyances in unregistered land must have been properly executed and stamped in order to constitute a good root of title
- Some third party rights in unregistered land may be protected by registration as land charges, including puisne mortgages (C(i)), estate contracts (C(iv)), restrictive covenants (D(ii)) and equitable easements (D(iii))
- Land charges searches should be obtained against all estate owners disclosed for their periods of ownership.
- A Class F and charge denotes a non-proprietary interest of a non-owning spouse who occupies the matrimonial home
- A buyer's solicitor may raise 'requisitions on title' and should report fully to his client on the title to be passed

Self-test questions

1 Is title deduced and investigated before or after exchange?

2 What is the difference between an epitome of title and an abstract of title?

3 Official copies of the register should not be too old. What age is considered too old?

4 Where title is held by co-owners, what does the absence of a restriction on the proprietorship register signify?

5 What two entries are commonly protected by way of notice on the charges register?

6 How are covenants which burden the property noted on the register?

7 What does 'qualified title' mean?

8 Must there be two or more personal representatives selling in order to overreach any beneficial interests?

9 Where someone (a donor) confers a general power of attorney on another (the donee), what is the consequence of the donor dying or becoming bankrupt?

10 Are positive covenants registrable?

11 What class of pre-root documents is a buyer entitled to see?

12 What two things need to be checked to ensure that the legal estate has been dealt with correctly?

13 What was the significance of a conveyance containing a 'certificate of value'?

14 There are three steps that a buyer of unregistered land must take in order to ensure that a joint tenancy has not been severed (under the Law of Property (Joint Tenants) Act 1964). Name two of them.

15 What is the protection period relevant to a land charges search?

16 What is a class C(iv) land charge?

17 What class of land charge is an equitable easement?

18 Is 'verification of title' of more importance in registered land or unregistered land? Why?

Answers to self-test questions

1. Before exchange, even though common practice used to be (and even a standard contract often provides for) after exchange
2. 'Epitome of title' refers to a chronological list of title documents and will attach copies of those documents. An abstract of title, on the other hand, is a carefully prepared synopsis of an owner's title, presenting only the relevant contents and features of the title documents required to establish a good root of title.
3. 12 months or more
4. That the co-owners hold the beneficial interest as joint tenants and the right of survivorship applies
5. Charges and restrictive covenants
6. They are referred to on the charges register by way of a notice and usually set out there in full or in a schedule of covenants
7. It means that the Registrar is unable to give absolute title, usually because title has only been established for a limited period of less than 15 years
8. No, one will suffice
9. The power is revoked and the attorney no longer has authority under it
10. They are not required to be registered but in practice the Land Registry will enter a 'Note' on the proprietorship register indicating the existence of positive and indemnity covenants and show details of the positive covenant in the charges register.
11. Relevant powers of attorney and pre-root documents referred to by a document in the epitome of title (s.45 LPA 1925)
12. That the relevant document was executed properly and stamped correctly
13. It meant that no ad valorem stamp duty was required to be paid. A PD stamp was still required however
14. He must:
    (1) obtain a clear bankruptcy search against the joint tenants for the survivor's period of ownership
    (2) check that no memorandum of severance has been endorsed on the conveyance to the joint owners
    (3) ensure that the conveyance to the buyer states that the seller is solely and beneficially entitled to the property
15. 15 working days
16. An estate contract
17. Class D(iii)
18. Unregistered land. In registered land, updated official copies are sufficient evidence of a seller's title

SPECIMEN EPITOME OF TITLE

of Joanna Brown
to freehold premises known as
8 Daisy Way
Hampton, Warchestershire

No of Document	Date	Description of document including parties or event	Evidence now supplied	Whether original will be handed over on completion
1.	14.03.64	Conveyance by Andrew Windsor to Arthur Hartley and Judith Hartley	Photocopy	No
2.	01.05.80	Land Charges Searches against names of Arthur Hartley and Judith Hartley	Photocopies	No
3.	06.05.80	Conveyance by Arthur Hartley and Judith Hartley to Freedom Development Company Limited	Photocopy	No
4.	26.08.80	Land Charges Search against name of Freedom Development Company Limited	Photocopy	Yes
5.	28.08.80	Conveyance by Freedom Development Company Limited to Lisa Dingle	Photocopy	Yes
6.	20.10.90	Land Charges search against the names of Lisa Dingle	Photocopy	Yes
7.	23.10.90	Conveyance by Lisa Dingle to Joanna Brown	Photocopy	Yes

SPECIMEN CONVEYANCE

THIS CONVEYANCE is made the Fourteenth day of March One Thousand Nine Hundred and Sixty-four BETWEEN HOLME FARM LIMITED whose registered office is situate at Holme Farm Hampton Warchestershire (hereinafter called "the Vendor") of the one part and ARTHUR HARTLEY and JUDITH HARTLEY of 16 Russ Street Hampton Warchestershire (hereinafter called "the Purchasers") of the other part.

WHEREAS:

The Vendor is seised of the Property hereinafter described for an estate in fee simple in possession free from incumbrances and has agreed to sell the same to the Purchaser for a like estate at the price of Fourteen Thousand Five Hundred Pounds (£14,500).

NOW THIS DEED WITNESSETH AS FOLLOWS:

1. IN CONSIDERATION of the sum of Fourteen Thousand Five Hundred Pounds (£14,500) paid by the Purchasers to the Vendor (the receipt of which the Vendor hereby acknowledges) the Vendor as beneficial owner HEREBY CONVEYS unto the Purchasers ALL THAT freehold Property in the parish of Hampton in the county of Warchestershire containing 4.00 acres or thereabouts and known as field number OS 86 and which is shown for the purpose of identification only edged red on the plan annexed to a conveyance dated the Sixth day of May One Thousand Nine Hundred and Six-two made between Orville Wright of the one part and the

Vendor of the other part (hereinafter called "the Property") TO HOLD the same unto the Purchasers in fee simple as beneficial joint tenants.

2. For the benefit and protection of the Vendor's adjoining property known as Holme Farm Hampton Warchestershire or any part or parts thereof and so as to bind the Property into whosoever hands the same may come the Purchasers hereby jointly and severally covenant with the Vendor that the Purchasers and the persons deriving title under them will at all times hereafter observe and perform the restrictive covenant set out in the First Schedule hereto.

3. The Vendor hereby acknowledges the right of the Purchasers to the production of the documents specified in the Second Schedule hereto and to delivery of copies thereof and hereby undertakes with the Purchasers for the safe custody thereof.

4. It is hereby certified that the transaction hereby effected does not form part of a larger transaction or of a series of transactions in respect of which the amount or value or the aggregate amount or value of the consideration exceeds fifteen thousand pounds.

IN WITNESS whereof the Vendor has ceased its common seal to be hereunto affixed and the Purchasers have hereunto set their hands and seals the day and year first before written.

THE FIRST SCHEDULE

Not to use the Property (or permit the Property to be used) other than as single private detached dwelling house

THE SECOND SCHEDULE

(Documents acknowledged for production)

Date	Document	Parties
06.05.62	Conveyance	Orville Wright (1) Holme Farm Limited (2)

THE COMMON SEAL of HOLME FARM)
LIMITED was hereunto affixed in the)
presence of:-)

I. James Director

R Tutin Secretary

SIGNED SEALED and DELIVERED
by the said ARTHUR HARTLEY in the
presence of:

P. Tweedy
16 Elm Grove, Hampton

Dinner Lady

A. Hartley

SIGNED SEALED and DELIVERED
by the said JUDITH HARTLEY in the
presence of:

Judith Hartley

P. Tweedy
16 Elm Grove, Hampton

Dinner Lady

9

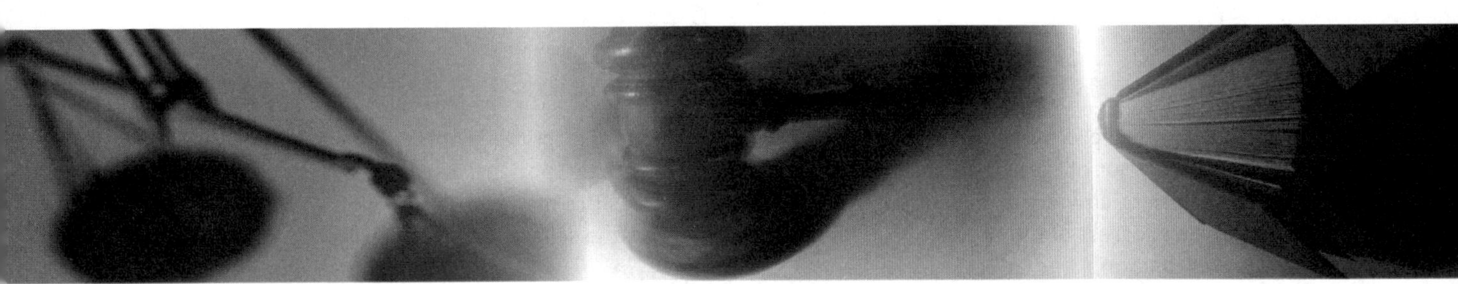

Pre-contract searches, enquiries and planning

Topic List

Chapter overview

This Chapter will:

- Identify the types of search that a buyer's solicitor will carry out as a matter of course and those that he might choose to carry out in addition
- Describe the scope and effect of each of those searches
- Explain the basic principles of planning law, including the circumstances in which planning permission is needed and how it is enforced
- Explain the relevance of building regulations
- Consider issues relevant to contaminated land
- Briefly identify matters relevant to new builds

There is no warranty by the seller that the property is legally or physically fit for the buyer's requirements. Investigation of title will reveal some but not all of the matters affecting a property. The buyer's inspection of the property, together with any survey undertaken, will reveal a great deal more. However, a critical part of the pre-exchange stage of conveyancing is the commissioning of enquiries and searches by the buyer's solicitor.

In view of the general principle of 'caveat emptor', the buyer's solicitor should examine the results of the following searches and enquiries before allowing the buyer to sign a binding contract.

Caveat emptor

Let the buyer beware

1 Enquiries

1.1 Pre-contract enquiries of the seller's solicitor

It is usual to ask the seller to answer questions on matters which may affect the property and which the seller is not obliged to disclose in any event. Although, strictly speaking, a seller is entitled to refuse to answer such enquiries, he is unlikely to do so as this may arouse suspicion and hinder the progress of the transaction. If incorrectly answered, the seller could face liability for misrepresentation.

1.1.1 Standard enquiries

The enquires are normally raised in a standardised form. The standard Property Information Questionnaire and the seller's Property Information Form will be used. Alternatively a solicitor may use his firm's own standard form or use one produced by a law stationer. Any such form will cover such matters as:

- The physical state of the property
- Whether the property has the benefit of any guarantees, eg for damp proofing
- Whether the property has been subject to any disputes
- Whether a third party has any rights over the property

1.2.1 Additional enquiries

In addition to these standard pre-contract enquiries, the buyer's solicitor will also raise additional enquiries with the seller's solicitors relating to any matters arising from the results of his searches, enquiries and title investigations, or the draft contract (see Chapter 10). He should also consider his initial interview with the client and whether there were any particular issues that needed to be pursued, either from the terms agreed (as understood by the client) or arising from the client's inspection of the property, for example regarding persons apparently in occupation or rights of way that seemed to affect the property.

1.2.3 Fixtures and fittings

In Protocol cases, the seller will also complete a Fittings and Contents Form detailing the items included in the sale. Remember the general rule that any items fixed to the property are included in the sale to the buyer unless specifically excluded and any items not fixed to the property are deemed excluded unless specifically included. The purpose of this form, therefore, is to confirm any fixtures which are being removed by the seller and any chattels being sold to the buyer.

2 Pre-contract searches

The buyer's solicitor should examine the results of the following searches before allowing the buyer to sign a binding contract.

- Local land charges search
- Enquiries of the local authority
- Drainage and water search
- Environmental search
- Land charges register search
- (Unregistered land only) Public index map search

These will be undertaken in every case, although remember that some of these will be carried out by the seller's solicitor.

- Coal mining search
- Chancel repairs liability search
- Company search
- Miscellaneous searches

These may be undertaken in certain cases

Note. Some of these searches can be carried out electronically where the relevant authority has made its data available in this way (if that is not the case, search results will be sent in the post).

2.1 Local land charges search (form LLC1)

An official search (on form LLC1) must be made of the Register of Local Land Charges maintained under the Local Land Charges Act 1975 ('LLCA 1975'). The register is kept by the relevant district or London borough council.

2.1.1 Scope of the search

The resulting search certificate, signed by an officer of the council, will reveal such matters as:

- Compulsory purchase orders
- Planning permissions and other planning charges, such as enforcement or stop notices
- Tree preservation orders (prohibiting the felling or lopping of the tree without permission)
- Smoke control orders (for example prohibiting the use of non-smokeless fuels and bonfires)
- Financial charges, such as road-making charges

2.1.2 Effect of the search

Note that the search certificate is not conclusive, but any person who enters into a contract to buy the property on the basis of a misleading or inaccurate reply is entitled to compensation (s.10 LLCA 1975). This does not have to be the person who instigated the search, which means that a lender can rely upon a buyer's search.

There is no priority period; the search is only meant to be accurate as at the date upon which the official certificate is issued. In practice, it is considered inadvisable to rely on a search that is more than **three months old** at the time of completion.

2.2 Local Authority Enquiries (form CON 29)

The local land charges search will reveal a limited number of very specific issues. However, a local authority also has at its disposal a vast amount of information on a broader range of issues and relating to the past and future, as well as the present, that may be of interest.

2.2.1 Scope of the enquiries

In order to tap into this, therefore, the buyer's solicitor, at the same time as requesting a local land charges search, will also raise enquiries with the local authority using form CON 29. This form is in two parts, dealing with regular (CON 29R) and optional (CON 29O) enquiries:

CON 29R: Standard enquiries, dealing with matters not directly covered by the local search, such as:

- The liability to maintain the roads adjacent to the property
- Whether there are any major proposals for roads or railways within 200 metres of the property
- Information on the drainage, eg does the property drain into a public sewer?
- Proposed enforcement and stop notices,
- Proposed compulsory purchase orders or tree preservation orders

CON 29O: Additional enquiries that may be raised in a particular transaction, depending upon the nature of the property and the buyer's proposals for the property. An additional fee is payable in respect of each optional enquiry raised. These may reveal matters such as:

- Whether the property is in a National Park
- Whether it is crossed by a public path or bridleway
- Whether any traffic schemes are proposed, for example, one-way streets or parking restrictions

Previously CON 29R and CON 29O were called Part I and Part II respectively of Form CON 29. Due to the introduction of HIPs, the structure was altered (because HIPs must contain the standard enquiries, but need not contain the optional enquiries, so the buyer may wish to submit CON 29O alone). It is quite possible, therefore, to submit CON 29O without CON 29R.

2.2.2 Additional enquiry 22

Note that **additional enquiry 22** replaces the Commons Registration Act Search that was abolished on 1 October 2007 and which related to the Commons Registration Act 1965 ('CRA 1965')(that was repealed by the Commons Act 2006 ('CA 2006')). S.25 CA 2006 will enable commons registration authorities to hold the registers in electronic form.

CON 22 asks whether the property, or any land adjoining it, is registered common land or town or village green under the CRA 1965 or CA 2006. An answer in the affirmative may mean that the subject land cannot be altered without consent or is subject to common rights (such as grazing rights or rights of way or rights of recreation). Copies of register entries can be obtained from the relevant commons registration officer and his details are also requested by CON 22.

Since CON 29O can be submitted without CON 29R (see above), if follows that CON 22 can be asked in isolation.

2.2.3 Other matters

In addition to these optional enquiries, it is always possible to raise individual enquiries with the local authority, again for an additional fee, although some local authorities will refuse to answer enquiries that are not on the standard form.

Note that both the LLCI and CON 29 will reveal information directly affecting the property. Apart from roads or railways within 200 metres, notices or proposals affecting land *nearby*, however, will not be revealed. For example, if a motorway is proposed half a mile from the property, it will not be revealed by these searches.

Further Reference
There are commercial suppliers of more far-reaching searches

2.3 Drainage and water (form CON 29DW)

Questions about drainage and water specific to the property are dealt with on form CON 29DW. This is sent to the water service company for the area. For example, in London the search would be raised with Thames Water. The search checks matters such as:

- Whether foul and surface water from the property drain to a public sewer
- Whether the property is connected to a mains water supply
- Whether there is a water main within the boundaries of the property

2.4 Environmental search

The Law Society requires the buyer's solicitor, in each transaction, to consider environmental matters that may affect the property. One reason for this is that an owner may be liable for the costs of cleaning up contaminated land, even if the owner has not been responsible for the contamination (see below).

Some information is given by the local authority on CON 29R, but this will be incomplete, so in practice the buyer's solicitor will commission a desktop environmental search. There are a number of search providers (and the information is readily available via the Government's land information database) and the searches are virtually instantaneous.

The results of the search will confirm if the property has ever been used for a contaminative use or if it is likely to flood or subside. It will also confirm land uses within, usually, a 250 metre radius of the property. For payment of a fee a property-specific search can be obtained.

If any information revealed by the search is adverse, further investigations should be undertaken, such as a contaminated land survey.

2.5 Land charges search

2.5.1 Registered land

Although not usually associated with registered land, it is considered good practice for a seller's solicitor to submit a search of the land charges register against the seller's name to ensure that there are no bankruptcy proceedings pending. Either Form K15 (full search) or form K16 (bankruptcy only) can be submitted to the Land Charges Department.

2.5.2 Unregistered land

As you learned in Chapter 8, a search should be carried out against the names of all estate owners revealed by the epitome of title. You will recall that a search result gives a priority period of 15 working days. Therefore the search should be repeated prior to completion if that falls outside the priority period. It is imperative that the estate owner's name is spelt correctly and that the period searched covers his period of ownership.

2.6 Public index map search (unregistered land only)

A search of the Public Index Map held by the Land Registry should be made (on form SIM) to check whether the land has already been registered (it should not have been) or if there is a pending application for, or caution against, first registration.

2.7 Coal mining search

Where the property is in an area likely to be affected by past or future coal-mining, enquiries should be made of the Coal Authority to see if the records or plans indicate:

- Any past or proposed mining underneath the property
- Any underground workings
- Whether previous compensation has been paid for subsidence, or if a claim is pending

Clearly, any such mining activity or underground workings may give rise to concerns about subsidence. The mining search may also reveal information about salt workings or tin or china clay mining in certain parts of the country. This search can also be made using the Coal Authority's on-line reports service.

2.8 Chancel repair liability search

The owner of a property may have a liability to contribute towards the cost of chancel repairs of the parish church. Any such liability attaches to the land and so even a new property could be affected. The land must be within the parish but might be at some distance from it and so care needs to be taken before assuming that it will not be relevant. In fact, following *Aston Cantlow and Wilmcote with Billesley Parochial Church Council v Wallbank 2003,* solicitors are well advised to carry out a ChancelCheck search to see whether the property is in a high-risk parish (which might be any parish with a mediaeval or older church). If it is, it may be appropriate to make further enquiries or to obtain insurance against the risk of liability for repairs.

The liability is not currently registrable and constitutes an overriding interest. However, from 2013, chancel repair liabilities will have to be registered at the Land Registry.

2.9 Land adjoining railway

Enquiries should be made of the seller's solicitors, for example with regard to any liability to maintain fences. Network Rail will no longer answer enquiries made of them.

2.10 Land adjoining water

Where the land adjoins a **canal**, enquiries should be made of British Waterways regarding responsibility for maintenance of riverbanks. In the case of **rivers**, enquiries should be made of the appropriate water authority.

2.11 Company search

Where the seller is a registered company, a company search should be made to ensure that the company is not in administration, liquidation or receivership and that there are no undisclosed fixed or floating charges that affect the land being sold. This search is likely to be repeated prior to completion since there is no priority period offering protection. A search is made at Companies House in London or Cardiff or online at www.companies-house.gov.uk or via NLIS.

3 Planning

3.1 The relevance of planning law

Various issues relating to planning may be revealed by the seller's replies to enquires and/or the search and enquiries of the local authority. It is important that you understand, and can advise upon, any such matters. You should also have a general knowledge of planning law, sufficient to give advice where relevant. Apart from the need to be satisfied that the property being bought complies with planning law, a buyer's solicitor may also need to address planning law in respect of any use or building works proposed by his client. Breach of planning law can incur heavy penalties and these can usually be enforced against the owner for the time being, even if committed by a predecessor. Any existing breach or irregularity should therefore be required to be made good by the seller prior to exchange of contracts.

Development and use of land and/or buildings is strictly controlled and there is a wide range of primary and secondary legislation that a solicitor may need to consult in relation to a transaction. The fundamental principles of planning law are set out here. They are not intended to be comprehensive.

3.2 The Need for Planning Permission

The fundamental principle is set out in s.57 Town and Country Planning Act 1990 ('TCPA 1990'), namely that planning permission is required for **'development'**.

Development is defined in s.55 TCPA 1990 as the:

- Carrying out of building, engineering, mining or other operations in, on, over or under land
- Making of any material change in the use of any buildings or other land

Planning permission is therefore required for any **building works** (including construction, demolition or alteration), or any **material change in use**. ('Material' is not defined but will be a question of fact in all the circumstances.)

Some works are specifically excluded from the scope of 'development' and, therefore, do not require planning permission or are deemed to be permitted without the need to apply for permission.

3.2.1 Excluded from 'development'

Such matters include:

- Works affecting only the interior, or not materially affecting the exterior, of the building
- The use of land or buildings within the curtilage of a dwelling house for any purpose incidental to the use of the dwelling house (for example, using a garage as a playroom)
- A change of use within a class of use as prescribed by the Town and Country Planning (Use Classes) Order 1987. For example, class A1 encompasses retail use, so a change from a hardware shop to a pharmacy would not require planning permission. However, a change of use from a restaurant (class A3) to a takeaway (Class A5) would be a material change of use and require permission.

3.2.2 Permitted development

Certain works and changes of use are deemed to be permitted without the need for express planning permission, under the Town and Country Planning (General Permitted Development) Order 1995 ('GPDO'). These include:

- The erection of fences up to a certain height
- Certain changes of use between use classes
- The erection of an extension to a residential property, provided the extension does not exceed 15% of the original volume of the property (or 10% in Conservation Areas or Areas of Outstanding Natural Beauty)

Care should be taken, however, since a local authority may restrict the scope of the GPDO within its area by use of an 'Article 4 Direction'. A local search will reveal whether the property is in an area subject to such a restriction.

3.3 Application for planning permission

Application is made to the local planning authority, usually by the landowner (but if not, notice of the application must be given to the landowner). There are certain rules governing the content and need to publicise the application.

3.3.1 Outline and full planning permission

'Outline' planning permission may be obtained initially without the need for detailed plans, which can be submitted at a later date on an application for 'full' or 'detailed' permission. The authority may impose conditions on the outline permission as to matters that must be dealt with on the later application. Planning permissions can be sold with the land and will greatly enhance its value.

3.3.2 Time limits

An outline permission is usually subject to a condition that an application for approval of reserved matters must be made within three years. A full permission is usually subject to a condition that development must commence within three years. The time limit applies to the commencement of works and not their completion, although if the works are not completed within a 'reasonable time', the authority may serve a completion notice specifying a period within which the works must be completed or the permission treated as withdrawn.

3.4 Enforcement of planning permission

3.4.1 Enforcement notices

The local planning authority may serve an **enforcement notice** on the landowner and occupier within **four years** from:

- Substantial completion of the works
- Change of use to a dwelling house

The time limit is **ten years** in respect of any other change of use or any condition attached to a planning permission.

3.4.2 Other remedies

The local planning authority may also:

- Serve a breach of condition notice
- Serve a stop notice, preventing further works or specified activities from being carried on
- Seek an injunction to prevent further breaches taking place

Non compliance with any of these notices may constitute a criminal offence.

3.5 Other consents

The property may be subject to further controls, in addition to the usual need for planning permission.

3.5.1 Listed building consent

Where the property is of outstanding historic or architectural interest, it (or a part of it) may be 'listed'. This will mean that the general exemptions mentioned above will not apply and listed building consent will be needed in relation to any development affecting it, even internally. The level of control will depend on the grade of listing.

3.5.2 Conservation area consent

A 'conservation area' is an area of 'special architectural or historic interest, the character or appearance of which it is desirable to preserve or enhance' as specified by a local authority (s.69 Civic Amenities Act 1967). Where the property is in a conservation area, even where it is not listed, any demolition of it will require consent and there may also be added restrictions on development generally. All trees within a conservation area are automatically protected and cannot be felled or lopped without permission.

3.6 Building regulations

All building works must comply with relevant Building Regulations (see the Building Act 1984 and Building Regulations 1991 and 2000), whether or not planning permission is required.

For example, if the building works form part of a permitted development, such as a small extension at the property, then planning permission will not be required but building regulation consent must be obtained.

Building regulations cover such matters as the choice of materials and methods of construction.

A person intending to carry out building works must serve notice on and deposit plans with the local authority before works are commenced. After satisfactory completion of the works, the local authority will issue a certificate of compliance.

3.6.1 Enforcement of building regulations

The local authority may prosecute for breach of the building regulations within 12 months of any infringement. However, s.36(6) Building Act 1984 still allows a local authority to apply to court to enforce the regulations by injunction at any time.

Alert

There is therefore effectively no time limit for the enforcement of building regulations

A solicitor must take all practical and reasonable steps to obtain copies of building regulation consent. Failure to do so may amount to negligence (*Cottingham v Attey Bower and Jones (a firm) 2000*).

Breach of building regulations is a strict liability offence.

3.6.2 Compliance with building regulations

In order to protect a buyer against the risks of enforcement where works may have been carried out, a buyer should ask the seller for confirmation of compliance. The seller should be asked to obtain a **regularisation certificate** or **final certificate** from the local planning authority. Where the seller cannot produce proof of compliance, regardless of how long ago the works were carried out, insurance may be obtained, although this will not normally cover personal injury or loss of profits due to closure while defective works are remedied for example.

Where building regulation consent is not available, the buyer should be concerned not just with the likelihood of enforcement action but also with the soundness of the property. Note that a lender may wish to reconsider his loan and/or impose conditions, for example, requiring that the property is made to comply with relevant building regulations (which could prove very expensive).

3.7 Contaminated land

One area relating to planning that requires special attention is the issue of contaminated land. The consequences of land being contaminated can be very dire, making it very difficult to sell the land or to offer it as security for a loan without the need for extensive and extremely expensive clean-up works. A solicitor must consider whether contamination may be relevant and must advise his client accordingly, in particular with regard to any potential liability.

3.7.1 Liability for contamination

Each local authority is required to inspect its area for contaminated land and to serve a 'remediation notice' on the 'appropriate person' where contamination is found. The appropriate person is either the person responsible for polluting the land in the first place, or the owner or occupier for the time being of the land (s78 Environmental Protection Act 1990). Civil liability may also exist in tort.

It is for this reason that a buyer's solicitor should make environmental searches and enquiries in respect of property, even where it is not immediately obvious that there is some degree of contamination.

3.7.2 Where contamination is revealed

If enquiries reveal the risk of liability for contaminated land, the buyer should be advised to obtain a survey carried out by environmental consultants. They will take soil samples and test them to discover the nature and extent of any contamination. Insurance should still be considered, even if the tests are negative, because there is always the risk that the samples miss pockets of contamination. The survey will report on the remedial works that are required and an estimate of costs can then be obtained.

3.7.3 Contamination and planning permission

Conditions may be imposed on any planning permission with regard to cleaning up contaminated land or requiring an investigation to be conducted into the possibility of contamination being present.

4 New builds

A lender will almost certainly require some form of structural guarantee and insurance before lending on the security of a new or recently constructed property. Clearly this is also in the buyer's interests in any event. The National House Building Council ('NHBC') provides a guarantee in two parts:

- First, an agreement by the developer to remedy all defects appearing within **two years** of purchase and a guarantee by the NHBC to do so if the developer defaults; and
- Secondly, a guarantee as to structural defects within the next **eight years** (making ten in all).

In addition, an NHBC guarantee given after 1 April 1999 will also cover the cost of cleaning up contaminated land.

Where your client is purchasing a new property (one built within the last ten years), you should have regard to the following matters in particular:

- Check that roads and drains are adopted or that agreements and bonds exist. If not, check that there are adequate rights of way belonging to the property and consider potential liabilities for contribution to upkeep
- Check that all necessary planning permissions and building regulation consents were obtained and complied with. If not, consider requiring retrospective consents or insurance or making good
- Require and check NHBC documentation.

5 Results of searches and enquiries

Once you have the results of searches and enquiries, you must report to your client. In so doing, you should draw his attention to matters of particular interest that have been revealed and advise on any problems arising as a result, for example lack of planning permission or the fact that there is a tree preservation order affecting a tree on the property. Obviously it is not enough to simply recite the entries, you must advise on their legal effect and, if appropriate, advise on steps that can be taken to improve your client's position.

If you are acting for both buyer and lender, remember that the lender must be kept informed and advised in the same way.

Summary

- Some searches and enquiries are made as a matter of course; others will be made as and when appropriate
- A local land charges search is always made, often together with standard and possibly additional enquires of the local authority
- Drainage and water and environmental searches will also be made. Note the risks relating to contaminated land
- Land charges searches will be made against all estate owners (unregistered land) or just the seller (registered land)
- Other possible searches include a public index map search, mining search, chancel repair search and company search
- Planning permission is required for any 'development' unless that development is 'excluded' or 'permitted'
- Breach of planning permission may result in service of an enforcement notice or stop notice, breach of condition notice or application for an injunction
- Building works must comply with building regulations even if planning permission is not required
- Where the property is a new build, consider the availability of NHBC documentation and roadways in particular

Self-test questions

1 What is the significance of a tree preservation order?

2 Is the result of a local land charges search conclusive?

3 How does a buyer's solicitor find out whether any planning enforcement notices have been served in respect of the property?

4 To whom is a drainage and water search sent?

5 Why should a land charges search be submitted in registered land?

6 When should a public map index search be made?

7 If a property is subject to a chancel repair liability, should that information appear on the register?

8 What search needs to be made when the seller is a company? How is it made?

9 Is planning permission needed when works are carried out to alter the internal layout of a property?

10 Does a change of use always require planning permission?

11 Does an extension to a residential property need planning permission?

12 Is there a time limit on a local authority serving an enforcement notice in respect of a breach of a condition attached to a planning permission?

13 Give two examples of the types of matter covered by building regulations.

14 What is the time limit for enforcement of building regulations?

15 How long is the protection offered by an NHBC guarantee in respect of structural defects?

Answers to self-test questions

1. It means that a tree cannot be felled or lopped without consent
2. No, but compensation may be awarded where someone enters into a contract on the basis of an inaccurate or misleading search result
3. This is one of the standard enquiries raised of the local authority on form CON29R
4. To the water service company for the relevant area
5. A search should be made against the seller to ensure that there are no bankruptcy proceedings pending. Form K16 can be used (bankruptcy only)
6. When the property to be bought is unregistered land
7. Not at present although this position is due to change in 2013
8. A company search needs to be made at Companies House (or online)
9. No. Such works are excluded from the scope of 'development' (unless it is a listed building). Building regulation consent is likely to be needed, however
10. No, not if it is a change of use within a class of use as prescribed by the Use Classes Order 1987 or a permitted change of use within the GPDO
11. Yes, if it exceeds 15% of the original volume of the property (or 10% in some cases)
12. Yes, ten years
13. Choice of materials and methods of construction
14. There is no time limit
15. Ten years

10

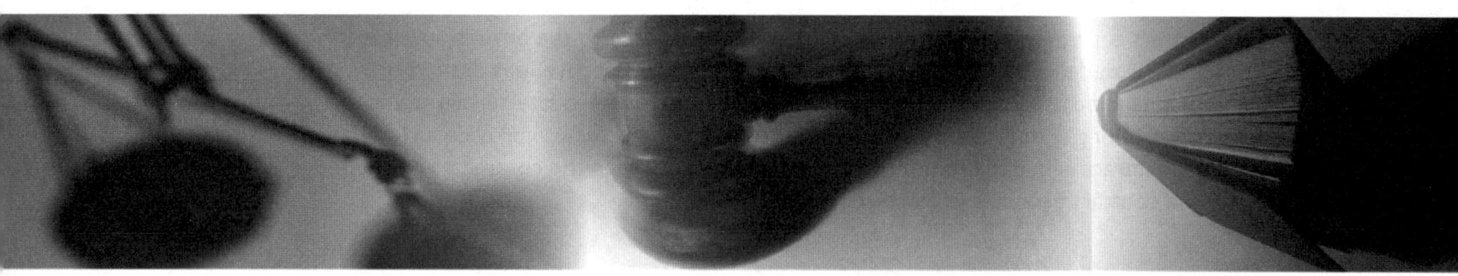

Drafting the contract and preparing for exchange

Topic List

Chapter overview

This Chapter will:

- Describe the scope and purpose of the contract for sale
- Describe a standard contract and comment on its principal terms
- Explain the procedural aspects of agreeing the contract, including considering the document from the buyer's point of view
- Outline the remaining pre-exchange steps to be taken by both parties once the contract is agreed

1 The scope and purpose of the contract

The purpose of the contract for sale is to create a legally binding agreement that gives effect to the terms agreed between the parties. Essentially it will identify the property to be sold and whether it is freehold or leasehold, identify the parties, set out the price and other terms on which the sale and purchase are to take place and record the parties' agreement to the transaction.

Like any contract, a contract for the sale and purchase of land must reflect agreement between the parties, be supported by consideration and be made with an intention to create legal relations. Likewise, the parties must have capacity to contract and the terms of the contract must be sufficiently certain.

The draft contract is prepared by the seller's solicitor and submitted to the buyer's solicitor for approval, usually with deduction of title. The buyer's solicitor may approve it as drafted or return it with amendments. Of course, the parties may continue to negotiate certain terms of the contract for as long as necessary. Once agreed, the seller's solicitor will provide a clean version of the contract in duplicate for signature and exchange. When the contracts are exchanged, the contract becomes legally binding.

2 The form of the contract

Under s.2 of the Law of Property (Miscellaneous Provisions) Act 1989 ('LP(MP)A 1989'), the contract must be in writing and contain all the terms agreed between the parties. Side agreements, letters of understanding and any oral agreements or representations are therefore excluded from the contract unless specifically incorporated.

In respect of residential and simple commercial property transactions, many solicitors will use a **standard form contract** which incorporates the Standard Conditions of Sale (4th edition) (SCS) prepared by the Law Society. Alternatively, a solicitor might use his own firm's standard contract. Even in this case, it is highly likely (although not essential) that it will incorporate the SCS by wording such as 'this contract is deemed to include the Standard Conditions of Sale, 4th Edition' (in order to comply with s.2 LP(MP)A 1989).

A copy of the standard contract that is commonly used is included below and its principal terms are described and commented upon. You will see that the front page of the standard form contract is to be 'filled in' for each transaction. The middle pages contain pre-printed standard conditions. The back page contains pre-printed special conditions with space for further special conditions to be drafted by the parties' solicitors, according to the specific features of the transaction.

Whichever form is used, the contract is likely to contain special conditions that vary or add to the standard conditions as required, in order to give effect to the parties' intentions.

There is also a set of standard conditions to be used in connection with commercial transactions (the 'Standard Commercial Property Conditions (2nd edition)'), but these are outside the scope of this Study Manual .

CONTRACT

Incorporating the Standard Conditions of Sale (Fourth Edition)

Date :

Seller :

Buyer :

Property (freehold/leasehold) :

Title number/root of title :

Specified incumbrances :

Title guarantee (full/limited) :

Completion date :

Contract rate :

Purchase price :

Deposit :

Chattels price (if separate) :

Balance :

The seller will sell and the buyer will buy the property for the purchase price.

WARNING This is a formal document, designed to create legal rights and legal obligations. Take advice before using it.	Signed Seller/Buyer

SCS1/1

STANDARD CONDITIONS OF SALE (FOURTH EDITION)
(NATIONAL CONDITIONS OF SALE 24th EDITION, LAW SOCIETY'S CONDITIONS OF SALE 2003)

1. GENERAL

1.1 Definitions

1.1.1 In these conditions:

(a) "accrued interest" means:

(i) if money has been placed on deposit or in a building society share account, the interest actually earned

(ii) otherwise, the interest which might reasonably have been earned by depositing the money at interest on seven days' notice of withdrawal with a clearing bank

less, in either case, any proper charges for handling the money

(b) "chattels price" means any separate amount payable for chattels included in the contract

(c) "clearing bank" means a bank which is a shareholder in CHAPS Clearing Co. Limited.

(d) "completion date" has the meaning given in condition 6.1.1

(e) "contract rate" means the Law Society's interest rate from time to time in force

(f) "conveyancer" means a solicitor, barrister, duly certified notary public, licensed conveyancer or recognised body under sections 9 or 23 of the Administration of Justice Act 1985

(g) "direct credit" means a direct transfer of cleared funds to an account nominated by the seller's conveyancer and maintained by a clearing bank

(h) "lease" includes sub-lease, tenancy and agreement for a lease or sub-lease

(i) "notice to complete" means a notice requiring completion of the contract in accordance with condition 6

(j) "public requirement" means any notice, order or proposal given or made (whether before or after the date of the contract) by a body acting on statutory authority

(k) "requisition" includes objection

(l) "transfer" includes conveyance and assignment

(m) "working day" means any day from Monday to Friday (inclusive) which is not Christmas Day, Good Friday or a statutory Bank Holiday.

1.1.2 In these conditions the terms "absolute title" and "official copies" have the special meanings given to them by the Land Registration Act 2002.

1.1.3 A party is ready, able and willing to complete:

(a) if he could be, but for the default of the other party, and

(b) in the case of the seller, even though the property remains subject to a mortgage, if the amount to be paid on completion enables the property to be transferred freed of all mortgages (except any to which the sale is expressly subject).

1.1.4 These conditions apply except as varied or excluded by the contract.

1.2 Joint parties

If there is more than one seller or more than one buyer, the obligations which they undertake can be enforced against them all jointly or against each individually.

1.3 Notices and documents

1.3.1 A notice required or authorised by the contract must be in writing.

1.3.2 Giving a notice or delivering a document to a party's conveyancer has the same effect as giving or delivering it to that party.

1.3.3 Where delivery of the original document is not essential, a notice or document is validly given or sent if it is sent:

(a) by fax, or

(b) by e-mail to an e-mail address for the intended recipient given in the contract.

1.3.4 Subject to conditions 1.3.5 to1.3.7, a notice is given and a document is delivered when it is received.

1.3.5 (a) A notice or document sent through a document exchange is received when it is available for collection

(b) A notice or document which is received after 4.00pm on a working day, or on a day which is not a working day, is to be treated as having been received on the next working day

(c) An automated response to a notice or document sent by e-mail that the intended recipient is out of the office is to be treated as proof that the notice or document was not received.

1.3.6 Condition 1.3.7 applies unless there is proof:

(a) that a notice or document has not been received, or

(b) of when it was received.

1.3.7 A notice or document sent by the following means is treated as having been received as follows:

(a) by first-class post:	before 4.00pm on the second working day after posting
(b) by second-class post:	before 4.00pm on the third working day after posting
(c) through a document exchange:	before 4.00pm on the first working day after the day on which it would normally be available for collection by the addressee
(d) by fax:	one hour after despatch
(e) by e-mail:	before 4.00pm on the first working day after despatch.

1.4 VAT

1.4.1 An obligation to pay money includes an obligation to pay any value added tax chargeable in respect of that payment.

1.4.2 All sums made payable by the contract are exclusive of value added tax.

1.5 Assignment

The buyer is not entitled to transfer the benefit of the contract.

2. FORMATION

2.1 Date

2.1.1 If the parties intend to make a contract by exchanging duplicate copies by post or through a document exchange, the contract is made when the last copy is posted or deposited at the document exchange.

2.1.2 If the parties' conveyancers agree to treat exchange as taking place before duplicate copies are actually exchanged, the contract is made as so agreed.

2.2 Deposit

2.2.1 The buyer is to pay or send a deposit of 10 per cent of the total of the purchase price and the chattels price no later than the date of the contract.

2.2.2 If a cheque tendered in payment of all or part of the deposit is dishonoured when first presented, the seller may, within seven working days of being notified that the cheque has been dishonoured, give notice to the buyer that the contract is discharged by the buyer's breach.

2.2.3 Conditions 2.2.4 to 2.2.6 do not apply on a sale by auction.

2.2.4 The deposit is to be paid by direct credit or to the seller's conveyancer by a cheque drawn on a solicitor's or licensed conveyancer's client account.

2.2.5 If before completion date the seller agrees to buy another property in England and Wales for his residence, he may use all or any part of the deposit as a deposit in that transaction to be held on terms to the same effect as this condition and condition 2.2.6.

2.2.6 Any deposit or part of a deposit not being used in accordance with condition 2.2.5 is to be held by the seller's conveyancer as stakeholder on terms that on completion it is paid to the seller with accrued interest.

2.3 Auctions

2.3.1 On a sale by auction the following conditions apply to the property and, if it is sold in lots, to each lot.

2.3.2 The sale is subject to a reserve price.

2.3.3 The seller, or a person on his behalf, may bid up to the reserve price.

2.3.4 The auctioneer may refuse any bid.

2.3.5 If there is a dispute about a bid, the auctioneer may resolve the dispute or restart the auction at the last undisputed bid.

2.3.6 The deposit is to be paid to the auctioneer as agent for the seller.

3. MATTERS AFFECTING THE PROPERTY

3.1 Freedom from incumbrances

3.1.1 The seller is selling the property free from incumbrances, other than those mentioned In condition 3.1.2.

3.1.2 The incumbrances subject to which the property is sold are:

(a) those specified in the contract

(b) those discoverable by inspection of the property before the contract

(c) those the seller does not and could not reasonably know about

(d) entries made before the date of the contract in any public register except those maintained by the Land Registry or its Land Charges Department or by Companies House

(e) public requirements.

3.1.3 After the contract is made, the seller is to give the buyer written details without delay of any new public requirement and of anything in writing which he learns about concerning a matter covered by condition 3.1.2.

3.1.4 The buyer is to bear the cost of complying with any outstanding public requirement and is to indemnify the seller against any liability resulting from a public requirement.

3.2 Physical state

3.2.1 The buyer accepts the property in the physical state it is in at the date of the contract unless the seller is building or converting it.

3.2.2 A leasehold property is sold subject to any subsisting breach of a condition or tenant's obligation relating to the physical state of the property which renders the lease liable to forfeiture.

3.2.3 A sub-lease is granted subject to any subsisting breach of a condition or tenant's obligation relating to the physical state of the property which renders the seller's own lease liable to forfeiture.

3.3 Leases affecting the property

3.3.1 The following provisions apply if any part of the property is sold subject to a lease.

3.3.2 (a) The seller having provided the buyer with full details of each lease or copies of the documents embodying the lease terms, the buyer is treated as entering into the contract knowing and fully accepting those terms.

(b) The seller is to inform the buyer without delay if the lease ends or if the seller learns of any application by the tenant in connection with the lease; the seller is then to act as the buyer reasonably directs, and the buyer is to indemnify him against all consequent loss and expense.

(c) Except with the buyer's consent, the seller is not to agree to any proposal to change the lease terms nor to take any step to end the lease.

(d) The seller is to inform the buyer without delay of any change to the lease terms which may be proposed or agreed.

(e) The buyer is to indemnify the seller against all claims arising from the lease after actual completion; this includes claims which are unenforceable against a buyer for want of registration.

(f) The seller takes no responsibility for what rent is lawfully recoverable, nor for whether or how any legislation affects the lease.

(g) If the let land is not wholly within the property, the seller may apportion the rent.

3.4 Retained land

Where after the transfer the seller will be retaining land near the property:

(a) the buyer will have no right of light or air over the retained land, but

(b) in other respects the seller and the buyer will each have the rights over the land of the other which they would have had if they were two separate buyers to whom the seller had made simultaneous transfers of the property and the retained land.

The transfer is to contain appropriate express terms.

4. TITLE AND TRANSFER

4.1 Proof of title

4.1.1 Without cost to the buyer, the seller is to provide the buyer with proof of the title to the property and of his ability to transfer it, or to procure its transfer.

4.1.2 Where the property has a registered title the proof is to include official copies of the items referred to in rules 134(1)(a) and (b) and 135(1)(a) of the Land Registration Rules 2003, so far as they are not to be discharged or overridden at or before completion.

4.1.3 Where the property has an unregistered title, the proof is to include:

(a) an abstract of title or an epitome of title with photocopies of the documents, and

(b) production of every document or an abstract, epitome or copy of it with an original marking by a conveyancer either against the original or an examined abstract or an examined copy.

4.2 Requisitions

4.2.1 The buyer may not raise requisitions:

(a) on the title shown by the seller taking the steps described in condition 4.1.1 before the contract was made

(b) in relation to the matters covered by condition 3.1.2.

4.2.2 Notwithstanding condition 4.2.1, the buyer may, within six working days of a matter coming to his attention after the contract was made, raise written requisitions on that matter. In that event, steps 3 and 4 in condition 4.3.1 apply.

4.2.3 On the expiry of the relevant time limit under condition 4.2.2 or condition 4.3.1, the buyer loses his right to raise requisitions or to make observations.

4.3 Timetable

4.3.1 Subject to condition 4.2 and to the extent that the seller did not take the steps described in condition 4.1.1 before the contract was made, the following are the steps for deducing and investigating the title to the property to be taken within the following time limits:

Step	Time Limit
1. The seller is to comply with condition 4.1.1	Immediately after making the contract
2. The buyer may raise written requisitions	Six working days after either the date of the contract or the date of delivery of the seller's proof of title on which the requisitions are raised, whichever is the later
3. The seller is to reply in writing to any requisitions raised	Four working days after receiving the requisitions
4. The buyer may make written observations on the seller's replies	Three working days after receiving the replies

The time limit on the buyer's right to raise requisitions applies even where the seller supplies incomplete evidence of his title, but the buyer may, within six working days from delivery of any further evidence, raise further requisitions resulting from that evidence.

4.3.2 The parties are to take the following steps to prepare and agree the transfer of the property within the following time limits:

Step	Time Limit
A. The buyer is to send the seller a draft transfer	At least twelve working days before completion date
B. The seller is to approve or revise that draft and either return it or retain it for use as the actual transfer	Four working days after delivery of the draft transfer
C. If the draft is returned the buyer is to send an engrossment to the seller	At least five working days before completion date

4.3.3 Periods of time under conditions 4.3.1 and 4.3.2 may run concurrently.

4.3.4 If the period between the date of the contract and completion date is less than 15 working days, the time limits in conditions 4.2.2, 4.3.1 and 4.3.2 are to be reduced by the same proportion as that period bears to the period of 15 working days. Fractions of a working day are to be rounded down except that the time limit to perform any step is not to be less than one working day.

4.4 Defining the property

4.4.1 The seller need not:

(a) prove the exact boundaries of the property

(b) prove who owns fences, ditches, hedges or walls

(c) separately identify parts of the property with different titles

further than he may be able to do from information in his possession.

4.4.2 The buyer may, if it is reasonable, require the seller to make or obtain, pay for and hand over a statutory declaration about facts relevant to the matters mentioned in condition 4.4.1.The form of the declaration is to be agreed by the buyer, who must not unreasonably withhold his agreement.

4.5 Rents and rentcharges

The fact that a rent or rentcharge, whether payable or receivable by the owner of the property, has been, or will on completion be, informally apportioned is not to be regarded as a defect in title.

SCS1/02

4.6 **Transfer**

4.6.1 The buyer does not prejudice his right to raise requisitions, or to require replies to any raised, by taking any steps in relation to preparing or agreeing the transfer.

4.6.2 Subject to condition 4.6.3, the seller is to transfer the property with full title guarantee.

4.6.3 The transfer is to have effect as if the disposition is expressly made subject to all matters covered by condition 3.1.2.

4.6.4 If after completion the seller will remain bound by any obligation affecting the property which was disclosed to the buyer before the contract was made, but the law does not imply any covenant by the buyer to indemnify the seller against liability for future breaches of it:

(a) the buyer is to covenant in the transfer to indemnify the seller against liability for any future breach of the obligation and to perform it from then on, and

(b) if required by the seller, the buyer is to execute and deliver to the seller on completion a duplicate transfer prepared by the buyer.

4.6.5 The seller is to arrange at his expense that, in relation to every document of title which the buyer does not receive on completion, the buyer is to have the benefit of:

(a) a written acknowledgement of his right to its production, and

(b) a written undertaking for its safe custody (except while it is held by a mortgagee or by someone in a fiduciary capacity).

5. **PENDING COMPLETION**

5.1 **Responsibility for property**

5.1.1 The seller will transfer the property in the same physical state as it was at the date of the contract (except for fair wear and tear), which means that the seller retains the risk until completion.

5.1.2 If at any time before completion the physical state of the property makes it unusable for its purpose at the date of the contract:

(a) the buyer may rescind the contract

(b) the seller may rescind the contract where the property has become unusable for that purpose as a result of damage against which the seller could not reasonably have insured, or which it is not legally possible for the seller to make good.

5.1.3 The seller is under no obligation to the buyer to insure the property.

5.1.4 Section 47 of the Law of Property Act 1925 does not apply.

5.2 **Occupation by buyer**

5.2.1 If the buyer is not already lawfully in the property, and the seller agrees to let him into occupation, the buyer occupies on the following terms.

5.2.2 The buyer is a licensee and not a tenant. The terms of the licence are that the buyer:

(a) cannot transfer it

(b) may permit members of his household to occupy the property

(c) is to pay or indemnify the seller against all outgoings and other expenses in respect of the property

(d) is to pay the seller a fee calculated at the contract rate on a sum equal to the purchase price and the chattels price (less any deposit paid) for the period of the licence

(e) is entitled to any rents and profits from any part of the property which he does not occupy

(f) is to keep the property in as good a state of repair as it was in when he went into occupation (except for fair wear and tear) and is not to alter it

(g) is to insure the property in a sum which is not less than the purchase price against all risks in respect of which comparable premises are normally insured

(h) is to quit the property when the licence ends.

5.2.3 On the creation of the buyer's licence, condition 5.1 ceases to apply, which means that the buyer then assumes the risk until completion.

5.2.4 The buyer is not in occupation for the purposes of this condition if he merely exercises rights of access given solely to do work agreed by the seller.

5.2.5 The buyer's licence ends on the earliest of: completion date, rescission of the contract or when five working days' notice given by one party to the other takes effect.

5.2.6 If the buyer is in occupation of the property after his licence has come to an end and the contract is subsequently completed he is to pay the seller compensation for his continued occupation calculated at the same rate as the fee mentioned in condition 5.2.2(d).

5.2.7 The buyer's right to raise requisitions is unaffected.

6. **COMPLETION**

6.1 **Date**

6.1.1 Completion date is twenty working days after the date of the contract but time is not of the essence of the contract unless a notice to complete has been served.

6.1.2 If the money due on completion is received after 2.00pm, completion is to be treated, for the purposes only of conditions 6.3 and 7.3, as taking place on the next working day as a result of the buyer's default.

6.1.3 Condition 6.1.2 does not apply and the seller is treated as in default if:

(i) the sale is with vacant possession of the property or any part of it, and

(ii) the buyer is ready, able and willing to complete but does not pay the money due on completion until after 2.00pm because the seller has not vacated the property or that part by that time.

6.2 **Arrangements and place**

6.2.1 The buyer's conveyancer and the seller's conveyancer are to co-operate in agreeing arrangements for completing the contract.

6.2.2 Completion is to take place in England and Wales, either at the seller's conveyancer's office or at some other place which the seller reasonably specifies.

6.3 **Apportionments**

6.3.1 Income and outgoings of the property are to be apportioned between the parties so far as the change of ownership on completion will affect entitlement to receive or liability to pay them.

6.3.2 If the whole property is sold with vacant possession or the seller exercises his option in condition 7.3.4, apportionment is to be made with effect from the date of actual completion; otherwise, it is to be made from completion date.

6.3.3 In apportioning any sum, it is to be assumed that the seller owns the property until the end of the day from which apportionment is made and that the sum accrues from day to day at the rate at which it is payable on that day.

6.3.4 For the purpose of apportioning income and outgoings, it is to be assumed that they accrue at an equal daily rate throughout the year.

6.3.5 When a sum to be apportioned is not known or easily ascertainable at completion, a provisional apportionment is to be made according to the best estimate available. As soon as the amount is known, a final apportionment is to be made and notified to the other party. Any resulting balance is to be paid no more than ten working days later, and if not then paid the balance is to bear interest at the contract rate from then until payment.

6.3.6 Compensation payable under condition 5.2.6 is not to be apportioned.

6.4 **Amount payable**

The amount payable by the buyer on completion is the purchase price and the chattels price (less any deposit already paid to the seller or his agent) adjusted to take account of:

(a) apportionments made under condition 6.3

(b) any compensation to be paid or allowed under condition 7.3.

6.5 **Title deeds**

6.5.1 As soon as the buyer has complied with all his obligations on completion the seller must hand over the documents of title.

6.5.2 Condition 6.5.1 does not apply to any documents of title relating to land being retained by the seller after completion.

6.6 **Rent receipts**

The buyer is to assume that whoever gave any receipt for a payment of rent or service charge which the seller produces was the person or the agent of the person then entitled to that rent or service charge.

6.7 **Means of payment**

The buyer is to pay the money due on completion by direct credit and, if appropriate, an unconditional release of a deposit held by a stakeholder.

6.8 **Notice to complete**

6.8.1 At any time on or after completion date, a party who is ready, able and willing to complete may give the other a notice to complete.

6.8.2 The parties are to complete the contract within ten working days of giving a notice to complete, excluding the day on which the notice is given. For this purpose, time is of the essence of the contract.

6.8.3 On receipt of a notice to complete:

(a) if the buyer paid no deposit, he is forthwith to pay a deposit of 10 per cent

(b) if the buyer paid a deposit of less than 10 per cent, he is forthwith to pay a further deposit equal to the balance of that 10 per cent.

7. **REMEDIES**

7.1 **Errors and omissions**

7.1.1 If any plan or statement in the contract, or in the negotiations leading to it, is or was misleading or inaccurate due to an error or omission, the remedies available are as follows.

7.1.2 When there is a material difference between the description or value of the property, or of any of the chattels included in the contract, as represented and as it is, the buyer is entitled to damages.

7.1.3 An error or omission only entitles the buyer to rescind the contract:

(a) where it results from fraud or recklessness, or

(b) where he would be obliged, to his prejudice, to accept property differing substantially (in quantity, quality or tenure) from what the error or omission had led him to expect.

7.2 **Rescission**

If either party rescinds the contract:

(a) unless the rescission is a result of the buyer's breach of contract the deposit is to be repaid to the buyer with accrued interest

(b) the buyer is to return any documents he received from the seller and is to cancel any registration of the contract.

7.3 **Late completion**

7.3.1 If there is default by either or both of the parties in performing their obligations under the contract and completion is delayed, the party whose total period of default is the greater is to pay compensation to the other party.

7.3.2 Compensation is calculated at the contract rate on an amount equal to the purchase price and the chattels price, less (where the buyer is the paying party) any deposit paid, for the period by which the paying party's default exceeds that of the receiving party, or, if shorter, the period between completion date and actual completion.

7.3.3 Any claim for loss resulting from delayed completion is to be reduced by any compensation paid under this contract.

7.3.4 Where the buyer holds the property as tenant of the seller and completion is delayed, the seller may give notice to the buyer, before the date of actual completion, that he intends to take the net income from the property until completion. If he does so, he cannot claim compensation under condition 7.3.1 as well.

7.4 **After completion**

Completion does not cancel liability to perform any outstanding obligation under this contract.

7.5 **Buyer's failure to comply with notice to complete**

7.5.1 If the buyer fails to complete in accordance with a notice to complete, the following terms apply.

7.5.2 The seller may rescind the contract, and if he does so:

(a) he may

(i) forfeit and keep any deposit and accrued interest

(ii) resell the property and any chattels included in the contract

(iii) claim damages

(b) the buyer is to return any documents he received from the seller and is to cancel any registration of the contract.

7.5.3 The seller retains his other rights and remedies.

7.6 **Seller's failure to comply with notice to complete**

7.6.1 If the seller fails to complete in accordance with a notice to complete, the following terms apply.

7.6.2 The buyer may rescind the contract, and if he does so:

(a) the deposit is to be repaid to the buyer with accrued interest

(b) the buyer is to return any documents he received from the seller and is, at the seller's expense, to cancel any registration of the contract.

7.6.3 The buyer retains his other rights and remedies.

8. **LEASEHOLD PROPERTY**

8.1 **Existing leases**

8.1.1 The following provisions apply to a sale of leasehold land.

8.1.2 The seller having provided the buyer with copies of the documents embodying the lease terms, the buyer is treated as entering into the contract knowing and fully accepting those terms.

8.1.3 The seller is to comply with any lease obligations requiring the tenant to insure the property.

8.2 **New leases**

8.2.1 The following provisions apply to a contract to grant a new lease.

8.2.2 The conditions apply so that:
"seller" means the proposed landlord
"buyer" means the proposed tenant
"purchase price" means the premium to be paid on the grant of a lease.

8.2.3 The lease is to be in the form of the draft attached to the contract.

8.2.4 If the term of the new lease will exceed seven years, the seller is to deduce a title which will enable the buyer to register the lease at the Land Registry with an absolute title.

8.2.5 The seller is to engross the lease and a counterpart of it and is to send the counterpart to the buyer at least five working days before completion date.

8.2.6 The buyer is to execute the counterpart and deliver it to the seller on completion.

8.3 **Consent**

8.3.1 (a) The following provisions apply if a consent to let, assign or sub-let is required to complete the contract

(b) In this condition "consent" means consent in the form which satisfies the requirement to obtain it.

8.3.2 (a) The seller is to apply for the consent at his expense, and to use all reasonable efforts to obtain it

(b) The buyer is to provide all information and references reasonably required.

8.3.3 Unless he is in breach of his obligation under condition 8.3.2, either party may rescind the contract by notice to the other party if three working days before completion date (or before a later date on which the parties have agreed to complete the contract):

(a) the consent has not been given, or

(b) the consent has been given subject to a condition to which a party reasonably objects.

In that case, neither party is to be treated as in breach of contract and condition 7.2 applies.

9. **COMMONHOLD LAND**

9.1 Terms used in this condition have the special meanings given to them in Part 1 of the Commonhold and Leasehold Reform Act 2002.

9.2 This condition applies to a disposition of commonhold land.

9.3 The seller having provided the buyer with copies of the current versions of the memorandum and articles of the commonhold association and of the commonhold community statement, the buyer is treated as entering into the contract knowing and fully accepting their terms.

9.4 If the contract is for the sale of property which is or includes part only of a commonhold unit:

(a) the seller is to apply for the written consent of the commonhold association at his expense and is to use all reasonable efforts to obtain it

(b) either the seller, unless he is in breach of his obligation under paragraph (a), or the buyer may rescind the contract by notice to the other party if three working days before completion date (or before a later date on which the parties have agreed to complete the contract) the consent has not been given. In that case, neither party is to be treated as in breach of contract and condition 7.2 applies.

10. **CHATTELS**

10.1 The following provisions apply to any chattels which are included in the contract, whether or not a separate price is to be paid for them.

10.2 The contract takes effect as a contract for sale of goods.

10.3 The buyer takes the chattels in the physical state they are in at the date of the contract.

10.4 Ownership of the chattels passes to the buyer on actual completion.

SCS1/03

SPECIAL CONDITIONS

1. (a) This contract incorporates the Standard Conditions of Sale (Fourth Edition).

   (b) The terms used in this contract have the same meaning when used in the Conditions.

2. Subject to the terms of this contract and to the Standard Conditions of Sale, the seller is to transfer the property with either full title guarantee or limited title guarantee, as specified on the front page.

3. The chattels which are on the property and are set out on any attached list are included in the sale and the buyer is to pay the chattels price for them.

4. The property is sold with vacant possession.

(or) 4. The property is sold subject to the following leases or tenancies:

Seller's conveyancers*:

Buyer's conveyancers*:

*Adding an e-mail address authorises service by e-mail : see condition 1.3.3(b)

2.1 Date

This remains blank until exchange of contracts. On exchange, the date is inserted, at which point a legally binding contract comes into existence and the parties are legally bound to complete the transaction in accordance with the contract's terms.

2.2 Seller

The **seller must have legal title** to the property and all legal estate owners must be a party to the contract.

Remember the following points, that have been addressed elsewhere, when inserting the name of the seller in the contract:

- If a grant is in favour of more than one PR, they must all be named in and execute the contract and the transfer. If a grant of representation is in favour of one PR only, he may act as seller
- The seller's solicitor should check that a mortgagee's power of sale has become exercisable

Alert

Note that a partnership is not a **separate legal personality**. In the case of partnership property, therefore, some or all of the partners, up to a maximum of four, will hold the legal title to partnership property personally and should be named as the buyer or seller accordingly

2.3 Buyer

The full names of **all** of the buyers must be set out in the contract.

2.4 Property (freehold/leasehold)

An accurate description of the property should be entered here. The title documents should be used as a starting-point (ie the description on the property register in registered land can be used or the description appearing in the root of title in unregistered land). In many cases a postal address (with postcode) will be sufficient. However, a plan is often desirable and, in many cases, essential, for example on a sale of part.

2.4.1 Easements and other benefits

The description of the property should also include reference to easements or other rights that benefit the property. Although this is not essential (since the benefit is likely to pass in any event, under the LPA 1925, see Chapter 3), it is considered good practice to do so.

2.4.2 Freehold/leasehold

Delete one or the other. This is straightforward and, in fact, will often be inserted within the description, eg 'The freehold land known as...'

2.5 Title number/root of title

Depending on whether the land is registered or unregistered, this will be amended as follows:

Registered land	Title number/~~root of title~~ AB 12345
Unregistered land	A conveyance of the Property dated 24th April 1963 and made between George Freeman (1) Michael Anderson (2)

2.6 Specified incumbrances

Note that SC 3.1.2 deems that the property is being sold subject to:

- Incumbrances mentioned in the contract
- Patent incumbrances (ie discoverable on inspection prior to exchange)
- Incumbrances that the seller neither knew nor could reasonably have known
- Entries made in public registers before contract (other than those maintained by Companies House, the Land Registry or Land Charges Department)
- Public requirements

At common law, the seller is only obliged to disclose latent encumbrances and defects in title. However, in light of SC3.1.2, it is advisable and general practice for the seller to disclose:

- All latent incumbrances affecting the property such as covenants and easements, including those revealed by an investigation of the title (ie land charges, matters on the register and companies register etc)
- Patent incumbrances
- Defects in title. Mention of a defect in title will often be accompanied by a special condition. For example where there is a defect in title due to a conveyance not having been executed properly, the contract might contain a clause such as:

  'the buyer shall assume that the conveyance dated .... and made between .... and .... was properly executed and shall raise no requisition or objection in relation to it'

Of course, up to exchange, this clause will have no effect and the buyer's solicitor can raise unlimited requisitions.

The seller need not include, however:

- Physical defects
- Local land charges
- Public notices and orders etc (that are usually revealed on enquiries of the local authority)
- Interests that will be overreached or discharged

2.7 Title guarantee (full/limited)

Whether full title guarantee or limited title guarantee is inserted here governs the covenants as to title that will be given in the transfer. The covenants are those set out in the Law of Property (Miscellaneous Provisions) Act 1994. Where the contract is silent, SC 4.6.3 provides that full title guarantee is to be given, subject to the effect of any incumbrances pursuant to SC 3.1.2.

Alert

Title guarantee should not be confused with the class of title given on registration by the Land Registry, eg Absolute Title, which is the State's guarantee as to the registered proprietor's interest in the land.

In the event of a breach of any of the terms of the guarantee, the buyer is able to sue the seller under the guarantee contained in the transfer. Also, under SC 7.4, he may sue for damages for breach of contract, since SC 7.4 excludes the doctrine of merger. (This doctrine would otherwise mean that once completion has taken place it would not be possible for the buyer to sue for damages under the contract because the contract 'merges' into the deed and in effect ceases to exist.)

The seller may choose to give full title guarantee, limited title guarantee or no title guarantee.

Type of guarantee	What it guarantees	Who might be expected to give this guarantee
Full title guarantee	▸ That the seller has the right to sell the property as he purports to ▸ That the seller will do all he reasonably can to transfer the title he purports to give ▸ That the land is sold free from incumbrances other than those the seller does not and could not reasonably know about (and except those disclosed by the seller or which the buyer knows about)	Owner-occupier Mortgagor offering a title guarantee on the security (a lender will normally require full title guarantee)
Limited title guarantee	▸ That the seller has the right to sell the property as he purports to ▸ That the seller will do all he reasonably can to transfer the title he purports to ▸ That the seller has not himself encumbered the land and is not aware that anyone else has done so since the last disposition for value	Trustees PRs Mortgagee exercising his power of sale (this might be expected but is not always given)
No title guarantee	Nothing	A donor giving the property for no value A mortgagee exercising his power of sale

2.8 Completion date

This is normally inserted immediately prior to exchange of contracts. If no date is inserted, SC6.1.1 provides that completion shall take place 20 working days after exchange. It also provides that time is not of the essence, which means that failure to complete on time gives the innocent party a right to compensation but not a right to repudiate the contract. This is explained in more detail in Chapter 14.

A special condition is normally inserted to specify a **time of day** for completion, for example 'completion shall take place by 1pm'. The buyer's solicitor will wish to ensure that he has sufficient time to transfer funds from a dependent sale and the seller's solicitor will wish to ensure that he has sufficient time to use the funds on a dependent purchase.

2.9 Contract rate

This is the rate of interest at which compensation for late completion is assessed (considered more fully in Chapter 14). The injured party does not have to show loss: the compensation is awarded as of right for late completion. The intention is to deter late completion.

Usually the interest rate is inserted into the contract at 3%–5% per annum above the base rate of one of the clearing banks. A fixed rate is not normally chosen because of the risk of interest rate fluctuation.

Where this is not done, SC 1.1.1(e) provides that the 'Law Society's interest rate from time to time in force' will apply. This rate is published weekly in the Law Society's Gazette.

2.10 Purchase price

This is the agreed amount payable for the property and it is the sum on which the rate of SDLT is assessed.

Where fittings or chattels are included in the purchase price, especially if they have a significant value, the purchase price may be apportioned between the value of the land and buildings (upon which SDLT is paid) and the value of the chattels (upon which SDLT is not paid). This is particularly beneficial where such an apportionment brings the purchase price into a lower band for SDLT (see Chapter 5).

Example

If the purchase price including chattels is £255,000, then SDLT at 3% (that is £7,650) is payable upon the unapportioned purchase price. If the chattels are valued at £6,000, then the purchase price may be apportioned £249,000 as to the land and buildings, and £6,000 as to the chattels, in which case SDLT based upon 1% of £249,000 (that is £2,490) is payable, a saving of £5,160.

Care must be taken to ensure that the apportionment of the purchase price is realistic: any overvaluation of the chattels would be treated as a fraud on HMRC.

2.11 Deposit

2.11.1 Amount of deposit

The agreed amount of the deposit to be paid by the buyer on exchange should be inserted here.

If nothing is inserted, SC 2.2.1 provides that the buyer must pay 10% of the total purchase price on or before exchange.

2.11.2 Capacity in which the deposit is held

A deposit may be held by the seller's solicitor as:

- **Stakeholder**, which means that the seller's solicitor is custodian of the deposit for both parties and the deposit may not be released to the seller until completion
- **Agent** for the seller, which means that the deposit is available to the seller from the moment of exchange

The buyer may have difficulties in recovering the deposit if the seller defaults, particularly if the seller has become insolvent, and hence the deposit is usually held as stakeholder. SC 2.2 provides for the deposit to be paid to the seller's solicitor to be held as stakeholder and on the basis that the deposit is released to the seller on completion with accrued interest.

2.11.3 Use of the deposit in a chain of transactions

Under SC 2.2.5, if the seller is buying another property in England and Wales as a residence, he may use all or part of the deposit received on his sale towards the deposit on his purchase. Furthermore, the person selling to the seller can use the deposit in the same way and the deposit can therefore travel part or all of the way up a 'chain' of transactions, the only requirement being that a stakeholder under 2.2.6 ultimately holds it.

2.12 Chattels price (if separate)

As mentioned above, a part of the agreed sale price might be apportioned to chattels – if so, that apportionment must be entered here as the 'chattels price' and **special condition 3** of the standard form contract should remain. The chattels must be listed. Remember that without such a provision the seller would be entitled to remove any chattels prior to completion. Even if no separate price is to be attributed to the chattels, for this reason they should still be listed.

The deposit payable upon exchange will include 10% of the chattels price.

2.13 Balance

This is simply the sum of the purchase price plus the chattels price, less the deposit.

2.14 Standard conditions

Many of the standard conditions have been mentioned above, in relation to the particulars of sale detailed on the first page of the standard contract. SC 1.1.4 provides that the standard conditions apply to the contract 'except as varied or excluded' by the contract, ie by the special conditions. Printed special condition 1 reiterates that the SCS are incorporated.

You should make sure that you understand all standard conditions and that they will apply as written unless they are expressly excluded or amended. It may be helpful to mention the following in particular:

1.5 The contract is personal to the buyer and cannot be assigned

4.3.2 A timetable is set out for preparation and approval of the transfer

4.4.1 The seller is not obliged to prove the exact boundaries of ownership of boundary structures beyond what he can reveal from information in his possession

5.1 The seller retains the risk as to the physical state of the property between exchange and completion but is under no obligation to the buyer to insure. This special condition is often excluded.

5.2 This sets out the basis on which the buyer occupies the property in the event that the seller allows him into occupation prior to completion

2.15 Special conditions

2.15.1 The purpose of special conditions

Each transaction is different and it is essential to ensure that the contract reflects the terms agreed between the parties. Where this is not achieved by the SCS, special conditions can be included to delete, amend or supplement them. For example, special conditions might address:

- Matters specifically agreed between the parties (for example if the seller has agreed to provide restrictive covenant indemnity insurance)
- Particular chattels included in the sale
- Fixtures excluded from the sale
- The exclusion or variation of statutory provisions, such as the Contracts (Rights of Third Parties) Act 1999 (which is commonly excluded)
- Occupiers at the property

2.15.2 Occupiers

Replies to pre-contract enquiries and/or inspection of the property may have revealed that there are non-owning occupiers at the property.

Although the printed special condition 4 (first alternative) states that the 'property is sold with vacant possession', a buyer is still well advised to obtain a written consent from occupiers rather than run the risk of having to go to court to oust someone from the property. If there are occupiers, the buyer should provide for a special condition to be inserted in the contract confirming that the occupier has no interest in the property and that the occupier agrees to vacate on completion. The occupier should then sign the contract to give effect to this provision.

Such a provision might take the following form:

'In consideration of the Buyer entering into this agreement, I [name of occupier] hereby agree to the sale of the Property on the terms herein contained and not to register any of my rights in relation to the Property, [including rights arising under the Family Law Act 1966] *(these words will only be appropriate where the occupier is a non-owning spouse or civil partner).* I also agree to the removal of any registration of such rights prior to completion and to give vacant possession of the Property on completion.'

3 The buyer's solicitor and the draft contract

The buyer's solicitor will examine the draft contract and will be concerned to ensure that its provisions accurately reflect both:

- His client's instructions and
- The title that has been deduced

If either is not the case, he must amend and return the draft contract and/or raise enquiries or requisitions on title as appropriate.

He may wish to negotiate some terms or make special provision, for example in relation to any of the following matters:

- The amount of deposit
- The contract rate
- The capacity in which the deposit is held
- Release of rights by occupiers (see above)
- Defective title indemnity insurance
- The obtaining of consents or insurance where there is a breach of covenant by the seller or his predecessor
- The procuring of a release or variation of a restrictive covenant at the Land Tribunal
- Making the contract conditional on a specified event, for example completion of building or remedial works (although conditional contracts are not generally regarded as satisfactory, particularly in residential transactions)

Obviously this list is not comprehensive. The buyer's solicitor needs to check very carefully to ascertain that his client will be satisfied and protected by the terms of the contract. All the results of his searches and enquiries, investigation of title, instructions received and his knowledge of land law principles will need to be applied in determining whether or not this is the case.

Remember that any provision that purports to make the buyer responsible for paying late stamp duty on a title document will be void.

Also, a clause that states that a sale by only one trustee will be sufficient if made by a trustee 'with the consent of all the beneficiaries', does not need to be accepted. S.42 LPA 1925 enables a buyer to insist upon the appointment of a second trustee in order to overreach any beneficial interests.

4 Once the contract is agreed

Once the contract is agreed, the parties are almost ready to exchange contracts and enter into the legally binding and enforceable contractual relationship (subject to the position in any related transactions and to any mortgage arrangements). However, the following matters need to be addressed by the parties' solicitors:

By the seller's solicitor	By the buyer's solicitor
Existing mortgage – Obtain a redemption figure from the existing mortgagee or mortgagees and ensure that the proceeds of sale will be sufficient to pay off all mortgages over the property. There is no obligation on the mortgagee to agree to this arrangement and the mortgagee's consent should therefore be obtained **before** exchange of contracts. The mortgagee may impose conditions, such as all or part of the sale proceeds being used to reduce the mortgage debt. It is likely that, if this is the position, it will already have been addressed as a result of enquiries raised by the buyer's solicitor.	**Enquiries and searches** – make sure that all have been obtained (and are sufficiently up to date at the time of completion) and that all matters arising have been dealt with.
Enquiries – deal with any outstanding replies to enquires or requisitions	**Survey** – make sure client has been advised and that if a survey has been commissioned, it has been received and that it is satisfactory
Engross contract – prepare final versions of the agreed contract (not necessary where the first draft was approved as drafted)	**Deposit** – does the client have sufficient funds? Are cleared funds in the solicitor's client account?
Instructions – Advise on contents of contract and steps following exchange. Obtain client's signature. Obtain instructions as to completion date. Obtain authority to proceed	**Mortgage** – check that mortgage offer has been received. Check whether there is any requirement for the borrower to formally accept the offer. Are terms and conditions satisfactory?
	Funding – prepare draft financial statement to check client will have sufficient funds to complete. Once exchange has taken place, the client is legally bound to complete the purchase.
	Instructions – Report to client on any remaining issues. Advise on contents of contract and implications of exchange. Obtain client's signature. Obtain instructions as to completion date. Obtain authority to proceed.

Summary

- The seller's solicitor prepares the draft contract
- A contract for the sale of land must be in writing and contain all the agreed terms. It becomes binding on the parties when the two parts are exchanged
- Many contracts use the Law Society's Standard Conditions of Sale. Additional 'special conditions' may be included
- Consider whether a plan is essential or desirable
- A seller should disclose latent and patent encumbrances and defects in title, having regard to SC 3.1.2
- Some sellers may only agree to giving limited title guarantee and some may refuse to give any at all
- There may be SDLT advantages to apportioning the purchase price in respect of chattels
- A deposit can be held as stakeholder or as agent
- Non-owning occupiers should sign the contract and agree to give vacant possession on completion
- Final checks need to be made and instructions obtained prior to actual exchange (for example in relation to mortgages)

Self-test questions

1. Who drafts the contract for sale?
2. A contract for the sale of land must be by deed. True or false?
3. Bloggs & Partners is a firm of solicitors. It is proposing to buy new office premises. Who will be named as the buyer?
4. Is a seller obliged to disclose patent encumbrances?
5. What percentage above a clearing bank's base rate is commonly expressed to be the 'contract rate'?
6. Is there any limit on how much of the purchase price can be apportioned in respect of chattels?
7. In what two capacities can a deposit be held?
8. Where there are non-owning occupiers at the property, is the buyer protected provided the contract provides for sale 'with vacant possession'?
9. Is a solicitor authorised to exchange contracts once the terms of it have been agreed?

Answers to self-test questions

1. The seller's solicitor
2. False. It must, however, be in writing and incorporate all the agreed terms
3. A maximum of four partners will hold the legal estate and they should be named as the buyer
4. Not at common law, but he should be advised to do so where the SCS are used
5. Between 3% and 5%
6. There is no monetary limit but any overvaluation of the chattels may be treated as a fraud on HMRC
7. As stakeholder or as agent
8. No. If the occupiers failed to vacate, the buyer may have a remedy for breach of contract against the seller but he would also need a court order to procure their removal. They should be parties to the contract in order to give a greater degree of protection
9. Although his instructions may have conferred this authority, as a matter of good practice he should obtain express authority to proceed to exchange

11

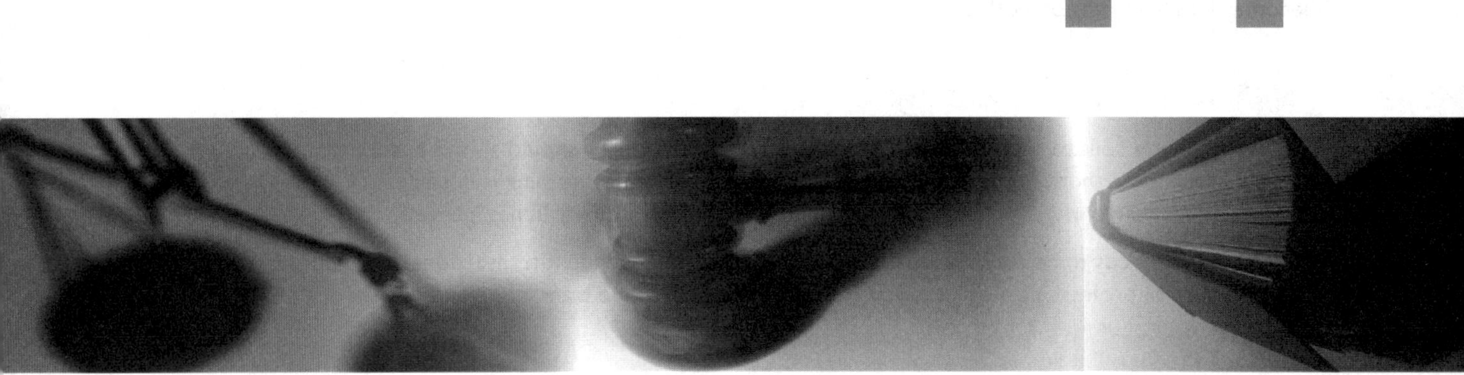

Exchange of contracts

Topic List

Chapter overview

This Chapter will:

- Explain what is meant by 'exchange'
- Explain the various ways in which exchange may be effected
- Consider the legal effects of exchange, including the position regarding insurance
- Consider whether and, if so, how the contract should be registered

1 Exchanging contracts

As you have learned, once **agreed, a contract for** sale is usually prepared and signed in duplicate. Each part of the contract is then dated and submitted to the other party. Since each party does this, the contracts are 'exchanged'. There is no legal requirement for a contract to be in two parts like this. There could be a single contract signed by both parties, but this is rare in practice. 'Exchange' or 'exchange of contracts' therefore refers to the point at which the contracts are dated and physically passed between the parties. As from this point in time, the contract becomes legally binding on both parties.

1.1 Authority to exchange

Remember that a solicitor, whether acting for the buyer or the seller, should always ensure that he has his client's authority to exchange, once he has ensured that everything is in place. Exchanging contracts without a client's authority may give rise to liability in negligence.

Particular care needs to be taken when acting for a client with dependent transactions. It would also be a case of professional negligence to commit the client to one transaction and not the other.

1.2 Methods of exchange

Contracts may be exchanged in several ways, namely:

- In person
- By post
- By telephone

It is up to the client's solicitor to decide which method of exchange to use (in the absence of express instructions).

Note that exchange is not effected by faxing copies of the signed contracts. Since contracts must be in writing, it follows also that contracts cannot be executed or exchanged via e-mail or the internet. However, it is proposed that 'electronic contracts' will become the norm for conveyancing in a few years' time.

1.2.1 Exchange in person

Ideally the two parts should be checked as being identical and properly executed and the deposit monies should actually accompany the buyer's part. These matters can only be dealt with satisfactorily where the solicitors meet in person in order to exchange contracts. However, due to the time involved, this is very rare in practice.

1.2.2 Exchange by post or document exchange ('DX')

Exchange by post normally occurs by the buyer's solicitor sending his client's part of the contract and deposit monies to the seller and the seller's solicitor then sending his client's part to the buyer's solicitor. Under the postal rule in *Adams v Lindsell 1818,* the contract becomes binding when the second part is posted.

This method is unsatisfactory because of the delay involved, the lack of certainty on the buyer's part once he has posted his part of the contract and because of the risk of post going astray. It is little used in practice and would never be sensible where there are linked transactions.

Similarly, exchange may take place by use of the solicitors' DX system. Where DX is used, the postal rule does not apply. If the SCS are used, SC 2.1.1 provides that the contract takes effect when the second contract is deposited at the exchange. If the SCS are not used, it is not altogether clear whether the contract is effective once the second contract is so deposited or when it is received by the buyer's solicitor.

1.2.3 Exchange by telephone

This is the most usual method of exchanging contracts and is, of course, *followed* by a physical exchange of documents through the post or DX system. The Law Society has set out prescribed formulae, designed to ensure consistency and certainty and to overcome, so far as possible, the risks involved by the lack of personal attendance. They rely on professional trust and solicitors' undertakings. The formulae are known as:

- **Formula A** – used where one solicitor (usually the seller's) holds both parts of the contract
- **Formula B** – used where each solicitor holds his own client's part
- **Formula C** – specifically designed for use in a chain of transactions

In each case, exchange is deemed to take place at the time specified by the solicitors as being the time of exchange. Any deviation from the formula used must be agreed between the solicitors and attendance notes must be made to record any such deviation and the fact of exchange.

Formula A

One solicitor holds both contracts and the deposit monies. Both solicitors agree the completion date and the seller's solicitor inserts the completion date into the contract. The buyer's solicitor releases the buyer's contract to the seller, the seller's solicitor confirms that his client's contract is in the agreed form and agrees to hold it to the order of the buyer's solicitor. They then agree that exchange should take place at that moment. The seller's solicitor dates each contract and undertakes to send the seller's contract to the buyer's solicitor that day.

Formula B

Each solicitor holds his client's contract and the buyer's solicitor holds the deposit funds.

Both solicitors confirm that they hold their clients' signed contracts in the agreed form and the buyer's solicitor confirms that he holds funds for the deposit. The completion date is agreed and inserted into the contract and exchange is agreed by each party agreeing to hold his client's contract to the other's order. The contracts are dated and each undertakes to send his contract (and deposit in the case of the buyer) to the other that day.

Formula C

This method of exchange is in two parts. In the first part, the solicitor at one end of the chain (eg the solicitor acting for the first time buyer) initiates a series of telephone calls by telephoning the seller's solicitor. Both solicitors confirm that their signed contracts are identical and agree the completion date. Both give **undertakings** to the other confirming that they will exchange with each other with completion for the agreed date, provided the seller phones back within a specified time. The same undertakings are given up the chain until the top of the chain is reached (ie the party that is selling but has no property to buy). At that point in this scenario, contracts are exchanged in the 'top' transaction pursuant to Formula A or B as appropriate.

The exchange of the 'top' contract then triggers the second part of Formula C. This involves the other contracts being exchanged one by one, all the way back to the first time buyer. Each solicitor in turn **undertakes** to forward the contract to the other party.

A deposit is always paid by the first time buyer, who may be obliged, at the direction of his seller's solicitor and in accordance with the contract terms, to send the deposit to a solicitor higher up the chain. It is likely that other buyers in the chain will need to add to the amount of deposit due on their sales in exchanging on their purchases.

1.3 After exchange

Once contracts have been exchanged, by whichever method is used, this fact should be reported to the client and an attendance note recorded on file. Solicitors must then perform the tasks that they have undertaken to do, ie send their clients' contracts and (in the case of the buyer's solicitor) the deposit monies.

2 Effect of exchange

Once contracts are exchanged, the terms of the contract become legally binding and any withdrawal from or failure to perform those terms will be a breach of contract.

2.1 Effect of death and bankruptcy

There may be a change in the parties, where one dies or becomes bankrupt, but the general position is that the contract remains valid.

2.1.1 Death of seller

Where the seller dies, his personal representatives ('PR's) should complete the sale. The buyer should see a copy of the death certificate and grant of representation.

If the seller is one of co-owners holding the property as joint tenants, his interest simply passes to the other joint tenant(s) and the buyer only needs to see a copy of his death certificate.

If he is one of legal co-owners also holding the property as tenants in common (and therefore one of the trustees), there must be two trustees in place to receive the purchase monies and overreach any beneficial interests (including his). If his death means that there is only one trustee remaining, another trustee will need to be appointed.

2.1.2 Death of buyer

The buyer's PRs will be bound to complete the contract and must be named as the buyer in the purchase deed. However, funding is likely to be problematic where the buyer's death results in a mortgage offer being revoked (as is likely to be the case) and even if completion is possible, there may be a delay caused by the need for PRs to obtain a grant of representation before they can proceed to completion.

Where the deceased buyer is one of joint buyers, the remaining buyer(s) will be obliged to complete. Again, there may be difficulty in doing so where the deceased was responsible, in whole or in part, for the mortgage or other funding.

2.1.3 Bankruptcy of seller

The buyer should learn of the seller's bankruptcy if there is a registered entry in respect of it in his official search or on the official copy entries. The buyer will then need to deal with the trustee in bankruptcy in whom the bankrupt's estate vests and not the seller. Although the trustee in bankruptcy is permitted to disclaim onerous property, this does not entitle him to default on the sale simply because he could obtain a better price elsewhere. He will normally proceed with the sale. (However, if the sale price is an 'undervalue', he is likely to apply to the court to set it aside.)

The purchase deed will need to name the trustee as the seller.

Where the seller is a tenant in common, the trustee will join in the purchase deed in order to overreach the beneficial interests. The legal estate is unaffected by a co-owner's bankruptcy.

2.1.4 Bankruptcy of buyer

The buyer's trustee in bankruptcy is legally bound to complete the purchase unless he disclaims it. In practice, the chances of him finding sufficient funding are extremely remote, particularly since any mortgage offer would be revoked on the buyer's bankruptcy.

The position is the same where the bankrupt buyer is one of co-buyers. His equitable interest under the contract passes to the trustee. The remaining buyers may be unable to complete because any mortgage may have been revoked by his bankruptcy.

2.1.5 Liquidation of seller

Where the seller is a company that goes into liquidation, the liquidator will usually go ahead and complete the sale. Usually the company will still be the seller and the liquidator will attest the company's seal (the legal estate is rarely vested in the liquidator personally).

2.1.6 Liquidation of buyer

Where the buyer is a company that goes into liquidation, the liquidator may complete the purchase or disclaim it as an onerous contract. It is highly probable that he will be unable to complete as he is unlikely to be able to provide sufficient funding.

2.2 Insurance

The question of insurance of the property between exchange and completion is an important one.

2.2.1 Common law position

At common law, the risk passes to the buyer who should, therefore, insure the property from exchange. In practice, the seller is likely to continue his policy of insurance, however, since he still owes a duty of care in respect of the physical condition of the property and will also wish to protect against the risk of the buyer defaulting on the purchase. It is also likely to be a condition of any mortgage that he maintains insurance.

2.2.2 Position under SCS

Under SC 5.1 the risk is expressed to remain with the seller but the seller owes no obligation to the buyer to continue to insure the property (although he is most likely to do so in order to bear this risk). SC 5.1 also provides that the buyer cannot claim on the seller's policy. SC 5.1 is often excluded or varied so that the risk is expressed to pass to the buyer on exchange.

Where a buyer is borrowing all or part of the purchase price, his lender is likely to require the buyer to insure the property from exchange.

2.3 Buyer's occupation before completion

Occasionally the buyer will request permission of the seller to occupy the property prior to completion, either to carry out works or to take up residence. The potential problem with this situation is that, once in occupation, the buyer may lose his incentive to complete the purchase. Also, the seller should consider the consequences of incomplete works or alterations in the event that completion does not take place.

To avoid such a situation, the seller should ensure that the buyer's occupation is as **licensee** and not tenant. SC 5.2 expressly states that the buyer's occupation is to be construed as a licence (but does not apply where the buyer is simply allowed access to carry out agreed works). The buyer is required to insure the property during the licence period and to pay a licence fee (at the contract rate based on the outstanding purchase price). The licence is expressed to end on the date of completion or rescission or on five days' notice, whichever is the earlier.

Where SC 5.2 is not used, the open contract position is that the seller may have to resort to obtaining a possession order from the court to regain possession of the property if completion does not take place and if the buyer will not vacate voluntarily.

3 Registration of contract

In practice, the contract for sale and purchase is rarely registered because the time lapse between exchange and completion is usually relatively short. However, it is possible to register, as follows:

Registered land	By a notice on the charges register of the seller's register of title
Unregistered land	By registering a class C(iv) estate contract land charge against the name of the seller

Registration may be advisable where:

- There is to be a long time before completion
- There is concern about the other party's trustworthiness in completing the transaction
- The parties are in dispute
- One party delays completion

Summary

- Contracts are dated and exchanged and become legally binding at that point
- Exchange takes place most commonly by telephone, supported by solicitors' undertakings and according to Law Society formulae A, B and C
- A contract is not invalidated by the death or bankruptcy of either party but special procedures will need to be followed as a result
- Who bears the risk and insures the property between exchange and completion should be set out clearly in the contract
- A contract for sale is not normally registered but registration may be advisable in certain circumstances

Self-test questions

1 Is it a legal requirement that a contract for sale is executed in duplicate and 'exchanged'?

2 Exchange can take place by fax. True or false?

3 When exchange takes place solely by post (with no telephone communication), at which point does exchange take place?

4 When is Law Society formula B used?

5 Does the buyer need to see anything other than the deceased's owner's death certificate when the owner was solely and beneficially entitled to the property?

6 If a prospective co-owner dies, is the other prospective co-owner legally bound to complete the purchase?

7 Can a seller's trustee in bankruptcy lawfully refuse to complete the sale?

8 At common law, who bears the risk of the property between exchange and completion?

9 What is the standard precaution taken when a buyer is permitted to occupy the property prior to completion?

10 How might a contract be registered in unregistered land?

Answers to self-test questions

1. No. It is common practice but it is possible for a single contract to be executed by both parties. The contract becomes binding once (executed and) dated
2. False
3. When the second part is posted
4. When each solicitor holds his own client's part
5. Yes, he should also see a copy of the grant to the owner's PRs
6. Yes
7. There are circumstances in which he may disclaim or apply to the court to have the contract set aside, for example if the proposed sale is at an undervalue
8. The buyer
9. It is usually provided that he will occupy as a licensee only, insure the property and pay a licence fee
10. By registration of a Class C (iv) land charge (estate contract)

12

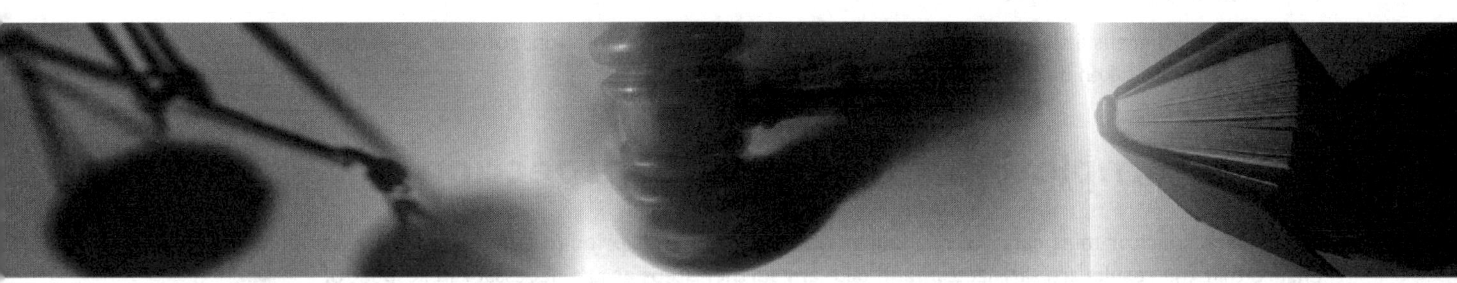

From exchange to completion

Topic List

Chapter overview

This Chapter will:

- Describe the pre-completion searches that need to be carried out, in relation to both registered and unregistered land
- Explain how the purchase deed should be drafted and prepared for completion
- Explain the rules regarding execution of the purchase deed
- Explain what is meant by the term 'requisitions on title' at this pre-completion stage
- Describe the steps that both solicitors should take in relation to the financial aspects of completion
- Describe how completion takes place

Chapter overview continued

Traditionally, completion would take place four weeks following exchange and the main task to be carried out in that period was deduction and investigation of title. Nowadays, title is dealt with before exchange and completion often takes place around 14 days later or even sooner (it can even be simultaneous). Although title has been largely dealt with by exchange, a buyer's solicitor (and to a lesser extent, a seller's solicitor) still has a number of matters to attend to and so must ensure that he has sufficient time to prepare as required. The principal matters are:

- Pre-completion searches
- Preparing the purchase deed
- Requisitions on title
- Attending to mortgages

In fact, where there is little (or no) time between exchange and completion, some or all of these measures may be taken before exchange.

1 Pre-completion searches and inspection

The buyer's solicitor must carry out a number of further searches prior to completion. He must ensure that the results are satisfactory and take any further steps as are necessary in respect of any entries that are revealed. Typically, he will make the searches around seven days before the contractual completion date as he must ensure that results are received in sufficient time. He may leave it a bit later where the search can be carried out by telephone, computer or fax. The searches are as follows:

Note

If the buyer's solicitor is also acting for the buyer's lender, he should also carry out a K16 bankruptcy only search against **the buyer** (whether registered or unregistered land).

Registered land	Land Registry search (OS1 or OS2)
Unregistered land	K15 against seller
Both registered and unregistered optional searches	Company search Local land charges search Inspection

If entries are revealed by pre-completion searches, the buyer's solicitor should deal with them (and keep his client informed) as appropriate. This may mean:

- Raising the matter with the seller's solicitor
- Obtaining an official copy of any land charge using form K19 (this should show the applicant and, therefore, the person to whom a request for removal of the land charge can be made)
- Requesting removal of the entry or an undertaking that it will be removed prior to, on, or immediately following completion

1.1 Registered land: OS1

Where the whole of a registered title is to be transferred, a search on form OS1 is carried out. The purpose of the search is two-fold to:

- Update the official copies on which title was investigated
- 'Freeze' the register in favour of the buyer (and lender) and gain priority over any applications lodged after the date of the search

Note

If the buyer's solicitor is also acting for the buyer's mortgagee, this search should be made in the name of the **lender** in order to protect both lender and buyer.

The priority period is **30 working days**. Provided the application to register the purchase, and any mortgage, is made within the priority period, registration will not be affected by any subsequent application. If registration is delayed beyond the expiry of the priority period, there is a possibility that it could be made subject to a third party entry for which application for

registration was made during the priority period or at any time thereafter up to the date of registration of the transfer.

1.2 Unregistered land: K15

Assuming land charges searches were properly carried out against all estate owners revealed in the title deduced to the buyer's solicitor, the buyer's solicitor need only carry out a K15 search against the current seller prior to completion. Again the purpose of this search is two-fold to:

- Update the search already carried out
- Obtain priority against later registrations

The priority period is **15 working days**. Completion should take place within this priority period in order to take free of any subsequent incumbrances for which application for registration is made.

Alert

The priority periods are extremely important. You should make a diary entry of the expiry of any relevant priority period

Remember that an official certificate of search is conclusive in unregistered land in favour of the searcher. He will therefore take free from any entries that should have been revealed (and the person with the benefit of the land charge may seek compensation from the Chief Land Registrar).

1.3 Acting for the lender: K16

The solicitor acting for the buyer's lender (very often the same as the solicitor acting for the buyer) should carry out a bankruptcy only search against the buyer on Form K16.

1.4 Company search

A company search against the seller, where the seller is a company, will reveal whether there are any fixed or floating charges against the company. As with company searches before exchange, any fixed charge will indicate that the mortgagee's consent is required to the transaction. If a floating charge is revealed, the solicitor will need to establish that the charge has not 'crystallised'. He should require a certificate of non-crystallisation.

Crystallisation

A floating charge is converted into a fixed charge that attaches to the relevant assets on the happening of certain events – it is said to 'crystallise'

The search will also reveal whether there are any insolvency proceedings pending against the company or indeed whether the company has been wound up.

1.5 Inspection

A further inspection is not normally considered necessary, although the buyer may wish to visit the property to take measurements, for example. However, it may be advisable in the following circumstances where:

- There has been an issue concerning occupiers other than the seller
- The seller has been constructing the property or carrying out works

2 The purchase deed

The buyer's solicitor will normally draft the purchase deed shortly after exchange and submit it to the seller's solicitor for approval. SC 4.3.2 provides that he should do so at least 12 working days before the contractual completion date and SC 4.3.2 provides that the seller's solicitor should return it amended or approve it within a further four working days. Once agreed, he will then engross it and each solicitor will arrange for his client to execute it if appropriate.

In some cases, the purchase deed might be prepared by the seller's solicitor, for example, where a developer is selling a number of houses and wishes to use standard documents for each.

2.1 Drafting the purchase deed

Under s.52 LPA 1925, property must be transferred by deed in order to pass the legal estate. The deed must be in accordance with the terms of the contract for sale.

2.1.1 Form of deed

In **registered land**, the purchase deed is called a **transfer** and is normally drafted using the Land Registry form TR1.

In **unregistered land**, the purchase deed was traditionally the '**conveyance**', for which there is no prescribed wording (although conveyances tended to follow a fairly standardised format). However, since any sale of unregistered land will now trigger compulsory first registration, the form TR1 is often used.

Land Registry form of Transfer TRI can be found on the Land Registry's website www.landregistry.gov.uk.

Some points to note are as follows:

- If an additional trustee has been appointed in order that beneficial interests are overreached, they should be included as one of the Transferors
- The Transfer is only dated at completion
- All buyers should be shown as Transferees
- The purchase price for the property needs to be inserted in words and figures. This is the amount excluding chattels, since it is the sum on which SDLT is calculated.
- The buyers can state whether they are going to hold as beneficial joint tenants or tenants in common. Again the appropriate box needs to be ticked. If the buyers are to hold the property as tenants in common in unequal shares, the third box should be ticked and the shares should be specified. If the trust is complex, a continuation sheet can be used or there may be a separate deed of trust 'behind the legal curtain'
- All transferors must execute. A transferee (or all transferees) must execute where he is entering into a covenant, making a declaration or making any sort of application to the Land Registry, for example for the noting of a restriction on the register.

2.1.2 Plans

Generally speaking, if the contract refers to a plan, the plan should be included in the transfer. If the transfer is of a whole registered title, no plan is needed.

2.2 Engrossing the purchase deed

Once the form of transfer has been agreed, the buyer's solicitor will engross the document in preparation for execution. He will then usually arrange for the buyer to execute it (leaving it undated) and send it to the seller's solicitor who will arrange for the seller to execute it.

SC4.3.2 provides that the engrossment must be delivered to the seller at least 5 working days before completion.

2.3 Execution of the purchase deed

Under s.1 Law of Property (Miscellaneous Provisions) Act 1989, in order to be valid, a deed must

- Indicate clearly that it is a deed
- Be signed by the necessary parties in the presence of a witness and
- Be delivered

2.3.1 Who must execute

The seller must always execute the purchase deed. Where the buyer is entering into any covenants, he too must execute the deed. In some cases, a third party may need to execute, for example a lender agreeing to release the property from a charge or a non-owning occupier to release his rights in the property. If the seller is a company in liquidation, for example, the liquidator will execute the deed if the court has ordered the company's property to be vested in him but, more commonly, he will attest the execution of the deed by the company.

2.3.2 The form of execution

The rules regarding execution of documents have already been covered in relation to investigation of title.

Although there is no statutory stipulation as to who can be a witness, it is generally regarded as good practice to ensure that a witness is independent (ie not a spouse or civil partner) and over 18 years of age.

3 Requisitions on title

You have already learned that title is deduced and investigated before exchange of contracts. Therefore 'requisitions on title', literally, are dealt with at that time. However, the buyer's solicitor will raise other matters with the seller's solicitor in between exchange and completion, and these are still referred to as 'requisitions on title' even though they relate to matters other than title, a hangover from the days when title requisitions were raised at this stage.

Requisitions on title typically deal with the following matters (and are usually submitted in a standard form):

- Arrangements for completion
- Request for an undertaking that the seller's mortgage will be discharged and the mechanics for dealing with the discharge on completion
- Bank details of the seller's solicitors
- Arrangements for handover of title and other completion documents (see 5.3 below)
- Information regarding handover or collection of keys to the property
- Confirmation that there has been no change to the title since it was deduced prior to exchange

Of course if there are any outstanding title matters, these will need to be dealt with at this stage. Under SC 4.2.2, where an undisclosed encumbrance is discovered after exchange, the buyer's solicitor should raise requisitions on it within 6 working days of becoming aware of it.

SC4.3.1 requires the seller's solicitor to reply to requisitions within 4 working days. Lateness in replying to requisitions could potentially provide a defence to a buyer who delays completion.

If any of the seller's replies to requisitions are unsatisfactory, the buyer's solicitor will need to raise further requisitions as appropriate.

4 Financial matters

The solicitors acting for both parties will need to attend to financial matters prior to completion, notably:

- A completion statement, as between the parties
- Discharge of the seller's mortgage and release of the deposit
- A statement and bill provided by the seller's solicitor to his client
- Obtaining the buyer's mortgage advance
- A statement and bill provided by the buyer's solicitor to his client

4.1 Completion statement

This is drawn up by the seller's solicitor and sent to the buyer's solicitor in response to the requisitions on title. A completion statement is only needed where the amount to be paid on completion is different from the balance shown on the contract. Items dealt with in a completion statement might include:

- Apportionment of income and outgoings
- Chattels
- Licence fee for occupation prior to completion
- Compensation in respect of delayed completion

4.2 Seller's finances

Mortgage	The seller's solicitor must obtain a redemption figure from the mortgagee, calculated up to the date of completion. The mortgagee will usually provide a daily redemption rate so that adjustments can be made easily in the event of completion taking place earlier or later than the contractual date for completion. The seller's solicitor might also need to prepare a form of discharge of the mortgage for signature by the lender, namely DSI or ENDI (see below).
Deposit	If the buyer's deposit is held by the seller's solicitor as agent, it can be released to the seller on completion without any further formality. Where the deposit is held as stakeholder, the seller's solicitor should obtain a written release from the buyer's solicitor, authorising payment to the seller (or as he directs). In practice this is hardly ever done and an oral release is considered sufficient. However, if the deposit is held by a third party, for example an estate agent, as stakeholder, then the buyer's solicitor should be required to provide a written release. If this is the case, the form of release should be drafted before completion and an undertaking to provide it may be required.

4.3 Seller's statement

The solicitor's financial statement to his client will incorporate the completion statement, showing the monies due from the buyer on completion. It will also set out deductions that need to be made from that balance, for example:

- Solicitor's costs
- Estate agent's commission
- Mortgage redemption

This statement is most likely to show an amount owing to the client unless there is less equity in the property than the sum of any outgoings, or indeed negative equity. If this is the case, the solicitor should obtain any monies due from the client (in cleared funds) prior to completion, so that he can redeem the mortgage and settle any agency fees or costs that are payable.

4.4 Buyer's finances

4.4.1 Mortgage

Mortgage funds	The buyer's solicitor must request the mortgage funds from the lender. This may have been done on the certificate of title or report on title form or the request may need to be made separately.
Mortgage deed	The mortgage deed must also be signed by the borrower, typically (as required by the lender) in the presence of his solicitor. Occasionally a mortgagee may require a non-owning spouse or adult dependant to sign a form of waiver in order to acknowledge the mortgagee's ultimate priority. In addition, a solicitor may be required to sign a confirmation that joint borrowers have been advised separately and/or that independent advice has been recommended or obtained.

4.4.2 SDLT form

The buyer's solicitor should also arrange for his client to execute a land transaction return (in form SDLT 1). (This will need to be sent to HMRC immediately following completion, see Chapter 13). A new mortgagee may *require* that this is done before completion but, in practice, it is likely to be done then anyway. The buyer's solicitor normally fills out the form (although, strictly speaking, it is the buyer who is personally responsible for its completion).

4.4.3 Cleared funds

The buyer's mortgage advance and any cash or cheques or transfers from the buyer's own accounts should be paid into the buyer's solicitor's client account and be cleared before the contractual completion date.

 **Alert**

If the buyer presents a large amount of cash or payment is made via a third party, the risk of money laundering should be given serious consideration

4.5 Buyer's statement

The buyer's solicitor will prepare a financial statement which sets out clearly how much money the buyer will need to pay his solicitor in readiness for completion. This will cover:

- The balance of the purchase price (as set out on the completion statement)
- The mortgage advance and any related costs
- SDLT
- Solicitor's costs
- Land Registry fees
- Other disbursements, including search fees

As noted above, the buyer's solicitor should require cleared funds in time for completion (and therefore needs to provide this statement in good time).

5 Method of completion

Completion normally takes place by post, although in some cases the solicitors may meet and complete in person (and either solicitor may appoint another person to do so on his behalf). SC6.2 actually provides that completion should take place at the seller's solicitor's office or at some other place that the seller reasonably specifies. It should take place on the completion date according to the contract. As mentioned above, exactly how and where completion is to take place is normally dealt with in the requisitions on title in between exchange and completion.

5.1 Completion in person

The completion documents will be checked and handed over, monies paid (usually) by banker's draft (or by telegraphic transfer) and the transfer dated. This method of completion is very rare, owing to the time involved.

5.2 Completion by post

Completion is usually conducted according to the Law Society's Code for Completion by Post, ie:

- The buyer's solicitor sends the completion monies to the seller's solicitor by telegraphic transfer
- The seller's solicitor sends the completion documents to the buyer's solicitor, using the post or DX system

5.3 Completion documents

Whether completion takes place in person or by post, the seller's solicitor will need to give a number of documents to the buyer's solicitor. Originals should be given unless the seller's solicitor has any reason to retain them (for example on a sale of part or where a power of attorney is not limited to the sale). If the original is not being provided, the buyer's solicitor should ensure that the copy is certified as a true copy.

The documents to be handed over are the deeds and documents according to a schedule of deeds including:

- Title deeds and documents
- An undertaking to discharge the seller's mortgage (in an appropriate form, depending on how discharge is to be dealt with, see below)
- An inventory of chattels sold
- A receipt for payment of the chattels price

5.4 Discharge of seller's mortgage

Almost without exception, the seller's solicitor will have undertaken to discharge any mortgages attached to the property. It is common practice to permit the seller to discharge his mortgage immediately after completion, by sending some or all of the proceeds of sale to his lender. In this situation, it will be agreed that the seller's solicitor will, on completion, providing an undertaking that he will:

- Upon receipt of the completion monies, discharge the seller's mortgage
- Forward either a receipted DS1 or a copy of the notice of confirmation from the lender that an Electronic Notice of Discharge (END) has been sent to the Land Registry, to the buyer's solicitor as soon as it is received by him

Discharge of the seller's mortgage is addressed in more detail in the next Chapter.

6 Effect of completion

In practical terms, the significance of completion is that it is the point at which the seller receives his money and the buyer moves in to his new property.

In legal terms, of course, the position depends on whether the property is registered or unregistered:

Registered land	The buyer becomes the new legal owner only once his name has been entered as registered proprietor on the register of title.
Unregistered land	The legal estate vests in the purchaser. (However, it is then rendered void if not registered within two months).

In both cases, the other legal effect is that the contract may merge with the purchase deed, which means that no action can be brought in respect of the terms of the contract following completion. However, in practice, this doctrine of merger is usually excluded (for example by SC 7.4) so that action can still be taken on the contract. The next Chapter will look at contractual and other remedies in the event of default.

Summary

- There is normally a period between exchange and completion when the parties' solicitors attend to pre-completion matters
- A buyer's solicitor should update his land registry or land charges searches
- These principal searches afford a period of protection: priority period.
- A lender's solicitor should carry out a bankruptcy search against the borrower
- A purchase deed is prepared and engrossed by the buyer's solicitor
- In registered land (and frequently in unregistered land) the purchase deed is a form TR1 transfer
- A transferor must always execute the purchase deed and a transferee must execute in certain circumstances
- 'Requisitions on title' deal primarily with arrangements for completion and are raised by the buyer's solicitor
- The seller's solicitor draws up a completion statement
- Completion usually takes place by post according to the Law Society's Code
- The legal estate is passed effectively once registration takes place

Self-test questions

1 There must be a period of at least 14 days between exchange and completion. True or false?

2 What is the main pre-completion search that a buyer's solicitor will make on a purchase of a registered title?

3 What search *must* a buyer's solicitor make if he is also acting for the lender?

4 What is the priority period on a Land Registry search?

5 What is the priority period on a land charges search?

6 How does a buyer's solicitor obtain further information about a land charge that is revealed by a search?

7 Does the buyer's solicitor always prepare the purchase deed?

8 When will the transfer or conveyance contain a 'declaration of trust'?

9 When must a transferee execute the purchase deed?

10 If a previously undisclosed encumbrance comes to light after exchange, can the buyer's solicitor raise a requisition in respect of it?

11 When should a buyer's solicitor provide a written release, authorising payment of the deposit to the seller (or as he directs)?

12 How does a seller's solicitor provide evidence of the discharge of his client's mortgage?

13 When does a buyer of registered land become the new legal owner of the property?

Answers to self-test questions

1 False. This is very often the case but it is not essential. Where there is little time, some or all of the pre-completion steps will be taken prior to exchange

2 Land Registry search on form OS1

3 A bankruptcy only search against the buyer on form K16 (whether the land is registered or unregistered)

4 30 working days

5 15 working days

6 By submitting form K19 to request an official copy of the land charge (which will reveal the applicant)

7 Usually but not always. A seller's solicitor may prepare it where, for example, the seller is selling a number of identical or similar properties

8 When the buyers are to hold the beneficial interest as tenants in common

9 When he is entering into a covenant or making a declaration of trust

10 Yes. Under SC4.2.2 he should do so within 6 working days of becoming aware of it

11 When the deposit is held as stakeholder, certainly if it is so held by a third party (such as an estate agent)

12 By forwarding to the buyer's solicitor a receipted DS1 or a copy of the lender's confirmation that an END has been sent to the Land Registry

13 Once he has been entered on the register of the relevant title as the new registered proprietor (ie following registration)

13

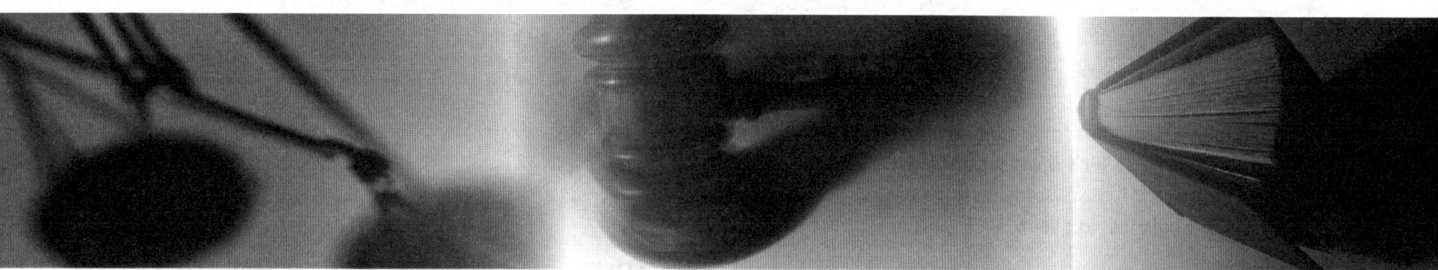

Post-completion

Topic List

Chapter overview

This Chapter will:

- Explain the steps that need to be taken following completion by the solicitors acting for the seller, buyer and lender with regard to money, mortgages and documents
- Explain the steps that need to be taken with regard to payment of SDLT and registration

1 Post-completion steps

Some of the steps that need to be taken following completion need to be taken as a matter of extreme urgency (for example passing received purchase monies up the chain on related transactions) or within certain time periods (for example payment of SDLT and registration). The consequences of being late in most of the post-completion steps can be extremely dire. It is therefore good practice to regard the post-completion stage as a matter of high priority in any transaction.

Broadly, these post-completion steps are as follows:

Seller's solicitor	Buyer's solicitor
1 Report to and advise client	1 Report to and advise client
2 Deal with money ▶ forward monies for onward purchase ▶ discharge seller's mortgage ▶ account for costs, commissions etc ▶ send balance to client	2 Deal with buyer's mortgage
3 Deal with documents	3 Deal with SDLT
	4 Register purchase and mortgage

2 Steps to be taken by the seller's solicitor

2.1 Seller's solicitor: report to and advise client

The seller's solicitor should report the fact of completion to his client immediately (and lender-client if appropriate), normally by telephone. He should also advise him (or remind him) to:

- Notify the local authority and utility suppliers of the change of ownership
- Cancel insurance on the property
- Remember to deal with accounting for CGT and/or VAT if appropriate

It goes without saying that where completion is by post, the seller's solicitor should also report immediately to the buyer's solicitor once the monies are received and completion (is taking or) has taken place. He may also need to report completion to the seller's estate agent, especially where the agent is holding the keys for release to the buyer.

2.2 Seller's solicitor: deal with money

2.2.1 Forward purchase monies

If the seller is also purchasing another property, it will be necessary to forward all or part of the sale proceeds to the next seller in the chain. This will need to be done in accordance with the contract and instructions received and is likely to have to be done as a matter of urgency in order to meet the contractual time of completion in the onward purchase.

2.2.2 Discharge seller's mortgage

The seller's solicitor must forward money to the seller's lender in the sum of the redemption figure as notified by the lender (adjusted as necessary if completion does not actually take place on the contractual completion date). This is done by client account cheque or direct transfer.

Where a separate solicitor is acting for the seller's lender, the seller's solicitor may request that separate transfers are made to each. It is more common that one solicitor will act for both seller and lender.

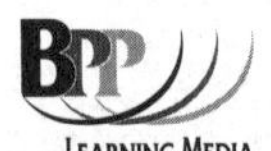

Of course he will need to be able to satisfy the buyer's solicitor that he has discharged the mortgage. This can be done in four ways:

DS1	by sending Form DS1 to the lender, requesting the lender to discharge the mortgage and return the receipted Form DS1 as soon as possible. Once received, and checked, he will then forward it to the buyer's solicitor
receipted mortgage deed	(unregistered land only) by asking the lender to complete the receipt clause on the reverse of the mortgage deed and return it. Once received, and checked, he will then forward it to the buyer's solicitor
END 1	by sending Form END 1, asking the lender to transmit the END

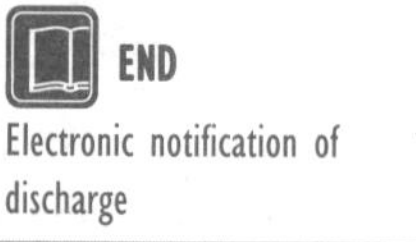

Electronic notification of discharge

Note that EDs are currently at a pilot stage and are expected to replace ENDs in due course, as part of the plans for electronic conveyancing. Under the EDs system, the lender sends a direct instruction to the Land Registry to cancel the charges entries in the register once the charge has been paid off. The Land Registry will process a number of automated checks and the entries will then be removed automatically.

2.2.3 Insurance policies

If the lender has insured the property, he should be advised to cancel that insurance. If a life policy was previously assigned to the lender by the seller, it should be re-assigned to the seller (or it may be appropriate for it to be assigned to a new lender on a related purchase).

2.2.4 Meet liabilities

It is likely that the seller's solicitor will have agreed to attend to the following:

Estate agent's commission	He should ask for a receipt.
Legal costs	These are likely to be retained from the sale proceeds. Provided he has authority, he may therefore transfer a sum representing legal costs and disbursements (already advised to the client) from client account to office account.

2.2.5 Pay balance

The seller's solicitor should then pay the balance of the sale proceeds to his client or otherwise as directed by him.

2.3 Seller's solicitor: deal with documents

Where completion takes place by post, the seller's solicitor will be required to forward the relevant documents to the buyer's solicitor in accordance with the schedule of deeds, in particular:

- The transfer, duly executed and dated
- Relevant title documents

Registered land	No title deeds are strictly necessary although old land/charge certificates may be supplied. Ancillary documents may be relevant, eg planning consents, power of attorney, grant of probate etc.
Unregistered land	Title deeds according to the epitome of title. Ancillary documents, eg planning consents, powers of attorney, grant of probate

Where the sale is of part only, the seller's solicitor will also need to attend to custody of the deeds relating to the retained land. Even on a sale of the whole, he might retain deeds, for example an original power of attorney that was not limited to the disposal. He should ensure safe custody in accordance with his client's instructions.

3 Steps to be taken by the buyer's solicitor

3.1 The buyer's solicitor: report to and advise the client

The buyer's solicitor must inform his client (and lender-client if appropriate) that completion has taken place immediately, normally by telephone. Where completion is by post, this will be as soon as the buyer's solicitor has been informed by the seller's solicitor that the monies have been received and the transfer dated.

He should advise his client to take meter readings and inform the local authority and utility suppliers of the change of ownership. He should also remind his client of his obligations with regard to VAT if appropriate (see Chapter 5).

3.2 The buyer's solicitor: deal with the buyer's mortgage

The buyer's solicitor must:

- Date the mortgage deed and complete any other details as appropriate
- Register the mortgage. (This will normally be done at the same time as registering the purchase).

Failure to register a charge created by a company within 21 days renders it void against any liquidator, administrator or creditor of the company. Company charges must be registered at the Companies Registry (s.860 Companies Act 2006).

If the buyer used **bridging finance** for the purchase, this will need to be accounted for and settled in accordance with any undertakings given.

 **Practice note**

Keep copies of the mortgage, transfer and relevant documents on file.

On receipt of the Form DS1 (or receipted mortgage deed), the buyer's solicitor should check it and release the seller's solicitor from his undertaking in respect of it.

Although not typical, a buyer's mortgage may involve the formal assignment to the lender of an endowment policy. If this is the case, notice of assignment must be given to the relevant insurance company and an acknowledgement of notice requested (usually by providing notice in duplicate with one part to be signed and returned).

3.3 Buyer's solicitor: account for SDLT

Any SDLT payable must be paid **within 30 days of completion** and the Land Transaction Return, in Form SDLT1, submitted. Failure to do so may result in penalties and interest charges. SDLT 1 must also be completed and submitted to HMRC even if no SDLT is payable.

The buyer's solicitor must send:

- A client account cheque
- The duly completed and signed SDLT1

Once processed, HMRC will certify payment by issuing SDLT 5 to the buyer's solicitor, who will need to submit it with the application for registration.

Note that SDLT 1 can be submitted electronically, using the Stamp Taxes Online service. Although the client must still sign a printed copy of it, this is retained on file and only the electronic version is sent to HMRC. Where this service is used, SDLT5 is also issued electronically and this is then printed off and sent to the Land Registry with the application for registration.

3.4 Buyer's solicitor: registration of title

Remember that the transfer of registered land is not effective to pass the legal estate until it is registered. On a first registration, failure to register within **two months** renders the transaction void.

Registered land	Registration should be made within the 30 days priority period given on the pre-completion OS1 search
Unregistered land	Registration should be made within 2 months of completion

The method of dealing with registration depends on whether the dealing is with unregistered land or land that is already registered. Some or all of the following documents, depending on the individual transaction, will need to be submitted to the relevant Land Registry for the property transferred:

Dealing with registered land	First registration (documents supplied must be listed in duplicate on form DL)
Form AP 1	Form FR 1
Transfer and certified copy	Transfer and certified copy *
Buyer's mortgage deed and certified copy *	Buyer's mortgage deed and certified copy *
Receipted Form DS1	Receipted seller's mortgage deed
SDLT 5	SDLT 5
Fee	Fee
Other relevant documents (which may also be relevant in a first registration of unregistered land): ▶ Official copy death certificate of a co-seller ▶ Official or certified copy grant of representation where the seller was the PR(s) of a deceased owner ▶ Original power of attorney (if special power limited to the transaction) ▶ Certified copy power of attorney (in other cases) ▶ Form D1 disclosing interests known to override registered dispositions	All title deeds and documents supplied by seller All results of all pre-contract searches and enquiries The contract Requisitions on title and replies All pre-completion search results Form D1 disclosing interests known to override first registration (if applicable)

* Where an original and a certified copy are submitted together, the Land Registry will normally return the original.

Where the contract for sale was registered, application should be made for removal of the notice or the estate contract land charge (as appropriate).

Once registration has been completed, the Land Registry will confirm this fact to the buyer's solicitor and provide a title information document. The buyer's solicitor should ensure that his client is now correctly shown as the registered proprietor and that all other details are correct.

The buyer's solicitor should also attend to custody of any deeds not submitted to or retained by the Land Registry. These may require to be stored by the mortgagee or by the solicitor or otherwise may be held as directed by the buyer.

Summary

- Post-completion steps should be taken as soon as possible
- The seller's solicitor needs to report to his client and attend to distribution of the sale proceeds
- A mortgage can be discharged and its discharge evidenced in a number of ways: DSI, END1 and a receipted mortgage deed
- The buyer's solicitor must report to his client and attend to payment of SDLT within 30 days, submitting form SDLT 1
- He must also attend to registration of the transfer (and mortgage).
- There are a number of prescribed documents that he must submit for registration.

Self-test questions

1 What is the time limit for payment of SDLT?

2 What is the time limit for applying for first registration?

3 Within what timescale should application for registration of a transfer in registered land be made?

4 What is the next step taken by a lender where the seller's solicitor sends form END1 to the lender?

5 Within what time limit must a company charge be registered?

6 What information is contained on Form D1?

Answers to self-test questions

1 Within 30 days following completion

2 2 months

3 Within the 30 day priority period given by the OS1 pre-completion search

4 The lender transmits the END (electronically) to the Land Registry

5 21 days

6 Interests known to override first registration or registered dispositions, as the case may be

14

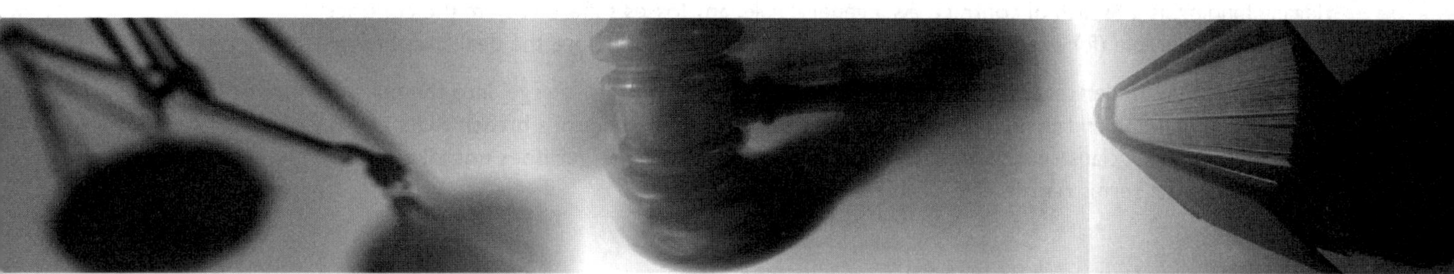

Remedies

Topic List

Chapter overview

This chapter will:

- Set out the potential situations in which a breach of contract might occur
- Explain the basic principles governing the remedies that are available in the event of breach, namely damages, specific performance and rescission
- Consider the consequences of a delay in completion
- Consider the consequences of a total failure to complete
- Explain what constitutes misrepresentation and indicate the remedies that may be available
- Examine some key standard conditions in the SCS
- Consider the steps that can be taken when an error occurs in the contract, purchase deed or register

Chapter overview continued

As outlined earlier in this manual, conveyancing is essentially the practical application of land law and the law of contract. We have seen in Chapters 10 and 11 how the contract is drafted and made binding by an exchange of parts. Chapters 12 and 13 then described the remainder of the conveyancing transaction on the basis of everything running according to plan. This Chapter will look at scenarios where problems occur and plans go awry.

1 Breach of contract

Any failure to adhere to and perform the terms of the contract, once that contract has become legally binding, is a breach of contract. As a general rule, any losses suffered *before* the contract are not recoverable (for example the costs of a survey carried out before the deal falls through).

Remember that, under general legal principles, the terms of a contract 'merge' into the purchase deed on completion and an action can no longer be brought in respect of a breach of its terms. However, where a clause of non-merger (such as SC 7.4) applies, merger does not take place and the contract terms remain enforceable.

1.1 Examples of breach of contract in a conveyancing transaction

There are many circumstances in which breach of contract may occur and the following are merely some examples:

Between exchange and completion

- Failure by either party to comply with the time limits set for preparing and agreeing the purchase deed, set out in SC 4.3.2
- The seller rendering the property 'unusable'
- The buyer altering the property whilst in occupation, in breach of SC 5.2.2

Arising at the time appointed for completion

- The buyer failing to produce the required completion monies by the day and time agreed
- The seller failing to produce the transfer duly executed or other completion documents
- The seller failing to give vacant possession
- The seller removing some fixtures or fittings that he agreed to leave behind

Only becoming apparent after completion has taken place

- The seller having failed to disclose something which should have been disclosed
- The seller having misrepresented something to the buyer

1.2 Remedies for breach of contract

The general position is that where one party commits a breach of contract, the other party may seek a legal remedy. The types of remedy will depend on the nature of the breach and the appropriateness of the remedy in redressing the consequences of the breach. A contract for the sale of land is no exception. Broadly, the relevant remedies are:

- Damages (with or without the termination of the contract, see below)
- Contractual compensation, pursuant to an express provision in the contract
- Specific performance

Service of a notice to complete, although not a 'remedy' in the same sense as those listed, is often the first step taken by a party in the event of the other party's delay (see para 3 below).

Whether a breach of contract entitles the injured party to treat the contract as discharged or merely to claim damages depends on the provision that has been breached and the extent to

which it is central or of material importance. Broadly speaking, contractual terms are sometimes categorised as either conditions, warranties or innominate terms.

- A **condition** is a fundamental term, of key importance to the contract. Breach of a condition entitles the innocent party to treat the contract as terminated and/or to claim damages.
- A **warranty** is a term of less importance and breach of a warranty gives rise to a claim in damages only.
- An **innominate term** is one that cannot easily be categorised as either a condition or a warranty and the remedy that is available in the event of breach will depend on the seriousness of the damage or loss suffered.

Whether or not a term is classed as a condition or warranty is to be determined having regard to all the facts and labelling them as one or the other in the contract will not be conclusive.

1.2.1 Damages

Damages for breach of contract are a monetary payment (usually a lump sum) designed to put the claimant in the position he would have been in, had the contract been properly performed.

Alert

Damages are really only relevant where contractual compensation is inadequate and/or where a party fails to comply with a notice to complete.

They may be claimed following any breach of warranty or breach of condition. Failure to complete on time is a breach of warranty, unless time is of the essence, in which case it is a breach of condition. Remember that any repudiatory breach, or breach of condition, entitles the innocent party to treat a contract as terminated in addition to claiming damages. Where this happens, such discharge of the contract as a result of the breach does not alter the contractual rights and obligations that have already arisen, but simply operates to discharge contractual obligations that have yet to be performed.

Damages are normally only available in respect of financial loss suffered and not emotional distress for example. Thus an award of damages might permit recovery of (*Bruce v Waziri 1982, Beard v Porter 1948*):

- The cost of alternative accommodation
- Additional legal costs
- Interest due on a mortgage or bridging finance
- Costs arising out of a related sale or purchase being affected

The claimant is expected to take reasonable steps to **mitigate**, or reduce, his loss. Thus, for example, a seller will be expected to re-market his property or a buyer will be expected to look at other properties. If a party fails to take steps to mitigate his loss, the level of damages may be reduced as a result.

Under the rule in *Hadley v Baxendale 1854,* the party in default will only be liable to pay damages in respect of:

- Losses arising naturally from the breach
- Losses that were reasonably foreseeable, having regard to all the circumstances and facts known at the time of the contract

Normally in the case of a breach of a contract for the sale of land, the amount of damages would be the difference between the contract price and the market price of the property at the date of the breach, plus any additional costs such as those mentioned above. Contractual damages will be assessed so as not to enable the innocent party to profit from the breach. Thus if a buyer defaults and the seller sells the property to another party for more money than he would have received from the buyer, any damages would be reduced by that extra amount.

Note that any compensation paid under SC 7.3 would also be taken into account (see 2.5 below).

1.2.2 Specific performance

Alert

A non-defaulting party is much more likely to serve a notice to complete than to seek a court order for specific performance.

The innocent party may seek an order of specific performance, although it is likely that service of a notice to complete will be a more attractive option (assuming time is not already of the essence), as it will be quicker and cheaper. The claimant may claim specific performance simultaneously with a claim for rescission or damages or on its own. It should be claimed within a reasonable time, as undue delay may result in it not being awarded.

It is an equitable remedy and is in the court's discretion. This means that it will not be awarded where, for example, damages would provide adequate compensation for the claimant's loss or a third party has acquired an interest for value in the property.

The court is empowered to award damages in lieu of specific performance (s.50 Supreme Court Act 1981), which it is likely to do where specific performance is not appropriate, for example where it would require some sort of ongoing supervision by the court.

However, in the case of a contract for the sale of land, damages will rarely be an adequate remedy and so the court will often award specific performance. (This is because it is unlikely that the claimant will be able simply to go out and buy an alternative plot of land that will satisfy his requirements.)

If a party fails to comply with a court order of specific performance, the claimant may submit a further claim for specific performance with damages (*Johnson v Agnew 1980*).

Note that the SCS do not make any express provision with regard to specific performance.

1.2.3 Contractual compensation

This may have the advantage of avoiding a common law court action that can be very time-consuming, costly and generally more onerous. It is payable irrespective of any loss and no loss needs to be proved.

SC 7.3 provides for contractual compensation and is considered at 2.5 below.

1.2.4 Rescission

The right to rescind arises in cases where a contract is rendered voidable by some vitiating factor such as fraud, misrepresentation or mistake. In these cases, the innocent party can elect to affirm the contract or to rescind the contract. Affirmation may be express or inferred from his actions. If he elects to rescind the contract, generally speaking, he should communicate that decision to the other party within a reasonable time.

Where a right to rescind is exercised, essentially it amounts to 'undoing' the contract and aims to restore the parties to the position they were in before the contract was made. It is likely that a court, in enforcing a claim to rescission, will also award the innocent party an indemnity or compensation (rather than 'damages', although the effect is similar).

Rescission is a creation of equity and may, therefore, be 'barred' in certain cases, namely where:

- The contract has been affirmed
- An unreasonable amount of time has lapsed
- *Restitutio in integrum* is impossible, ie the parties cannot be restored to their original position
- A third party has acquired an interest in the property for value

Unfortunately, the word 'rescission' is often used, incorrectly, to refer to the election of the innocent party to treat a contract as terminated where a breach of condition occurs. As the House of Lords recently made clear in *Johnson v Agnew 1980*, whereas such repudiatory breach simply brings a contract to an end at the time of breach and does not destroy the rights and obligations under the contract up to that point, rescission cancels a contract retrospectively in its entirety.

In any event, note that a right to 'rescind' may arise because a **contract expressly provides** that it shall. For example, the SCS provide for 'rescission' in four situations, namely where:

- The property is rendered unusable prior to completion (SC 5.1)
- An error or omission is fraudulent or reckless or where it would result in the buyer accepting property substantially different (in quality, quantity or tenure) from what the error or omission had led him to expect (SC 7.1)
- Either party fails to comply with a notice to complete (SC 7.5, 7.6)
- A licence to let, sublet or assign is required and is not obtained (SC 8.3)

1.3 Exclusion clauses

It is possible that the contract for sale will contain an exclusion clause. To the extent that this relates to a breach of a contractual term, it may be effective (provided there is no question of undue influence or duress for example). The Unfair Contract Terms Act 1977 ('UCTA') does not apply to contracts for the sale of land.

However, where it seeks to limit or restrict liability for breach of contract arising out of legal principles outside the actual terms of the contract (for example misrepresentation), then the exclusion clause will need to satisfy the reasonableness test under UCTA in order to be valid.

Note that SC 7.1 is an exclusion clause, in providing that damages are only available where there is a **material** difference in the tenure or value of the property and that rescission is only available where there is fraud or recklessness or a **substantial** difference in quantity, quality or tenure.

1.4 Limitation periods

Generally speaking, an action for breach of contract must be brought within six years of the breach (or 12 years where the contract is made by deed) under the Limitation Act 1980.

2 Delay in completion

Typically it will be the buyer who commits a breach of contract by delaying completion, where he fails to produce the completion monies in time. However, the seller may also cause a delay, for example by not having the transfer executed in time.

Late completion might only be a delay of a day or two but, even then the inconvenience as well as the cost involved should not be underestimated, particularly since a residential sale is very often part of a chain of transactions where the delay can have a knock-on effect on parties up and down the chain.

2.1 When completion should take place

The remedies for delay will apply wherever completion does not take place at or before the **time** specified for completion on the **date** specified for completion. These are likely to be expressly provided for in the contract (see Chapter 10). By way of reminder:

- **The completion date** is:
  - The date specified in the contract (often inserted immediately prior to exchange)
  - (Where SCS apply) if no date is specified, then 20 working days after exchange (SC 6.1.1)
  - Where the contract is silent, a 'reasonable time' after exchange, under the common law. (Obviously this is very unsatisfactory, which is why a specific date is almost invariably provided.)

  Note that the completion date may be subject to a condition being satisfied (for example 'within x days from planning permission being obtained'). Any such condition should be sufficiently clear so as not to be declared void for uncertainty.

- **The completion time** is:
  - The time inserted in the contract
  - (Where SCS apply) 2pm, following which completion is treated as having taken place on the next working day (SC 6.1.2). This means that a delay of minutes gives rise to an entitlement to at least one day's compensation under SC 7.3. However, this rule does not apply where the delay is due to the seller not having vacated the property by that time, where he was under an obligation to do so.

  Note that any variation in an express term concerning the contractual completion date should be dealt with by amending the contract and arranging for the parties to exchange contracts again, in order to incorporate the variation in accordance with s.2 LP(MP)A 1989. A mere exchange of solicitors' letters recording the variation is not sufficient *(McCausland v Duncan Lawrie Ltd 1997)*.

2.2 The remedies for delay

Clearly the non-defaulting party who is delayed from completing on time can face quite significant losses as well as substantial inconvenience. His choice of remedy may depend on the extent of those losses.

First, however, the remedies available depend on whether or not time is 'of the essence' (which is actually highly unlikely in a residential or simple commercial transaction).

Is time of the essence?	Yes	He may treat the contract as discharged and/or claim damages (essentially for breach of condition) or seek an order for specific performance
	No	He may either: ▸ Claim damages ▸ Claim contractual compensation if available ▸ Both of the above ▸ Serve a notice to complete (see paragraph 3 below) ▸ Seek an order for specific performance

2.3 When is time of the essence?

Time may be of the essence in three situations, namely when:

- The contract **expressly** so provides – this is unusual
- It is **implied** (unless SCS apply *) – for example, where the sale is linked to a particular event taking place
- A **notice to complete** is served – see 3.2 below

* SC 6.1.1 provides that time is of the essence only where a notice to complete is served; it cannot be implied.

2.4 Whether to claim damages or contractual compensation

A non-defaulting party is often faced with a choice between claiming damages or contractual compensation.

The advantage of claiming compensation under the terms of SC7.3 (or a similar clause) is that there is little room for dispute, either over the amount of compensation that is payable or over whether there is any entitlement to it. In addition, it is not necessary to show any loss, nor to take any steps to mitigate any loss.

The disadvantage is that the amount payable may not be sufficient to compensate the innocent party for the losses suffered. In these circumstances, he may be advised to seek damages in a common law action in addition to, or instead of, claiming the contractual compensation. In fact he would be well advised to do so additionally, because he is likely to receive payment more promptly under the contract's express provision (and therefore recover some of his loss more quickly).

2.5 SC 7.3: contractual compensation

Under SC 7.3, compensation is payable at the **contract rate** on the total purchase price:

- (Land and chattels), where the seller is in default
- Less any deposit paid, where the buyer is the party in default

The contract rate is normally specifically stated. Where none is stated and the SCS apply, SC 1.1.1 provides that it is the Law Society's interest rate from time to time in force (currently 4% pa above the base rate of Barclays Bank plc).

Where only one party is responsible for the delay, compensation is paid for the period from the contractual completion date (which takes account of the time) to actual completion. Where both parties are at fault, the party who must pay the compensation is the party who has caused the greatest delay and the period in respect of which the compensation must be paid is as above or, if longer, the period by which the paying party's default exceeds the receiving party's default.

Note that where a party rescinds the contract, he cannot also claim compensation under SC 7.3.

The period is calculated on a whole day basis and not just on working days (so, for example, if completion is due by 2pm on a Friday and actually takes place at 4pm, compensation will be payable for three days, not one).

Example

A contract for sale between Simon and Boris provides for completion at 1pm on Thursday 15 September. The purchase price is £500,000 and the contract rate is 8% pa. Boris's bank fails to transfer the purchase monies in time and they reach Simon's solicitor at 3pm on Friday 16 September.

Under SC 6.1.1 completion is treated as taking place on 19 September (as the completion time on the next working day has also not been met). Boris must pay compensation of £438.36 (4 days).

Remember

The non-defaulting party may seek an order for specific performance. In practice he is more likely to serve a notice to complete

2.6 Delay and chain transactions

Of course if a client is faced with a delay in the completion of his sale or purchase, he may need to consider the effect on a related sale or purchase in a chain of transactions. There are two options: either to default on the related transaction or to make arrangements to enable the related transaction to proceed. In the first, he will incur liability and in the second, he will incur costs. In both cases, he would seek to pass on this liability or cost to the party causing the initial default. However, even if legal principles dictate that recovery should be possible, the prospect of time-consuming litigation to achieve that result is likely to be unattractive.

Example

Nadeen is selling and buying. His purchaser fails to produce the purchase monies on time. In order to proceed with his purchase, he will need to obtain bridging finance and will end up owning two houses at once. Compare the likely costs and prospects of recovery between taking this action and delaying his purchase.

Owen is also selling and buying. His seller fails to complete on time. In order to proceed with his sale he will need to find alternative accommodation and will be homeless until completion can take place. Is this a better course of action than delaying his sale?

A solicitor must act in his client's best interests and it will be essential, therefore, to consider the options very carefully with his client. It could actually be less risky to incur a liability to compensation on the related transaction than to face escalating costs and inconvenience. This will be a matter of considering all the relevant facts, including the reason for the delay and the likely length of the delay.

3 Failure to complete

Where it becomes clear that the defaulting party is not going to complete at all - which may come after a period of delay or become apparent immediately on (or even before) the contractual date for completion, the breach of contract is a matter of **failure to complete**. For example, a party may expressly communicate the fact that he has no intention of completing or this may be implied, perhaps by the seller selling to another party or the purchaser buying another property. It is also a matter of failure to complete where time is of the essence or where a party fails to comply with a notice to complete.

3.1 Notice to complete

The service of a notice to complete has the effect of making time of the essence. It may be appropriate where completion is being delayed with no real prospect of the delay being brought to an end and has the advantage of achieving a greater level of certainty for both parties. However, the party serving a notice to complete must always bear in mind that it essentially makes time of the essence for **both** parties and so he should ensure that he will be able to comply with it himself. It is not open to him to withdraw it once it has been served.

Service of a notice to complete is an option under general legal principles relating to contracts. However, it will normally be served pursuant to SC 6.8 or similar express provision. SC 1.3 governs the method of service and specifies times when a notice will be deemed to have been received. Note that a notice received on a non-working day or after 4pm on a working day shall be deemed to have been received on the next working day (SC 1.3.5).

3.2 Effects of a notice to complete served pursuant to SC 6.8

Under SC 6.8, service of a notice to complete:

- Makes time of the essence
- Provides for completion 10 working days after service (excluding the day of service)
- Provides for the buyer to make up any shortfall in payment of a deposit equivalent to 10%

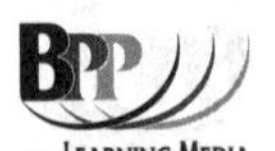

3.3 Remedies for failure to complete

3.3.1 Where SC 6.8 applies

The consequences of a failure to comply with a notice to complete pursuant to SC 6.8 are as follows:

Failure by the buyer	Failure by the seller
The seller:	The buyer:
▶ May rescind the contract	▶ May rescind the contract
▶ May keep the deposit and any accrued interest	▶ Is entitled to repayment of the deposit with interest
▶ May resell the property and any chattels included with it	▶ Must return any documents received from the seller
▶ May claim damages	▶ Must cancel any registration of the contract (at the seller's expense)
▶ Must return any documents received from the buyer	
▶ Must cancel any registration of the contract	

3.3.2 Where there is no express provision

Failure to complete, where time is (or has been made) of the essence or where a party makes clear his repudiatory breach, does not automatically terminate the contract but the innocent party may choose to treat the contract as discharged and/or claim damages. Where the buyer fails to complete, the seller is entitled to retain any deposit paid. Where the seller defaults, the buyer is entitled to recover any deposit paid.

(S.49(2) Law of Property Act 1925 allows an application for the return of a deposit which has been forfeited. Case law suggests that the court has discretion only to order the return of the whole, not part, of the deposit, although the court has ordered return of a deposit on condition that the buyer must reimburse certain expenses to the seller (see *Universal Corporation v Five Ways Properties 1979*).)

As mentioned, it is also open to an innocent party to seek an order of specific performance, even once a notice to complete has been served and not observed (since his other rights and remedies are not affected).

4 Misrepresentation

A party may seek redress where the other party has misrepresented something or omitted to disclose something that he should have disclosed. Misrepresentation often arises in relation to replies to enquiries or replies to requisitions and may come to light before or after completion. Where the SCS apply, he is likely to pursue a remedy under SC 7. Where the SCS (or similar) do not apply, he may pursue an action for misrepresentation in equity or under the Misrepresentation Act 1967 ('MA 67').

Doctrine of laches

This is similar to the law of limitations but is equitable rather than statutory. Undue delay will prejudice or even provide a complete defence to a claim

Where a claim is based on a contractual provision, it must be made within six years (or 12 years if the contract is by deed) but if it arises from the general law of misrepresentation, the doctrine of laches applies and a claim must be made within a reasonable time.

4.1 Misrepresentation and SC 7

The misrepresentation and remedies under SC 7 apply to any misleading or inaccurate plan or statement in the contract or pre-contract negotiations caused by an error or omission and the remedies depend on the effect of such error or omission:

Damages	Where there is a **material difference** between the description or value of the property (or of any of the chattels included in the contract) as represented and as it is
Rescission	Where the error or omission results from fraud or recklessness or where the error or omission would lead him to expect a property differing substantially (to his detriment) in quantity, quality or tenure, from the property that he would be obliged to accept

The remedies specified in SC 7 will also be relevant to cases of:

- **Misdescription**, for example where the particulars of sale are incorrect, perhaps by inaccurately describing the extent of the property or giving an incorrect title number or statement of tenure
- **Failure to disclose**, for example failure to disclose a latent defect or the fact of a third party's occupation of the property

It may be considered more straightforward and, therefore, advisable to pursue a remedy under SC 7 rather than under common law principles relating to breach of contract or misrepresentation.

Note that, under SC 7, there is no requirement for the buyer to prove that he was induced to enter into the contract by the information supplied by the seller, as is the case under the general law.

4.2 Where the SCS do not apply

Under the general law, misrepresentation occurs where one party makes a statement of fact that turns out to be untrue and the other party enters into the contract in reliance on it. The statement must be of fact, not of law or opinion.

A misrepresentation may be:

- Fraudulent, ie deliberately dishonest
- Negligent, ie careless or reckless
- Innocent, ie genuinely mistaken

4.2.1 Common law remedies

In the case of fraudulent misrepresentation, rescission and damages are available in the **tort of deceit**. However, due to the onus of proving fraud, seeking a remedy under the express terms of the contract or MA 1967 is likely to be a more sensible route.

4.2.2 MA 1967

The court has a discretion to award rescission and so, if any of the equitable bars to rescission apply, it is unlikely to be ordered. S2(1) MA 1967 also provides that the court may award damages in lieu of rescission. In practice, rescission is only likely to occur where the misrepresentation **substantially deprives** the innocent party of the benefit of the contract.

Damages under MA 1967 are assessed as tortious damages, ie with the aim of putting the claimant in the position he would have been in if the tort had not been committed. The principle that a claimant cannot recover more than once for his loss applies.

Where the misrepresentation has become a term of the contract, the claimant may pursue an action either based on breach of contract or under s.1 MA 1967.

Note that where a solicitor gives an incorrect reply, this is treated as a reply of the client's and so the client may incur liability for misrepresentation. The solicitor would, of course, be open to a claim in negligence.

If a client makes a misrepresentation to the other party that is corrected by his solicitor, the other party is deemed to be aware of the corrected statement, even if he is not advised of it by his own solicitor and he cannot, therefore, bring a claim for misrepresentation in respect of it.

4.3 Exclusion clauses

As noted earlier, a clause that attempts to restrict or exclude liability for misrepresentation (including the provisions of SC 7.1) will be valid only if it satisfies the reasonableness test under UCTA 1977. This will be a question to be determined on the facts of each case and based on the circumstances known to the parties when the contract was made. The same applies to any exclusion clause contained in replies to enquires (*Walker v Boyle 1982*).

Note
No exclusion clause is contained in the seller's Property Information Form.

5 Particular conditions arising under the SCS

Delay in completion, failure to complete and misrepresentation are undoubtedly the principal causes of breach of contract. However, there are of course a number of other possible scenarios where one party fails to perform the contract according to its agreed terms. For the purposes of this Study Manual, however, it will be sufficient to address in addition only the following instances, where the consequences are governed by special conditions.

5.1 Where the property becomes 'unusable' between exchange and completion (SC 5.1)

You will recall that, in normal circumstances, the seller retains the risk until completion. If, prior to completion, the physical state of the property renders it unusable for its purpose (as intended at the date of the contract), then SC 7 provides that :

- The buyer may rescind
- The seller may rescind, where the cause is a problem against which he could not reasonably have insured or where it is not legally possible for him to make good the damage (for example, where listed building consent would be necessary for the relevant work but cannot be obtained)

Note that fair wear and tear is excluded. The property becoming unusable might be as a result of the seller's conduct or due to storm damage or flooding, for example.

5.2 Where the seller commits a breach of any of the implied covenants as to title

SC 7.1 may provide a remedy in cases where it turns out that the seller's covenants as to title have been breached. The nature and extent of those covenants will depend on whether the seller is selling with full or limited title guarantee which were explained in Chapter 12. Damages are likely to be the most appropriate remedy or the seller might be asked to execute documents in order to perfect the title defect.

6 Rectification

6.1 In the contract or purchase deed

It is open to the parties to apply to court for rectification of any error appearing in the contract or purchase deed (where something agreed has been either inaccurately represented or omitted altogether). Such an order is in the court's discretion and where rectification is made, the court may issue an order declaring the date on which a contract shall be deemed to have become legally effective or enforceable (s.2(4) LP(MP)A 1989).

6.2 In the register

Under the LRA 2002, application can be made to the Office of the Adjudicator to rectify any error appearing on the register of title. An error might be a simple mistake or typographical error, or a failure to update the register or properly to give effect to an existing estate, right or interest.

The Land Registry can indemnify any person who suffers loss due to any of the reasons contained in Sch 8 para 1 including:

- Rectification of the register
- A mistake in an official search or official copy
- Loss or destruction of a document lodged at the Land Registry
- Any failure by the registrar to give notice of any statutory charge (in accordance with s.50 LRA 2002)

Remember

A solicitor owes a duty of good faith and should, therefore, always point out errors or omissions in documentation of which he is aware

Summary

- Breach of contract may arise in many situations, most notably delay in completion or failure to complete at all
- Provided there is no merger, an action for breach of the contract terms can still be taken following completion
- Remedies are normally pursued according to express contractual provisions but are also available in common law (damages) and equity (specific performance and rescission)
- Any breach of contract gives rise to a liability in damages, assessed under the rule in *Hadley v Baxendale*. If the breach is very serious, it also entitles the innocent party to treat the contract as discharged
- Rescission 'unwraps' the contact and is relevant to misrepresentation, fraud and mistake. Under SCS, 'rescission' is also available in four cases including situations of fundamental breach (for example failure to comply with a notice to complete)
- Enforcement of the right to rescind, like specific performance, is subject to general equitable principles and is in the court's discretion
- Contractual compensation arises as of right and irrespective of loss but may be inadequate in monetary terms
- UCTA does not apply to contracts for the sale of land but insofar as an exclusion clause relates to legal liability arising outside the express contract terms, it must be 'reasonable' if it is to be effective
- Actions for breach of contract must be brought within six years (or 12 years if by deed)
- Service of a notice to complete makes time of the essence and non-compliance with it entitles the innocent party to treat the contract as discharged and/or claim damages or to rescind under SC 7.1. He may also seek an order for specific performance.
- Remedies for misrepresentation can be pursued under any express provision (such as SC 7.1), the MA 1967 or under general law. Damages or rescission are the most appropriate remedies
- Other special conditions make express provision for remedies in particular cases, such as the property becoming unusable after exchange or for breach of title covenants
- Rectification may be an appropriate remedy

Self-test questions

1 What remedy is available at common law for breach of warranty?

2 How are damages assessed, ie what is their aim?

3 Is a claimant under a duty to mitigate his loss in the case of:

(a) Common law damages
(b) Contractual compensation under SC 7.3?

4 When is a court most likely to refuse to award specific performance?

5 An exclusion clause in a contract for the sale of land is void under UCTA 1977. True or false?

6 What is the time limit for bringing an action for breach of contract under the Limitation Act 1980?

7 Where time is expressed to be of the essence and a party defaults on completion, what remedy is appropriate and available to the other party?

8 What is the principal reason for pursuing a claim in damages rather than contractual compensation?

9 Where the seller is in default, what sum is the contract rate applied to, under SC 7.3?

10 Can a notice to complete be withdrawn, once it has been served?

11 What remedies are available for fraudulent misrepresentation where there is no express provision in the contract?

12 What is the most likely remedy where a seller commits a breach of an implied covenant as to title?

13 What remedy is available to a buyer who has suffered loss as a result of an error appearing on an official certificate of search?

Answers to self-test questions

1 Damages

2 To put the claimant in the position he would have been in if the contract had been performed

3 (a) Yes
(b) No

4 When damages would provide an adequate remedy or where a third party has acquired an interest in the property

5 False. UCTA does not apply to contracts for the sale of land

6 Six years

7 To treat the contract as discharged and/or claim damages

8 To recover a greater financial amount than is available under the express contract provision

9 The whole purchase price including deposit, land and chattels

10 No. It binds both parties

11 Rescission and damages in the tort of deceit

12 Damages (or a seller might be required to execute certain documents in order to perfect the title, if appropriate)

13 He may be compensated for, or indemnified against, any loss by the Land Registry

Part C
Leases and Leasehold Conveyancing

Part C: Leases and leasehold conveyancing

Overview

So far this Study Manual has concentrated on the law and conveyancing practices relating to freehold interests. We now turn to the leasehold estate which, you will remember from Chapter 1, is the only other type of legal estate that can be created. There are many different types of lease and a variety of reasons for dealing with a leasehold, rather than a freehold, estate. Leases are commonly encountered in commercial and residential developments, where there are common parts used by all occupiers in the development, but also in stand-alone premises and also in agricultural property.

Legislation relating to leases is extensive and this part of the Study Manual is by no means comprehensive. However, it will introduce you to the concept of leases (Chapter 15), lease covenants and their enforcement (Chapters 16 and 17) and how, as a matter of conveyancing, leases are created and transferred (Chapter 18).

Test requirements

The QLTT Test Specification does not address the law or conveyancing practices relating to freehold and leasehold separately, except to identify that your knowledge of the basic principles of land law and the manner in which they apply to conveyancing transactions may be tested by questions on leases.

However, many of the issues addressed in the Test Specification and set out at the beginning of Part B of this manual can also be applied to leasehold property and leasehold conveyancing.

15

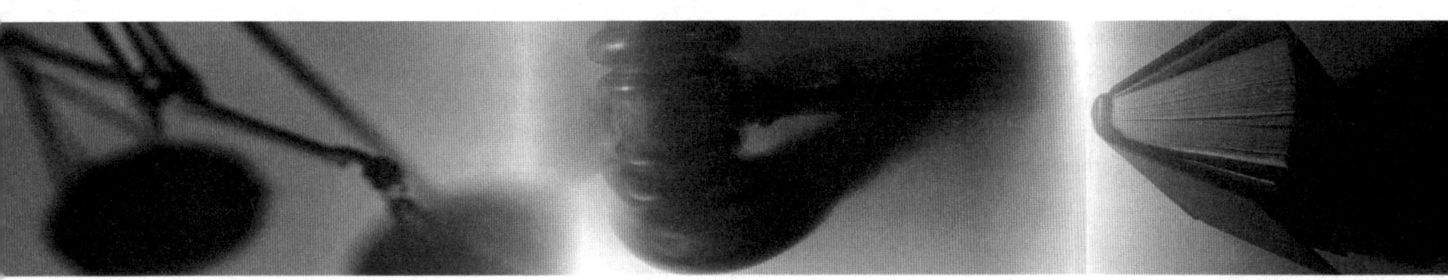

Leases

Topic List

Chapter overview

This chapter will:

- Define a lease and explain its key features
- Describe several different types of lease
- Distinguish between a legal and equitable lease and state the registration requirements
- Clarify the terminology used in discussing the law relating to leases
- Consider when a leasehold estate might be created, rather than disposing of the freehold estate
- Explain how a lease may be terminated

1 What is a lease?

A lease is the grant of **exclusive possession** of land for a **term that is certain**. These characteristics, of exclusive possession and certain duration, are essential in any lease. Without both, the interest is not a lease.

Although payment of rent has been held to be a non-essential element of a lease (*Ashburn Anstalt v Arnold 1989*), a covenant to pay rent is almost invariably contained in a lease and its absence is likely to make it harder to draw the conclusion that the arrangement is a lease.

1.1 Exclusive possession

A person is granted exclusive possession if he has the right to exclude all other persons, including the landlord, from the property. If in fact the landlord is able to enter the property (other than in the event of breach) at any time, or if he retains control over the property or a part of it, then there is no exclusive possession and the arrangement cannot be a lease (*Wells v Kingston-upon-Hull Corporation 1875*) and will be construed as a licence (see paragraph 6 below).

1.2 Term that is certain

Remember that the legal estate, although commonly referred to as 'leasehold', is referred to as a 'term of years absolute' by the LPA 1925. This expression requires that the duration of the arrangement is fixed, or capable of being ascertained with certainty. Thus a purported lease 'for the duration of the war', for example, will not satisfy the requirement for a term that is certain (*Lace v Chantler 1944*). Likewise, a 'tenancy' of land until such time as the landlord required it for road improvement works, with payment of an annual rent, was held to be a periodic tenancy, and not a lease. The reason given was that an agreement for indeterminate occupation can never constitute a lease (*Prudential Assurance Co Ltd v London Residuary Body 1992, House of Lords*).

Furthermore, the certain length of the term must be known at the commencement of it and the date of commencement must also be fixed or capable of being ascertained with certainty. Thus a lease that is expressed to commence on a given date is quite acceptable, even where that date is a date in the future (in which case the lease is called a '**reversionary lease**'), provided the commencement date is no later than **21 years** after the date of the instrument purporting to create it (s.149(3) LPA 1925).

2 The nature of the leasehold estate

A lease can be legal or equitable.

2.1 The legal lease

As mentioned, the LPA 1925 provides that a lease can exist as a legal estate. There are two ways in which a legal lease can be created:

(1) By deed (s.52 LPA 1925)

(2) Orally or in writing, provided (s.54(2) LPA 1925) the lease:

- Takes effect in possession (ie immediately, not in reversion)
- For a term not exceeding three years **
- At the best rest reasonably obtainable (ie a full market rent)
- Without taking a fine (ie a premium)

** This includes fixed terms of three years or less. Note that it also includes periodic tenancies, even though they may continue indefinitely (see 5.2 below).

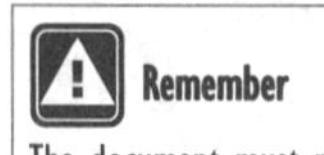

Remember

The document must make clear on its face that it is intended to be a deed and must be validly executed as such (s.2 LP(MP)A 1989)

Note that if the lease is for more than seven years, the legal estate will not pass until it is registered (see paragraph 3.1 below).

2.2 The equitable lease

Where a lease fails to satisfy either of the requirements above, no legal estate will pass and the lease is said to be void at law. Instead, it will take effect as an equitable interest only, namely a contract to grant a lease. This contract is actually treated as 'an equitable lease', under the doctrine of *Walsh v Lonsdale*, which provides that the parties will be treated as if the necessary formalities had been observed and a legal estate had been created, ie equity will recognise what the common law refuses to recognise.

Provided the agreement is at least in writing, incorporates all the agreed terms and is signed by both parties (in accordance with s.2 LP(MP)A 1989), its terms will be enforceable in equity, ie by an order for specific performance. Normal equitable principles will apply (*Coatsworth v Johnson 1886*).

3 Registration of leases

Most leases can be registered, according to the following rules:

3.1 Legal leases over seven years

Under s.4 LRA 2002, a lease for more than seven years must be registered and the legal estate will not pass until registration is effected. It will be registered with its own separate title and also entered as a notice on the charges register of the freehold title, provided that the freehold is registered of course. Thus it is that one piece of land can have at least two registered title numbers applicable to it.

An existing unregistered legal lease also needs to be registered where it is transferred (for value or by way of gift) or where a first legal mortgage is created over it, provided it has more than seven years to run at the time of such transfer or mortgage.

Note that leases granted before 13 October 2003 had to be registered only if they were for a term of years exceeding 21 years. It is anticipated that the threshold will actually be reduced to three years at some point in the next few years.

3.2 Reversionary leases

A lease (for any term) that takes effect in possession more than three months following the date of the grant must also be registered.

3.3 Legal leases for less than seven years

A legal lease for less than seven years cannot be registered with a separate title. However, provided it is for more than three years, it can be protected by entry of a notice on the charges register of the superior title where that is registered (s.32 LRA 2002).

In any event, a lease for a term of not more than seven years is an interest which overrides first registration (Sch 1 para 1 LRA 2002) and registered dispositions (Sch 3 para 1 LRA 2002).

3.4 Equitable lease

An equitable lease is not capable of substantive registration, ie with a title of its own. Its registration depends on whether the freehold reversion is registered or unregistered.

Registered freehold	It should be protected by entry of a notice on the charges register of the freehold title. It may be an overriding interest if the tenant is in occupation of the property
Unregistered freehold	It should be registered as a Class C(iv) estate contract land charge against the freeholder's name

3.5 Class of title

A leasehold estate may be registered with one of four different classes of title (s.10 LRA 2002):

- Absolute title
- Good leasehold title
- Qualified title
- Possessory title

These have been explained (in Chapter 2) but by way of reminder:

Absolute title	This is given where the registrar is satisfied with the lessor's title in granting the lease and is satisfied that the lessee's title is such as a willing buyer could properly be advised to accept.
Good leasehold title	This is given where the registrar considers that the lessee's title is such as a willing buyer could properly be advised to accept. It does not, however, make any guarantee as to the reversionary title.
Qualified title	This is given where the registrar believes that the lessee's title or the lessor's title has been established only for a limited period or is subject to certain reservations which cannot be disregarded.
Possessory title	This class is registered where the lessee is in actual possession of the land, or in receipt of rents and profits from it, but none of the other classes is appropriate.

4 Terminology

4.1 Basic terminology

You should be aware that several terms are used interchangeably and, whilst one might be more appropriate than another depending on the context in which they are used, they have essentially the same meaning. For example:

Landlord	Lessee	Lease	Sublessee	Sublease
Lessor	Tenant	Tenancy	Subtenant	Subtenancy
Grantor	Grantee	Demise		Underlease
Reversioner				

A landlord retains the 'reversion' when he grants a lease. If he owns the freehold, this is often referred to as 'the freehold reversion'. The reversion to a sublease may be called the 'superior reversion' or 'superior leasehold reversion' or 'headlease'. The reversion incorporates the owner's rights to enforce the lease and to enjoy the property free of the lease when the lease comes to an end.

Note that where there is more than one lease, the lease granted by the freeholder is called the 'headlease' (it is not normally referred to as a 'headtenancy'). The 'headlessee' or 'headtenant' is then the reversioner and landlord to the sublease.

A lease may be 'granted' or 'created' or 'carved out of' the superior title (which may be freehold or leasehold).

A lease may be 'transferred', 'sold' or 'assigned' by the tenant (who is therefore the 'assignor' or 'transferor' or 'seller') to a third party who then becomes the next tenant. He is also the 'transferee' or 'assignee' or 'buyer'. The purchase deed is called a 'transfer' or 'assignment'.

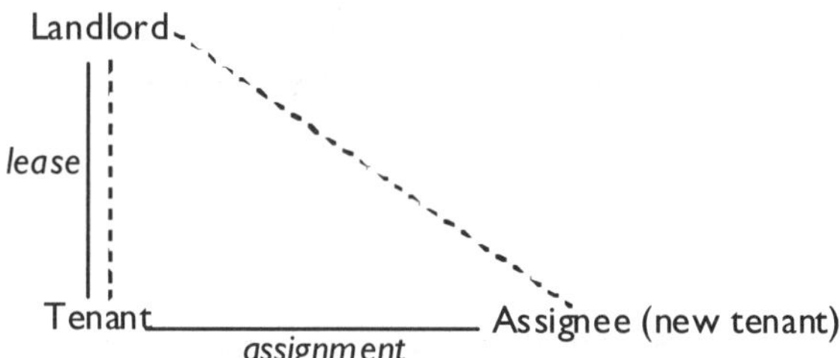

Terms used to describe different types of leases and also licences are explained in the remainder of this chapter.

4.2 Security of tenure

'**Security of tenure**' is a form of statutory protection that is afforded to a tenant in certain circumstances and gives him the right to remain in possession notwithstanding the termination of the tenancy at common law. Thus a tenant is entitled to remain in possession unless the landlord can prove one of the grounds for recovering possession under the:

- Rent Act 1977, the Housing Act 1988 and the Housing Act 1996 (private sector tenants of residential property depending on when the tenancy was granted)
- Housing Act 1985 (council tenants in residential premises)
- Landlord and Tenant Act 1954 Part II (commercial tenants)

4.3 Commercial leases

Some terminology is especially (though not exclusively) relevant to **commercial leases**. Thus

- The '**FRI** ('full repairing and insuring') lease' is one where the tenants either directly or indirectly (through reimbursement, usually via a service charge) pays for the upkeep and insurance of the property and the landlord has no financial liabilities of his own in respect of the lease. An FRI lease, therefore, ensures a clear income stream or 'clear rent', not reduced by running costs. Institutional and investor landlords will be particularly concerned to deal only in FRI leases so that the ultimate investors' interests are protected.
- '**Covenant strength**' refers to the ongoing ability of the tenant to pay the rent and perform the other obligations of the tenant under the lease. A '**good covenant**' is an expression for a tenant who has good covenant strength
- The '**current**' or '**passing**' rent usually describes the market rent from time to time. '**Market rent**', refers to a full commercial rent whereas **ground rent** refers to a very low rent (sometimes called a 'peppercorn') relevant to a lease where the premium is the main consideration.
- '**Rental yield**' is the ratio of rent to capital value of the property.
- A **'rent deposit'** is an amount of money to be paid to the landlord prior to the grant or assignment of a lease. It is held by him for the duration of the tenant's ownership of the lease and drawn upon if the tenant defaults. Alternatively another party, a '**guarantor**', may be required to guarantee the performance of the tenant's or assignee's obligations under the lease.

4.4 Quarter days

References to **quarters** or **quarterly** periodic tenancies or **quarter days** refer to the following:

25 March
24 June
29 September
25 December

5 Types of tenancy

There are several types of tenancy, or arrangements in the nature of landlord/tenant relationships, that you may encounter.

5.1 Fixed term lease

A lease may have a fixed term either by virtue of the express wording used or by operation of law.

5.1.1 Express fixed term

This is perhaps the most common type of lease and forms the core of this section of the manual. The term may be long or short. Essentially, the term can be of any length, although there are certain conventions that apply depending on the sector of the property market. For example, residential properties have been traditionally let (at a premium) on long leases of, say, 999 years. Commercial properties are more likely to be let on shorter terms (at a market rent) of, say, 25 years.

Note that the inclusion of a 'break clause' in a lease (allowing early termination of the lease in accordance with its terms) does not prevent a lease being a fixed term lease.

5.1.2 Fixed terms by operation of law

Two types of lease are effectively converted into fixed term tenancies by statute, namely:

- A lease granted for a term that is measured by someone's **life or marriage** becomes a lease for **ninety years**, terminable by one month's notice following the relevant life or marriage (as the case may be) under s.149(6) LPA 1925.
- A **perpetually renewable** lease becomes a lease for **two thousand years** under s.145 LPA 1922. Note that the courts will endeavour not to interpret a lease as a perpetually renewable lease in view of the rather extreme effect of this provision (*Burnett (Marjorie) Ltd v Barclay 1980)*.

  Great care needs to be taken in drafting a lease so as to avoid a perpetually renewable lease arising inadvertently. For example, in *Northchurch Estates Ltd v Daniels 1947*, a term of one year containing an option to renew 'on identical terms and conditions' was held to be a perpetually renewable lease and was converted pursuant to s.145, even though it was at least arguable that only one further term of one year had been intended.

5.2 Periodic tenancy

A periodic tenancy may be created expressly or by implication. Essentially, the term runs from one defined period to another, for example from month to month or year to year, until it is brought to an end by either party serving a notice to quit on the other. Periodic tenancies are usually yearly, quarterly, monthly or weekly.

If rent is paid and accepted on a periodic basis, without reference to an overall fixed term, this may create an implied periodic tenancy, provided this can be presumed to have been the intention of the parties. The courts have shown an increasing reluctance to imply a periodic

tenancy, no doubt due to the statutory protection afforded to tenancies, but it may be that no other conclusion can be drawn from the circumstances.

Remember that a periodic tenancy is a curious creation in that it can be legal even without execution of a deed. Any assignment of a periodic tenancy, however, must be by deed in order to pass a legal estate to an assignee.

5.3 Tenancy at will

A tenancy at will arises where the tenant occupies land with the consent of the landowner for an indefinite period and either party can terminate the arrangement at any time without notice. The tenancy is treated as creating 'a personal relation between the landlord and his tenant' (*Wheeler v Mercer 1957*) and the tenant has no estate. He cannot, therefore, transfer or sublet his interest and the agreement will come to an end if the landlord sells his reversion or if either party dies. However, owing to his undoubted possession of the land, he can take action for trespass against anyone who enters, except the landowner.

A tenancy at will is relatively uncommon and slightly obscure. Its principal application is when a tenant stays in occupation after the expiry of his term, with the landlord's consent. It is similar to a licence in that it is a personal relationship but is not for a defined duration. Like a periodic tenancy, it is terminable by either party but, unlike a periodic tenancy, no notice is required.

5.4 Tenancy by estoppel

Where someone purports to grant a lease when he is not actually entitled to an estate in land, it operates as a tenancy by estoppel and both parties are 'estopped' from denying its existence (even if they were aware of the deficiency in the landlord's title). In effect, they are treated as parties to an imaginary lease.

In the event that the landlord later becomes entitled to that estate, the estoppel is 'fed' and his reversionary interest and the tenant's lease take effect 'in interest and not by estoppel' (*Cuthbertson v Irving 1859*).

6 Licences

Where a person is not given exclusive possession but otherwise the arrangement is in the nature of a lease, he is considered to have a 'licence' to occupy the property. Essentially, a 'licence' is a grant of permission to exercise some right in respect of the licensor's land which would otherwise amount to a trespass. It does not create an interest in land and does not give rise to security of tenure.

6.1 Nature of a licence

Where the landlord has the right to control or enter the premises (other than in the event of breach) the arrangement is likely to be a licence rather than a lease.

However, it is not only in these circumstances that a licence can be created legitimately. For example, in *AG Securities v Vaughan 1988*, a four-bedroom flat was occupied by four unrelated people, who entered into agreements on different dates and with different rents. It was up to the occupants to decide which room each person occupied. It was held that they did not have exclusive possession and each had a licence to occupy only.

6.2 A lease or a licence?

A landlord may seek to create a licence instead of a lease in order to deprive the 'tenant' of security of tenure (see 4.2 above). However, it is immaterial whether the document or the parties call the arrangement a lease or a licence. It is a question of fact, dependent on all the circumstances (*Street v Mountford 1985*). A court will have regard to all relevant facts, including the relationship between the parties, the nature of the premises, how the arrangements were intended to operate and how they do operate in practice.

Street v Mountford 1985

A person was given the right to occupy a room on payment of a weekly 'licence fee'. The agreement was called a personal licence that was non-assignable and terminable on 14 days' notice. It also contained an acknowledgement by the 'licensee' that it did not create 'a tenancy protected under the Rent Acts'.

On the facts, however, it was considered that the person did have exclusive possession for a fixed term on payment of a rent and, in the absence of any actual derogation from that entitlement, the agreement was held to be a lease.

Similarly, if the purported document contains provisions designed to deny exclusive possession, with the intention that the arrangement will be construed as a licence and not a lease, they will be disregarded if they are revealed to be nothing but a sham in practice and the arrangement will be a lease (*Antoniades v Villiers 1988*).

Antoniades v Villiers 1998

A couple entered into identical 'licences' of a one-bedroom flat. The document provided that the landlord could share occupation with them. The court considered the arrangements in practice and the fact that there was only one bedroom, albeit with a sofabed in the lounge.

It was held that the clause was a sham, designed to prevent the couple having protection under the Rent Acts and that the couple were joint tenants of a lease of the flat.

Generally speaking a licence is not enforceable against successors in title as it is a personal arrangement only. Certainly where it is a **bare licence** (ie there is no consideration, so that the licence is nothing more than a permission or a privilege) this will be the case. However, there may be cases where the courts will seek to protect the validity and endurance of a contractual licence (ie one supported by consideration) or a licence protected by the doctrine of estoppel, by imposing a constructive trust on the licensor (*Bannister v Bannister 1948*) or a successor in title (*Binions v Evans 1972*). A licence may arise by estoppel where one party relies on representations made by another to his detriment. For example where A allows B to spend money in the belief that his licence will continue, A cannot then deny the existence of the licence and seek to terminate it prematurely (*Inwards v Baker 1965*).

7 The leasehold market

As mentioned above, typically you will come across leases in dealing with commercial property , residential developments and agricultural property.

Note that a landlord in any sector may be a private sector individual or company, as a developer or one-off landlord, or a public sector body such as a local authority or social landlord. Commercial sector landlords are most likely to be institutions (rather than individuals) involved in the investments market.

7.1 The scope of this manual

Much of what is covered in this manual, particularly with regard to lease covenants and conveyancing procedures, will be of general relevance in commercial and residential transactions, unless otherwise mentioned.

Historically, houses were often sold on long leases at a premium and for a ground rent, although this is rarely done now. Whilst the conveyancing aspects relating to the **sale** of such leases are addressed in Chapter 18, the **grant** of such leases is outside the scope of this manual.

More commonly, houses might be let on very **short term leases**, for example six month lets. A short term lease has no capital value, but is granted at a full open market rent. In these cases, the conveyancing matters hardly apply, since a tenant will not generally make any searches and is likely not even to instruct a solicitor. The landlord is likely to appoint letting agents to deal with the leasing arrangements and will mainly be concerned with the tenant's covenant strength. As a property lawyer, you are more likely to be involved with regard to matters of security of tenure. For this reason, such leases are not covered in detail in this manual.

7.2 Reasons for granting a lease

There are certain circumstances where there is little option but to grant a lease, but it is worth considering the positive reasons why a freeholder might choose to grant a lease, beyond considering the nature of the property. Some of these will also be applicable to a superior leaseholder granting a sublease rather than assigning his leasehold interest.

Value	It may be that the grant of a lease at a substantial premium (that may even be close to the freehold value) together with the future prospect of receiving rent on the property and other benefits is more attractive to the grantor from a financial perspective
Development	Where a landlord retains ownership of adjoining premises or common parts, it is likely to be more attractive to grant a lease rather than sell part of the development outright (however note that a commonhold scheme might be most suitable)
Interest	By granting a lease rather than selling his existing estate or interest, a grantor retains an interest in the property which he can either retain or sell as a capital asset.
Control	He also retains some control over who occupies the land (both initially and subsequently), its use and any alterations to it
Responsibility	He is in a position to pass responsibility for maintenance and repair of the property, or at least the cost of it to the tenant(s)
Covenants	Leasehold covenants are considerably easier to enforce than freehold covenants (see Chapter 17) against a successor in title

7.3 Disadvantages of a lease

It may be worth pointing out that there are certain disadvantages also, although none may be substantial enough to rule out a leasehold transaction. Financial and commercial considerations are likely to dictate how land is dealt with.

Of course, from the tenant's point of view, he faces the converse of the reasons stated above, ie he is restricted in what he can do to the property and how he can deal with his interest in it. His obligations as to repair and maintenance will also be significantly more onerous than any he might have as a freeholder.

A landlord should consider the tax implications of granting a lease, including income tax assessed on incoming rents. Negotiation of the lease can be extensive. He should also be aware that enforcement of covenants (including payment of rent) can sometimes involve expensive and time-consuming litigation.

8 Termination of a lease

A lease may come to an end in several ways and these are summarised below:

Method of termination	Notes
Expiry of the term	A lease expires automatically when a term expires, save in specific cases where a tenant has **security of tenure**. Even where security of tenure provisions do not apply, a landlord can only enforce recovery of residential premises let 'as a dwelling' by means of court proceedings (Protection from Eviction Act 1977). A term of 25 years commencing on 1 April 2010 will terminate at midnight on 31 March 2035.
Exercise of a 'break clause'	A break clause is commonly found in a long commercial lease and usually provides for either party to determine the lease at one or more intervals before the expiry of the term (for example at five yearly intervals).
Notice to quit	A periodic tenancy may be terminated by notice to quit served by either party. The notice must be properly served and provide for termination on the correct date, ie at the end of one of the periods. At common law, one full period is required as notice (except that half a year is required on a yearly tenancy) so, for example, a monthly periodic tenancy is terminable on one month's notice. However, in residential premises, a minimum of four weeks is imposed by the Protection from Eviction Act 1977.
Repudiatory breach	Most breaches of covenant entitle the innocent party to damages only. However, in extreme cases, the courts may rule that breach of a fundamental term entitles him to treat the lease as terminated and to sue for damages (*Chartered Trust plc v Davies 1997*). Breach is discussed in Chapter 17.
Forfeiture	The right to forfeit a lease in the event of a tenant's breach of covenant is nearly always expressly provided for in the lease. However, the exercise of the right is generally subject to fairly extensive restrictions, particularly in the case of residential premises and breach of repairing covenants in a commercial lease. Forfeiture is described in more detail in Chapter 17.
Surrender	A surrender may take place by deed or be implied, for example by the tenant removing all his possessions and returning the key. In either case, the surrender is only effective if it is accepted by the landlord. If he does not accept it, rent continues to be payable (*Bellcourt Estates Ltd v Adesina 2005*).
Disclaimer	Typically disclaimer arises in cases of insolvency. A tenant's liquidator or trustee in bankruptcy may disclaim a lease if it is considered to give rise to a 'liability to pay money or perform any onerous act' or if the property is 'not readily saleable' (Insolvency Act 1986). Such a disclaimer extinguishes the lease and releases the tenant from any further liability.
Frustration	Like any contract, an entire lease may be discharged by frustration, provided the frustrating event brings about a sufficiently fundamental change in circumstances as to justify treating the lease as at an end (*National Carriers Ltd v Panalpina (Northern) Ltd 1981*).

Method of termination	Notes
Statutory termination	Sometimes a specific statutory provision will operate to terminate a lease (for example s7 Housing Act 1988).
Enlargement	A lease granted for over 300 years, with at least 200 years to run, may be 'enlarged' into a freehold estate, under a procedure in LPA 1925 (s.153).
Merger	If the tenant acquires the landlord's reversionary interest, the lease 'merges' into the freehold and is extinguished.
Leasehold enfranchisement	Certain statutory provisions enable the tenant to purchase the freehold reversion, thus merging the lease. This is termed 'leasehold enfranchisement' and arises under provisions of the Leasehold Reform Act 1967 (applicable to houses let at low rents for over 21 years) and The Housing Act 1985 (the public sector tenant's 'right to buy').

Summary

- A lease is the grant of exclusive possession for a term that is certain, or capable of being ascertained with certainty
- The term commencement date must also be certain or capable of being ascertained with certainty and can be up to 21 years in the future
- To be legal, a lease must be created by deed or be a full market rent lease not exceeding 3 years that takes effect in possession without a premium (including periodic tenancies)
- Any other lease will be an equitable lease, provided it satisfies LP(MP)A 1989
- Legal leases **over** 7 years are registrable – as a separate title number and on the charges register of the superior title
- Legal leases **under** 7 years are usually overriding
- A lease over 3 years can be entered on the charges register
- Equitable leases are protected by entry of a notice on the charges register or by registration of a C (iv) land charge
- A lease may be registered with any of four classes of title
- Security of tenure entitles a tenant to remain in possession notwithstanding the termination of the tenancy at common law
- A perpetually renewable lease will be converted into a lease for 2000 years
- A periodic tenancy runs from one fixed period to another. It can arise expressly or by implication. Although it does not need to be created by deed, it should be transferred by deed
- A tenancy at will may arise where a tenant remains in occupation following the expiry of a term, with the landlord's consent
- A tenancy by estoppel may arise where the landlord does not actually have title to grant the lease
- A licence does not give exclusive possession and is a personal interest only
- The parties' label is not conclusive. Whether an arrangement is a lease or licence is a question to be determined on all the facts.
- A lease may come to an end in a variety of ways. A surrender must be accepted. A notice to quit applies to periodic tenancies. A break clause may be found in commercial leases.

Self-test questions

1 What are the two essential elements of any lease?

2 Can a lease be expressed to commence on a date 15 years later?

3 Must a lease be created by deed in order to be a legal estate?

4 Does a lease for 5 years need to be registered?

5 Does a reversionary lease need to be registered?

6 How is an equitable lease protected in unregistered land?

7 What class of title is relevant only to leaseholds?

8 Give two other words meaning 'sublease'

9 What do the letters 'FRI' stand for?

10 A perpetually renewable lease may be converted into a fixed term of how many years?

11 How long should a notice to quit be in the case of a quarterly periodic tenancy?

12 Does a tenancy at will amount to a proprietary interest?

13 To what does 'feeding the estoppel' refer?

14 If a document is called a licence and is signed by both parties, will that be conclusive?

15 Can a tenant choose to surrender his interest in a lease at any time by vacating the premises and returning the keys?

16 What is the consequence of a tenant purchasing his landlord's reversionary interest?

Answers to self-test questions

1 Exclusive possession and certain term of years

2 Yes. The maximum time limit for the term commencement of a reversionary lease is 21 years

3 No. There is an exception for leases not exceeding 3 years, taking effect in possession at the best rent reasonably obtainable and without taking a fine

4 It can be protected by entry of a notice on the charges register of the superior title but is not capable of substantive registration

5 Yes, if it is to take effect later than 3 months following the date of the grant

6 By registration as a Class C (iv) land charge (estate contract)

7 Good leasehold title

8 Subtenancy and underlease

9 'Full repairing and insuring'

10 2,000 years

11 One quarter

12 No, it is a personal interest only which is non-assignable

13 When a purported landlord later becomes entitled to the estate out of which the purported tenancy was created.

14 No. Whether it is a lease or a licence will be determined as a matter of fact in all the circumstances

15 No. Such a purported surrender would need to be accepted by the landlord in order to be effective

16 The lease 'merges' into the freehold and is extinguished

16

Lease covenants

Topic List

Chapter overview

This Chapter will:

- Set out and explain the principal covenants on the part of the tenant, both express and implied
- Set out and explain the principal covenants on the part of the landlord, both express and implied
- Describe other key clauses such as rent review, service charge and forfeiture

Chapter overview continued

A lease is normally a very long document. Most of its length comprises covenants on the part of the tenant and the landlord. Although some covenants are implied by law in the absence of express provision, most leases will expressly set out the rights and obligations that are to govern the relationship between the parties. Statutory duties also apply and these will only be affected by express provision where the relevant statute so permits.

1 The demise of the premises

The actual 'leasing' of the premises is done at the beginning of the lease, where the 'parcels clause' identifies the premises to be let and then the 'demise' actually grants a lease of that property for a term of years.

Example

This lease is made the 25th day of October 2007 between X ('the Landlord') of [address] and Y ('the Tenant') of [address]

In consideration of the sum of £ (receipt of which the Landlord acknowledges) and of the rent reserved and of the covenants by the Tenant contained in this lease, the Landlord hereby demises [description of property] ('the Premises') to the tenant with [full/limited] title guarantee for a term of 25 years commencing on and from 1 January 2007.

1.1 Consideration

A long residential lease is likely to provide for payment of a capital sum, or 'premium', in addition to a rent, but a commercial lease is more likely to be in consideration of a 'rack rent' or 'market rent' only.

1.2 The parcels clause

The precise extent of the premises must be clearly set out. Where it is a lease of the whole, this is straightforward and similar to any freehold transfer. Where, as is more likely, the lease is of part of a building or development, great care needs to be taken to ensure that the tenant receives what he is expecting, both in terms of the actual demise and also rights granted and reserved. Any less and he may be unable to enjoy the premises to the full. Any more and he may find himself liable to unduly onerous repair obligations, a greater rent on review and a higher level of service charge.

Alert

Always bear in mind the correlation between the parcels clause and the repairing covenants.

1.3 Rights

Any rights being granted with the premises should be stated in the parcels clause or, if long or complex, in a schedule to the lease. Rights reserved to the landlord will be dealt with similarly. To a large extent, the question of rights is a matter of common sense. Think about the property and its location within the building or development: does the tenant have all the rights he needs fully to use and enjoy the let premises? As a minimum, he will need rights (in common with the landlord and other tenants) to use the common parts and conducting media for utilities and services and also have rights of access to view the state of repair and carry out any necessary works.

It is a good idea to ensure that there is sufficient flexibility in the drafting to enable the parties to accommodate any new technological services or benefits. Careful consideration may need to be given to refuse collection, vehicular access, loading and car parking arrangements. For example, a

specific car space might be included in the demise but if the landlord is merely giving a right to park a car somewhere on the development, this will simply be a right granted as a benefit with the demised premises in the lease.

Premises on the top floor of a building should normally be stated to exclude the roof space and, likewise, premises on a ground floor will normally be defined so as to exclude any scope for extension downwards. On a lease of part, the demised premises will normally be defined to include plasterwork and floor coverings, but to exclude the external and structural parts of the building. A plan is likely to be essential on a lease of part.

1.4 Term

The term commencement date needs careful drafting. 'From 1 January' would be interpreted to mean 'commencing on 2 January', whereas 'on 1 January' or 'from and including 1 January' would mean a commencement date of 1 January.

2 Implied covenants

2.1 Covenants implied on the part of the landlord

There are three principal covenants that are implied where there is no express provision to the contrary, namely:

- Quiet enjoyment
- Not to derogate from the grant
- To repair

2.1.1 Quiet enjoyment

This is essentially a covenant to allow the tenant to enjoy his exclusive possession of the premises for **ordinary and lawful use** without interruption or interference from the landlord or anyone claiming under him (which means that the landlord must prevent his other tenants from causing a breach of this covenant also).

It bars acts of harassment or eviction, such as the cutting of services or removing the tenant's belongings (*Perera v Vandiyar 1953)* and impeding access to the tenant's premises by the erection of scaffolding (*Owen v Gadd 1956*). There is no breach of the covenant where interference with the tenant's quiet enjoyment stems from the landlord carrying out works that he is obliged to carry out, provided that the landlord takes steps to avoid excessive disturbance (*Goldmile Properties Ltd v Lechouritis 2003*).

Generally speaking, there must be some form of **physical interference** with the tenant's use and enjoyment of the premises and mere inconvenience is unlikely to constitute breach of covenant (*Browne v Flower 1911*).

Note that intimidating or harassing conduct towards a **residential tenant** (ie withholding services or acts that are likely to interfere with his 'peace and comfort') could constitute a criminal offence under s.1(3) Protection from Eviction Act 1977.

2.1.2 Not to derogate from the grant

This covenant prohibits the landlord from doing anything that materially detracts from the purpose of the grant and often overlaps with the covenant of quiet enjoyment. Basically the landlord is bound not to engage in conduct which renders the property materially less fit for, or which is inconsistent with, the purpose for which it was demised. Allowing a competitor to occupy and trade from neighbouring premises is not a breach of this covenant (*Port v Griffith 1938)*.

Harmer v Jumbil (Nigeria) Tin Areas Ltd (1921)

A landlord was held to be in breach of the covenant not to derogate from grant, where he leased land for the storage of explosives and then permitted the use of adjoining property for mining operations.

2.1.3 Concerning fitness for habitation and state of repair

The law relating to implied covenants of repair is extremely convoluted and unsatisfactory (which is one reason why express covenants are usually included).

Common law

Traditionally the courts have been reluctant to impose any obligation on the landlord as to repair, on the basis that 'fraud apart, there is no law against letting a tumble-down house' (*Robbins v Jones 1863*). However, the common law has embraced an implied condition of fitness for human habitation in the case of a furnished dwelling-house and a duty of care (owed only to the tenant) in respect of essential facilities enjoyed by the tenant (*Liverpool City Council v Irwin 1977*). He may also face liability in tort where his negligence causes loss or damage to the tenant during the term of the lease (*Sharpe v Manchester CC 1977*).

Statutorily implied covenants

Statute has, however, intervened to imply a number of statutory obligations including:

- **s.11 LTA 1985** (dwelling house for less than 7 years *) – to keep in repair the structure, exterior and service installations and appliances. **Note that the tenant cannot be required to pay for works within this implied covenant**. The landlord is not obliged to make good repairs that are necessitated by the tenant's misuse of the premises and the tenant must allow the landlord entry to view the state of repair. The landlord is only responsible for defects of which he has notice.
- **LTA 1985, s8** (dwelling houses, where the rent is below (very low) prescribed levels) – that the house is and will be kept fit for human habitation at the commencement of and during the tenancy

* Note that a lease for more than seven years, which is terminable by the landlord within the first seven years falls within this provision, Equally, a term for less than seven years where the tenant has the option to renew it (to make it an extended term of over seven years) is not caught by this provision.

(See also s.4 Defective Premises Act 1972, s.4 Health and Safety at Work Act 1974 and ss1–7 and 28–35 Housing Act 2004.)

2.2 Covenants implied on the part of the tenant

Perhaps not surprisingly, given that it is the landlord who provides the form of lease for negotiation and approval (and is often the party with the greater bargaining strength), the tenant's obligations are usually set out at length and relatively comprehensively. The following covenants are, nonetheless, implied at common law, to the extent that they are not overridden by any express provision.

- To pay rent
- Not to deny the landlords' title
- Not to commit waste (concerning repair)

2.2.1 To pay rent

In the absence of any contrary provision (as there usually is), the obligation will be to pay rent in arrears rather than in advance.

2.2.2 Not to deny the landlord's title

If the tenant claims to be entitled to the reversion for example, or supports a third party's claim to it, he will be in breach of this covenant and the landlord will be automatically entitled to forfeit the lease (see paragraph 7 below).

2.2.3 Not to commit waste

This is essentially a covenant concerned with the state of repair of the premises and the tenant's obligations will vary, depending on the nature of his lease. A fixed term tenant, for example, will generally owe more extensive duties than a periodic tenant, including a duty not to allow the property to deteriorate through lack of attention and a duty not to make alterations that detract from the value of the property. A monthly or weekly periodic tenant, on the other hand, is simply required to 'take proper care of the place' (*Warren v Keen 1954).*

A lease will normally contain an express provision dealing with alterations and improvements.

2.2.4 Statutorily implied covenant

Under s.11 Housing Act 1988, where the landlord is obliged to repair the premises, whether by an express or an implied covenant, the tenant must permit him to enter the demised premises in order to inspect the state of repair.

3 Express covenants on the part of the tenant

Even in the case of covenants implied by law, the tendency is to deal comprehensively with the parties' rights and obligations. In addition to those already mentioned, a lease might typically contain the following express covenants on the part of the tenant. Normally these follow the operative words.

3.1 To pay rent

In most cases, the covenant will provide for payment **in advance** and should stipulate the manner of payment (eg by standing order).

In commercial leases, the rent may be linked to the tenant's business turnover, for example a rent of '£X or Y% of turnover, if greater'.

3.1.1 Reservation of payments as rent

The landlord will wish to reserve other payments as rent, including insurance and service charge, in order to take advantage of the remedies available for rent default. Furthermore, the lease may provide that the rent is to be paid 'without deduction or set off' in order to counter any rights that the tenant may have to reduce the rent payable in circumstances where the landlord is in breach of covenant. Remedies and rights of set off are discussed in the next Chapter.

3.1.2 VAT

In some cases, a landlord may seek to charge VAT on rent, for example to facilitate the recovery of VAT on his development costs (by 'opting to tax' or 'waiving the exemption' for the property). However, he should consider this carefully where the property is likely to be used by tenants who are unable to recover VAT, because of the adverse effects on marketing the premises and the depressing effect that this could have on rent review.

3.1.3 Rent abatement

The tenant should negotiate a rent suspension and/or abatement clause to provide that the rent ceases to be payable in the event of the premises being damaged or destroyed (as they will otherwise continue to be payable unless the lease is actually frustrated). The landlord will seek to restrict such a clause to damage caused by 'insured risks' only (see 4.1.1 below).

3.2 To repair

The precise extent of the tenant's obligations will be spelt out. The landlord will wish to ensure that the tenant is required to maintain the property during the term sufficiently to protect the capital value of the property. He will also aim to ensure that all costs of repair and maintenance are borne by the tenant(s), either by the tenant having responsibility for undertaking such matters at his own cost or by providing for reimbursement (usually via a service charge) where the landlord undertakes the relevant works himself.

Since the repairing covenant is linked to the parcels clause, the tenant should ensure that the definition of 'the premises' in the demise is accurately drafted so that he does not inadvertently undertake to repair more than he is actually going to be occupying.

3.2.1 Meaning of 'repair'

'Repair' is generally taken to mean replacement and renewal rather than renovation or creation. Note that a covenant to '**keep in repair**' requires the tenant only to ensure that the property does not fall into a worse state of repair than it was in at the beginning of the term. An obligation '**to repair**' or 'put in repair', on the other hand, will require him to put the property into a state of repair and thereafter maintain it and deliver it up in that repaired state at the end of the term. In such cases, the tenant should be fully aware of the state of the premises at the commencement of the term. Sometimes a 'schedule of condition' is attached to the lease and specifically referred to in the repairing covenants, for the avoidance of doubt.

A landlord should always include a self-help provision which enables him to enter on the premises to view the state of repair and to carry out any works not carried out by the tenant in breach of the tenant's covenant, with provision to recoup the costs of such works.

3.2.2 Fair wear and tear

A tenant will wish to include a provision that 'fair wear and tear' is excluded from his repairing obligations. If so, he will not be obliged to make good any disrepair arising from his ordinary use of the premises. He will, however, be required to make good consequential damage from disrepair caused by forces outside his control, for example to prevent the premises becoming uninhabitable as a result of a few tiles being blown off the roof in strong winds (*Regis Property Co Ltd v Dudley 1959*).

3.2.3 Latent defects

He may also seek to exclude any responsibility pertaining to damage arising from latent defects (ie defects in the design or construction of the building that are not readily apparent on an inspection). Often a landlord will not accept this, as to do so would impinge on his objective of achieving a clear rent.

3.2.4 Insured risks

The tenant is likely also to seek to exclude responsibility for any disrepair arising out of 'insured risks', a term which he will also want to be defined sufficiently widely (see 4.1.2 below).

3.2.5 Notification of defects

The landlord should impose a covenant on the tenant to notify the landlord of any defect or want of repair for which the landlord is responsible, insofar as it is visible or apparent on or from the premises within the tenant's control.

3.3 To yield up

A lease will usually contain a covenant to yield up the premises at the end of the term in the state of repair required by the lease. The tenant must, therefore, make good any state of disrepair at that point. If he fails to do so, the landlord may claim for 'dilapidations', assessed as the amount that the landlord would have to spend in carrying out the necessary work, together with compensation for loss of rent while those works are carried out.

3.4 To decorate

Decoration is not generally regarded as part of an obligation to repair. Typically a lease will provide for the tenant to redecorate the interior of the premises at least once every five years. Except where the lease is of part of a building or development, he will also covenant to decorate the exterior, say, at least once every three years.

3.5 Not to assign or sublet (the 'alienation' covenant)

A lease is freely transferable subject to any restrictions contained in it. However, the landlord will usually want some control over who is in occupation of the property and so, in most cases, there will be either:

- An **'absolute' prohibition** which means that the landlord may refuse a request to give consent for any reason whatsoever. He may choose to waive the prohibition by giving consent on any occasion, although this would not alter the prohibition in respect of future dealings or
- A **'qualified' covenant** that permits dealing with the tenant's interest only with the landlord's consent or
- A **'fully qualified' covenant** that permits dealing with the tenant's interest only with the landlord's consent and such consent shall not be unreasonably withheld

Alienation

This refers to the tenant dealing with the demised premises - by assigning, subletting, mortgaging or otherwise parting with possession of them.

Of course a lease might provide for unrestricted alienation, for example, a long residential lease (although there may still be restrictions on subletting or alienation of part). In such cases, there will at least be provision for **registration** of any dealing with the landlord so that he is fully aware of his tenant's identity and details at any given time.

Although an absolute covenant may appear most favourable to the landlord, he should always have regard to the likely effect on rent review and a tenant or prospective assignee (or his lender) may refuse to accept such a clause.

Note

A landlord's consent is normally in the form of a legal document called a 'licence to assign'

Most leases will provide for an absolute prohibition on subletting of part, however, as the landlord will not wish for a multiplicity of tenants where he originally chose to have one!

3.5.1 Statutory provisions relevant to qualified alienation covenants

Where the alienation covenant is **qualified**, the following statutory provisions are relevant:

S.144 LPA 1925	The landlord cannot demand a fine or premium in exchange for giving consent, unless the lease expressly so provides. However, he may demand payment of his legal costs incurred in granting consent.
S.19LTA 1927	The qualified covenant is deemed to include the proviso that the landlord cannot unreasonably withhold consent, thus making it a fully qualified covenant. Whether a landlord's decision is reasonable or not will be a question of fact. There is authority that refusal may be **reasonable** where it is because the proposed assignee's references are unsatisfactory (*Shanley v Ward 1913*) or where the assignee would be entitled to security of tenure whereas the original tenant was not. Refusal may be **unreasonable**

	where it is because the landlord wishes to have use of the property himself (*Bates v Donaldson 1896)* or would prefer a different tenant for reasons linked to the rental value of his other property. A refusal on discriminatory grounds based on sex or race is likely to be **unreasonable** and may also offend the Sex Discrimination Act 1975 or Race Relations Act 1976 (as appropriate). In all cases, the reason for refusing consent cannot be reasonable if it has nothing to do with the landlord/tenant relationship (*International Drilling Fluids Ltd v Louisville Investments (Uxbridge) Ltd 1986)*. Note, however, that in the case of **commercial leases** granted **after 1 January 1996**, it is open to the parties to negotiate and agree **specified conditions** to govern the question of alienation and those express conditions are not required to be 'reasonable' (s.22 Landlord and Tenant (Covenants) Act 1995). Such conditions are likely to provide that the landlord can withhold consent where the tenant is in arrears or where it appears that the assignee would be unable to perform the tenant's covenants under the lease. He may also demand payment of a rent deposit by the assignee. As a result of this statutory modification, a landlord will almost invariably require the assigning tenant to enter into an 'authorised guarantee agreement' (described in the next Chapter) before giving consent.
S1(3) LTA 1988	The landlord must respond to a written request for consent within a reasonable time, giving reasons for any refusal. (28 days was considered to be reasonable in *Dong Bang Minerva (UK) v Davina 1996)*. He will need to show that his refusal was reasonable or that any conditions attached to his consent were reasonable and that he responded within a reasonable period. Whether his decision to refuse or grant permission is reasonable will be a question of fact, based on all the circumstances known to him at the time. Breach of these requirements may render him liable for tortious damages for breach of statutory duty.

3.6 User

Typically a lease will contain a covenant 'not to use the premises other than as...' (because a positively-worded covenant, ie ' to use as ...' would mean that any period of non-user would constitute a breach).

3.6.1 The scope of any restriction

The extent of the restriction is a matter of balance in negotiations. The more restrictive the user clause, the greater the degree of control the landlord has, but also the more adverse the effect on any rent review and the less attractive it is to a tenant and potential assignees. A tenant will need to ensure that the clause is not too restrictive, either for his own intended use or with a view to possible developments or assignability during the term.

As a minimum, a user clause will normally prohibit illegal and immoral use. A landlord is also usually advised not to permit commercial use within a development intended for residential use (save perhaps for certain types of professional or home-working use).

3.6.2 Qualified covenants

Where the covenant is qualified, ie 'not to use the premises other than as...without the landlord's consent', s.19(3) LTA 1927 prohibits the landlord from demanding a fine or premium for giving consent (as in the qualified alienation covenant) This prohibition only applies where the proposed alteration to user does not involve any structural alteration of the premises and does not preclude the landlord from demanding legal expenses or a reasonable sum in respect of the

resulting diminution in the value of his premises. The section does *not* imply a proviso that the consent shall not be unreasonably withheld.

The tenant should seek to include the words 'or delayed' where there is a qualified covenant that consent is not to be unreasonably withheld, since there is no corresponding provision to s.1 LTA 1988 in the case of user.

3.6.3 Not to vitiate insurance

The lease will probably contain a clause prohibiting the tenant from doing anything that might vitiate the insurance effected by the landlord.

3.7 Not to make alterations

Without express provision in the lease, the tenant is entitled to alter the premises as he wishes. Not surprisingly, therefore, there will usually be a covenant restricting this freedom, either to prohibit absolutely any alterations or to permit them only with the landlord's consent. Furthermore, the clause may be drafted so as to deal differently with structural and non-structural alterations, for example to permit non-structural changes subject to the landlord's consent but to prohibit absolutely any changes to the structure of the property. It is also likely to provide for the tenant to reinstate the premises at the end of the term.

Clearly a tenant must ensure that the premises are adequate for his use over the term, that he has sufficient flexibility to make adaptations and that his interest is not so restricted as to make it difficult to sell. A landlord should also consider the depressing effect on rent review of an absolute prohibition or unduly restrictive regime for alterations and improvements.

There are certain statutory provisions relevant to covenants concerning alterations.

3.7.1 Absolute prohibition

Notwithstanding any absolute prohibition against alterations, a tenant can seek a court order to permit works that are:

- Needed to comply with the Fire Precautions Act 1971
- '**Improvements**' (and, at the end of the lease, may apply for compensation if the property has increased in value as a result of the improvements)

Where works are needed to comply with the Disability Discrimination Act 1995, the lease shall be deemed to contain a covenant that the landlord shall not unreasonably withhold his consent to the tenant (where the tenant is an employer with 15 or more employees) carrying out those works.

3.7.2 Qualified covenant as to 'improvements'

Where the clause requires a landlord's consent to **improvements**, it will be deemed to be subject to a proviso that that consent shall not be unreasonably withheld (s.19(2) LTA 1927). The courts have interpreted 'improvement' widely to include any works which, from the tenant's point of view, can be said to improve the property (*Lambert v FW Woolworth & Co Limited 1938*).

The landlord cannot demand a fine or premium for giving consent, but he is entitled to require payment of legal expenses and a reasonable sum in respect of the resulting diminution in the value of his premises. He may also, provided it is reasonable, require the tenant to agree to reinstate the premises.

The tenant should seek to include the words 'or delayed' where there is a qualified covenant and consent is not to be unreasonably withheld, since there is no corresponding provision to s.1 LTA 1988 in the case of alterations.

4 Express covenants on the part of the landlord

4.1 To insure

Typically the landlord will covenant to insure the premises in order to protect his capital asset. (There are very real practical considerations and problems involved where it is intended that each *tenant* in a building or development insures his own demise, even where the landlord insures the common parts separately.) He is likely to reserve insurance costs as rent, so that the remedies that are specifically available for non-payment of rent will also apply where a tenant fails to reimburse the insurance costs (see Chapter 17).

4.1.1 Insured risks

The lease is likely to specify the 'insured risks', including (as a minimum) fire, flood, riot, storm, burst pipes and earthquakes. In fact a typical insurance clause in a lease might list the following insured risks:

'fire, lightning, explosion, aircraft and articles dropped from them, riot, civil commotion, malicious damage, storm, tempest, flood, earthquake, bursting or overflowing of water tanks, apparatus and pipes, impact by any vehicle and such other risks as the landlord may reasonably consider necessary to insure'

4.1.2 Tenant's drafting considerations

The tenant should consider negotiating the following provisions, if they are not already in the draft lease.

- That insurance is effected with a reputable insurer
- That insurance is in the parties' joint names (or at least that the tenant is noted on the landlord's policy)
- That the landlord should produce a copy of the policy to the tenant (and on each renewal if any changes are made)
- That, where the premises form part of a building or development, the landlord also covenants to insure the common parts
- That the rent, including any insurance and service charge, should be suspended or reduced in the event that the premises are destroyed or made unusable (the landlord will wish to limit this to damage caused by insured risks)
- Wider insured risks, where his repairing obligations exclude damage by insured risks or where a rent abatement clause is limited by reference to insured risks
- That the landlord covenants to reinstate the premises in the event of damage (and, if possible, agrees to fund any shortfall from his own monies)
- That the level of insurance is linked to the full cost of reinstatement ('full reinstatement value' normally covers the cost of demolition, site clearance and professional fees and makes provision for inflation)
- Provision for termination of the lease where the landlord cannot or does not reinstate within the rent suspension period or a reasonable period

4.2 To repair and maintain structure and common parts

The scope of any implied covenant in respect of common parts is unsatisfactory and so should be expressly included in the lease. Clearly the tenant will be concerned to ensure that he has full use of the premises as intended and this will involve use of staircases, fire exits, the structure of the building, routes of access and egress and so on. Exactly what is needed will depend on the property being demised. He must also ensure that the landlord is under an obligation fully to

repair and maintain all parts of the building and/or development, to the extent that responsibility has not been accepted and undertaken by the tenant. Where provision is made for these obligations to fall on a management company, the tenant should be satisfied that they are still properly enforceable.

The landlord will seek to recover the cost of such maintenance from his tenant(s), normally through a service charge (see paragraph 6 below). For this reason, a tenant is not advised to insist on too onerous a covenant on the landlord's part – he may accept having to repay the cost of repairs and maintenance but may not wish to repay the cost of improvements or annual decoration etc! Sometimes qualifying such a covenant will suffice (for example 'to repair and maintain and, so far as necessary or desirable to keep the building/development in good and substantial repair, to review and improve ...').

5 Rent review

A commercial lease will usually contain a rent review clause, designed to bring the rent payable under the lease up to a full open market rent at specified intervals (typically every five years in a fifteen or twenty-five year lease).

A ground rent lease (and therefore most residential leases) will not usually contain a rent review clause, although there may be provision for increasing the ground rent at specified intervals (for example, £50 per annum for the first ten years, £100 per annum for the next ten years etc).

5.1 Upward only

The clause will provide that the review can result only in an increase in the level of rent or no change, but never a decrease. This enables the landlord to have a degree of security over the yield from his investment.

5.2 Formula for rent review

The mechanics for review vary. A simple form might link the review to the Retail Prices Index. A more complex form (that is more common) is to provide for an independent valuer to revalue the open market rent of the premises as at the date of each review, ie to assess the level of rent that would be paid by a 'hypothetical tenant' (assuming the parties cannot agree on a revised rent). The valuer will be a surveyor and, where the rent is high or unusually complex, the clause is likely to specify minimum qualifications that he must possess.

The clause effectively comprises a set of instructions to the valuer at that time to consider a hypothetical letting, based on the actual lease, but also 'assuming' and 'disregarding' certain matters. These will be aimed at removing any untypical aspects of the letting or the market at the time that might distort the rent to be assessed. For example, a common **assumption** is that the tenant has fully performed his covenants under the lease. Not to include such an assumption would enable to the tenant to benefit from his own breach, since the hypothetical bid from a hypothetical tenant would clearly be lower if the premises were in a state of disrepair for example. A common **disregard** is to ignore the impact on rent of other premises in the development being unlet.

You will appreciate that negotiations on the assumptions and disregards, in particular, can be intense and the relative bargaining strengths of the parties will be critical.

Practice note. The whole rent review clause is one of the most heavily negotiated provisions in a lease. You should be very conscious of the fact that although the initial rent is agreed without your input, the level of rent being paid or received by your client, probably for the greater part of the term, will depend very much on your drafting and negotiating skills.

6 Service charge arrangements

As already mentioned, where the lease is of part of a building or development, the landlord usually covenants to repair and maintain the structure and common parts and to provide services, both in the buildings and outside. The landlord will be concerned to ensure that all related costs will be recovered from the tenants. This is normally done via a 'service charge', which is usually reserved as rent. The tenant will need to ensure that all required services and facilities are expressly covered and provide for a sufficient standard of work. He should also require the landlord to be 'reasonable' in arranging for the works to be carried out and in administering the service charge, so that the landlord does not have a completely free rein to run up massive costs unnecessarily.

6.1 Calculation of service charge

Each tenant's contribution to the costs is normally calculated on the basis of the internal area of his premises as against the total internal area of lettable premises. Here again, the wording is critical. Compare the results if, instead, the contribution was assessed as a fraction of the total let area or the total internal area of the development.

Example

A tenant lets a retail unit of 2,000m^2 in a shopping mall of ten shops. The total internal floor area is 50,000m and the total internal area of all retail stores is 42,000m. At rent review, only 8 of the shops are let. The internal area of the two unlet shops is 6,000m. The landlord's costs total £100,000. See how the wording of the clause can affect the tenant's liability (and therefore the landlord's exposure to cost):

$$\frac{\text{Tenant's area}}{\text{Total lettable area}} \quad \frac{2{,}000}{42{,}000} \times 100{,}000 = £4{,}761.90$$

$$\frac{\text{Tenant's area}}{\text{Total let area}} \quad \frac{2{,}000}{36{,}000} \times 100{,}000 = £5{,}555.56$$

$$\frac{\text{Tenant's area}}{\text{Total internal area}} \quad \frac{2{,}000}{50{,}000} \times 100{,}000 = £4{,}000.00$$

Alternatively, service charge may be assessed on a fixed or equal percentage or on the basis of a 'fair proportion' (which permits flexibility but also huge scope for argument!). In either case, the formula might also take into account the exact location of the demised premises (for example a ground floor tenant may object to contributing to the costs of lifts or a tenant with no allocated parking space may object to contributing to the costs of maintaining a car parking area). A landlord should normally expect to have to bear the cost of unlet lettable space, at least in the initial phase of letting a development. Thereafter, and in relation to contributions to any sinking-fund in particular, express provision must be made.

6.2 Certification of service charge

The lease usually sets out a mechanism for a service charge certificate to be produced, showing and justifying the amount owing. The landlord will wish to provide that such a certificate is deemed to be conclusive. The tenant should ensure that it is provided by an independent party, rather than the landlord or his employee or associated company.

In the absence of such a provision, a **residential** tenant is entitled to request a written summary of the costs incurred (s.21 Landlord and Tenant Act 1985). Provided there are over four tenants required to pay a service charge, the summary must be certified by an independent qualified accountant.

The lease will normally provide for payment of service charge **in advance**, usually on the basis of projected expenditure, with a balancing calculation to be made at the end of the year. Any overpayment by the tenant is usually credited to his account for the following year, rather than being refunded. Any underpayment will normally be demanded as an immediately payable lump sum.

6.3 Reserve or sinking fund

A lease may also provide for the landlord to establish a 'reserve fund' or 'sinking fund', into which tenants contribute, via the service charge. The purpose of the fund is to make anticipatory provision for items of expenditure that are both major and irregular (for example re-roofing or installing a new air-conditioning system). Such a fund has the advantage of avoiding unexpected large service charge liabilities and providing a fairer basis for liability, having regard to changes in the identity of tenants. For example, an assignee could face a huge service charge liability in his first year if the landlord opts to renew the roof that year, whereas the previous tenants (who enjoyed the benefit of the roof) will have paid nothing. However, many larger and wealthier tenants will not wish to be paying (or 'lending') money to the landlord in this way. As with so many points, it comes down to the relative bargaining strengths of the parties!

Any reserve fund should be held 'on trust', as this will provide some protection from the landlord's creditors in the event of his insolvency. The lease should make clear in what circumstances the landlord is **entitled** to use monies in the fund and in what circumstances he is **obliged** to use the fund.

7 Forfeiture

Forfeiture is one of the remedies available to a landlord and enables him to terminate the lease before the expiry of the term in the event of certain events or breach of covenant by the tenant. For this reason, it is regarded as the most draconian remedy available. There is no right to forfeit implied in a legal lease; it must be expressly provided for.

In forfeiting a lease, a landlord must observe statutory procedures. These differ, depending on whether the forfeiture is for non-payment of rent or for other reasons, and are described in detail in the next Chapter.

Summary

- The parcels clause (that describes the demised premises and rights) must be drafted and interpreted in conjunction with the parties' repairing and insuring obligations and also the rent review and service charge provisions
- A landlord covenants to give quiet enjoyment and not to derogate from grant, as these are implied in every lease
- A landlord also owes implied covenants as to repair, although express covenants will normally be included. Be aware of the difference between covenants to 'repair' or 'put in repair' or 'keep in repair' and of the impact of provisions relating to 'insured risks'
- A tenant also has implied covenants, including not to deny the landlord's title and to repair, but virtually all leases will actually set out the tenant's obligations expressly and in full (don't forget the lease is prepared by the landlord!)
- Insurance and service charge are often 'reserved as rent' in order to take advantage of remedies for non-payment of rent
- The alienation covenant may provide an absolute or qualified provision (which LTA 1927 renders fully qualified). Statute provides for no premium (but costs permitted) on giving consent (unless expressly provided for) and for consent to be given (or refused with reasons) within a reasonable time
- A qualified user covenant is not rendered fully qualified by statute but the landlord is not allowed to take a premium for giving consent (where no structural alteration is involved)
- An alterations covenant is likely to differentiate between structural and non-structural alterations. A qualified covenant as to *improvements* is rendered fully qualified by statute
- In addressing the balance between freedom for and restriction of the tenant, always bear in mind the impact on marketability, assignability and rent review
- The landlord will normally insure and recover the cost from the tenant
- The landlord should repair and maintain the structure and common parts. The extent of his obligations will impact directly on the tenant's financial liabilities through a service charge
- A rent review normally provides for a valuer to assess the market rent on the basis of a hypothetical tenant, assuming and disregarding certain factors
- Service charge is normally calculated on the basis of the internal floor area of the demised premises compared to the total lettable area of the development
- A reserve fund, or sinking fund, may be established to meet items of major expenditure

Self-test questions

1 What does the 'parcels clause' in a lease deal with?

2 What type of lease is commonly granted in consideration for a premium?

3 What is the term commencement date for a term of thirty years 'from 10 April 1995'?

4 What is meant by the covenant of quiet enjoyment?

5 In the absence of express provision, is a tenant required to pay rent in advance or in arrears?

6 What is meant by a covenant 'not to commit waste'?

7 Does a covenant to 'keep in repair' imply an obligation to put the premises into a good state of repair and thereafter to maintain that level of repair?

8 What is meant by a claim for dilapidations at the expiry of a lease?

9 What is the proviso to be implied into a qualified alienation covenant by s.19 LTA 1927?

10 Why is a restrictive user clause potentially disadvantageous to a landlord?

11 In the case of a qualified covenant against alterations, does statute imply a proviso that consent shall not be unreasonably withheld?

12 What is the normal formula for calculation of a service charge in a development?

13 What is a sinking fund?

Answers to self-test questions

1. The location and extent of the premises being demised
2. A long residential lease
3. 11 April 1995
4. That the tenant shall be allowed to enjoy his exclusive possession of the premises without interruption or interference form the landlord or anyone claiming under him
5. In arrears
6. Broadly, it is a covenant to repair. The extent of the obligation will depend on the nature of the tenancy
7. No. It is interpreted only as an obligation not to allow the property to fall into a worse state of repair
8. A claim by the landlord for an amount equal to the cost of necessary works (and loss of rent while the works are carried out) caused by the tenant's failure to yield up the premises in the appropriate state of repair
9. That consent shall not be unreasonably withheld
10. Because it is likely to have an adverse effect on rent review
11. No, but this is the case for a qualified covenant against *improvements*
12. The ratio of the tenant's internal floor area to the total lettable floor area applied to the total costs
13. It is an account to which tenants contribute in respect of occasional items of major expenditure

17

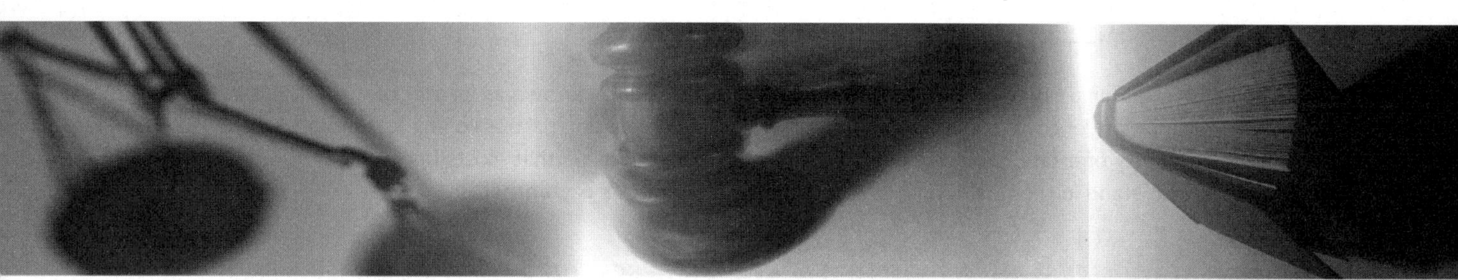

Enforceability and enforcement of leasehold covenants

Topic List

Chapter overview

This Chapter will:

- Consider the enforceability of lease covenants as between the original landlord and tenant and their successors
- Consider the mutual enforceability of covenants between tenants in a building or development
- Explain the changes to the law brought about by the Landlord and Tenant (Covenants) Act 1995
- Explain the method for forfeiting a lease for non-payment of rent or other breach
- Set out and explain the nature and scope of other remedies available to both landlord and tenant in the event of a breach of covenant

1 Enforceability of covenants

Before considering the specific remedies available in the event of a breach of covenant by either the landlord or tenant, we shall consider to what extent those covenants can be enforced between both the original parties and, where one or both transfer an interest, by and against successors in title.

For these purposes it is helpful to identify the various parties as follows:

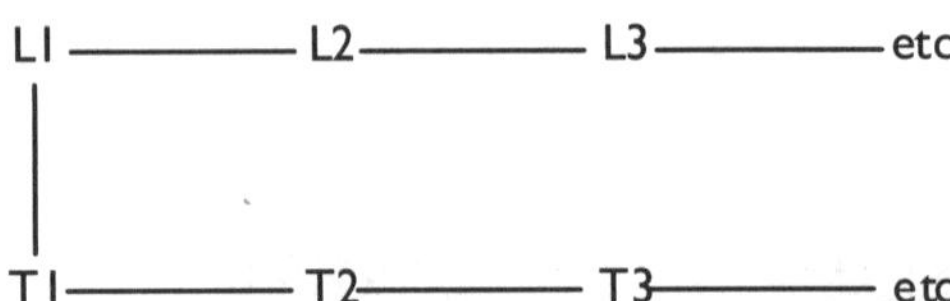

In any contract, either party may sue and be sued on its terms. This is known as 'privity of contract'. Such privity of contract exists between the *original* contracting parties to any leasehold relationship. 'Privity of estate' is a term used to describe the relationship that exists between two parties who stand in the position of landlord and tenant vis-à-vis each other.

1.1 Between L1 and T1 prior to any transfer

Here the question of enforcement is entirely straightforward and is simply a matter of contract law. Either party may sue and be sued on the covenants, since there is privity of contract between them.

1.2 Between L1 and T1 after a transfer

Until recently, it was the case that this original liability endured throughout the term of the lease, notwithstanding any transfer(s) of either or both interest(s). The Landlord and Tenant (Covenants) Act 1995 ('LTCA 1995') has changed the law. The new law, however, is different for leases granted before 1996, called 'old tenancies' and leases granted on or after 1 January 1996, called 'new tenancies'.

1.2.1 LTCA 1995

Essentially, the Act was designed to relieve the original tenant of the onerous continuing liability brought about by the application of the doctrine of privity of contract and, in turn, to strengthen the landlord's control over assignments of the lease.

Benefit and burden passes

Under LTCA 95, the benefit and burden of all landlord and tenant covenants are transmitted to successors in title unless they are expressed to be personal only. There is thus no need to determine whether the covenants touch and concern the land or whether they 'have reference to the subject matter' of the lease as used to be the case; the emphasis has been shifted to put the onus on the parties to indicate where the covenant is *not* intended to run.

Covenants included in the lease that relate to premises other than those assigned are not included (so, for example, if T has a lease of units A and B and assigns B only, the assignee of B will not be bound by covenants in so far as they relate to unit A).

Authorised guarantee agreement ('AGA')

Where an outgoing tenant enters into an AGA, he guarantees performance of the tenant's covenants by his immediate successor only. The possible obligations that can be covered by the agreement are set out in s16 LTCA 1995, but a tenant cannot be bound by anything more onerous than the covenants contained in the lease.

A landlord can demand that the outgoing tenant enters into an AGA only in the following circumstances, where the:

- Lease contains an absolute prohibition on assignment
- Alienation covenant is qualified and expressly provides that the landlord may demand an AGA as a condition of giving consent
- Alienation covenant is qualified and the demanding of an AGA is reasonable (notwithstanding that it is not expressly mentioned).

An outgoing tenant who is obliged to enter into an AGA may require an express indemnity covenant from his assignee. However, even if he does not, he may still recover any money that he has had to pay under the agreement, under the law relating to guarantees. (S.77LPA 1925 and s.134 LRA 2002, referred to below, no longer imply statutory indemnities because they are no longer needed under the new regime.)

1.2.2 Old tenancies: L1 and T1

Basically, T1 remains liable throughout the term, even where the breach is committed by T2 or T3. Similarly L1 remains liable to T1, even where a breach is committed by L2 or L3.

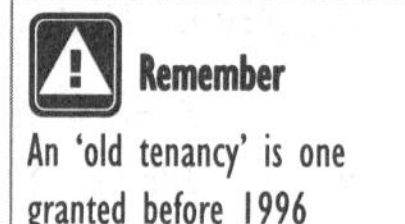

An 'old tenancy' is one granted before 1996

However, the Act did make a few changes that apply to tenancies already in existence. In particular it introduced a requirement that T1 should be given notice, as a warning, that action is going to be taken against him for the breach of covenant by T2 (or T3 or T4 etc). Where the breach is of a covenant to pay rent, service charge or any other liquidated sum under the lease or interest, L1 must serve this notice within six months of the so-called 'fixed charge' becoming due. This has the effect of limiting the tenant's liability to the arrears attributable to that six month period. This applies to old tenancies as well as to new tenancies.

Where a tenant or guarantor receives notice requiring payment of such a fixed charge, he may, within 12 months of making payment, require the grant of an **overriding lease** to him by the landlord (s 19 LTCA 1995). Such an overriding lease effectively 'slots in' above the assignee's lease, which therefore becomes a sublease. If the assignee's default continues, this means that the tenant with the overriding lease can take action against him. It gives him some degree of control in return for his liability.

The effect of this is that a landlord may choose to sue the original tenant or a subsequent tenant and, where one is insolvent, he has a viable alternative. He may recover only once in respect of his loss, however, and will normally take action against the tenant who is actually in breach. Where T1 is sued, he (T1) may claim under an indemnity from T2. Such an indemnity covenant may be:

- Express (this is common practice on any assignment)
- Implied

Remember

A 'new tenancy' is one granted on or after 1.1.1996

Registered land	s.134 LRA 2002 implies an indemnity on the assignment of a registered lease
Unregistered land	s.77 LPA 1925 implies an indemnity on an assignment for value

1.2.3 New tenancies: L1 v T1

The LTCA 1995 made the fundamental change of providing that the tenant is to be released from any liability for tenant's covenants once he assigns his interest. Any attempt to exclude, modify or frustrate this provision will be void. However, the release does not apply in three cases, namely where:

- The assignment from T1 to T2 is in breach of covenant
- The assignment from T1 to T2 takes place by operation of law

- T1 enters into an AGA (as he will often be required to do as a condition of the landlord granting his consent to assign). Under such an agreement, T1 is made liable for the default of T2 but not of T3 and, in the case of liquidated sums (ie the 'fixed charge' of rent and service charge, for example) this is restricted to the six months prior to the 'warning notice' referred to at 1.2.2 above.

Similarly, when T2 assigns to T3, T2 will be likely to enter into an AGA to guarantee T3's performance of the tenant's covenants.

1.2.4 New tenancies: T1 v L1

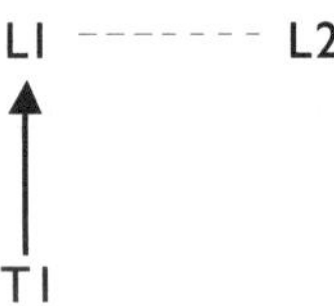

There is no corresponding provision for L1 to be released from his liability. Instead, he is entitled to apply to T1 for a release (s8 LTCA 1995). He must make such application before or within four weeks following his assignment and he will be released from any ongoing liability in the following circumstances:

- Where T1 consents
- Where T1 fails to give a written notice of objection within four weeks
- Where the court rules that L1's request is 'reasonable'

Note that any release under LTCA 1995 will not be effective in relation to any breach occurring before the relevant assignment.

1.3 Between successors in title to both parties' interests

Where one is talking about enforcement of covenants by a successor to either the original landlord or the original tenant (or both), privity of contract is no longer relevant. Instead it is a matter of privity of estate.

1.3.1 LTCA 1995

Again one needs to consider the question of enforceability depending on whether the lease pre-dates or post-dates 1 January 1996.

Old tenancies

Under the rule in *Spencer's case 1583* and the doctrine of privity of estate, landlord and tenant covenants run with the land so as to bind successors in title, provided the:

- Relevant assignee takes a legal estate in the land
- Covenants 'touch and concern' the land demised

A covenant is said to 'touch and concern' the land, if it can be said to affect 'the landlord in his normal capacity as landlord or the tenant in his normal capacity as tenant' (*Hua Chiao Commercial Bank Ltd v Chiaphua Industries Ltd 1987*). In addition, ss.141 and 142 LPA 1925 provide that the benefit and burden of leasehold covenants pass to new owners of the reversionary and leasehold interests where the covenant 'has reference to the subject-matter' of the lease. This wording is generally regarded as meaning the same as 'touch and concern'.

Note, however, that the benefit of a surety covenant (ie a guarantor's covenant as to performance of the tenant's covenants) is enforceable by a landlord's successor under the doctrine of privity of estate but not under s141 LPA 1925 (*Swift (P & A) Investments v Combined English Stores Group plc 1989).*

Again, a tenant may be able to enforce an indemnity covenant against his assignee.

New tenancies

Since LTCA 95 transmits the benefit and burden of all landlord and tenant covenants to successors (unless they are expressed to be personal only), it follows that successors in title can enforce them as if they were the original contracting parties. Thus L3 can sue T3 if they are in privity of estate at the time (ie landlord and tenant together). The above considerations relating to AGAs apply.

The various scenarios are set out below.

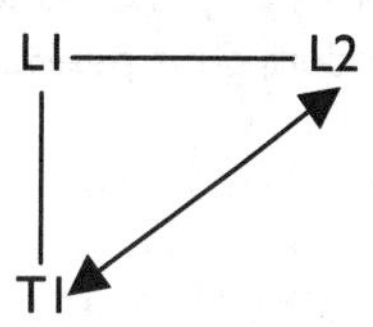

1.3.2 Old tenancies: T1 and L2

Both at common law and under LPA 1925, all covenants that touch and concern the land (or 'have reference to the subject matter of the lease' (s.141,142 LPA 1925)) bind L2.

By way of exception, if the nature of the provision requires registration, for example an option for the tenant to renew the lease or to acquire the landlord's reversion, then L2 will only be bound by it if registration was effected as it should have been.

Remember

An option should be protected by entry of a notice on the reversionary title or by registration of a C(iv) land charge

L2 acquires the exclusive right to sue for breach of covenant arising prior to the transfer, provided L1 did not waive the breach (*Re King 1963*), even where T1 had subsequently assigned the lease (*Arlesford Trading Co Ltd v Servansingh 1971*). L1 is no longer entitled to sue in respect of it because the benefit has passed to L2.

1.3.3 New tenancies: T1 and T2

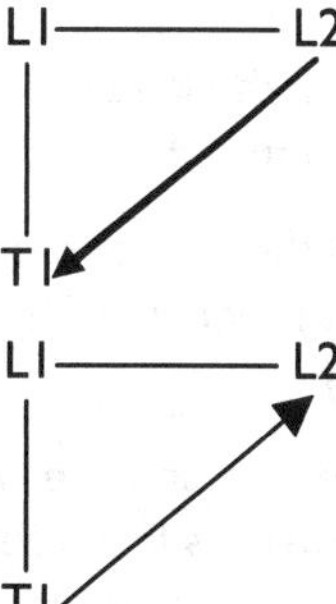

L2 v T1. L2 can sue on the tenant's covenants unless they are expressed to be personal only. A right of re-entry also passes to him and is not restricted to breaches occurring after he acquired his interest. L2 also takes the benefit of any guarantor of T1's covenants.

T1 v L2. L2 can be sued on the landlord' covenants unless they are expressed to be personal or unless they require registration and have not been registered (see above).

1.3.4 Old tenancies: L1 and T2

L1 can sue T2 by virtue of privity of estate. He can also sue T1 (but will need to serve a warning notice as described above)

T2 can sue L1 by virtue of privity of estate.

1.3.5 New tenancies: L1 and T2

T2 v L1. T2 can sue on the landlord's covenants unless they are expressed to be personal only

L1 v T2. L1 can sue on the tenant's covenants unless they are expressed to be personal only

1.3.6 Old tenancies: T2 and L2

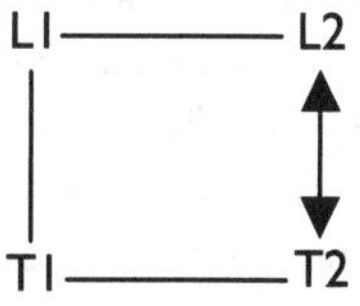

Under the doctrine of privity of estate, both L2 and T2 can enforce covenants against the landlord or tenant for the time being, as the case may be, provided they touch and concern the land. Generally speaking, each successor will only be liable, however, in respect of breaches committed during his possession of the land (*Duncliffe v Caerfelin Properties Ltd 1989*).

Note, however, that where a party has commenced legal proceedings against another and then assigns his interest, that assignment will not mean that he cannot continue those proceedings (as in *City and Metropolitan Properties Ltd v Greycroft Ltd 1987* where the court rejected L1's argument that T2's assignment of the lease to T3 meant that T2 could not continue his action against L1 for breach of covenant).

1.3.7 New tenancies: T2 and L2

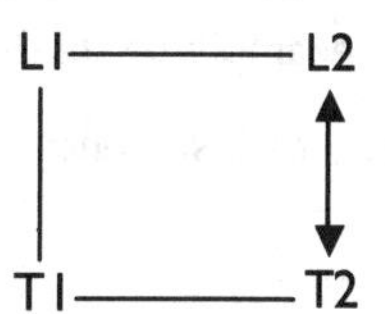

As above, the benefit and burden of landlord and tenant covenants pass to successors in title to each party. Therefore either party may sue on the other's covenants unless they are expressed to be personal only.

As mentioned already, where a transfer or assignment relates only to part of the assignor's interest and the covenants can be said to relate to land that was not assigned, then they will not pass. Remember that each successor is liable only in respect of breaches committed during his period of possession, unless he enters into an AGA in respect of his assignee.

1.4 Landlord and a sub-tenant

There is neither privity of contract nor privity of estate between a landlord and a sub-tenant. However, a sub-tenant is deemed to have notice of all covenants in the headlease and the landlord may be able to enforce them against a sub-tenant (*Hall v Ewin 1888*).

1.5 Mutual enforceability of covenants between tenants

A tenant of a flat in a block of flats or in a retail unit in a shopping centre, for example, will be concerned to see that his covenants are duplicated in the other tenants' leases and also that he has a means of enforcing them. He should seek:

- An obligation on the landlord to impose the same or substantially the same covenants on other tenants within the building or development
- A covenant on the part of the landlord to enforce a covenant against another tenant on the (reasonable) request of the tenant (possibly at the tenant's expense in very limited circumstances)
- There may also be a scheme which enables tenants to enforce their covenants directly against each other (as in a freehold building scheme). The lease should provide that it is the parties' intention that the covenants be mutually enforceable

Alternatively, the covenants could be expressed to benefit 'the tenants for the time being of the other units in the building/development' so that the provisions of the Contracts (Rights of Third Parties) Act 1999 might be applied.

2 Forfeiture

As explained in the previous Chapter, forfeiture is the remedy exercisable by the landlord that results in termination of the lease.

Generally speaking, a landlord may forfeit a lease either by peaceable re-entry or by court proceedings. However, in the case of lawfully-occupied **residential premises**, a landlord cannot enforce forfeiture without court proceedings (s.2 Protection from Eviction Act 1977). If peaceably re-entering, a landlord must always have regard to potential criminal liability when he considers re-entry (Criminal Law Act 1977). In the case of commercial premises, liability can normally be avoided by re-entering outside the tenant's business hours.

A right to forfeit must be expressly provided in the lease.

2.1 Events giving rise to forfeiture

Typically, events expressed to give rise to the right to forfeit will include:

- The tenant being in arrears of rent for, say, 14 or 21 days
- Breach of any covenant or agreement (clearly the tenant will seek to limit this type of provision, for example to *substantial* breach of *specified* covenants)
- The bankruptcy or insolvency of the tenant

2.2 Forfeiture for non-payment of rent

Where the landlord intends to forfeit for breach of the covenant to pay rent, he must first serve a 'formal demand' for rent, unless there is provision to the contrary or unless more than six months' rent is in arrears and there is insufficient distress to be found on the premises (s.210 Common Law Procedure Act 1852). In practice, most leases will obviate the need for such formal demand; the tenant is expected to know, without being reminded, when he is in arrears.

There is an exception, however, in the case of **long residential leases** (generally over 21 years) where the landlord must serve a notice specifying a date for payment within 30 and 60 days from the notice (Commonhold and Leasehold Reform Act 2002). The arrears must be over a prescribed level in terms of lateness, before the landlord can exercise a right of re-entry.

2.3 Forfeiture for breach other than non-payment of rent

The landlord must serve a written notice on the tenant pursuant to s.146 LPA 1925 (commonly referred to as a 's.146 notice') prior to re-entry, whether by court action or peaceably. This notice must:

- Specify the breach complained of and
- If it is capable of remedy, require it to be remedied
- State the period within which it must be remedied (which must be a reasonable time)

The notice may also require the tenant to make monetary compensation for the breach.

2.3.1 'Capable of remedy'

Whether or not a breach is capable of being remedied is really a question of whether the landlord can be restored to the position he was in prior to the breach within a reasonable length of time. Provided compliance following the notice, together with monetary compensation, makes good the harm suffered by the landlord, the breach will be regarded as capable of being remedied.

Breach of a positive covenant is likely to be capable of remedy, simply by late performance. Breach of an ongoing negative covenant is also likely to be capable of being remedied, provided the consequences of breach can be restored and rectified. However, a 'one-off' negative covenant (for example a covenant not to assign the lease) is likely to be regarded as incapable of remedy (*Scala House & District Property Co Ltd v Forbes 1974*). Care needs to be taken because if a breach is deemed capable of remedy and the s.146 notice does not specifically require it to be remedied, the notice will be void and no possession order will be granted (*Glass v Kencakes Ltd 1966*).

Glass v Kencakes Ltd 1966

The landlord sought to forfeit the tenant's lease on the basis of the subtenant having used the premises as a brothel, in breach of the covenant not to use them for illegal or immoral purposes. The s.146 notice did not require the breach to be remedied. The court held that the breach was capable of remedy (and had in fact been remedied by the subtenant having vacated the premises) and would not grant possession since the notice was void as a result.

2.3.2 Breach of repairing covenant

Where the notice is served in respect of a breach of a repairing covenant, it must point out the tenant's rights under the Leasehold Property (Repairs) Act 1938 ('LPRA 1938'), provided it is a **lease of at least seven years with at least three years to run** at the relevant time. Where it applies, this Act provides that a landlord must obtain a court order before pursuing forfeiture or damages for failure to repair.

2.3.3 Breach of covenant to pay service charge

In this case, the s.146 notice must inform the tenant that the landlord cannot proceed to forfeit the lease unless and until a court or leasehold valuation tribunal confirms the tenant's liability to pay the service charge in question.

2.3.4 Long residential leases

In the case of a long lease of residential premises, a landlord cannot serve a s.146 notice, unless the fact of the tenant's breach has been accepted by a court or leasehold valuation tribunal, or acknowledged by the tenant (s.168 Commonhold and Leasehold Reform act 2002).

2.3.5 Effect of the notice

The aim of the notice is really to give the tenant 'one last chance'. It gives him an opportunity to remedy his breach and if he doesn't, or if he can't, to seek relief from the court before the landlord proceeds to forfeit his lease.

The LPRA 1938 provides that a tenant may, within 28 days of service of the s.146 notice, serve a counter notice on the landlord requiring him to obtain a court order before re-entering the premises. The landlord must then prove one of the grounds under the 1938 Act in order to obtain an order for possession (s.1(5) LPRA 1938).

2.4 Relief from forfeiture

The tenant is entitled to apply to the court for relief from forfeiture (s.146 (2) LPA 1925). If relief is granted, the lease is effectively reinstated and continues as if there had never been any breach. Whilst the courts have a general equitable jurisdiction to grant relief, the main jurisdiction stems from the following.

2.4.1 Non-payment of rent

Generally speaking, provided the tenant pays all arrears of rent, together with costs, before the date set for trial, the court will grant relief by preventing the landlord from proceeding.

The relevant statutory provisions are ss.210 and 212 Common Law Procedure Act 1852, where the landlord has commenced proceedings in the High Court, and s.138 County Courts Act, where proceedings are in the County Court.

The court also has a discretion to grant relief within six months of the landlord re-entering the premises, provided the tenant pays costs and arrears (and, in High Court proceedings, provided there is more than six months' arrears of rent).

2.4.2 Breach of other covenants

Immediately following service of a s146 notice, the tenant is entitled to apply to the court for relief. This right continues until either the:

- Landlord has obtained a possession order and entered into possession
- Tenant has failed to seek relief within a reasonable period following the landlord having peaceably re-entered the premises (*Billson v Residential Apartments Ltd 1992)*

The courts will look at the seriousness of the breach, the extent of the damage caused and its detrimental effect on value and consider whether forfeiture is appropriate. Generally speaking, provided the landlord's interest has not been irrevocably damaged, relief will be granted, although the tenant's conduct may also be taken into account (*Akici v LR Butlin Ltd 2005*). Certainly where the breach is relatively minor or was unintentional or where remedial steps have already been taken, relief is likely to be granted. An irremediable breach, however, is unlikely to give rise to relief being given.

2.4.3 Breach of a covenant to decorate

S.147 LPA 1925 contains a specific provision that applies where the breach complained of is one of a **covenant to decorate** the premises. The tenant may be granted relief where the landlord is shown to be acting unreasonably. This applies to commercial and residential leases regardless of the length of term.

2.5 Residential leases

As mentioned above, a landlord cannot enforce a right to re-enter premises which have been let, in whole or in part, as a **dwelling**, without a court order (s.2 Protection from Eviction Act 1977). To do so is to commit a criminal offence under that Act. In the case of tenancies protected by the Rent Act 1977 or Housing Acts 1985 and 1988, there are more restrictions that apply, even where a tenant is in substantial default. A tenant who is unlawfully evicted is likely to be able to recover substantial damages in civil proceedings.

2.6 Waiver of the right to forfeit

The landlord will lose his right to forfeit the lease, where he can be said to 'waive' the right, either expressly or by implication, in circumstances where he is aware of the breach. For example, accepting rent will constitute a waiver of the right to forfeit, as will making demands that a breach is remedied or commencing proceedings for an injunction (*Iperion Investment Corporation v Broadwalk House Residents Ltd 1992).*

A waiver will not have any effect on **subsequent** breaches of covenant. Nor will it prevent the landlord from seeking alternative remedies in respect of the breaches for which the right to forfeit has been waived.

2.7 Effect of forfeiture

Once the landlord has re-entered, the tenant becomes a trespasser and the landlord may use such force as is reasonably necessary to remove him.

Any **sublease** is automatically terminated by forfeiture of a headlease. However, a subtenant may seek relief independently (s.146(4) LPA 1925) and the court may choose to invest a new lease of the premises in the subtenant.

A **mortgage** is also destroyed by forfeiture of the lease, but a legal mortgagee may also apply for relief independently. An equitable mortgagee may join the tenant in claiming relief or seek relief under s.138 County Courts Act 1984.

3 Other remedies of the landlord

A landlord has various remedies available in the event of a tenant's breach, namely:

For non-payment of rent	**For breach of other covenant**
Forfeiture	Forfeiture
Distress	Damages
Action for debt	Self-help
	Injunction
	Specific performance

3.1 Forfeiture

Forfeiture has already been explained. Remember that where forfeiture is used for non-payment of rent, no s.146 notice is required to be served. Also, breach of the implied covenant not to deny the landlord's title gives rise to an automatic right to forfeit the lease, but in other cases the right to forfeit must be expressly reserved.

3.2 Distress for arrears of rent

Distress is a common law remedy that allows the landlord to seize goods belonging to the tenant found on the demised premises and to sell them in order to recoup arrears of rent.

The landlord is not required to obtain a court order first, although the exercise of the remedy is restricted as to the time and method of execution and the nature of goods that can be seized. The landlord must give notice to the tenant of his intention to sell the goods (s.1 Distress for Rent Act 1689). Landlords are, not without good cause, reluctant to use distress as a remedy, in part due to these restrictions and in part due to a concern that challenges could be brought under the European Convention on Human Rights (for example, the guarantee of a right to a 'fair and public hearing', Art 6) or the Human Rights Act 1998 (see *Fuller v Happy Shopper 2001*).

3.3 Action for arrears of rent

As an alternative to distress, a landlord may sue for unpaid rent. There is no need to re-enter the premises. There is also authority for saying that, even where the tenant abandons the premises, a landlord is not under a duty to mitigate his loss by re-letting the premises (*Boyer v Warbey 1953*).

The landlord must commence proceedings, in the County Court or High Court as appropriate, within six years of the date of default (s.19 Limitation Act 1980).

3.4 Damages for a breach of covenant other than the covenant to pay rent

Where the landlord has suffered loss as a result of the tenant's breach, he may seek an award of damages. As a general rule, damages will be such amount as would put the landlord in the position he would have been in had there been no breach. If the covenant breached is a covenant to keep or put premises in repair, statute provides (s.18 LTA 1927) that:

- The level of damages cannot exceed the amount by which the value of the reversion has been diminished through the breach
- No damages will be awarded where it was intended to demolish the premises, or to make such substantial alterations as to render the subject repairs valueless, at or shortly after the termination of the lease

3.5 Self-help

The landlord may choose to exercise any rights set out in the lease for him to re-enter the premises and carry out the repairs himself. He will then sue the tenant to recover his costs. This approach has the advantage that the costs are recoverable as a debt and not as damages (*Jervis v Harris 1996*), which means that they are not subject to the limitation under s.18 LTA 1927 (see 3.4 above).

3.6 Injunction

It may be appropriate for the landlord to seek an injunction to restrain an anticipated or ongoing breach of covenant. An injunction is an equitable remedy within the discretion of the court.

3.7 Specific performance

Similarly, it may be appropriate for a landlord to seek an order of specific performance (or a mandatory injunction) to compel a tenant to comply with his covenants, particularly where the lease does not include a forfeiture clause or other provision for re-entry enabling the landlord to carry out essential repairs *(Rainbow Estates Ltd v Tokenhold Ltd 1998)*. However, such an award is unlikely to be made, and generally will not be made where monetary damages are considered to be an adequate remedy, or where the clause breached is a 'keep open' covenant (*Co-operative Insurance Society Ltd v Argyll Stores (Holdings) Ltd 1998*).

Co-operative Insurance Society Ltd v Argyll Stores (Holdings) Ltd 1998

A tenant closed its supermarket in a shopping centre after 15 years of a 35 year lease, on the basis that it was running at a loss. The court refused the landlord's application for a mandatory injunction, on the grounds that it was an established principle that a defendant should not be required positively to carry on a business.

The decision has been widely criticised, not least because the effect on the remainder of the landlord's investment in the shopping centre can be, as in this case, substantially detrimental.

4 Remedies of the tenant

A tenant will often be concerned with a landlord being in breach of his repairing covenants, but of course he may also seek to enforce his remedies in respect of the landlord's other covenants. The likely remedies are:

- Damages (or to treat the lease as terminated and sue for damages)
- Injunctions and specific performance
- Self-help and set off

4.1 Damages

Where the tenant has suffered loss as a result of the landlord's breach of covenant, he may seek an award of damages. These will be assessed as such amount as would restore the tenant to the position he would have been in had the landlord performed his obligations.

Where the landlord's breach is so fundamental as to amount to a repudiatory breach, the tenant may be entitled to reject the entire lease and sue the landlord for damages.

4.2 Specific performance and injunctions

Although these are equitable remedies within the court's general discretion, s.17(1) LTA 1985 specifically provides that the court may order specific performance where a tenant of a **dwelling** claims for breach of the landlord's **repairing covenant**, notwithstanding any equitable rule restricting the scope of the remedy.

4.3 Self-help and set off

In cases of breach of the landlord's **repairing covenant**, a tenant has the right, at common law, to withhold payments of rent of an amount equivalent to the reasonable cost of him carrying out necessary repairs that the landlord has failed to carry out (*Lee-Parker v Izzet 1971*).

He also has the right, in equity, to set off an unliquidated claim for damages in respect of the landlord's breach against the landlord's demand for arrears of rent. This right is not available against a successor of the landlord, however (*Edlington Properties Ltd v JH Fenner & Co Ltd 2006*).

Summary

- Covenants between the original tenant and original landlord prior to any transfer of either party's interest are enforceable by virtue of privity of contract
- Once either party has assigned his interest, the LTCA 95 governs the enforceability of covenants. For old tenancies, the parties remain liable but warning notices and overriding leases provide some protection for the tenant. For new tenancies, T1 is usually released from liability, subject to any AGA, and L1 can apply to be released
- An AGA guarantees the performance of an immediate successor only. It can only be required of the tenant in certain circumstances
- Covenants in old tenancies between L2 and T1 or L1 and T2 or L2 and T2 are generally enforceable by virtue of privity of estate
- In new tenancies, such covenants are enforceable unless they are expressed to be personal only
- A landlord may generally enforce headlease covenants against a subtenant
- A tenant in a development should ensure that there is a scheme for enforcement of covenants against other tenants
- A landlord may forfeit a lease either by court proceedings or peaceable re-entry, except that a court order is essential in respect of a dwelling. First he must serve a formal demand for rent (unless this requirement is excluded) or a s.146 notice
- A s.146 notice must contain prescribed information in certain cases
- A tenant may apply to the court for relief from forfeiture. A landlord may waive his right to forfeit
- Distress is the seizure of the tenant's goods for sale
- A landlord may sue for arrears of rent and may seek damages for any other breach of covenant
- The landlord may also seek an injunction or an order for specific performance or he may exercise self-help rights reserved in the lease
- A tenant may seek damages for breach of covenant, or an injunction or specific performance
- A tenant may be entitled to withhold rent or to set off a sum against a claim for arrears in cases where the landlord is in breach of his repairing covenants

Self-test questions

1. What is meant by the term 'privity of estate'?
2. For a lease granted in 1991, can T1 sue L1 where L2 commits breach of covenant?
3. Can an indemnity from T2 in favour of T1 be implied where there is no express provision?
4. For a lease granted in 1989, what test must be satisfied for landlord and tenant covenants to bind successors to the legal estate?
5. For a 'new tenancy', in what circumstances will a tenant not be released from his original liability (except where he enters into an AGA)?
6. What do the letters AGA stand for?
7. Where L1 applies to T1 to be released from liability on a transfer of his interest to L2, but T1 gives notice of refusal, can L1 still be released?
8. Where an alienation covenant is qualified but does not specifically mention AGAs, can a landlord still demand that a tenant enters into an AGA?
9. Is L2 bound by T1's option to renew the lease?
10. Under LTCA 1995, in new tenancies, when do leasehold covenants *not* bind successors in title?
11. In what two ways can a landlord forfeit a lease?
12. Must a landlord always serve a formal demand for rent before forfeiting for non-payment of rent?
13. When is a breach of covenant unlikely to be capable of remedy?
14. What is the effect of a tenant's counter notice served under LPRA 1938 following service of a s.146 notice for breach of a repairing covenant?
15. When a headlease is forfeited, what is the position of a subtenant?
16. What limit is imposed on damages for a tenant's breach of his repairing covenant?
17. In what circumstances is a tenant most likely to succeed in seeking an order for specific performance?

Answers to self-test questions

1. It is the relationship that exists between a landlord and tenant for the time being
2. Yes
3. Yes. An indemnity covenant is implied on an assignment of a registered lease or (in unregistered land) on an assignment for value
4. That the covenants 'touch and concern' the land or 'have reference to the subject matter of the lease'
5. Where the assignment is in breach of covenant or where it takes place by operation of law
6. Authorised guarantee agreement
7. Yes, if the court rules that his request is reasonable
8. Yes, provided that it is reasonable to do so
9. Yes, provided it is registered
10. When they are expressed to be personal only
11. Peaceable re-entry or court order
12. Not if the lease expressly provides that he need not do so or if arrears exceed six months and there is insufficient distress on the premises
13. When it is a one-off negative covenant
14. The landlord must then prove one of the grounds set out in the 1938 Act before he can re-enter the premises
15. His sublease is automatically terminated but he may apply for relief
16. Damages cannot exceed the amount by which the reversion is diminished through the breach
17. A tenant of a dwelling claiming in respect of a landlord's breach of repairing covenants

18

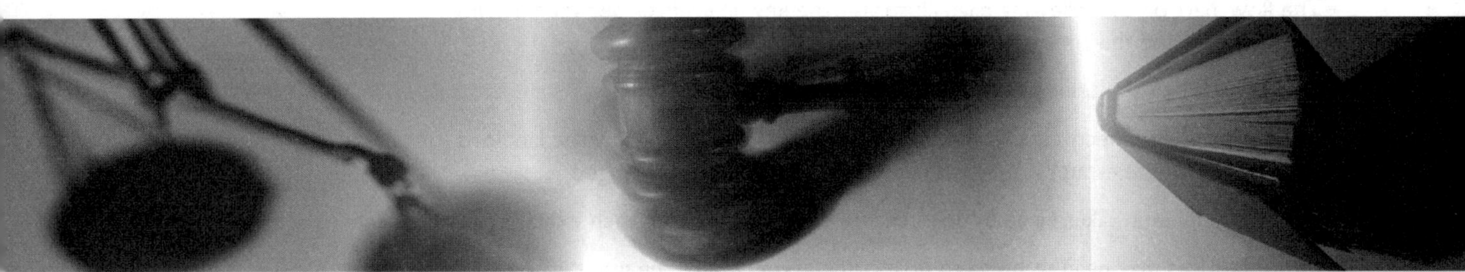

Leasehold conveyancing

Topic List

Chapter overview

This Chapter will:

- Address conveyancing matters relevant to the grant of a new lease or sublease
- Address conveyancing matters relevant to the sale of an existing lease

Chapter overview continued

Section B of this Study Manual took you through the conveyancing procedures in relation to freehold title and, so far in section C, you have learned the basic legal principles relating to leases. This final Chapter now brings the two together and addresses the ways in which leasehold conveyancing differs from freehold conveyancing. In many respects the two are the same and where differences are not highlighted (or are not assumed to be obvious), you may assume that what you learned in relation to freehold conveyancing is still applicable.

1 The grant of a lease

The flowchart on the following page illustrates the key differences between freehold conveyancing and the grant of a lease.

You will see that the principal differences are that:

- The lease (effectively the creation of an estate) is drafted (i) by the landlord (or person creating the estate) (ii) prior to any agreements being exchanged
- Completion takes place by an exchange of the lease parts, each executed by one party
- Notices may need to be given post completion (where the grant is of a sublease and/or where a mortgage is involved)

1.1 Taking instructions

You will need to have details of the parties and the terms that they have agreed, including as to the extent of the demise, the rent and the length of term.

Clearly you should also take instructions as to the covenants appearing in the intended lease. If you are acting for the landlord, you might take him through your office's standard form lease and, to the extent that its terms do not reflect your client's instructions, you will need to adapt them. If you are acting for the tenant, you will need to report on the terms of the draft lease that you have received, advise as appropriate and amend it according to your instructions. In either case you will usually negotiate terms with the other party's solicitor, acting in your client's best interests and seeking instructions intermittently on key points rather than on every proposed amendment.

Perhaps the landlord's prime objectives will be to achieve an FRI lease with a clean rent, ie with no residual responsibility for outgoings. He will also wish to have a suitable degree of control over key areas such as alienation, user and alterations. Conversely, a tenant will be concerned to ensure that the lease allows him sufficient flexibility (again, particularly with regard to alienation, user and alterations) but also that his financial commitments are both clearly ascertainable and manageable.

1.2 Professional conduct

The rules relating to acting for both seller and buyer also apply to acting for both landlord and tenant. Thus you should not act for both unless the limited exceptions of rule 3 apply (see Chapter 7). Similarly, the rules on acting for a landlord and his lender or a tenant and his lender (only likely to be relevant to the grant of a lease at a premium) also correspond.

Flowchart 1

Grant of lease

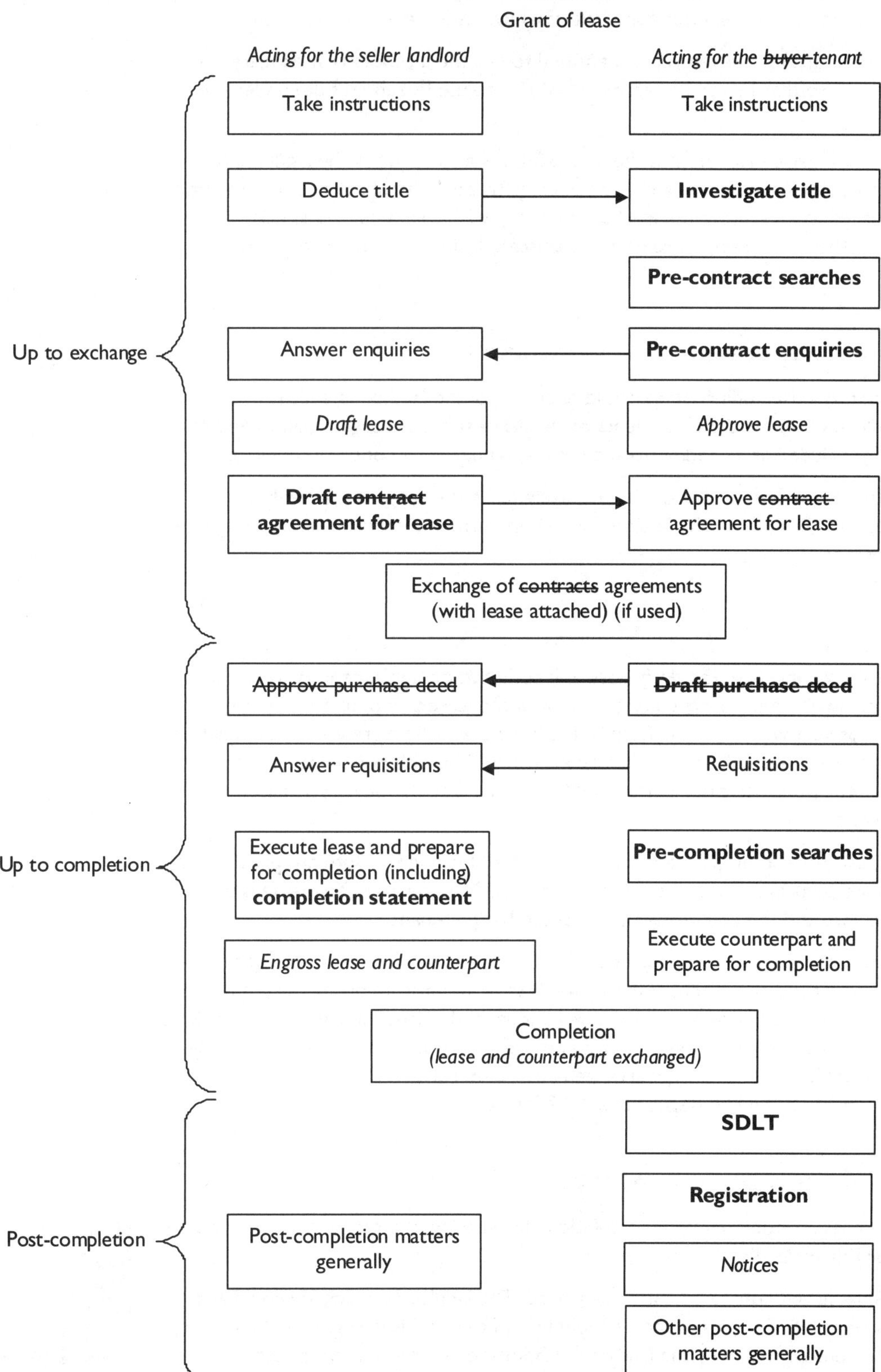

1.3 Title

The landlord's solicitor will deduce title (after studying it himself) and the tenant's solicitor will investigate it, as in freehold conveyancing. Note that if the property is subject to a mortgage, the lender's consent is likely to be required to the grant of a lease.

A tenant of a lease for less than seven years is not entitled to call for deduction of the freehold reversionary title on the grant of a lease (s.44 LPA 1925), although (where the lease is a sublease) he is entitled to see the superior lease out of which his lease is to be granted.

A tenant of a lease for more than seven years is entitled to see the freehold reversionary title and any superior leases (so that he can be registered with absolute leasehold title) under the LRA 2002.

Where an agreement for lease incorporates the SCS, SC 8.2.4 also requires the landlord to deduce such title as would enable the tenant to obtain registration with absolute leasehold title. A headtenant who failed to investigate the freehold title may wish to amend this special condition, therefore, where the freehold remains unregistered, since he would be unable to comply with it.

1.4 Pre-contract searches and enquiries

The buyer's solicitor may raise additional leasehold enquiries of the landlord's solicitor, concerning the landlord's insurance arrangements or details of service charge liabilities and so on. These are usually included as an additional section on standard pre-contract enquires.

Otherwise, pre-contract searches and enquiries are likely to be the same as for freehold conveyancing, except possibly where the lease is for a short term and certain searches might not be considered necessary.

1.5 Agreement for lease and lease

The landlord's solicitor will prepare the draft lease and contract, or 'agreement for lease'. In some cases, the parties will simply proceed to the grant of the lease and omit the contract. Where a contract is used, it will annex the form of the lease that will be granted on completion and so its terms must have been fully agreed before exchange. This differs from freehold conveyancing, where the purchase deed is prepared for approval by the buyer's solicitor following exchange of contracts.

The landlord's solicitor will also prepare engrossments of the documents. Both are prepared in duplicate and the lease parts are referred to as the 'lease' and 'counterpart'. The lease is executed by the landlord and the counterpart is executed by the tenant.

Where a HIP is required, it must contain details of the proposed lease and estimates of the total costs that might be demanded of the tenant during the first 12 months following the grant of the lease, including rent, insurance and service charge. Additional authorised information will include details of any licences affecting the property, information regarding any management company and further details about any service charge arrangements. Other matters might be required and reference should be made to the HIP Regulations 2007 for details.

1.6 Pre-completion and completion

Pre-completion searches are the same as for freehold conveyancing, the search being carried out against the superior title or landlord.

On completion, the lease and counterpart are exchanged. The landlord's solicitor should also hand over originals or certified copies of the freehold title (if the land is unregistered) and a certified copy of the consent issued by the landlord's landlord or lender, if appropriate.

Alert

This is a physical exchange of the lease and the counterpart. Do not confuse it with 'exchange of contracts'

The monies to be paid on completion will be any premium that is payable and/or an apportionment of rent from the date of completion to the next quarter day (or other date specified in the lease for payment of rent).

1.7 Post completion

1.7.1 SDLT

As for the purchase of a freehold estate, a land transaction return must be sent to HMRC following the grant of a lease and SDLT may be payable. SDLT is charged on any premium in the same way as for the purchase price in a freehold purchase. It is also charged on rent according to a complex formula (the HMRC website has a helpful procedure for calculating the rate of SDLT). Broadly speaking, SDLT is payable on the 'net present value' (the 'NPV') over certain thresholds. The NPV is calculated by reference to the total rental liability over the term of the lease minus rental payments arising in future years (discounted on the basis of an annual percentage), at the same time making provision for rental increases over the period of the term.

1.7.2 Registration

A lease for **seven years or less** is not substantively registrable but takes effect as an unregistered disposition that overrides first registration or subsequent registered dispositions. Provided it is for over three years, however, it should be protected by entry of a notice on the charges register of the superior title, where that is registered. In unregistered land, a legal lease is deemed to bind the whole world.

A lease for **more than seven years** is a registrable disposition. It must, therefore, be registered with its own title number, even where the interest out of which it is granted is unregistered. It will also be noted on the charges register of the superior title where that is registered. As in freehold conveyancing, application should be made within the priority period of any pre-completion search and, in the case of a first registration, within two months of completion.

1.7.3 Notices

If the tenant has a mortgage in respect of any premium, notice should be given to the landlord. This might be a requirement of the lease but is likely to be a requirement of the lender in any event. The landlord should be asked to sign one copy of the notice by way of acknowledgement and return it to the tenant's solicitor.

If the lease granted is a sublease, notice is likely to be required to be given to the headlandlord in accordance with the provisions of the headlease. Notice is usually given in duplicate and the headlandlord asked to sign and return one part by way of acknowledgement.

The obligation to give notice of a disposition is usually coupled with an obligation to pay a fee (in respect of the landlord's administrative costs).

2 The assignment of a lease

The following flowchart illustrates the key differences between freehold conveyancing and the assignment of a lease. In fact, there is relatively little difference, since an assignment is simply the sale of the remainder of a term granted by a lease. One can refer to an assignor and assignee, transferor and transferee or seller and buyer.

Flowchart 2

Assignment of lease

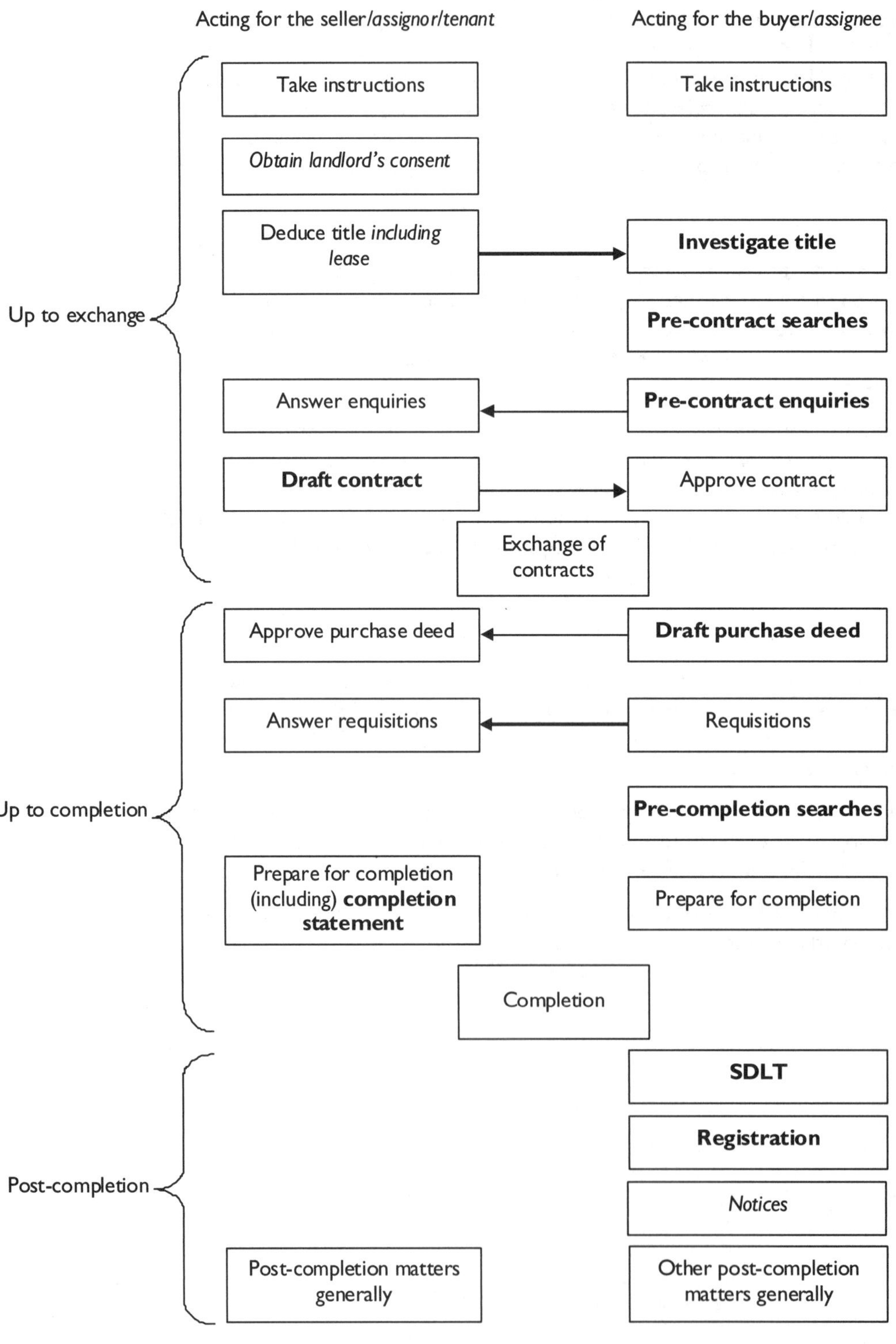

You will see that the principal differences are the:

- Likely requirement to obtain a licence to assign
- Need to give notice to the landlord following assignment

2.1 Instructions

Both solicitors will need to obtain details of the lease being sold and of any particular terms that the parties have agreed, as in freehold sales. Both will be concerned, in particular, with the alienation covenant in the lease and whether it permits assignment.

2.1.1 Licence to assign

If the alienation covenant contains an absolute prohibition on assignment, the landlord is under no obligation to give consent. Even if he waives the prohibition on one occasion, there is no obligation on him to do so again and so an assignee should proceed with extreme caution. Any lender (to the assignee) is likely to refuse to lend on the basis of a lease with such a covenant.

If the alienation covenant contains a qualified or fully qualified covenant, the seller's solicitor should seek the landlord's consent. Remember that s.19 LTA 1927 adds to a qualified covenant the proviso that consent shall not be unreasonably withheld. The landlord is required to give his consent within a reasonable time or to give reasons where he is refusing consent. He is not entitled to charge a premium as a condition for giving consent unless the lease expressly allows him to do so. He may, however, require payment of his costs in giving consent. Breach of the landlord's obligations under the statutory provisions is actionable in tort for breach of statutory duty.

Where a contract for sale incorporates the SCS, SC 8.3 provides that the seller shall use all reasonable efforts to obtain consent at his own expense. The buyer is required to provide all information and references that are reasonably required. Where consent has not been given (or given only subject to a condition to which the buyer reasonably objects), the SCS also provide that either party may rescind the contract by notice. It is best practice not to exchange contracts until consent has been given, particularly where dependent transactions are involved.

The buyer may also be required to enter into a direct deed of covenant with the landlord. This is particularly common in the case of long residential leases and some commercial leases.

2.1.2 The seller's solicitor

The seller's solicitor should obtain from his client the original lease and any related title documents. He should also ask for details of insurance and service charge so that he is in a position to provide the buyer's solicitor with the information that he will require.

Where the Protocol applies, the seller should complete the Seller's Leasehold Information Form in addition to the Seller's Property Information Form. Where a HIP is required, this should contain copies of the lease, rules and regulations concerning management of the property, details of service charge liabilities over the past three years and details of other costs and contributions required from the tenant over the previous twelve months. Other information may be required under the HIP Regulations 2007, which should be checked for details.

2.1.3 The buyer's solicitor

The buyer's solicitor should study the lease carefully and ensure that his client both understands and is prepared to purchase the lease on its terms. Since the lease has already been granted, he is not at liberty to negotiate the provisions of the lease, although the landlord could always be approached to consider a variation of the lease where there is something that the prospective assignee cannot accept.

2.2 Title

The buyer's solicitor will investigate title, deduced by the seller's solicitor, in the same way as for freehold conveyancing.

Where the lease is registered with absolute leasehold title, official copies of the register will be provided in the normal way (together with a copy of the lease) and there is no need for the assignee to investigate the freehold title.

Where the lease is registered with good leasehold title, the tenant should ask for the freehold title to be deduced in addition to the leasehold title. Of course, if the freehold is registered, he will be able to obtain official copies even if the seller does not provide evidence of this title. However, if it is unregistered, the assignee will be dependent upon the seller deducing title to it as he is only entitled to call for the lease and all assignments of that lease for the previous 15 years (so as to show a good root of title) but is not entitled to see title to the freehold. If the selling tenant cannot or will not do so, the assignee will need to take a view on whether he is prepared to purchase a lease with good leasehold title only. To do so is likely to be unacceptable to a lender.

2.3 Pre-contract searches and enquiries

These will normally be the same as for a freehold purchase (except possibly where there is only a short unexpired term), save that pre-contract enquiries will also cover leasehold matters.

2.4 Contract and purchase deed

2.4.1 Breach of covenants

It is common for a contract for the sale of a leasehold estate to contain express provision that the buyer shall take the property in its existing state of repair, in order to avoid any possible breach of the covenants for title where the seller is in breach of his repairing covenants to any degree. If so, this should also be mentioned in the purchase deed. Typically a clause might state that the covenants for title implied under s.4 LP(MP)A 1994 shall not be deemed to imply that the tenant has complied with his covenants for repair or decoration.

Where the seller is in breach of any other covenants, the buyer should seek to address them in the same way, since the statutory provision implies a covenant that there is no subsisting breach of any tenant's obligation (and nothing which would render the lease liable to forfeiture). Of course a buyer would not be advised to purchase a lease where the seller is in breach of covenant (save perhaps in relation to the repairing covenant and to the extent described above) and should, instead, require the seller to rectify the breach first.

2.4.2 Indemnity

You will remember that, following the LTCA 1995, in respect of a lease granted on or after 1.1.1996, a tenant is released from his liabilities under a lease where he assigns his interest, unless that assignment is in breach of the alienation covenant or arises by operation of law or unless the tenant assumes an ongoing liability, usually by virtue of entering into an AGA. Where he does enter into an AGA, the tenant should require an indemnity from the assignee. Provision for such an indemnity should be made in the contract and the purchase deed will set out the indemnity covenant in full.

Where the assignment is of a lease granted before 1996, an indemnity covenant is likely to be implied (although not in the case of an assignment of unregistered land otherwise than for value). However, in practice, an express covenant for indemnity is usually included.

2.4.3 The purchase deed

The form of the purchase deed will depend on whether the lease is already registered. If it *is*, then form TR1 will be used, just as on a transfer of the freehold. If it is *not* currently registered,

then if the lease is for seven years or less, an assignment will be used (which normally follows the format of a freehold conveyance). If the unregistered lease is for more than seven years, its sale will trigger compulsory first registration and so a TR1 is likely to be used (although it is not essential).

2.5 Pre-completion and completion

2.5.1 Pre-completion searches

Pre-completion searches will be made in the same way as for freehold conveyancing. However, if the lease is unregistered or registered with good leasehold title only, the buyer should also commission a land charges search against the estate owner of the unregistered freehold reversion.

2.5.2 Documents on completion

On completion, in addition to the documents to be supplied in the same way as a freehold sale, the seller should provide the **licence to assign**. If this contains direct covenants by the assignee, it should be drawn up as a deed and the assignee will need to execute it. It will normally be engrossed in two parts, a licence and a counterpart. The original licence will be given to the buyer on completion and the counterpart, executed by the buyer, will be retained by the landlord.

The seller's solicitor should also provide evidence of the superior title (where the lease is unregistered or only registered with good leasehold title) if this has been deduced, a copy of the landlord's insurance, receipts for rent, insurance and other outgoings and any other documents relating to the lease (for example previous assignments or notices that have been served under the lease informing the landlord of any dispositions).

2.5.3 Completion monies

Rent and other outgoings on the lease will need to be apportioned as at the date of completion. The apportionment will be included on the completion statement prepared by the seller's solicitor and relevant receipts and demands should be handed over on completion. Where it is not possible to give an apportionment with certainty, for example in relation to a service charge where the figures are not available, an apportionment should be made on the basis of a 'best estimate', as in SC 6.3.5. This condition also provides for an adjustment to be made at a later date and payment made as appropriate within 10 days of the final apportionment.

2.6 Post-completion

SDLT is payable in exactly the same way as on a freehold sale.

2.6.1 Registration

If the lease is registered, application should be made to register the purchase within the priority period of the pre-completion search. If the lease is unregistered but has over seven years to run, application should be made for first registration within two months. The lease will also be noted on the reversionary title if that is registered. If it has less than seven years to run, it will not require registration but will be an overriding interest. A lease for a term of more than three years can, however, be protected by the entry of a notice on the superior registered title.

2.6.2 Notice of assignment

Notice of the assignment (and any mortgage) should be given to the landlord. (In most cases this is required by the terms of the lease but is good practice in any event.) This notice will normally be provided in duplicate and the landlord asked to sign one and return it to the assignee by way of acknowledgement. A fee may be payable.

Summary

On a grant of a lease:

- The landlord's solicitor drafts the lease for approval by the tenant
- The agreed form of lease is attached to the agreement for lease
- A tenant is only entitled to see title to the freehold reversion in the case of a lease for more than seven years or if SC 8.2.4 (or similar) applies
- Pre-contract enquiries include a leasehold section
- A lease is engrossed in duplicate. The lease is executed by the landlord and the counterpart by the tenant. They are exchanged on completion
- Completion monies will be apportioned as to rent, insurance, service charge and any other outgoings on the date of completion
- SDLT may be payable on the grant of a lease, based on the NPV
- A lease for more than seven years must be registered
- Notice of a mortgage or notice of a sublease should be given to a landlord/headlandlord following completion

On an assignment of a lease:

- A licence to assign is likely to be required and a deed of covenant may be required. The original(s) will be handed over on completion
- Where the lease is unregistered or registered with good leasehold title only, the assignee should endeavour to obtain evidence of title to the freehold reversion (and search against it prior to completion)
- A transfer, or 'assignment', is likely to modify the implied covenants as to title with regard to any breach of the repairing covenant
- An indemnity is usually implied for an assignment of 'old tenancies' and is not usually required on an assignment of a 'new tenancy' unless the tenant enters into an AGA
- A TRI is likely to be used as the purchase deed, except perhaps in the case of a lease of unregistered land for seven years or less
- A registered lease, or an unregistered lease with more than seven years to run, should be registered. A lease of registered land for over three years should be entered on the charges register of the superior title
- Notice of the assignment (and any mortgage) should be given to the landlord

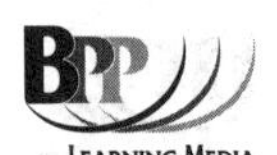

Self-test questions

1 Is a solicitor prohibited from acting for both landlord and tenant?

2 Is a tenant entitled to call for deduction of the freehold reversionary title where the lease is for more than seven years?

3 When is a tenant unlikely to commission pre-contract searches?

4 Who prepares the agreement for lease?

5 On the grant of a lease, what consents might need to be handed over on completion?

6 Is SDLT payable on the grant of a lease?

7 Does a four year lease of unregistered land trigger compulsory registration?

8 Is a landlord allowed to charge a premium for giving consent to assign?

9 What are the consequences of a landlord (reasonably) refusing consent?

10 Should an assignee of a registered lease (with absolute title) also ask for deduction of title to the freehold?

11 What special provision should a seller include where he is in breach of his repairing obligations?

12 When is an indemnity covenant not implied in an assignment?

13 What form will an assignment of a 12 year lease take?

14 To whom should notice of assignment be provided in duplicate?

Answers to self-test questions

1. Generally speaking he cannot, but there are exceptions in the same way that there are for acting for both seller and buyer
2. Yes (and title to any superior lease)
3. When the lease is for a very short term (for example a six month tenancy)
4. The landlord's solicitor. It has the agreed form of lease attached
5. Consent from the landlord's mortgagee and/or from a headlandlord where the lease is a sublease
6. Yes, on the NPV
7. No. As a legal lease, it binds the world without registration. (It also overrides first registration.)
8. Only if the lease expressly provides for him to do so (otherwise he is prohibited by statute)
9. The assignee should not proceed. SC 8.3 provides for rescission of the contract
10. No, it is not necessary
11. He should modify the covenants as to title implied under s.4 LP(MP)A 1994, by providing that the assignee shall take the property in its existing state of repair
12. On an assignment of unregistered land to a purchaser not for value
13. Form TR1
14. The landlord

Section 2
Wills, Probate and Administration

Section overview

Test requirements

The QLTT Test Specification provides that candidates should be able to demonstrate:

- An understanding of the principles involved in wills and estate planning
- An understanding of the principles involved in drafting wills and codicils
- A broad understanding of the nature of estates
- An ability to ascertain the value of estates and liabilities
- An understanding of how to obtain a grant of representation
- An understanding of the principles involved in winding-up estates

The specification also provides that candidates' knowledge may be tested by questions that require them to demonstrate that they are able to:

(a) Identify the beneficiaries of a range of testate and intestate estates by applying relevant succession law and the rights of the family and dependants of the deceased under inheritance legislation

(b) Identify the formalities for the creation of a will and the effect of its principal provisions

(c) Identify the powers and duties of personal representatives and possible problems in obtaining a grant of representation and in the administration of the estate

(d) Distinguish between the assets and liabilities to be excluded from the estate or the statement of assets and liabilities, by applying the relevant principles of inheritance tax and succession law

(e) Identify the circumstances in which the submission of an HMRC account will be required and show an understanding of the information to be provided

(f) Describe the methods for transferring assets to beneficiaries and for varying the devolution of assets, having regard to the effect of capital gains tax and inheritance tax

19

Freedom of testamentary disposition

Topic List

Chapter overview

This Chapter will:

- Introduce the fundamental principle of freedom of testamentary disposition.
- Introduce the Intestacy Rules
- Make it clear that a person can, in effect, 'opt out' of the intestacy rules by making a valid will
- Introduce the concepts of a total intestacy and partial intestacy
- Explain that certain assets do not pass under a will or the Intestacy Rules
- Introduce the Inheritance (Provision for Family and Dependants) Act 1975 and show that this legislation has an impact on freedom of testamentary disposition
- Introduce post-death disclaimers and variations
- Introduce inheritance tax and the fact that certain death transfers are taxable and certain death transfers are exempt for inheritance tax purposes

1 Freedom of testamentary disposition

In England and Wales, we have **freedom of testamentary disposition**.

This means that a person is free to give those assets by will (which are capable of being disposed of by will), to whomever he pleases, providing the person making the will has the required capacity, which means that he must be aged 18 or over and have the necessary mental capacity (known as testamentary capacity in the case of testamentary dispositions) to make a will. Capacity is dealt with in more detail in Chapter 20.

In other words, if a person (known as the **testator**) has made a valid will, which deals with all those assets which can be left by will, no relative of the testator has an automatic right to receive any of the deceased's estate on his death, unless of course they are a **beneficiary** under the will or the assets pass to them automatically through other rules of succession.

Example

Sarah is married and has two sons. She has made a will leaving her entire estate to a named charity. Assuming that she had testamentary capacity at the time she made the will, she had the intention to make the will and it was executed in accordance with the correct formalities (intention and formalities are covered in detail in Chapter 20), the will is valid and neither her husband, nor her sons, have any automatic right to inherit her estate; those assets which are capable of passing by will shall be inherited by the named charity, subject to the payment of debts and testamentary expenses (the meaning of 'testamentary expenses' is explained in Chapter 22).

However, it should be noted that Sarah's husband and sons may be entitled to claim against her estate under the **Inheritance (Provision for Family and Dependants) Act 1975** ('IPFDA 1975') (see paragraph 4 below).

---

2 The Intestacy Rules

If a person dies without a valid will, either because no will has been made or, alternatively, because the will is invalid for some reason (for example, due to a lack of testamentary capacity), the **Administration of Estates Act 1925** ('AEA 1925') determines who is entitled to the deceased's residuary estate (which is broadly the deceased's assets, after the payment of debts and testamentary expenses). Such a deceased person is said to have died **intestate** and the rules governing the distribution of the estate contained within the AEA 1925 are known as the **Intestacy Rules.** Essentially, the intestacy rules ensure that the deceased's **next of kin** (closest relatives including spouse or civil partner) share in his estate, or at least those assets which are capable of passing under the Intestacy Rules.

It is important that these fixed rules of inheritance under the Intestacy Rules are not confused with a system in which the provisions of a valid will are overruled by a 'forced heirship' system, particularly if you are from a jurisdiction where there are such fixed rules of inheritance.

In other words, the provisions of a valid will (which effectively deals with all the deceased's assets which are capable of passing by will) overrule the Intestacy Rules.

Example

If Sarah (above) dies intestate, her husband and sons will share in her estate under the Intestacy Rules, although whether her sons will inherit will depend upon the value of Sarah's estate, as will be seen.

The intestacy rules are considered in more detail in Chapter 23.

You should also be aware that a person can die **partially intestate**.

This can happen if they left a valid will which disposes of some, but not all, of their assets which are capable of passing by will. This may arise due to poor will-drafting or because a beneficiary has predeceased the testator.

In these circumstances, any assets which are effectively dealt with by the will are inherited according to its provisions and the remaining assets are inherited in accordance with the Intestacy Rules.

Example

Michael died leaving a valid will in which he gives £10,000 to his cousin Martin and the residue of his estate (broadly all his other assets after the payment of liabilities and testamentary expenses) to his cousin John. John predeceased Michael and, if there is no substitution provision in the will, the residue of Michael's estate passes under the Intestacy Rules. It may well end up passing to Martin, but that depends upon which other relatives survived Michael.

3 Assets

We have seen that a person is free to give those assets by will (which are capable of being disposed of by will), to whomever he pleases, providing the person making the will has the required capacity and intention.

The Intestacy Rules ensure that the deceased's next of kin share in the deceased intestate's assets which pass under the Intestacy Rules.

There are certain assets which pass independently of the terms of a valid will or the Intestacy Rules. These assets are considered in more detail in Chapter 20, although you should by now (if you have studied Part 1 of this Study Manual) be familiar with the concept of survivorship.

Example

Ena and Samir own their home as beneficial joint tenants. Ena has made a will in which she leaves her entire estate to her daughter, Punita. On Ena's death, the house passes automatically to Samir by survivorship as it was owned by them as beneficial joint tenants. If Ena wishes to leave her beneficial 'share' of the house to her daughter, she will need to **sever the beneficial joint tenancy**.

4 Inheritance (Provision for Family and Dependants) Act 1975

IPFDA 1975 has had an indirect impact on the principle of freedom of testamentary disposition.

IPFDA 1975 gives the court powers to order financial provision to be made from the estate of a deceased person for the benefit of **certain specific categories of applicant**, if it can be shown that **reasonable financial provision** was not made. An application will not automatically be successful.

Notably, an application under IPFDA 1975 can be made against the estate of a person who dies testate (with a valid will which effectively disposes of all their assets which can be disposed of by will), intestate or partially intestate.

IPFDA 1975 is considered in more detail in Chapter 26.

5 Post-death disclaimers and variations

Not all beneficiaries wish to accept their inheritance under a will or under the Intestacy Rules; an alternative distribution of the deceased's estate may be preferable for some reason.

For example, a surviving wife who inherits all of her husband's estate may wish to make some provision for their children, or a beneficiary may wish to pass some of his inheritance to his own children.

Of course, there is generally no reason why a simple gift cannot be made by the beneficiary during their lifetime.

However, it may be preferable for **tax** reasons to 'wrap' such a gift in a formal **disclaimer** or **variation**.

These are essentially methods by which a beneficiary under a will, or indeed the Intestacy Rules, can pass his inheritance to another person and, for tax purposes (inheritance tax and/or capital gains tax), arrange for it to be treated as if it passed directly from the deceased to that third person.

It is therefore possible, through the use of variations and disclaimers, to do some post-death estate planning.

Post-death disclaimers and variations are considered in more detail in Chapter 26.

6 Inheritance tax

Although inheritance tax is not directly related to the principle of freedom of testamentary disposition, it is worth commenting upon in this Chapter, as the impact of inheritance tax on a deceased's estate cannot be ignored. In fact some people might argue that it is an indirect impact on their freedom of testamentary disposition!

Inheritance tax is considered in depth in Chapter 24.

Example

Kristina and Bruno are a wealthy married couple, with adult children. They each have significant assets in their respective sole names. Kristina wishes to leave her assets to her children on her death and not to her husband. We have see that she can do this due to her freedom of testamentary disposition. However, there may be an inheritance tax charge on her death if she does so (depending upon the value of those assets, the inheritance tax allowance and the value and nature of any gifts made by her during her lifetime, which may have used up part or all of her allowance). This charge could be avoided if she leaves her assets by will to her husband because of the **spouse exemption**. There is no such inheritance tax exemption for children.

It should also be noted that if Kristina leaves her assets to her children only, her husband would be entitled to make a claim against her estate under the provisions of IPFDA 1975 (spouses are eligible to claim under IPFDA 1975), although this does not necessarily mean he would be successful.

Summary

- In England and Wales, we have freedom of testamentary disposition.
- The Intestacy Rules govern the devolution of a person's estate if they die without a valid will. A person may also die partially intestate.
- A person can effectively 'opt out' of the Intestacy Rules by making a valid will which effectively disposes of all their assets which can be disposed of by will.
- Not all assets are capable of passing by will or under the Intestacy Rules; some assets pass according to their own succession rules.
- Despite the principle of freedom of testamentary disposition, certain categories of person are able to claim against the estate of a deceased person for reasonable financial provision.
- A beneficiary under a will or the Intestacy Rules can disclaim their interest or enter into a post-death variation; if certain conditions are met, such gifts will be treated for inheritance tax and/ or capital gains tax purposes as gifts on death by the deceased rather than by the beneficiary.
- Inheritance tax should be considered when a person is making a will.

Self-test questions

1 Which of the following statements is true:

(a) A person can leave all his assets to his children by will, but his personal possessions will pass automatically to his spouse, regardless of the terms of his will.

(b) A person can leave all his assets to his children by will, but his wife will be able to successfully claim against his estate for financial provision.

(c) A person can leave all his assets by will to his children, except any assets he holds as beneficial joint tenants.

2 How old must a person be to make a valid will?

3 Give two reasons why a person might die partially intestate.

4 Which legislation sets out the Intestacy Rules?

5 If a person dies leaving a valid will which effectively disposes of all their assets are the Intestacy Rules relevant?

6 Can a claim under IPFDA 1975 be made against the estate of a person who has died intestate?

7 If a person makes a post-death variation, who is making the gift: the testator or the person making the variation?

8 If a person owns a property as beneficial joint tenants with someone else, but wishes to leave their 'share' in that asset by will, what must they do?

9 Does the inheritance tax spouse exemption on death apply to registered civil partners?

10 What do we call the person who makes a will?

Answers to self-test questions

1 (c)

2 18 years old.

3 They left a valid will, but it disposes of some, but not all of their assets because of (a) poor drafting or (b) because a beneficiary has predeceased the testator. (It should be noted that there are other reasons and they will be covered later in this Study Manual.)

4 AEA 1925.

5 No.

6 Yes.

7 The person making the variation, although for tax purposes (inheritance tax and/or capital gains tax) it can be treated as if it passed directly from the deceased to the donee of the gift. This is an important distinction.

8 Sever the beneficial joint tenancy.

9 Yes.

10 The testator. Testatrix is sometimes used for female testators, but is generally considered to be old-fashioned.

20

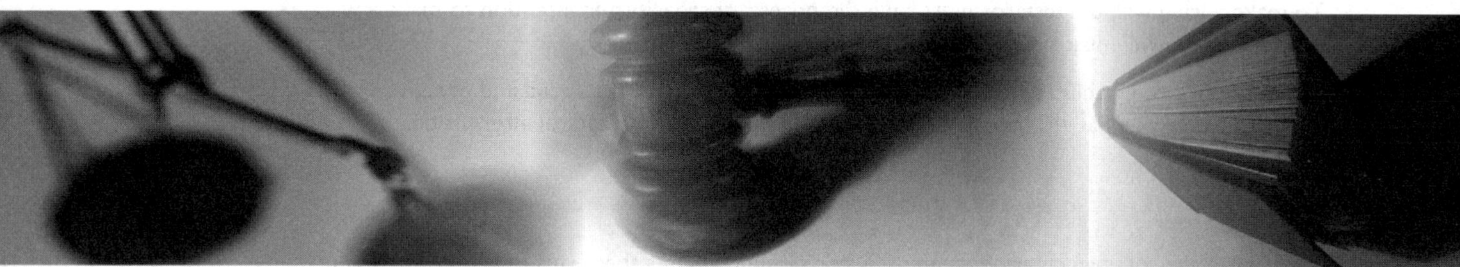

Wills: introductory matters

Topic List

Chapter overview

This chapter will:

- Explain what a will is and what a codicil is
- Specify some types of property that pass automatically, notwithstanding the terms of any will or the Intestacy Rules
- Explain a solicitor's duties and describe various relevant conduct issues in relation to the preparation of wills
- Explain the meaning of testamentary capacity and the impact of the Mental Capacity Act 2005
- Explain that without the necessary intention to make a will the will will not be valid
- Describe the formalities for execution of a will
- Describe the ways in which a will can be revoked
- Set out the basic structure of a will
- Explain the rules concerning alterations in wills
- Explain the doctrine of incorporation

1 What is a will?

1.1 Wills

A will is a written declaration of the intentions of the person making the will (the testator) which are to take effect on his death and which can be revoked at any time until his death. It is a testamentary document. Whilst the testator is alive, the people named in his will generally have no interest or rights to his property and the testator can, therefore, during his lifetime (*inter vivos*), dispose of his assets as he wishes. (Although if an asset is given in a will by way of a **specific** gift and it is no longer owned by the testator at his death, the gift will fail; this is known as **ademption**. This is covered in more detail in Chapter 22)

To make a valid will, the testator must have the necessary capacity and intention to make a will. In addition, the will must satisfy certain statutory formalities.

It is important to establish whether or not a deceased person has left a valid and effective will, in order to establish what will happen to the deceased's property (the estate) after his death.

1.2 Codicils

A codicil is also a testamentary document. A codicil supplements the terms of an existing will (eg by adding to it or by amending it). To make a valid codicil, the testator must have the necessary capacity and intention to make a codicil. The same formalities apply to the execution of a codicil as to the execution of a will and it is usually a relatively short document to prepare.

The main disadvantage of a codicil is that the will and codicil(s) must be read together and sometimes this gives rise to ambiguity or inconsistency between the two.

Only minor adjustments should, in practice, be made by a codicil; any major changes should be incorporated into a new will.

Example

Tamar James made a valid will dated 13 August 2006 in which she appoints her brother Anthony as her sole executor (the person entitled to administer her estate after her death – see Chapters 22 and 25), gives £10,000 to her friend Lucy Hines (known as a pecuniary legacy: a gift of money) and leaves the rest of her estate (the residue: the remainder of her estate after payment of debts and testamentary expenses) to her brother Anthony. Tamar no longer wishes to make a gift to Lucy. She can make this change using a codicil, which could be drafted as follows:

'I Tamar James of 12 Brook Lane Hale, Cheshire WA15 6TU declare this to be a first codicil to my will dated 13 August 2006

1. I revoke the legacy of £10,000 given to Lucy Hines by clause 2 of my said will

2. In all other respects I confirm my said will

**Signed by the above named Tamar James
in the presence of two witnesses who
signed in the presence of the above
named Tamar James and each other'**

Provided that Tamar has testamentary capacity and intention, and the codicil is executed correctly, it will be valid. On Tamar's death, the codicil will be read together with her will; Anthony will be entitled to act as her executor and will inherit the residue of her estate. Lucy will receive nothing.

However, as a will is a **public document** (*after* death), it may be preferable for Tamar to make a new will.

2 Testate, intestate and partially intestate

When a person dies, they may die 'testate', 'intestate' or 'partially intestate'. The meanings of these terms are as follows:

Testate	A person dies testate if he left a valid will and that will effectively disposes of all his assets, which are capable of being disposed of by will. If a person dies testate his assets, which can pass by will, are inherited in accordance with the provisions of his will.
Intestate	A person dies intestate if he did not leave a will or if he left a will which is invalid for some reason. If a person dies intestate, all his assets, which could have passed by will, are instead inherited according to the statutory rules known as the Intestacy Rules.
Partially intestate	A person dies partially intestate if he left a valid will, but it disposes of some, but not all, of the deceased's property that could have passed by will. In these circumstances, any assets which are effectively dealt with by the will are inherited according to its provisions and the remaining assets are inherited in accordance with the Intestacy Rules.

It is important to remember that some types of assets can never pass under a will or in accordance with the Intestacy Rules, regardless of whether the deceased died testate, intestate or partially intestate; they are considered later in this Chapter.

3 Who can make a will?

In general, to make a valid will a person must:

- Be aged 18 years or over when he executes his will
- Have the required level of testamentary capacity to make a will
- Intend to make a will

These issues will be considered later in this Chapter.

4 Reasons for making a will

If a person does not make a will, the following problems (amongst others) may arise:

- On death, the property, which could have passed under the deceased's will (had he made one), will be distributed according to the Intestacy Rules. As a result, the property will usually be shared between the nearest relatives on specified terms, which may not reflect the wishes of the deceased.
- The deceased's family may waste time trying to find out whether the deceased made a will and they may have to spend time and money tracing relatives.
- If there is no will, it may take longer and cost more to 'prove' the estate (this being the administrative process which has to be completed before the estate can be distributed).
- Without a will, the deceased's next of kin (often the spouse) will usually be appointed by the court, according to statutory rules, to administer the deceased's estate. This may not be appropriate. If the deceased had made a will, he could have exercised his own choice by appointing executors to administer his estate and trustees to administer any trusts

which arise under his will. (Usually the same persons are appointed as both executors and trustees.)

- If the deceased has children who are under the age of 18, he can appoint legal guardians by will. In the absence of an express appointment, the court may appoint guardians for children under the age of 18 whose parents have died.
- The deceased may have had express wishes as to the burial and disposal of his body on death.
- Administrators and trustees of trusts arising under the Intestacy Rules have only the powers given to them by statute. Making a will provides an opportunity to consider the statutory powers of the executors and trustees and extend, limit or exclude them where appropriate.

5 Assets

5.1 General

A person's **assets** are his property or other items of value which are owned by him. His **estate** is the entirety of his assets.

If a testator makes a will in which he disposes of all his estate, the will (and/or the Intestacy Rules, if applicable) will operate on his death to dispose of *most* types of asset which he then owns in his **sole** name, for example:

- Cash
- Money in bank and building society accounts
- Shares
- Other investments
- Real property
- Chattels (see below)

The will (and/or the Intestacy Rules, if applicable) will also operate on his death to dispose of:

- His beneficial interest in any property held by him as tenants in common with one or more person(s)

5.2 Meaning of 'chattels'

Chattels are personal property such as household and personal goods. Will-drafters often adopt the definition of 'personal chattels' given by **s.55 (1)(x) AEA 1925**:

'Personal chattels' mean carriages, horses, stable furniture and effects (not used for business purposes), motor cars and accessories (not used for business purposes), garden effects, domestic animals, plate, plated articles, linen, china, glass, books, pictures, prints, furniture, jewellery, articles of household or personal use or ornament, musical and scientific instruments and apparatus, wines, liquors and consumable stores.......'

Example

'I give my personal chattels as defined by s.55(1)(x) Administration of Estates Act 1925 to Mary Smith of .... absolutely'

(You will also see reference to this definition in relation to the Intestacy Rules.)

This is often a convenient way of dealing with the testator's personal possessions. However, it may not always be appropriate if a testator does not wish to give all their personal possessions by way of one gift.

Example

'I give all my jewellery to Catriona Dort of ……………….. outright'

5.3 Particular assets with their own rules of succession

There are some types of assets which pass on death, independently of the terms of the will or the Intestacy Rules. These include:

- Joint property
- Life insurance policies written in trust for a named beneficiary or beneficiaries
- Death in service payments, which have been nominated to a beneficiary or beneficiaries

These will now be considered in turn.

5.3.1 Joint property

Where a property is held by more than one person as beneficial joint tenants, on the death of one joint tenant his interest passes automatically by survivorship to the surviving joint tenant(s), regardless of the terms of the will (or the Intestacy Rules, if applicable). The same rule applies to other jointly held assets such and bank and building society accounts and chattels.

Example

Ela makes a will leaving all her estate to her sister, Julie. Ela and her boyfriend, Dave, have a joint bank account and own a house together as joint tenants in equity. On Ela's death, her interests in the house and the bank account will pass automatically to Dave, not to her sister, Julie.

Where land is held by more than one person as tenants in common, the share of each tenant in common passes on his death under his will or under the Intestacy Rules.

It is possible to sever the beneficial joint tenancy in real property, but it is important to note that a beneficial joint tenancy cannot be severed by will, it can only be severed *inter vivos*. If a testator wishes to leave his share in a property which is held as beneficial joint tenants by will, he should sever the joint tenancy during his lifetime.

In *Kecskemeti v Rubens Rabin and Co (1992)* a solicitor failed to advise his client that certain land would pass by survivorship and not by will. In his will the testator gave half of the land to his son. As a beneficial joint tenancy cannot be severed by will, the son did not receive the land. The son was able to recover his loss against the solicitor.

5.3.2 Life insurance policies

If a person takes out a simple life insurance policy, on his death, the policy matures and the insurance company will pay the proceeds to the personal representatives of his estate who will distribute the money according to the terms of his will (or the Intestacy Rules, if applicable).

However, a life insurance policy may be expressly written in trust for a named beneficiary or named beneficiaries. If this is done, on the death of the life assured, the policy matures and the insurance company will pay the proceeds to the named beneficiary/beneficiaries, regardless of the terms of the deceased's will (or the Intestacy Rules, if applicable).

5.3.3 Death in service payments

Many pension schemes provide for the payment of benefits if an employee dies whilst 'in service'.

These schemes usually allow the employee to indicate to the trustees of the scheme those persons he would like to benefit. This is usually done using a simple nomination or expression of wishes form. The pension fund trustees will normally follow the deceased's wishes, although they are not bound to do so. Such benefits do not belong to the employee during his lifetime and pass on his death independently of the terms of his will (or the Intestacy Rules, if applicable).

5.3.4 Inheritance tax

Note that some property which falls outside the estate for succession purposes may, nevertheless, form part of the estate for inheritance tax purposes. This is discussed in more detail in Chapter 24.

6 Solicitor's duties

A solicitor has various duties in connection with the preparation of a will, which include ensuring that:

- Instructions for the will are taken directly from the client.
- The instructions are not affected by duress or undue influence.
- The testator has the necessary capacity to make the will.
- The testator has the necessary intention to make a will.
- The will accurately reflects the client's instructions.
- The will is prepared with reasonable speed.
- The will complies with the formalities required by **s.9 Wills Act 1837** ('WA 1837').

6.1 Instructions for the will are taken directly from the client

Although it is acceptable to take instructions from a client in writing or over the telephone, it is preferable to see the testator in person.

This is particularly important if you have any doubts or concerns in relation to the testator's mental capacity or you are concerned that there may be undue influence.

Note that the testator is the client. **Rule 2.01** of the **Solicitors' Code of Conduct 2007** makes it clear that, where instructions are given by someone other than the client (for example, a relative), you must confirm the instructions directly with the testator before you proceed.

6.2 Duress or undue influence

It is also clear from **Rule 2.01** that, where you know or have reasonable grounds for believing that the client's instructions may be affected by **duress** or **undue influence**, you must not act on those instructions until you have satisfied yourself that they represent the client's wishes. In such circumstances it would be wise to see the client alone. It is important to be satisfied that the client is giving their instructions freely. Solicitors should be conscious of particularly vulnerable clients such as the elderly or those with language or learning difficulties or disabilities.

If a client makes a will under the undue influence of a third party (who may also be attempting to give instructions for the will (see above) and/or may be benefitting under the will) then, on death, probate of the will (see Chapter 25) may be refused if undue influence can be proved.

It should also be noted that if a testator makes a will as a result of force, fear or fraud, the will will not be valid.

6.3 Capacity

A solicitor must make sure that the testator has the requisite level of testamentary capacity to make a will, otherwise the will will not be valid. Capacity is considered in more detail later in this Chapter.

6.4 Intention

The testator must intend to make a will as opposed to any other kind of document and must know and approve its contents. This is considered in more detail later in this Chapter.

6.5 The will must accurately reflect the client's instructions

Will drafting issues are covered in Chapters 21 and 22.

Ross v Caunters (1980) established the principle that an intended beneficiary who, through the solicitor's negligence, fails to receive his gift, may recover his loss in an action against the solicitor.

6.6 The will must be prepared with reasonable speed

Having taken instructions, the solicitor is under a duty to prepare the will with reasonable speed.

In the case of *White v Jones (1995,)* the testator died before the solicitor had prepared the will. The court held the firm liable to compensate the disappointed beneficiaries.

It is generally considered that the will should be prepared within a week, but if there is a significant risk that the client will die imminently, the will should be prepared immediately. A handwritten (*holographic*) will can be valid.

6.7 The will must comply with the formalities required by s.9 Wills Act 1837

The formalities for execution of a valid will are set out in s.9 WA 1837 and are discussed later in this Chapter.

It is preferable for the solicitor to oversee the execution of the will, either in the office or at the testator's home. If the client prefers to execute the will at home, without the solicitor present, he should be sent instructions explaining how to execute the will. The solicitor should check the will after execution to satisfy himself that it has been validly executed and that none of the beneficiaries (or the spouse or civil partner of a beneficiary) has acted as a witness.

In *Ross v Caunters*, a solicitor was found to be negligent in circumstances where he had failed to warn the testator that a spouse of the beneficiary should not witness the will, had failed to observe that one of the witnesses was the spouse of a beneficiary and had failed to check whether the will was properly executed.

The effect of a beneficiary (or their spouse or civil partner) witnessing a will is dealt with later in this Chapter.

7 Accepting gifts from clients

Where a client proposes to make a gift on death (or a lifetime gift) to, or for the benefit of, the solicitor, any principal, owner or employee of the solicitor's firm or a family member of any of the aforementioned people, and the gift is of a significant amount, either in itself or having regard to the size of the client's estate and the reasonable expectations of the prospective beneficiaries, **Rule 3.04** of the **Solicitors' Code of Conduct 2007** requires a solicitor to advise the client to take independent advice about the gift, unless the client is a member of the beneficiary's family.

If the client refuses, you must stop acting for the client in relation to the gift and it would be wise to stop acting for the client in connection with the preparation of their will.

It should be noted that a solicitor is not prevented by **Rule 3.04** from including a professional charging clause in the will if he or the partners (or anyone else within the firm) is appointed as executors and/or trustees of the will.

8 Capacity

In order to make a valid will, the testator must satisfy the age requirement and testamentary capacity requirements.

8.1 Age

The testator must not have been under the age of 18 at the date of the execution of the will (unless he was able to make a 'privileged will' as a soldier on actual military service or a seaman at sea, which is outside the scope of this Study Manual), otherwise the will will not be valid.

8.2 Testamentary capacity

8.2.1 The basic rule

The basic rule is that the testator must have the required testamentary capacity when he executes the will, otherwise the will will not be valid.

Before the **Mental Capacity Act 2005** ('MCA 2005') came into force on 1 October 2007, the test for testamentary capacity was solely a common law test set out in the case of *Banks v Goodfellow (1870).*

Banks v Goodfellow defined testamentary capacity as 'soundness of mind, memory and understanding'. This means that the testator must have understood three things, namely the:

- Nature of the act of making a will and its effect
- Extent of his property (although he does not need to be able to recall every item)
- Moral claims to which he ought to give effect (even if he decides to ignore such claims and leave his property to other beneficiaries)

Insanity or insane or irrational delusions do not automatically mean that a testator lacks capacity. Delusions are only material if they affect the disposition of property in the will.

8.2.2 The rule in *Parker v Felgate (1883)*

Generally, testamentary capacity must have existed at the date of execution. Under the rule in *Parker v Felgate*, a will might be valid even though the testator had lost capacity by the time the will was executed provided:

- The testator had the requisite capacity at the date he instructed a solicitor to prepare a will
- The will was prepared in accordance with those instructions
- At the time of execution he was able to understand that he was signing a will for which he had given instructions and that he believed the will to be in accordance with those instructions

8.2.3 The Mental Capacity Act 2005

As noted above, MCA 2005 came into force on 1 October 2007. Its main aim is to provide a statutory framework for people who *lack capacity* to make decisions for themselves. The legal framework provided by MCA 2005 is supported by the Code of Practice. The Code of Practice provides guidance and information about how MCA 2005 works in practice.

MCA 2005 sets out a clear test for assessing lack of capacity. The definition of capacity in MCA 2005 is in line with existing common law tests (including *Banks v Goodfellow*) and it does not replace them. When cases come before the court on the above issues, judges can adopt the new definition if they think it is appropriate, however, it seems likely that practitioners will continue to adopt the *Banks v Goodfellow* test and that is the approach taken in this Study Manual.

However, the MCA 2005 test in effect adds a new layer to the *Banks v Goodfellow* test and the following points should be noted:

- There is no such thing as 'generally lacking capacity'; capacity is time-specific and decision-specific so the question will be whether the client has testamentary capacity to execute a particular will at a particular time. It is likely that the rule in *Parker v Pelgate* will still be applicable in certain circumstances.
- A lack of capacity cannot be established merely by reference to a person's age or appearance, or a condition of his, or an aspect of his behaviour, which might lead others to make unjustified assumptions about his capacity.
- A person must be assumed to have capacity unless it is established that they lack capacity (on the balance of probabilities).
- A person is not to be treated as incapable of making a will unless all practicable steps to help him to do so have been taken without success.
- A person is not to be treated as incapable merely because their instructions seem unwise.

8.2.4 Expert opinion

Although the test for testamentary capacity is a legal test, the Code of Practice reiterates the common law 'golden rule' (*Kenward v Adams (1975)*) that where a person's capacity to sign a will could later be challenged, an expert should be asked for their opinion. It is wise therefore, if there is doubt in relation to testamentary capacity (for example, if the testator has a history of mental illness, has been diagnosed with a mental illness or physical illness that could affect their mental ability or appears confused) to ask a medical practitioner to confirm that the client has testamentary capacity at the time he is making the will. In addition, if in doubt about capacity, the golden rule requires solicitors to discuss any earlier will with the client and the reasons for changing it and to take instructions from the testator without any prospective beneficiary being present and in the absence of anyone who may have influence over the testator.

8.2.5 Burden of proof

The propounder of the will (ie the person(s) seeking to prove it eg the executors) must normally prove the existence of the necessary testamentary capacity. However, if a duly executed will appears to be rational on its face, capacity is presumed. It is then up to those opposing the will to rebut this presumption by proof of incapacity at the time the will was made.

8.2.6 Statutory Wills

If it is established that a person lacks testamentary capacity, an application can be made to the Court of Protection for a statutory will to be made. The Court has power under MCA 2005 to make a statutory will on behalf of the incapable person. The Court will try to make a will which the person lacking capacity would have made if acting reasonably and on competent legal advice, had he enjoyed a brief lucid interval.

9 Intention; knowledge and approval

The testator must have both general and specific intention at the time he executes his will. This means that the testator must intend to make a will as opposed to any other type of document and that he must have the specific intention to make the will he is now executing, which means that he must know and approve its contents. If the testator does not have this intention the will is not valid.

The burden of proof generally lies on the propounder of the will, but in practice there is usually a presumption that a testator who had the necessary capacity and who properly executed the will did so with the necessary intention and knowledge and approval of its contents. It would be for those opposing the will to prove that the testator lacked intention.

There is no presumption of knowledge and approval where the testator is blind or illiterate or the will is signed by someone other than the testator on his behalf (see paragraph 10 below). In such cases, affidavit evidence of knowledge and approval will be required on death when an application is made to the Probate Registry for the grant of representation (see Chapter 25). However, in these cases a presumption can be raised if the will is 'read over' in the presence of the testator and witnesses and the testator indicates his approval of the contents. The attestation clause should be adjusted to indicate that this was done (see Chapter 21).

In addition, there is no presumption of knowledge and approval where there are suspicious circumstances. These arise where the will substantially benefits the person who prepared or drafted it (or a close relative of such person) or someone who took a hand in obtaining its execution. A solicitor should take appropriate practical steps to remove this suspicion, for example, discussing the matter fully with the testator alone, and making detailed file notes which can be produced should the will be challenged after death.

The solicitor should always explain to the client the meaning and effect of all the clauses in the will and check that it fully complies with the testator's wishes. It is preferable to ask the testator to read the will before he executes it.

10 Formalities of execution

S.9 WA 1837 provides that no will shall be valid unless:

- It is in writing, signed by the testator or by some other person in his presence and at his direction.
- It appears that the testator intended by his signature to give effect to the will.
- The signature is made or acknowledged by the testator in the presence of two or more witnesses present at the same time.
- Each witness either attests and signs the will (or acknowledges his signature) in the presence of the testator but not necessarily in the presence of any other witness.

10.1 In writing

A will can be handwritten, typed or printed.

10.2 Signed by the testator

A testators should preferably sign with his usual signature. However, any mark made by the testator intended to be his signature will be effective.

Another person (including a witness, although this is not ideal) can, if required, sign on behalf of the testator, provided that this is done in the presence and at the direction of a testator with

testamentary capacity. The person signing on behalf of the testator can sign in their own name or the name of the testator, although the former is preferable.

10.3 Intention

The testator must intend to give effect to the will. There is no requirement for the signature to be at the end of the will, but this is advisable, otherwise the intention of the testator may have to be established by an affidavit of due execution (from the attesting witnesses or others present at the execution) where this cannot be presumed from the face of the will, eg if the signature appears in an unusual position. The affidavit must prove that the testator intended to execute the whole will including that part of it following the signature.

10.4 Witnesses

The most appropriate signing procedure is as follows:

- The testator signs the will in the presence of two witnesses, who should watch him sign (and date – see Chapter 21) the will.
- The witnesses then each sign whilst the testator watches.
- All three should remain together and alert throughout the entire execution procedure.

The witnesses must be both mentally and physically 'present' and not therefore drunk, mentally incapable or asleep! A blind person cannot be a witness because he cannot be physically 'present' (ie have the opportunity of seeing the signature).

Under **s.15 WA 1837**, a gift to a beneficiary fails if the beneficiary (or his/her spouse or civil partner) witnesses the will. The attestation of the will and therefore the will remains valid; it is the gift to the beneficiary which fails. The critical time is the date of execution of the will, so that if a witness marries or forms a civil partnership with one of the beneficiaries after that date, the gift is not affected. The gift is saved (ignoring the attestation by the witness or his or her spouse or civil partner) where there are at least two other non-beneficiary witnesses.

10.5 Attestation clause

A well-drafted attestation clause (whilst not required by s.9 WA 1837) recites that the will was executed in accordance with the requirements of s.9 WA 1837 and raises a presumption of proper (due) execution. It can also be used, suitably amended, to raise a presumption of knowledge and approval in the case of a blind or illiterate testator or if the testator is not signing personally. Attestation clauses are considered in more detail in Chapter 21.

11 Revocation

A will remains revocable during the testator's lifetime. Even if the testator has contracted not to revoke his will he may still do so, though his estate may be liable for his breach of contract; this is not considered further in this Study Manual.

A will may be revoked in the following ways:

- By marriage or the formation of a civil partnership
- By implied revocation
- By express revocation
- By destruction

11.1 Marriage or civil partnership

Generally, the marriage or formation of a civil partnership of the testator automatically revokes his will. The exception to this is where it appears from the will that, at the time it was made, the testator expected to be married or enter into a civil partnership to/with a particular person and he intended that the will should not thereby be revoked by that marriage/civil partnership. This is considered in more detail in Chapter 21.

It should be noted that divorce or the dissolution of a civil partnership does not revoke a will. The effect of divorce or the dissolution of a civil partnership is considered in more detail in Chapter 22.

11.2 Implied revocation

Where a new will is executed and it does not include an express revocation clause (see below) the new will revokes any earlier will or codicil to the extent that it is inconsistent with or merely repetitive of the provisions in the earlier will. This 'implied' revocation raises problems of inconsistency and ambiguity and so it is good drafting practice always to include an express revocation clause in the will.

11.3 Express revocation

If a new will is made and it includes an express revocation clause, this will revoke all earlier wills and codicils. This is considered in more detail in Chapter 21.

11.4 Revocation by destruction

The whole or any part of the will or codicil is revoked by burning, tearing or otherwise destroying the will/codicil by the testator, or by some person in his presence and by his direction, with the intention of revoking the will/codicil.

Some actual burning, tearing or destroying is necessary; merely writing across the will words such as 'revoked' or 'cancelled' is not sufficient.

Destruction by someone other than the testator carried out not in his presence or without his direction is not effective to revoke and cannot be later ratified by the testator.

Example

Jack telephones his solicitor and instructs his solicitor to destroy his will and the solicitor confirms that this has been done. There is no valid revocation of the will. If Jack dies, there could, however, be problems of proof because the will is no longer in existence.

The testator must intend to revoke the will at the time of the destruction. It follows that a will cannot be revoked by accidental destruction, nor where it is destroyed under the mistaken belief that is invalid or has already been revoked. Again, there could be problems of proof because the will is no longer in existence. The level of mental capacity to revoke a will is the same as for making a will.

A will last known to be in the testator's possession but which cannot be found at the date of his death is presumed to have been destroyed by the testator with the intention of revoking it. This presumption may be rebutted by evidence to the contrary and the contents proved by means of a copy or draft.

12 Basic will structure

Although the content of a will may vary from case to case, it will usually follow the following pattern:

- Commencement and date
- Revocation clause
- Appointment of executors (and trustees)
- Appointment of guardian(s) (where appropriate)
- Non residuary gifts (if any) (eg specific and pecuniary gifts)
- Residuary gift
- Administrative powers
- Attestation clause

It may also include wishes with regard to the disposal of the body and, if so, it is preferable to include these near the beginning of the will so that they are not missed.

Examples

'I wish my body to be cremated.'

'I wish my body to be buried at Southern Cemetery, Crouch End, London'

If the wishes are lengthy or detailed, it may be preferable to include them in a side letter of wishes (which is not a testamentary document, but rather a non-binding expression of wishes) to be stored with the will; in this way they can be updated without changing the will. See Chapter 21 for more detail.

13 Alterations

An alteration made before the will was executed is valid.

An alteration made after the will was executed is not valid unless it has been executed in the same manner as is required for a will (attested). In practice, it is sufficient if the testator and witnesses place their initials in the margin along side the alteration.

If the alteration is unattested, it may be that it was made before the will was executed and is therefore valid. However, there is a rebuttable presumption that an unattested alteration was made *after* the execution of the will (ie the presumption is that the alteration is invalid). This presumption may be rebutted by intrinsic evidence (ie from the will itself) or by extrinsic evidence (eg from the attesting witnesses or others present at the execution of the will). In practice, therefore, any alteration to a will should be initialled by the testator and the witnesses. Alterations should be confined to the correction of minor errors.

If the alteration is invalid (or presumed invalid and this presumption cannot be rebutted) the effect is as follows:

- Where the original wording is 'apparent' (ie decipherable by natural means) the original wording is admitted to probate and the beneficiary receives the original amount. For this purpose 'natural means' includes, *inter alia*, holding the will up to a light, the use of a magnifying glass, but does not include extrinsic methods, eg chemicals or infra-red photography.

- Where the wording is not apparent, that it has been obliterated, the basic rule is that the will is admitted to probate with a blank space and the beneficiary receives nothing.

14 Incorporation

A document which has not been executed in accordance with s.9 WA 1837 cannot be admitted to probate unless it can be included under the doctrine of incorporation by reference, which requires the following three conditions to be satisfied:

- The document must be clearly identified by the will
- The document must already exist at the date of execution of the will
- The document must be referred to in the will as pre-existing the will

Therefore a reference to 'the persons set out in a memorandum which I shall prepare and keep with my will' does not validly incorporate the memorandum as the words refer to preparation of it in the future.

Example

'I give the sum of £30,000 to be divided equally between the persons set out in a note which I shall prepare and keep with my will.' The gift would fail.

It is safer to include all the testator's dispositions of property expressly in the will. Many dangers arise, including the fact that the document referred to may be lost, or the testator may subsequently wish to effect changes simply by substituting a new document. If the testator insists on using incorporation then great care must be taken to incorporate the correct document and avoid ambiguity.

It is common to give personal chattels to someone (eg a trusted friend or the executors) and express the wish (without imposing any binding obligation, as this could inadvertently create a trust which would need to be administered after death and may have tax consequences) that they distribute the chattels in accordance with any wishes which the testator may make known to them before their death. They may then prepare a document (a letter of wishes) setting out their wishes, the original of which should be kept with their will.

Provided the personal chattels have been given to the chosen trusted beneficiary outright, the doctrine of incorporation is not relevant.

Example

'I give my personal chattels as defined by s.55(1)(x) Administration of Estates Act 1925 to my executors and express the wish but without imposing any binding obligation on them that they shall follow my wishes which I make known to them with regard to the distribution of my personal chattels'

Summary

- A will does not take effect until death and can be revoked in a number of ways at any time before death.
- A codicil is a supplementary testamentary instrument which is read together with the will and which must be executed in the same manner as a will.
- A person may die testate, intestate or partially intestate.
- There are many advantages to making a will, rather than dying intestate.
- A person can give by will those assets which are capable of passing by will; some assets have their own succession rules.
- A solicitor has various duties in connection with the preparation of wills.
- Care should be taken if the testator wishes to leave the solicitor a gift in his will.
- The test for testamentary capacity was established in the case of *Banks v Goodfellow (1870);* MCA 2005 has had an impact on this test.
- A testator must have general and specific intention to make a will for the will to be valid.
- Certain formalities for execution must be observed.
- An alteration to a will should be initialled by the testator and the witnesses.
- Unexecuted documents cannot be admitted to probate unless they are properly incorporated by reference.

Self-test questions

1. If a person has made a will in which they give all their jewellery to a named beneficiary, can they give that jewellery to someone else during their lifetime?
2. What is a codicil?
3. If a person dies having made a valid will, do the Intestacy Rules apply?
4. Which assets pass under their own rules of succession, regardless of the terms of a will and/or the Intestacy Rules?
5. Which of the following is not a personal chattel as defined by s.55 AEA 1925?

   (a) A necklace
   (b) A car
   (c) Cash
6. When is it appropriate to draft a will solely based on instructions from someone other than the testator?
7. Which case established the common law test for testamentary capacity?
8. In which of the following situations would you formally assess a person's testamentary capacity?

   (a) When they are old
   (b) When they are excluding their children from benefit
   (c) When they have been diagnosed with dementia
9. Can a beneficiary witness a will?
10. You are making a will for a testator who is physically disabled and unable to sign or mark a will. How would you arrange for the will to be executed?
11. Your client rings you just before he is about to execute his will. He tells you that he wants to change the amount of one of the legacies. There is no time to send him an amended will as he is going on holiday. How can you make sure that any manuscript amendment made by him is not invalid?
12. Another client rings you from the airport and asks you to immediately tear up his will as he no longer wishes to leave everything to his brother. Is the will revoked if you do so?

Answers to self-test questions

1 Yes; the legacy is likely to fail due to the doctrine of ademption.

2 A codicil is a testamentary instrument, which supplements the terms of an existing will. It must be executed in the same way as a will if it is to be valid.

3 It depends whether the will, as drafted and in the circumstances, effectively disposes of all the testator's assets which can be disposed of by will; if not, then the Intestacy Rules will apply in relation to the undisposed assets: there is a partial intestacy.

4 Property held as beneficial joint tenants; life insurance policies written in trust and death in service payments which have been nominated.

5 (c)

6 Never.

7 *Banks v Goodfellow (1870)*

8 (c)

9 Yes, although the gift to them will fail unless there are two other witnesses: s15 WA 1837.

10 The will can be signed by another person in the presence and at the direction of the testator. However, the presumption of knowledge and approval will not apply. The attestation clause should be amended to raise a presumption of knowledge and approval.

11 It is preferable for him to make the alteration before the execution of the will. The simplest way to ensure the alteration is presumed valid is for your client and his witnesses to initial the alteration.

12 No, as you are not tearing it up in his presence. If someone other than the testator tears up a will it must be in the testator's presence and at his direction for the will to be revoked.

21

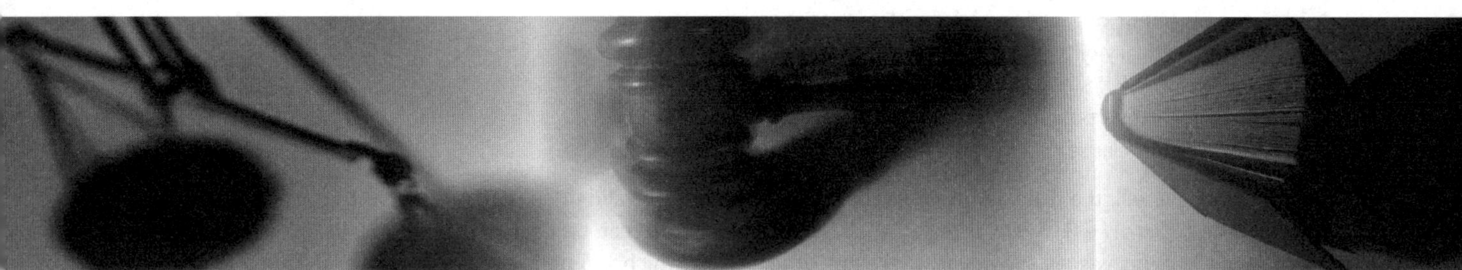

Will drafting

Topic List

Chapter overview

This Chapter will:

- Describe a solicitor's objectives in drafting a will
- Explain the information that should be obtained from the client
- Outline the format of a typical will
- Consider the non-beneficial provisions of a typical will, including the introductory words, provisions regarding the disposal of the body, the express revocation clause, the appointment of executors and trustees, the appointment of guardians, some administrative provisions which are often included in wills and the attestation clause

1 Introduction

A solicitor must draft a will reflecting the client's instructions.

In practice, a solicitor will normally use and adapt precedents to meet the needs of a particular client's circumstances.

We have already seen that, although the content of a will may vary from client to client, all wills usually follow the following pattern:

- Commencement and date
- Revocation clause
- Appointment of executors (and trustees)
- Appointment of guardian(s) (where appropriate)
- Non residuary gifts (if any) (eg specific and pecuniary gifts)
- Residuary gift
- Administrative powers
- Attestation clause

When drafting a will, the main aim of the solicitor is to produce a valid document which, on the death of the testator, effectively disposes of all his property which can be disposed of by will, in accordance with his wishes. However, there are other issues which will need to be dealt with, for example the appointment of executors and trustees.

The solicitor must identify and anticipate all foreseeable events and problems which might arise after the will has been executed and ensure that the will is clear as to what should happen in the event of these problems arising. This requires the solicitor to be both precise, yet flexible, so that future changes in family and property circumstances are catered for.

A will should be reviewed regularly, particularly when the testator's circumstances change or there is a change in the law. Examples of a change of circumstances include:

- Entering into a marriage or civil partnership (which would generally revoke an existing will)
- Divorce
- The birth of children and/or grandchildren
- A change in financial circumstances

Note: in the example clauses which follow, the use of capital letter in some clauses in purely a matter of style. It is a technique which is commonly adopted to highlight important parts of the will, but is not strictly necessary.

2 Taking instructions

In addition to the matters considered in the previous Chapter, a solicitor must obtain accurate details of the testator's property, family, testamentary wishes and intended beneficiaries. The solicitor's role goes further than simply recording what the client tells him. He should also draw the testator's attention to legal provisions of which the client may be unaware and explain the succession and tax consequences of the client's suggestions and possibly suggest alternatives.

In particular, the solicitor should obtain information regarding:

- Whether the client has made any previous wills.
- The client's family.
- The client's property.
- The client's instructions for the will.

2.1 Previous wills

It is important to ascertain whether the client has made a previous will (and codicils).

If there is a previous will, it should be expressly revoked in the new will. In any event, it is good drafting practice to always include an express revocation clause, even if the solicitor believes this to be the client's first will. This will prevent difficulties if it subsequently transpires that there is in fact an earlier will.

It is sensible to ask see a copy of the existing will and, if the terms of the will are significantly different to terms of the proposed new will, this should be discussed with the client and reasons for the changes recorded, particularly if there are any doubts about the testator's capacity or a perceived risk of undue influence.

2.2 Family details

Full details of the testator's family and dependants and personal circumstances (eg a forthcoming marriage or civil partnership) should be obtained.

You should bring to the attention of the testator IPFDA 1975, particularly if the testator is omitting from benefit a member of the family or a dependant who might expect to be included in the will.

If the testator is excluding a person from benefitting who might expect to be included in the will then they may wish to prepare a document setting out the testator's reasons for the lack of provision which should be kept with the will. Such a document will usually be admissible in any subsequent claim under IPFDA 1975, although is unlikely to carry much weight in court proceedings.

2.3 Assets

The size and nature of the testator's estate should be established, including its approximate value, the different types of assets within it and how those assets are owned (eg in the testator's sole name or jointly owned). This will enable the solicitor to give advice on the succession to property and also give inheritance tax advice . It may also be appropriate to ask the client if any lifetime gifts have been made as this could impact on the inheritance tax advice (see Chapter 24).

2.4 Will instructions

The solicitor will need to take full details of the client's instructions with regard to the will.

Remember that the usual will structure is as follows:

- **Commencement and date**
- **Revocation clause**
- **Appointment of executors (and trustees)**
- **Appointment of guardian(s) (where appropriate)**
- Non residuary gifts (if any) (eg specific and pecuniary gifts)
- Residuary gift
- **Administrative powers**
- **Attestation clause**

Non-residuary gifts and gifts of residue are dealt with in the next chapter. The non-dispositive provisions are dealt with in this chapter.

3 Commencement and date

3.1 General

The commencement clause should accurately identify the testator by including his full name and address.

Although a will does not need to be dated to be valid, it should always be dated to prevent problems if more than one will is found at the testator's death. The date can be included here or at the end of the will. Therefore a draft will should always have a blank space for the date on which the will is to be executed.

Example

'THIS IS THE LAST WILL of me JACOB OSBORNE of 12 Mountford Street, Otley, West Yorkshire LS11 1TG which I make this …….. day of …………… 2009'

3.2 Use of another name

If the testator uses a name, other than his real name, or owns property in a different name, although not necessary, it is preferable to refer to this in the will. This simplifies matters when applying for the grant of representation after the testator dies.

Example

Kathryn Jones instructs you to make a will for her. She has recently married Keith Jones and has taken his surname. Her maiden name was Davis. She has no middle name. She still has assets in her maiden name. She also tells you that she has a building society account in the name of Kate Davis. The commencement clause of her will could be drafted as follows:

'THIS IS THE WILL of me KATHRYN JONES (formerly known as KATHRYN DAVIS and also known as KATE DAVIS) of ………………………………………dated ………………………………… 2009'

3.3 Occupation or description

The testator's occupation or description is sometimes included in the will (for example 'Doctor' or 'Retired Professor'). This is old-fashioned and unnecessary, but can be included if the client so wishes.

3.4 Evidence of intention

One of the requirements for a valid will is that the testator had the general intention to make a will. Referring to the will as the testator's 'will' or 'last will' helps show that the testator had the general intention to make a will. However, you should note that a reference to the will as the 'last will' or the 'last will and testament' does not automatically revoke any earlier will or codicil(s) and therefore an express revocation clause should always be included.

3.5 Forthcoming marriage/civil partnership

The basic rule is that marriage or the formation of a civil partnership automatically revokes an existing will. This does not apply if the testator makes the will in anticipation of a forthcoming marriage or civil partnership with a particular person.

Under **s.18(3) WA 1837**, where it appears from a will that, at the time it was made, the testator expected to be married or form a civil partnership with a particular person and that he intended that the will should not thereby be revoked by the marriage/civil partnership, the will shall not be revoked by the subsequent marriage/civil partnership.

It should be noted, however, that a general intention to marry or form a civil partnership with an unidentified person is not sufficient; therefore it is advisable only to include such a clause if a date has been set for the wedding/registration of civil partnership.

Examples

'I make this Will in expectation of my marriage to Jennifer Almeida on ……….. and I intend that this Will shall not be revoked by that marriage'

'I make this Will in expectation of my formation of a civil partnership with Arnold Peters on …………….. and I intend that this Will shall not be revoked by that civil partnership'

This provision can be included as a separate clause (as above) or incorporated into the introductory words.

Example

'I Jennifer Goodwin of 12 Briony Grove Cheltenham CH1 1JF make this my last will dated ………… 2009 in expectation of my marriage to Peter Fields on ………….. and I intend that this will shall not be revoked by that marriage'

If a person marries/forms a civil partnership with someone else, that marriage/civil partnership will revoke the will.

If the testator is in a relationship, but an expectation of marriage/civil partnership clause is not appropriate because there are no immediate plans to get married or form a civil partnership, then it should be brought to the attention of the testator that if they do marry or form a civil partnership in the future, the will will be revoked and a new will should be made. Any such advice should be confirmed in writing.

It should be noted that divorce or the dissolution of a civil partnership does not revoke a Will (see Chapter 22 for its effect).

4 Express revocation clause

It is advisable to include an express revocation clause in the will. If omitted, implied revocation may mean that parts of an earlier will survive.

The revocation clause can either form part of the opening words or can be included as a separate clause.

Examples

'I REVOKE all former wills and codicils'

'I REVOKE all former wills'. This would revoke wills <u>and</u> codicils.

'I REVOKE all former testamentary dispositions'. This would also revoke all earlier wills and codicils.

'THIS IS THE LAST WILL of me JACOB OSBORNE of .... which I make this .... day of .... 2009 by which I revoke all former wills and codicils'

---

5 Disposal of the body

If the client has any particular wishes regarding the disposal of his body, these can be included in the will. Such wishes are not legally binding on the executors and are usually expressed as wishes or requests.

Examples

'I request that my body shall be cremated'
'I request that my body shall be cremated and my ashes scattered in the River Mersey'
'I wish my body to be buried at Highfield Cemetery in Kendal'

If the wishes or requests are detailed or likely to change, it may be preferable to include them in a side letter of wishes, to be stored with the will; they can then be updated at any time without the need to change the will.

6 Appointment of executors and trustees

6.1 General

Executors are the people appointed by will to administer and wind up a person's estate after his death. If executors are not appointed, the testator will have no control over who is entitled to administer his estate and the people entitled are set out in the **Non-Contentious Probate Rules 1987** ('NCPR 1987') (see Chapter 25).

Trustees will be required to administer any trust which will come into effect when the administration of the estate is complete.

A trust will arise in the following situations:

- If a trust is expressly created, for example a life interest trust or a discretionary trust (see Chapter 22).
- If a gift is made contingent (conditional) on a beneficiary attaining a certain age and on the death of the testator the beneficiary has not yet attained that age (see Chapter 22).
- If a gift is to a minor (vested) and the minor is under the age of 18 when the testator dies (see Chapter 22).

In these situations, trustees should be appointed in addition to executors.

The same people are usually appointed as executors and trustees.

If the estate is straightforward one executor may be sufficient.

Although any number of executors may be appointed, only four may take out the grant.

It is worth considering the appointment of two primary executors so that if one dies (or cannot act for any reason or renounces probate) there is still one who can act in the administration. It may also be worth considering the appointment of substitute executors.

If trustees are also being appointed, it is advisable to appoint two executors/trustees since two trustees are required to give a good receipt for the proceeds of the sale of land.

Examples

'I APPOINT my wife .... of .... to be the sole executor of my will'

I APPOINT my son Marcus Smith of .... and my daughter Gemma Adams of .... to be the executors of my will but if either or both of them predecease me renounce probate or do not act for any reason I appoint Harvey Hargreaves of .... as executor of my will'

'I APPOINT Brian Gold and Susanna Gold both of .... as the executors and trustees of my will'

'I APPOINT my wife AVRIL OSBORNE of ....and my children FINBAR OSBORNE of .... and ALEX OSBORNE of .... (together called 'my Executors') to be the executors and trustees of my Will'

6.2 Choice of executor/trustee

A testator can appoint anyone to be an executor or trustee. However, as minors and mentally incapable persons cannot take out a grant, it would be advisable not to appoint them.

The relative merits of possible appointees must be considered. The choice will be influenced by a number of factors including, among other things:

- The availability and willingness to act of suitable persons, bearing in mind the size and nature of the estate.
- The possibility of a conflict of interest arising.
- Cost.
- Age and the possibility of the appointees predeceasing the testator. (This may be overcome by appointing substitutional appointees or the partners in a firm of solicitors as at the date of the testator's death.)

Two of the most common categories of appointee are:

- Members of the family or friends
- Professional executors/trustees, eg solicitors

If the client wishes to appoint professionals as executors/trustees they can either choose named individual professionals or appoint the firm.

If named individual professionals are chosen then the possibility of the appointment failing should be considered, as discussed above.

To prevent this, the firm could be appointed. The appointment of a firm is, in fact, the appointment of the partners at the date the will is made. It is therefore preferable to appoint the partners at the date of death, and provision should also be made for change of name or status of the firm.

It is common for the testator to request that only two of the partners take out the grant of probate, but, if there is no such request, the partners in the firm will decide who is going to take out the grant and will usually decide that an application should be made by two of them, with power reserved to the others (see Chapter 25).

Examples

'I APPOINT the partners at the date of my death in the firm of ………………….. of ………………….. or in the firm or practice which at my death carries on its practice to be the executors of my will'

' I APPOINT my wife………………….. of ………………….. and the partners at the date of my death in the firm of ………………….. of ………………….. or the firm which at that date has succeeded to and carries on its practice to be the executors and trustees of this will and I express the wish that one and only one of those partners (or if the appointment of my said wife fails for any reason to take effect then two and only two of them) shall prove the will'

6.3 Charging clause

Where professionals are appointed, an express charging clause is usually included and should be brought specifically to the attention of the testator. Without such a clause, the professional executor may be reluctant to act in the administration of the estate and may renounce probate.

If there is no charging clause then, under the **Trustee Act 2000** ('TA 2000'), an executor or trustee acting in a professional capacity is entitled to receive 'reasonable' remuneration for his services. However, it is preferable to include an express charging clause in order to overcome the constraints of TA 2000. An express charging clause will usually be drafted to allow a professional executor/trustee to charge for the work done as if he were instructed by the executors to carry out the work required.

7 Appointment of guardians

The appointment of a guardian or guardians should be considered where the testator has minor children.

The appointment is automatically conditional upon the minor's surviving parent failing to survive, provided that surviving parent has parental responsibility for the minor, which we will assume is the case. It should be noted that the court could override the appointment in the event of a dispute.

The appointee should always be consulted to ensure willingness to act as guardian.

Consideration should also be given to the provision of finance for the guardians (eg extending trustees' powers to advance capital to them for the maintenance of the minors.).

Example

'IF MY WIFE dies before me I APPOINT NATHANIEL HORTON and MATILDA HORTON both of …………………….. or the survivor of them to be the guardians or guardian as the case may be of such of my children who are under 18 at the date of my death'

8 Administrative provisions and powers

Personal representatives ('PRs') (eg executors) and trustees have statutory powers which enable them to carry out the administration of the estate and run any trusts arising under the will.

However, consideration should be given to the desirability of excluding, amending or extending some of the various powers conferred by the general law on PRs and trustees. Some of the more common provisions are discussed below.

8.1 Inclusion of an infant receipt clause

If the testator has made an absolute (vested) gift to a beneficiary, whether it is a non-residuary gift or a residuary gift and that beneficiary is under the age of 18 when the testator dies, the beneficiary cannot, under the general law, give a good receipt for capital money until he is 18 (unless he is married or in a civil partnership). However, the parents or guardian(s) have the right to receive the assets and may demand that the assets are paid to them; otherwise the PRs will have to hold the assets until the minor reaches the age of 18.

It is good practice in such situations to include an infant receipt clause in the will so that the PRs have express power to accept a receipt from the parents or guardian(s) or minor if aged 16 or over.

Example

'ANY vested gift made by this will or any codicil to it to someone who is a minor may be paid or delivered by my executors to anyone who appears to them to be a parent or guardian of the minor or to the minor himself if of the age of 16 and that person's receipt shall be a good discharge to them for the gift'

There may be circumstances where the testator may not be happy to allow the parent or guardian to receive the gift and so he may wish to consider making the gift contingent of the minor attaining the age of 18 (or indeed a later age).

8.2 Inclusion of a professional charging clause

As discussed above, where professionals are appointed, a charging clause should also be included to overcome the limitations of TA 2000.

8.3 Inclusion of a receipt clause for gifts to charities or other organisations

If the testator is making a gift to a charity or another organisation, a receipt clause should be included.

Example

'THE RECEIPT of anyone purporting to be the treasurer or other proper officer of any charitable or other body to which any gift is made by this will or any codicil to it shall be a good discharge to my executors for the gift'

8.4 Extension of s.41 AEA 1925

S.41 AEA 1925 gives the PRs power to appropriate (transfer) any part of the estate in or towards satisfaction of an interest in the estate provided that this does not prejudice any specific beneficiary. The consent of the beneficiary to whom the appropriation is being made must be obtained. This provision is often extended so that the PRs do not have to seek consent, although it is nevertheless good practice to discuss this with the beneficiary concerned.

Example

'THE POWERS given to personal representatives by section 41 of the Administration of Estates Act 1925 may be exercised by my executors without obtaining any of the consents required by that section and even though one or more of them may be beneficially interested'

Note: there is no reason why an executor/trustee cannot be a beneficiary under a will.

8.5 Extension of ss.31- 32 Trustee Act 1925 ('TA 1925')

In summary, by **s.31 TA 1925** where trustees are holding property on trust for an infant beneficiary, the trustees have power to apply income from that trust property for the maintenance, education or benefit of the infant, subject to certain limitations.

By **s.32 TA 1925**, trustees (and PRs) have power to advance capital for the benefit of a beneficiary of any age, provided he has an interest in the capital of the trust fund, whether it be vested or contingent, subject to certain limitations.

It is common to extend the powers of the trustees so that they can apply income and advance capital from the trust property to the beneficiary at their absolute discretion, with no limitations. If the beneficiary is under the age of 18, then an infant receipt clause (see paragraph 8.1 above) should also be included.

9 Attestation clause

An attestation clause is not required by s.9 WA 1837, but the inclusion of a well drafted attestation clause (essentially reciting the s.9 procedure) will raise a presumption of proper execution (due execution), in the absence of evidence to the contrary.

Example clauses

'Signed by the above named testator in our joint presence as witnesses and then by us in his'

'Signed by the testator John Smith in our joint presence and then by us in the presence of the testator'

'Signed by the testator John Smith in our joint presence and then by us in the presence of each other and the testator'

The usual clause should be amended where the testator is blind or illiterate or where the will is signed by someone other than the testator (to show that the will was read over to the testator who indicated his knowledge and approval of it) to reflect the procedure that was followed.

It is preferable to supervise the execution of the will, but if the will is to be sent to the client for execution, a covering letter should explain clearly the requirements of s.9 WA 1837 (and the effect of s.15 WA 1837).

If the client is not informed of the correct procedure or the vitiating effect of s.15, this may give rise to an action for professional negligence by a beneficiary who is prejudiced as a result.

If the will is sent to the client for signing, the solicitor should check that it has been executed correctly and that s.15 WA 1837 will not be applicable.

Summary

- A will should be a clear, comprehensive and unambiguous document which accurately reflects the testator's wishes.
- The solicitor should ascertain whether the client has an existing will and discuss any changes with him.
- Full details of the testator's relatives and dependants should be obtained and advice in relation to IPFDA 1975 given if appropriate.
- Full details of the testator's property (including details of lifetime gifts) should be obtained so that advice can be given in relation to succession and inheritance tax.
- The testator should be accurately identified in the will.
- The will should be dated.
- Marriage or the formation of a civil partnership revokes a will unless it is made in expectation of that marriage or civil partnership.
- An express revocation clause should be included.
- The client may wish to include requests with regard to the disposal of his body.
- Executors and trustees (often the same people) should be chosen carefully and their powers extended if appropriate.
- Consideration should be given as to whether guardians should be appointed.
- A properly drafted attestation clause should be included to raise a presumption of due execution.

Self-test questions

1. List the categories of person entitled to claim against a deceased's estate for reasonable financial provision.
2. Does a will have to be dated to be valid?
3. Must a will refer to itself as being a 'will' in order to be valid?
4. Is a will revoked on divorce?
5. If Pria makes a will in expectation of her marriage to Sam and then marries Simon, is the will revoked?
6. How many executors can be appointed in a will?
7. If two executors are appointed and one of them predeceases the testator, can the surviving executor act in the administration of the estate?
8. Can professional executors/trustees charge for the work they do?
9. When would it be appropriate to extend ss.31 and 32 of TA 1925?
10. Why is it sensible to include an attestation clause in the will?

Answers to self-test questions

1 See Chapter 26. Note that these people are not automatically entitled to benefit, but are eligible to make a claim against the estate and will be successful only if the can prove that reasonable financial provision has not been made for them.

2 No. s.9 WA 1837 does not state that a will has to be dated to be valid, but it is sensible to date a will to prevent difficulties in the event that there is more than one will in existence at the testator's death.

3 No, but it is preferable for it to do so as this helps show that the testator had the general intention to make a will.

4 No, but the ex-spouse is treated as pre-deceasing the testator and their appointment as executor/trustee will fail, as will any gift to them in the will (see Chapter 22).

5 Yes.

6 Any number of executors can be appointed, but as only four can take out the grant it is usual to limit it to a maximum of four, although two is more common, unless the appointment is of the partners in a firm.

7 Yes.

8 Yes, under TA 2000 they can, but there are limitations, which is why it is sensible to include an express charging clause in the will when professionals are appointed.

9 When minor children will be entitled under the will or where there are contingent interests under the will.

10 To raise a presumption of due execution.

22

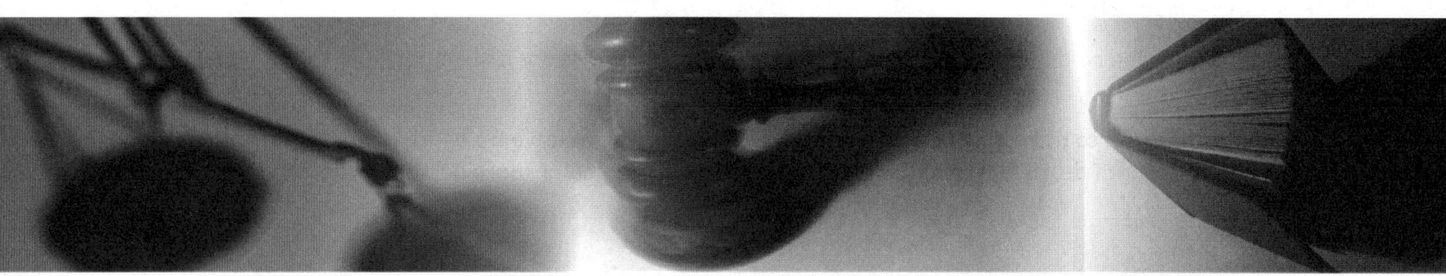

Gifts in wills

Topic List

Chapter overview

This Chapter will:

- Explain the difference between non-residuary and residuary gifts
- Explain the difference between vested and contingent gifts
- Consider various rules in relation to children and minors
- Explain why it is important to identify the beneficiary or beneficiaries of a will
- Consider the different types of gifts in wills, drafting issues and reasons why gifts in wills fail
- Consider the use of express trusts in wills
- Describe particular consideration in relation to gifts of property and gifts to charities and other organisations

1 General

We have already seen that, although the content of a will may vary from case to case, the structure will usually be as follows:

- Introductory words
- Revocation clause
- Appointment of executors (and trustees)
- Appointment of guardian(s) (where appropriate)
- **Non residuary gifts (if any) (eg specific and pecuniary gifts)**
- **Residuary gift**
- Administrative powers
- Attestation clause

The items shown in bold are sometimes known as the dispositive provisions or beneficial provisions.

A testator may wish to make a number of gifts by will or may prefer to leave his entire estate (after the payment of debts, funeral and testamentary expenses) to one or more persons.

1.1 Non-residuary gifts

These are gifts of particular specified amounts or assets.

Examples

' I give £10,000 to John Jones of ....'

' I give all my jewellery to Amanda Hurst of ....'

' I give £30,000 to such of my children alive at my death and if more than one in equal shares'

1.2 Residuary gifts

A gift of residue is a gift of the remainder of the estate, in other words all the property which has not already been given away. The gift of residue should be carefully drafted to avoid a partial intestacy.

Example

'I give the residue of my estate after the payment of debts funeral and testamentary expenses ('the residue') to my sister Mary Adams of .... but if she does not survive me or this gift fails for any other reason I give the residue to my cousin Austin Ramsbotham of ....'

---

2 Legacies and devises

Gifts in wills are often described as **legacies** or **devises.** The expression 'gift' is often used for both.

A **legacy** is a gift in a will of personalty (eg chattels, cash etc)

A **devise** is a gift of realty (eg land).

Non-residuary gifts can be classified as:

- Specific (legacy or devise)
- General (legacy)
- Demonstrative (legacy)
- Pecuniary (legacy)

Residuary gifts are classified as residuary legacies.

3 The payment of debts, funeral and testamentary expenses

The deceased may have outstanding debts at the date of his death, for example unpaid utility bills, credit card debts, bank loans, a mortgage, unpaid income tax or capital gains tax. There will also be expenses related to the administration of the estate, funeral costs and possibly inheritance tax payable. The expression 'testamentary expenses' includes inheritance tax and these liabilities are usually referred to as 'debts, funeral and testamentary expenses' .

If the will is silent on the payment of the debts, funeral and testamentary expenses the burden usually falls on residue, but it is common to make express provision in the gift of residue for payment of these expenses.

Example

'I give the residue of my estate after the payment of debts funeral and testamentary expenses to .... of...................'

In relation to non-residuary gifts, the beneficiary is not required to pay the inheritance tax attributable to that gift unless the will provides otherwise. If the testator wishes to alter this statutory position, he should make the gift 'subject to tax'.

Example

I give £10,000 to Alice Cooper of .... subject to tax'. Alice would bear the inheritance tax on the property which has been left to her.

However, it is common for non-residuary gifts to be made 'free of tax', effectively stating the statutory provision and for the gift of residue to be made subject to the payment of inheritance tax. Nevertheless, the testator's instructions should be taken on this point.

It should be noted that debts charged on a specific property are payable from that property. If a specific devise is made of a property which is subject to a mortgage, **s.35 AEA 1925** provides that the burden of the mortgage is borne by the property and the beneficiary would be liable to pay the mortgage debt. The testator's instructions should be taken as to where the burden of the mortgage is to fall and this should be expressly stated in the will. This is covered in more detail later in this Chapter.

4 Vested and contingent gifts

A testator might wish to make the gift in question, whether it is a non-residuary gift or a gift of residue, vested or contingent, depending on the circumstances.

4.1 Vested gifts

A gift is vested if, by the terms of the gift, the entitlement of the beneficiary depends *only* on them being alive at the testator's death.

Even if the beneficiary dies before obtaining possession of the gift, the benefit of the gift devolves as part of the **beneficiary's** estate (either by their will, or under the Intestacy Rules, or by a combination of the two if there is a partial intestacy).

Examples

'I give £10,000 to my son Michael James of ....'

'I give £10,000 to my son Michael James of .... vested'

'I give £10,000 to my son Michael James of .... outright'

'I give £10,000 to my son Michael James of .... absolutely'

'I give the residue of my estate after the payment of debts funeral and testamentary expenses to Jane Smith of ....'

'I give the residue of my estate after the payment of debts funeral and testamentary expenses to my wife .... of ....outright'

'I give the residue of my estate after the payment of debts funeral and testamentary expenses to such of my children who are alive at my death and if more than one in equal shares'

4.2 Contingent gifts

A contingent gift can, by the terms of the gift, only vest when some future condition is satisfied. Such a gift will not vest until that condition is satisfied. Typically, a gift will be made contingent on the beneficiary attaining a certain age.

If the beneficiary dies before attaining a vested interest, the gift fails and will not pass to the deceased beneficiary's estate. Instead, what will happen to that gift will be determined by the provisions of the testator's will.

Examples

'I give £10,000 to my son Michael James of ....if he attains the age of 25'

'I give £10,000 to my son Michael James of .... if he attains the age of 18'

'I give the residue of my estate after the payment of debts funeral and testamentary expenses to Jane Smith of .... if she attains the age of 21'

'I give the residue of my estate after the payment of debts funeral and testamentary expenses to such of my children who are alive at my death and attain the age of 25 and if more than one in equal shares'

5 Gifts to minors

If the testator has made a vested gift to a beneficiary, whether it is a non-residuary gift or residuary and that beneficiary is under the age of 18 when the testator dies, the beneficiary cannot, under the general law, give a good receipt for capital money until he is 18 (unless he is married or in a civil partnership). However, the parents or guardian(s) have the right to receive the assets and may demand that they are paid to them; otherwise the PRs will have to hold the assets until the minor reaches the age of 18.

It is good practice in such situations to include an infant receipt clause in the will so that the PRs have power to accept a receipt from the parent or guardian (or minor if aged 16 or over) (see Chapter 21).

There may be circumstances where the testator may not be happy to allow the parent or guardian to receive the gift and so he may wish to consider making the gift contingent of the minor attaining the age of 18 (or indeed a later age) (see above).

6 Rules relating to children

Unless the will provides otherwise, a gift to the child or children of the testator or of someone else includes adopted children, illegitimate children (those born outside of marriage/civil partnership) and children *en ventre sa mere* (conceived but not yet born).

Examples

Daniel dies leaving a valid will in which he gives 'the residue of my estate after the payment of debts funeral and testamentary expenses to such of my children alive at my death and if more than one in equal shares'. He dies survived by a wife (who is pregnant) and two daughters (one of whom was adopted). The residuary estate will be divided in three equal shares between the two daughters and the unborn child.

Arthur dies leaving a valid will in which he gives 'the residue of my estate after the payment of debts funeral and testamentary expenses to such of my grandchildren alive at my death and if more than one in equal shares'. He dies survived by his son, his son's girlfriend (who is pregnant) and his son's adopted daughter. The residuary estate will be divided in equal shares between the adopted daughter and the unborn child.

---

7 Identity of the beneficiary

The beneficiary should be clearly identifiable from the description in the will; otherwise the gift may fail for **uncertainty** or for the reasons described below.

7.1 Gifts to a single individual

The beneficiary should be identified by naming him and including his address.

Example

'I give £5,000 to Charles Brooks of 1 Pleasant Grove, Muswell Hill, London N11 7YH'.

A postcode, whilst probably not required in terms of identification, will assist the PRs in the administration of the estate.

'I give £5,000 to Charlie' will fail for uncertainty. Who is Charlie?

7.2 A gift to a person by description

In this case a will is construed at the date it is made unless there is contrary intention.

Example

'I give £50,000 to my sister's youngest son'. At the date of the will the testator's sister had two sons. This is construed as being a gift to the youngest son at the date the will is made. If that son predeceases the testator, the gift fails and does not pass to his sister's other son.

This result could have been avoided in either of the following ways:

'I give £50,000 to my sister's youngest son Thomas Oaks of ....'

'I give £50,000 to the son of my sister who is her youngest son at the date of my death'

7.3 Gifts to a class

The testator may wish to make a gift to a class of beneficiaries. See below.

8 Class gifts

8.1 Class closing rules

A class gift is a gift to a group of people satisfying a general description, for example 'my children', 'my sister's children', 'my grandchildren' etc.

The class closing rules need to be borne in mind. These rules apply whether the gift is non-residuary or residuary. The effect of the rules is to close the class as soon as there is one beneficiary entitled to immediate distribution. The effect of the rules will vary according to whether the gift is vested or contingent.

The need for these rules is illustrated by the following example.

Example

John dies leaving a valid will in which he gives 'the residue of my estate after the payment of debts funeral and testamentary expenses to my grandchildren in equal shares'. He dies survived by his son Jack and his son's daughter. Until Jack dies it is possible that the number of people fulfilling the description of John's 'grandchildren' will increase and the PRs of John's estate would have to wait until Jack's death before they could ascertain the members of the class.

The effect of these rules in relation to vested gifts and a contingent gifts is illustrated in the examples below.

8.1.1 Immediate class gifts

Example

Jill dies leaving a valid will in which she gives '£30,000 to be divided equally between the children of my friend Peter Parks of 1 The Mount, Macclesfield, Cheshire'. If there is a child of Peter alive at Jill's death, the class closes and the PRs distribute to the members of the class then in existence. If Peter has no children at Jill's death, the class closing rules do not apply and the class stays open until Peter dies.

8.1.2 Contingent class gifts

Example

Jill dies leaving a valid will in which she gives '£30,000 to be divided equally between the children of my friend Peter Parks of 1 The Mount, Macclesfield, Cheshire who reach the age of 21'. If there is a child of Peter alive at Jill's death who has reached the age of 21, the class closes and will include any child of Peter living at that date who reaches the age of 21. If a child of Peter dies without fulfilling the contingency, that child's 'share' is divided amongst the other member of the class who fulfil the contingency. If no child of Peter has reached the age of 21 at the date of Jill's death, the class remains open until a child reaches the age of 21 and will include any child living at that date who reaches the age of 21.

8.1.3 Drafting

It is far preferable to avoid these class closing rules by drafting the will clearly!

Example

'I give the sum of £50,000 to such of my grandchildren alive at my death and if more than one in equal shares'.

By defining the class of grandchildren as being those alive at the death of the testator, the class closing rules are avoided and the gift is shared between those grandchildren alive at the death of the testator.

8.2 Identity of the class

Care should be taken if a class gift is made so that the named class reflects the wishes of the testator.

Example

Harvey has instructed you to make a will for him. His brother, Michael, has three daughters and Harvey wants to make a non-residuary gift to Michael's children of £30,000, with the residue of his estate passing to Michael. Should the will be drafted so that this is a gift to his nieces *or nephews* and *nieces?* Take instructions and draft the will accordingly.

9 Nature of non-residuary gifts

Non-residuary gifts can be classified as:

- Specific
- General
- Demonstrative
- Pecuniary

9.1 Specific gifts

This is a gift of a particular item of property owned by the testator, distinguished from other property of the same kind owned by him, and usually described by words of ownership or possession.

Examples

'I give my engagement ring to Mary Jones of...............'

'I give all my shares in National Grid PLC to John Smith of...............'

'I give my house to Sam Peters of...............'

Specific gifts are subject to **ademption** - the gift will fail (adeem) if the property described does not form part of the testator's estate at his death.

9.2 General gifts

This is a gift of property not distinguished from property of a similar type.

Examples

'I give 2000 shares in National Grid plc to John Smith of...............'

This is a gift of any 2,000 shares in National Grid PLC.

General gifts do *not* adeem. In the above example, even if the testator possessed no shares in National Grid PLC at his death, the gift would not adeem. The fact that, at the time of making the will, the testator owned exactly 2,000 shares in the company, is not sufficient to turn it into a specific legacy.

In these circumstances the PRs would have to buy 2000 shares in National Grid PLC to give to John (unless they exercise their discretion to appropriate assets from the estate in John's favour pursuant to s.41 AEA 1925) (see Chapter 21).

9.3 Demonstrative legacies

This is a general legacy directed to be paid from a specific fund.

Example

'I give £1,000 to John Smith of .... payable out of my deposit account with Abbey'

Such legacies do not suffer ademption if the fund no longer exists and are payable from the estate like a general legacy.

Demonstrative legacies are uncommon and are best avoided (particularly due to the inherent difficulties if the specified fund exists, but is not large enough to satisfy the gift).

9.4 Pecuniary legacies

A pecuniary legacy is a gift of money and is usually general in character.

Example

'I give £1,000 to John Smith of...............'

However, a pecuniary legacy may be specific in nature.

Example

'I give the money under my bed to John Smith of...............'

A pecuniary legacy may also be demonstrative as has been seen.

Example

'I give £1,000 to John Smith of .... payable out of my deposit account with Abbey'

---

10 Residuary gifts

The gift of residue is a gift of all the testator's remaining assets and provision is normally made that all the debts of the estate, funeral and testamentary expenses are to be paid before residue is distributed.

If no non-residuary gifts are made, a gift of the whole estate is a residuary gift.

Examples

'I give the residue of my estate after the payment of debts funeral and testamentary expenses to Jane Smith of...............'

'I give the residue of my estate after the payment of debts funeral and testamentary expenses to Jane Smith of...............outright.'

'I give the residue of my estate after the payment of debts funeral and testamentary expenses to Jane Smith of...............absolutely.'

'I give the residue of my estate after the payment of debts funeral and testamentary expenses to such of my sisters as survive me and if both in equal shares.' This avoids the class closing rules: 'as survives me'.

'I give the residue of my estate after the payment of debts funeral and testamentary expenses to my wife Maureen Peterson of...............'

---

11 Reasons why gifts in wills fail

There are a number of reasons why gifts in wills may fail, including:

- Ademption
- Lapse
- Divorce
- Failure to fulfil a contingency
- Uncertainty
- S.15 WA 1837

Alterations and the doctrine of incorporation were discussed in Chapter 20.

It should be noted that if a non-residuary gift fails it falls into residue unless the testator has included a substitutional gift. If a gift of residue fails, unless there is an effective substitution provision, the property passes under the Intestacy Rules.

11.1 Ademption

We have already considered the difference between **specific gifts** and **general gifts**.

A **specific** gift will fail if the subject matter of the gift does not form part of the estate of the testator at his death, for example because it has been sold or given away before death. The gift adeems and the beneficiary receives nothing.

General gifts do not adeem if the if subject matter of the gift does not form part of the estate of the testator at his death. In these circumstances the PRs would have to buy the subject matter of the gift and give it to the beneficiary (unless they exercise their discretion to appropriate assets from the estate in favour of the beneficiary pursuant to s.41 AEA 1925).

The distinction between specific and general gifts is academic in the context of ademption if the testator owns the property in question at the date of his death.

S.24 WA 1837 states:

'A will shall be construed to speak from the death of the testator. Every will shall be construed, with reference to the real estate and personal estate comprised in it, to speak and take effect as if it had been executed immediately before the death of the testator, unless a contrary intention shall appear by the will.'

Examples

A gift of 'all my jewellery' means all jewellery owned by the testator at the date of death. Ademption will only occur if there is no jewellery at all at the date of death.

A gift of 'all my estate' passes all the property owned by the testator at his death.

However, if a person makes a gift of a **single item** of property, the use of the word 'my' indicates contrary intention to s.24 WA 1837. It is assumed that the gift is the item owned at the date of the will with the likely result that if the specific item no longer forms part of the estate at death, the gift will adeem.

Example

'I give my watch to John Smith of...............'

If on death, the testator does not own the particular watch he owned at the date of the will, the gift adeems even if the testator owns another watch at his death.

The doctrine of ademption and the above rules should be explained to a testator so that instructions can be given in relation to the proposed gift.

Examples

- Simon has 1,000 shares in X plc which he wants to give to Alice. Instructions should be taken from the testator as to whether the gift should be specific, for example, 'I give all my shares in X plc...' or general, ie 'I give 1,000 shares in X plc...'
- If John makes a gift of 'my car,' this may be construed as being his car at the date of the will. Consider avoiding the danger of ademption by using wording such as 'I give any car which I may own at the date of my death'.
- Consider the use of substitutional gifts. 'I give my shares in X plc to Martha Davis of .... but if I do not own any shares in X plc at my death I give the sum of £10,000 to the said Martha Davis'.

- If the testator is gifting his main residence, the gift will fail if the testator has moved house before he dies. The testator may wish to make provision for this: 'I give my house known as...... or such other property that at my death I am living in as my main residence to .... of ....'

11.2 Lapse

Lapse occurs when a beneficiary dies before the testator. Lapse therefore applies in the context of non-residuary and residuary gifts and vested and contingent gifts.

If a non-residuary gift lapses, it falls into residue. If a gift of residue lapses, the property passes under the Intestacy Rules.

11.2.1 Substitutional gifts

A substitutional gift can be included in the will to take effect if the original beneficiary dies before the testator.

Example

'I give £20,000 to Mary Hargreaves of............... but if Mary dies before me or if the gift to her fails for any other reason then I give £20,000 to Mary's son Michael Hargreaves of...............'

11.2.2 Gifts to more than one named person

If the gift is made to more than one beneficiary as joint tenants the gift will only lapse if all of the named joint tenants have predeceased the testator.

Examples

If the gift is made to 'Carl and Peter jointly', if Carl dies before Peter, Peter will take the whole gift. The gift will only lapse if neither Carl nor Peter survive.

If the gift is made 'to such of Carl and Peter as survive me and if both in equal shares', then if Carl dies before Peter, Peter will take the whole gift. The gift will only lapse if neither Carl nor Peter survive.

If the gift includes words of severance the beneficiaries take as tenants in common. This means the share of any beneficiary who dies before the testator will lapse.

Example

If the gift is made 'to Sam and Lilly in equal shares' and Lilly dies before the testator, her gift lapses and Sam takes only his share.

Example

'I give the residue of my estate after the payment of debts funeral and testamentary expenses in equal shares to my niece Jane Mallott and my nephew Monty Mallott'.

If Monty predeceases the testator, his share lapses and there will be a partial intestacy. This could have been avoided by drafting the clause as follows:

'I give the residue of my estate after the payment of debts funeral and testamentary expenses to such of my niece Jane Mallott and my nephew Monty Mallott as survive me and if both in equal shares'.

11.2.3 S.33 WA 1837

An important exception to the doctrine of lapse is contained in **s.33 WA 1837**.

Gifts in a will to the testator's child or remoter issue (eg grandchildren, great grandchildren etc) who **predecease** the testator leaving issue living or *en ventre sa mère* at the testator's death do not lapse but take effect as gifts to such issue in equal shares, vested.

S.33 applies unless there is a contrary intention appearing from the will. This is usually shown by including an express substitution provision.

S.33 applies to both vested and contingent gifts, provided that the beneficiary dies before the testator.

It should be noted that s.33 does not apply to gifts to other relatives.

Example

Stephen leaves his entire estate to his daughter Jacinta. Jacinta has predeceased Stephen, but both Stephen and Jacinta are survived by Jacinta's daughter, Ruby. The gift does not lapse; instead under s.33 Ruby receives her mother's entitlement outright.

If a gift is made to a class of beneficiaries consisting of children and/or remoter issue of the testator and a member of the class dies before the testator leaving issue at the testator's death, the deceased beneficiary's share passes to the remoter issue in equal shares.

Example

Lucas leaves £300,000 to 'such of my children as survive me and if both equally'. He is survived by his son Jonah, but his daughter, Sasha, died before him. Sasha's share passes to her own children in equal shares, vested. Had Sasha dies without children, Jonah would have received all the £300,000.

Example

Lucas leaves £300,000 to ' Sasha and Jonah in equal shares'. He is survived by his son Jonah, but his daughter, Sasha, died before him. Sasha's share passes to her own children in equal shares, vested. Had Sasha died without children, her share would have lapsed and Jonah would have received £150,000.

S.33 only applies if there is no contrary intention in the will and this would usually be shown by including an express substitution provision, sometimes coupled with an express exclusion of s.33.

Example

'I give £50,000 to my son Oscar Hayes but if my said son does not survive me my wife Anne Hayes shall take the sum of £50,000 and I declare that s.33 Wills Act 1837 shall not apply to this will'

Even if the wishes of the testator appear to correspond with the effect of s.33, it is preferable to nevertheless include express provision to ensure that any ambiguities in the application of s.33 are avoided and to bring the issue to the attention of the testator.

Example

'I give the residue of my estate after the payment of debts funeral and testamentary expenses to such of my children as survive me and if more than one in equal shares but if any child of mine dies before me or the gift to them fails for any other reason leaving a child or children surviving him or her then such children shall take and if more than one in equal shares the share of my estate which is or her parent would have take had he or she survived me or had the gift to him or her not failed'

---

s.33 does not apply if the child dies after the testator but before attaining a contingency.

Example

'I give £30,000 to my daughter Meryl Partridge if she attains the age of 25'

If Meryl survives the testator, but dies with children before attaining 25, s.33 does not apply.

If it is the testator's wish that Meryl's children should inherit in such circumstances, express provision should be made:

'I give £30,000 to my daughter Meryl Partridge if she attains the age of 25 but if she dies before me or before attaining a vested interest or the gift to her fails for any other reason leaving a child or children surviving her then such children shall take by substitution and if more than one in equal shares if they attain the age of 25'

If the gift to the deceased beneficiary is contingent (but he/she died before the testator) it is not clear whether the substituted children take on the same contingency as their deceased parent. This is another reason why it is preferable to make express provision in the will and avoid the rule under s.33.

11.3 Divorce

If, after the date of the will, the testator gets divorced or their civil partnership is dissolved then any gift to the former spouse/civil partner shall lapse (they are treated as predeceasing the testator) (except insofar as contrary intention appears in the will) (**s.18A WA 1837**). This means that any gift to the former spouse/civil partner lapses and any appointment as executor/trustee fails.

Example

Tom dies leaving a valid will dated 4 June 2004 in which he gives '£50,000 to my wife Daneille Parker' and 'the residue of my estate after the payment of debts funeral and testamentary expenses to such of my children as survive me and if more than one in equal shares'. Tom and Danielle divorced last year. The gift to Danielle lapses and falls into residue. However, the will remains valid.

Example

Lloyd dies leaving a will dated 3 July 2005 in which he gives '£50,000 to my son Nathaniel Clark' and 'the residue of my estate after the payment of debts funeral and testamentary expenses to my wife Jennifer Clark'. Lloyd and Jennifer divorced last year. The gift to Jennifer lapses and devolves in accordance with the Intestacy Rules: there is a partial intestacy. The will remains valid.

Example

Kat dies leaving a valid will dated 2 June 2007 in which she gives 'the residue of my estate after the payment of debts funeral and testamentary expenses to my civil partner Carolyn Heart but if she predeceases me to my brother Michael James'. Kat and Carolyn's civil partnership was dissolved last month. The gift of residue is saved from lapse and passes to Michael because Carolyn is **treated as predeceasing** Kat and this wording is therefore sufficient.

11.4 Failure of a contingency

A contingent gift will fail if the beneficiary dies after the testator, but before attaining the contingency. Remember that s.33 WA 1837 is of no application here.

If a substitutional provision is used, it is important that it applies whether a beneficiary predeceases a testator or whether they survive the testator, but die before attaining the contingency.

Example

'.....provided that if the said Susan Sumner dies before me or before attaining a vested interest or this gift fails for any other reason then....'

11.5 Uncertainty

Where it is not possible to identify the subject matter of the gift or the object of the gift, it may fail for uncertainty.

Example

A gift of 'some of my best pottery', will fail for uncertainty.

Example

'I give my ring to Miranda Carr of ....' .

If the testator had a number of rings at the date of the will, the gift will fail for uncertainty.

Example

'I give £1,000 to my niece'.

If the testator has two nieces at the date of the will, the gift will fail for uncertainty.

11.6 S.15 WA 1837

A gift to a beneficiary fails if the beneficiary or his spouse/civil partner witnesses the will (s.15 WA 1837). The attestation of the will remains valid; it is the gift which fails.

Example

Jada dies leaving a will in which she gives 'the residue of my estate after the payment of debts funeral and testamentary expenses to my brother Tyson Bell of ....'. Tyson is one of the two witnesses to the will and so the gift to him fails; as there is no substitution provision, the residue of Jada's estate passes under the Intestacy Rules.

Any substitution provision should be worded so that it takes effect should the gift fail for any reason. For example: ' provided that if ...... dies before me or the gift fails for any other reason....'.

12 Express trusts

It is possible that the testator may wish to set up an express trust in his will. Trusts usually arise in the context of residuary gifts, although trusts can arise in the context of non-residuary gifts.

Where a trust is created, trustees should be appointed in addition to executors (and they are usually the same people). It should be noted that trusts can also arise where a vested gift is made to a minor and where contingent gifts are made, but here we will consider two of the most common types of express trust.

12.1 Life interest trust

The testaor may wish to leave assets to a beneficiary for his life only and this is known as a **life interest trust**. In its most simplistic form, the benficiary will be entitled to the income from the assets for his life (or will be entitled to live in any property comprised in the trust during his life). On his death, the underlying capital in the trust will pass to other beneficiaries named in the will, on such terms as the testator selects. The person with the life interest is know as the **life tenant** and the ulmimate beneficiary or beneficaries, the **remainderman** or remaindermen (as recipient(s) of the interest in remainder).

The advantage of this arrangement is that the testator effectively retains an element of control after death.

Example

Susan and Jake are married and do not have children, but Jake has children from an earlier marriage. He may wish to leave his estate to Susan for her life, but that on her death it passes to his children. Susan will have a life interest and Jake's children will have an interest in remainder.

You should bear in mind that Susan may feel that reasonable finanicial provision has not been made for her and make a claim under the IPFDA 1975.

12.2 Discretionary trust

Some testators prefer to retain flexibility by leaving assets to trustees who can decide at their absolute discretion how income and/or capital from the trust assets can be distributed among the class of beneficiaries.

This post-death flexibility can be achieved by leaving assets on discretionary trusts. The trustees are given absolute discretion regarding the distribution of capital and income from the trust amongst the class of beneficiaries.

The testator will often prepare a non-binding letter of wishes explaining how they wish the trustees to exercise their discretion.

Example

Gideon makes a will leaving his entire estate to his nephews and nieces on a discretionary trust, appointing his brother and sister as trustees. None of the nephews and nieces has any entitlement to income or capital and will only receive income and/or capital if the trustees exercise their power in their favour.

13 Gifts to charities and other organisations

Whenever there is a gift to a charity or other organisation the solicitor should:

- Confirm the organisation's existence and correct name and address. The gift may fail if it is not correctly identified under the will.
- Consider the inclusion of a receipt clause discharging the PRs by the receipt of the person 'appearing to be the secretary, treasurer, or other proper officer of the institution' to overcome the difficulty of the executors ascertaining who can give receipt for the legacy on behalf of the organisation.
- Consider the possibility of the organisation changing name or merging with another organisation and make provision for such a situation.

14 Gifts of real property

14.1 Mortgages

If a specific devise is made of a property and that property is subject to a mortgage, the property will pass to the beneficiary subject to the mortgage by virtue of s.35 AEA 1925. If the testator wishes to place the burden of the mortgage on residue, this should be expressly stated in the will.

Example

'I give my house known as 53 Cross Street Manchester M2 6YH to Bethany Hodge of .... and I direct that any charge on the house shall be discharged out of the residue of my estate'

Even if the testator wishes to pass the burden of the mortgage to the beneficiary it is preferable for this to be expressly stated in the will for the avoidance of doubt.

Example

'I give my house known as 53 Cross Street Manchester M2 6YH to Bethany Hodge of ....subject to mortgage'

The solicitor should also check whether the testator has taken out a life insurance policy with a view to the proceeds paying off the mortgage in the event of his death. If so, consideration should be given to writing the policy in trust for the beneficiary who suffers the burden of the mortgage.

There are inheritance tax reasons for writing the policy in trust, rather than it being paid to the estate (see Chapter 24).

14.2 Ademption

The possibility of ademption should always be considered and the testator may wish to make provision for this.

Example

'I give to Mathilda Singer of .... my house known as .... or such other property as at my death constitutes my principal residence.'

14.3 Contents

A gift of a property does not include its contents. Instructions should therefore be taken as to whether the testator wishes to make a gift to the beneficiary of the contents of the house.

14.4 Inheritance tax

In view of the likely value of the property, the testator may wish to make the gift subject to inheritance tax and instructions should be taken on this point. Even if the testator wishes to make the gift free from inheritance tax, this should be expressly stated in the will for the avoidance of doubt.

Examples

'I give my house known as 53 Cross Street Manchester M2 6YH to Bethany Hodge of .... free of tax'

'I give my house known as 53 Cross Street Manchester M2 6YH to Bethany Hodge of .... subject to tax and subject to mortgage'

14.5 Life interest

It is not uncommon for a testator to leave his house on a life interest trust for a beneficiary, rather than outright.

Example

Lewis lives with his girlfriend Nicole. He makes a will leaving a life interest in his house to Nicole, with gift in remainder and the residue of his estate to his brother.

Summary

- A testator may wish to make non-residuary gifts in his will and should also make a gift of residue which should be drafted to avoid a partial intestacy arising.
- Gifts in wills are often described as legacies or devises.
- Provision is usually made for the payment of debts, funeral and testamentary expenses (including inheritance tax) to be from residue before distribution to the residuary beneficiaries, although consider s.35 AEA in relation to mortgages.
- Gifts in wills can be vested or contingent.
- There are particular rules relating to gifts to children.
- The beneficiaries should be accurately described.
- Non-residuary gifts in wills can be classified as specific, general, demonstrative or pecuniary.
- There are many reasons why gifts in wills can fail and these need to be considered in relation to will drafting and beneficial entitlement. These include ademption, lapse, divorce, failing to fulfil a contingency, uncertainty and the rule in s.15 WA 1837. The doctrine of incorporation and the rules in relation to alterations may also cause gifts in wills to fail.
- The rule in s.33 WA 1837 is an important exception to the doctrine of lapse.
- Divorce does not revoke a will, but the ex-spouse/civil partner is treated as predeceasing the testator.
- Express trusts are sometime used in wills, notably life interest and discretionary trusts.
- Particular considerations apply in relation to gifts to charities and gifts of houses.

Self-test questions

1 Why is it important that a will disposes of all the assets which are capable of being disposed of by will?

2 Peter's will leaves 'the residue of my estate after the payment of debts funeral and testamentary expenses to my children in equal shares'. At Peter's death, he is survived by his wife, Annabelle, who is pregnant and two children, Beau, aged 5, and Maisie, aged 16. Who is entitled to Peter's estate? Are their interests are vested or contingent?

3 Samira dies leaving a will in which she leaves '£10,000 to my father'. Samira is adopted. Is her natural father or adoptive father entitled?

4 Derek dies leaving a will in which he leaves '£20,000 to my daughter Megan if she attains 21'. Megan dies 3 months after Derek, aged 20. Will this affect the beneficial entitlement under Derek's estate?

5 Hal dies leaving a valid will in which he leaves '£10,000 to Mia Denver'. Mia survives Hal, but dies a year later aged 12. Will this affect the beneficial entitlement under Hal's estate?

6 Joe died leaving a will in which he leaves the residue of his estate 'to my sisters Hannah and Fiona in equal shares'. Fiona predeceased Joe, leaving a daughter of her own. Are the Intestacy Rules applicable?

7 Does divorce revoke a will?

8 Jack makes a will leaving '10,000 shares in Harris Homes Limited to Margo Fontner'. It transpires after Jack's death that he has sold the shares. What does Margo receive?

9 When might a life interest trust in a will be appropriate?

10 Martina dies leaving a will in which she leaves 'my house to Ross' and the residue of her estate to Janhavi. At her death she owns the house valued at £200,000, with an outstanding mortgage of £100,000, together with other assets valued at £300,000. Explain the beneficial entitlement to Martina's estate.

Answers to self-test questions

1 To avoid a partial intestacy.

2 His three children (including the unborn child) and their interests are vested.

3 Adoptive father.

4 Yes, she had only a contingent interest and, as she died before attaining the contingency, the gift will fail. Derek's estate will be redistributed on the basis that Megan predeceased him. The beneficial entitlement will depend upon the provisions of the will, but it is likely that the funds will pass to the residuary beneficiary/beneficiaries.

5 No, Hal's estate is not affected. Mia had a vested interest and the assets will pass in accordance with the Intestacy Rules applicable to her estate (she was too young to have made a valid will).

6 Yes, there is a partial intestacy of Fiona's share – it does not automatically accrue to Hannah and s.33 WA 1837 is not applicable as Fiona is not 'issue' of Joe. That share will be redistributed according to the Intestacy Rules applicable to Joe's estate and the beneficial entitlement to that share will depend upon who survived Joe – it might be that Hannah will inherit under the Intestacy Rules (see Chapter 23).

7 No.

8 It is a general legacy and so does not adeem. The PRs must buy 10,000 shares in Harris Homes Limited for Margo or use their powers of appropriation under s.41 AEA 1925 to transfer assets to her in satisfaction of the general legacy.

9 If the testator wishes to retain control over the ultimate destination of the capital comprised in the gift, in effect protecting the inheritance of the remaindermen beneficiaries.

10 Ross receives a net gift of £100,000 as the house passes to him subject to mortgage (s.35 AEA 1925). Janhavi receives £300,000. Was this Martina's intention?

23

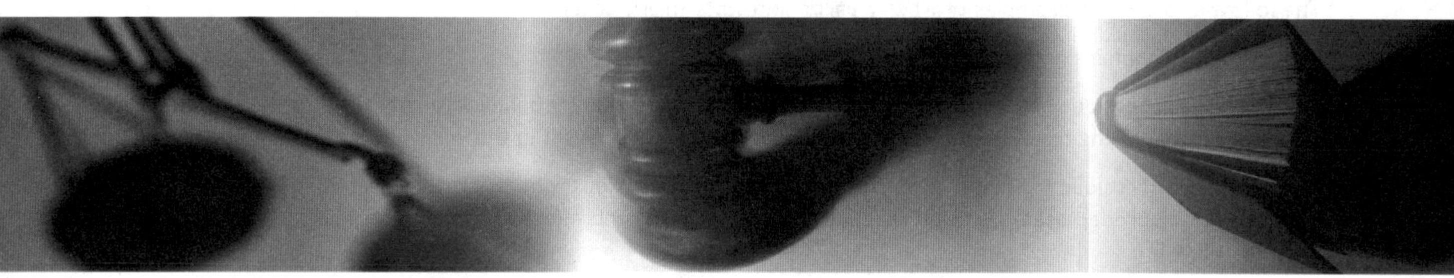

Intestacy

Topic List

Chapter overview

This Chapter will:

- Describe when a total intestacy arises and when a partial intestacy arises
- Describe the property which does not pass under the Intestacy Rules, but rather passes under its own succession rules
- Explain the meaning of the 'statutory trusts'
- Explain who is entitled where there is a surviving spouse/civil partner
- Describe the additional rights of the spouse/civil partner
- Explain who is entitled where there is no surviving spouse/civil partner
- Describe how entitlements may change under the Intestacy Rules

1 When are the Intestacy Rules relevant?

A **total intestacy** arises where the deceased dies without having disposed of any of his property by a valid will. This may be because the deceased never made a will or because the will is invalid for some reason, for example, the testator lacked testamentary capacity.

A **partial intestacy** arises where the deceased has left a valid will which does not dispose of his entire estate which is capable of being disposed of by will. This might be because the will was drafted in such a way that all of the assets were not disposed of in the will, or because events have occurred since the will was drafted which have caused all or part of the gift of residue to fail.

The following are some examples of when a partial intestacy might occur:

- The will contains no residuary gift.
- The gift of residue has failed, wholly or in part, because a residuary beneficiary has predeceased the testator and there is no effective substitutional gift in the will.
- The gift of residue has failed, wholly or in part, because a residuary beneficiary is treated as having predeceased the testator (eg divorce) and there is no effective substitutional gift in the will.

The assets not passing under the will pass according to the Intestacy Rules which lay down an order of entitlement.

Examples

- Archie made a will on 4 December 2004 leaving his entire estate to his daughter, Florence. Archie was married last year. The will was not made in expectation of his marriage. It has been revoked by his marriage and on his death the entire estate is distributed in accordance with the Intestacy Rules.
- Brian by will leaves £5,000 to his friend, Michael, and the residue of his estate to his sister, Pippa. Pippa dies before Brian. On Brian's death, £5,000 passes under his will to Michael and the rest of Brian's estate passes under the Intestacy Rules. This result would have been avoided if Brian's will had contained a substitutional gift of residue to take effect if Pippa died before him. If Michael had died before Brian, but Pippa had survived, on Brian's death his estate would pass to Pippa and the Intestacy Rules would not be applicable.
- Simon made a will leaving his personal chattels to his sister and the residue of his estate to his brother, Peter. Peter was one of the witnesses to the will. Although the will remains valid, under s.15 WA 1837 Peter is treated as predeceasing Simon and so the residue of the estate passes under the Intestacy Rules.
- Tim leaves all his estate to 'my brother Daniel and sister Harriet in equal shares'. Daniel dies before Tim. Therefore, on Tim's death, half his estate passes to Harriet, but Daniel's half share lapses and passes according to the Intestacy Rules. This result would have been avoided had Tim left his estate to 'such of my brother Daniel and sister Harriet as survive me and if both in equal shares'. If Daniel predeceased Tim, Harriet would inherit all of Tim's estate.
- Under her will, Natasha leaves all her estate to 'my nephews Reuben Felix and Jared jointly'. The gift contains no words of severance and, therefore, Natasha's nephews take as joint tenants. Reuben dies before Natasha. All Natasha's estate passes to Felix and Jared, as joint tenants, and the Intestacy Rules do not apply.

2 Type of assets passing on intestacy

The Intestacy Rules only apply to property which is capable of being passed by will.

For example, property owned beneficially as joint tenants passes under a right of survivorship and not according to the Intestacy Rules. A life insurance policy written in trust for a third person will not pass under the Intestacy Rules. Similarly, a death in service payment which has been nominated to a third person passes independently of the Intestacy Rules.

Examples

John dies intestate, survived by his wife, Martina, and their sons, Johnny, Jack and Tim. Martina and John owned their own house as beneficial joint tenants. The Intestacy Rules do not affect John's 'share' of the house, which passes automatically to Martina by survivorship.

Brendan dies intestate, survived by his parents and brother. Brendan had taken out a life assurance policy for £200,000, which is written is written in trust for his boyfriend, Jonas. The Intestacy Rules do not apply to the life insurance policy, which passes to Jonas under the terms of the trust.

---

3 S.33 AEA 1925

S.33 AEA 1925 places a statutory trust over all the property in respect of which the deceased died intestate. This statutory trust provides that the PRs must pay the debts, funeral and testamentary expenses of the deceased. The balance remaining is the 'residuary estate', which is divided between the deceased's family under the rules set out in **s.46 AEA 1925**.

4 The 'statutory trusts'

As will be seen, certain categories of beneficiary are entitled on the 'statutory trusts', which are set out in **s.47 AEA 1925**.

The statutory trusts dictate who is a member of the class of beneficiaries and how they will inherit.

The expression 'on the statutory trusts' means:

- Equally for all members of the class of relatives concerned, living or *en ventre sa mere* (ie conceived, but not born, at the death of the intestate) at the date of the intestate's death.
- The interests of the beneficiaries are contingent upon them attaining the age of 18 or earlier marriage/civil partnership.
- The issue of any class members who pre-decease the intestate take their parent's share provided that they attain 18 or marry/form a civil partnership earlier.

The term 'issue' means all direct descendants of the deceased ie children, grandchildren, great grandchildren etc.

The application of the statutory trusts will be considered later in this Chapter.

5 The rules of intestacy

The right of a person to benefit on intestacy depends on that person's relationship with the deceased and which other relatives are alive at the death of the deceased. The law aims, in the first instance, to protect the deceased's immediate family, ie his spouse/civil partner and children.

People who are not part of the deceased's family (for example, an unmarried partner) have no automatic right on intestacy, although they may have a claim against the estate under IPFDA 1975 (see Chapter 26).

S.46 AEA 1925 lists the categories of beneficiaries in order of priority. The general principle is that the estate is shared by the relatives in the highest category, excluding those in a lower category from benefiting.

If, however, there is a surviving spouse or civil partner, the division is more complicated. The surviving spouse or civil partner (if there is one) takes priority over all the other categories of beneficiary, although the surviving spouse or civil partner may have to share the residuary estate with other beneficiaries.

6 Where there is a surviving spouse/civil partner

The entitlement of the intestate's spouse or civil partner is conditional upon the spouse or civil partner surviving the intestate for 28 days. Where the spouse or civil partner dies within 28 days of the intestate, the estate devolves as if the spouse or civil partner had not survived the intestate. Note that this condition applies to a spouse's or civil partner's rights on intestacy and not to those arising by will.

The entitlement of the surviving spouse or civil partner depends upon whether he survives together with 'relevant relatives'. Essentially the distribution is different, depending on whether the spouse or civil partner survives with or without issue.

6.1 Spouse/civil partner and issue

If there is a surviving spouse/civil partner and issue, the estate is shared between them to the exclusion of any other relatives. The spouse/civil partner is entitled to the following:

- **Personal chattels**, as defined by s.55(1)(x) AEA 1925 absolutely; and
- A **'statutory legacy'** of **£250,000** absolutely, free of tax and costs, with interest from the date of death until payment. This means that, if the residuary estate, apart from the personal chattels, is worth less than £250,000, the spouse/civil partner receives it all and the issue receive nothing; and
- A **life interest**, ie the right to the income, in one half of the remainder.

The issue are entitled to the:

- Other half of the remaining amount; and
- Interest in remainder in the life interest trust for the spouse/civil partner - this is the underlying capital in the life interest trust on the death of the spouse/civil partner, although, as will be seen, it is likely that the spouse/civil partner will elect to capitalise the life interest.

Issue are entitled on the **'statutory trusts'**.

Examples

- Andrew dies intestate and his only surviving relatives are his wife, Kirsty, and their son, Bruno (24). Andrew's residuary estate is worth £525,000 (in his sole name), which includes personal chattels worth £15,000. Without taking into account debts, funeral and testamentary expenses, Kirsty will be entitled to the personal chattels (worth £15,000), the statutory legacy of £250,000 and a life interest in £130,000. Bruno is entitled to £130,000 on the statutory trusts which, in this case, means, as he is aged 24, he has a vested interest. Bruno also has an interest in the remainder in the life interest trust for

his mother, which means that he will inherit the underlying capital on her death (although it is likely that his mother will elect to capitalise the life interest – see below).

- Cain dies without a will, survived by his mother, brother, wife Briony and granddaughter Ceri (aged 12) (the daughter of his son Max, who died last year). His assets at his death are all in his sole name and amount to £655,000 (including personal chattels worth £5,000). As Cain died intestate, the Intestacy Rules govern the devolution of his estate. Although Cain is not survived by any children, he is survived by his wife and issue (the daughter of his deceased son Max). Ignoring the incidence of debts, funeral and testamentary expenses, his wife Briony is entitled to his personal chattels, a statutory legacy of £250,000 and a life interest in half the remaining amount (£200,000). As Max predeceased Cain, because of the application of the statutory trusts, Ceri is entitled to her deceased father's entitlement, which means that she is entitled to £200,000 on the statutory trusts. In view of Ceri's age, her interest is contingent on her attaining the age of 18. Ceri is also entitled to the interest in remainder in the life interest trust for her grandmother on her grandmother's death, again on the statutory trusts.
- Norman dies intestate survived by his wife Aggie, son Marcus (40), daughter Wendy (38) and grandson Ben (19). Ben is the son of his daughter Charlotte who died several years ago. Norman's wife is entitled to his personal chattels, a statutory legacy of £250,000 and a life interest in half the remainder. The other half passes to the issue on the statutory trusts. This means that each of Marcus and Wendy are entitled to one–third of this amount, vested as they are 18 or over. The other one-third, which would have passed to Charlotte had she survived Norman, is instead inherited by Ben because of the substitutional effect of the statutory trusts and his interest is vested as he is over the age of 18. The issue are also entitled on the statutory trusts, to an interest in remainder in the life interest trust for Aggie.
- Stephen dies leaving a valid will in which he gives a legacy of '£10,000 to my son William' and the residue of his estate to his wife Hilda. Hilda was one of the two witnesses to the will and therefore the gift to her fails and there is a partial intestacy. Stephen's only surviving relatives are Hilda, William (19) and Stephen's brother, Alexander. Stephen's assets at his death are a house owned as beneficial joint tenants with Hilda and other assets in his sole name amounting to £365,000 (including his personal chattels worth £5,000). The house will pass to Hilda automatically by survivorship, regardless of the terms of the will or the Intestacy Rules. William will receive £10,000 under the will and his interest is vested. Ignoring the incidence of debts, funeral and testamentary expenses, the assets which have not been disposed of, amounting to £355,000, will pass in accordance with the Intestacy Rules. Hilda will receive Stephen's personal chattels (worth £5,000), a statutory legacy of £250,000 and a life interest in £50,000. William will receive £50,000 vested and is also entitled to the interest in remainder in the life interest trust for his mother.

6.1.1 Capitalisation of life interest

The spouse/civil partner may prefer to receive a capital sum, rather than a life interest.

Under s.47 AEA 1925, the spouse/civil partner can elect to convert the life interest into a capital sum. The election must be made in writing to the PRs within 12 months of the date of the grant of representation (or later at the court's discretion).

If the spouse/civil partner is the sole PR, the election is made to the Senior Registrar of the Family Division of the High Court. A complex formula for determining the capital amount is set out in statutory instruments and is not considered further in this Study Manual. If all affected beneficiaries are adults and mentally capable they can avoid this and agree the value between them.

The effect of this election is that, instead of receiving the income only from one half of the residue for life, the spouse/civil partner will instead receive a capital sum absolutely. Where the spouse/civil partner so elects, it may have inheritance tax implications since less of the deceased's estate will pass under the spouse/civil partner exemption, however the spouse/civil partner is not treated as making a 'transfer of value' (see Chapter 24).

Example

The residue of a deceased's estate, after deducting the personal chattels and statutory legacy, is £100,000 and the surviving spouse is entitled to a life interest in £50,000. Instead of receiving the income from this amount, he can capitalise the life interest and receive a lump sum instead. The remaining estate is held on the statutory trusts for the issue.

6.1.2 Appropriation of matrimonial home

The surviving spouse/civil partner also has the right to require the PRs to appropriate (transfer) the 'matrimonial home' in total or partial satisfaction of any absolute or capitalised interest in the estate. If this is not sufficient the spouse/civil partner can make up any deficiency from his own resources.

The surviving spouse/civil partner may wish to make the election if the house was owned in the deceased's sole name or as tenants in common.

The house is valued at the date of the appropriation, not death.

Example

Pearl is entitled under the Intestacy Rules to her deceased's husband's personal chattels, a statutory legacy of £250,000 and a life interest in half the remainder, which she has capitalised to give a cash sum of £150,000. The matrimonial home is worth £400,000. Pearl can require the PRs to appropriate the matrimonial home to her in satisfaction of her statutory legacy and capitalised amount. She does not receive the house *in addition* to these amounts.

If the house is valued at £600,000 Pearl can still require the appropriation, but must pay 'equality money' of £200,000 to make up the shortfall. The 'traded' capital sums (and equality money, if applicable) are held for the issue on the statutory trusts.

Example

Megan is entitled under the Intestacy Rules to her deceased's husband's personal chattels, a statutory legacy of £250,000 and a life interest in half the remainder, which she has capitalised to give a cash sum of £50,000. The matrimonial home is worth £600,000 and was held by Megan and her late husband as beneficial tenants in common in equal shares. Megan can require the PRs to appropriate her husband's half-share in the matrimonial home to her and, in this example, will not be require to pay any equality money into the estate.

Such election must normally be made within 12 months of the date of the grant (or later at the court's discretion) in writing to the PRs. No formal election is required should the surviving spouse/civil partner be the sole PR.

It should be noted that the surviving spouse/civil partner has this right if he survives, not with issue, but with surviving parents or brothers and sisters (see below).

6.2 Spouse/civil partner and no issue

Where there is a surviving spouse/civil partner with no issue, but the deceased is survived by parents and/or brothers or sisters of the whole blood (same parents as the deceased) or their issue, the spouse/civil partner takes the following:

- **Personal chattels**, as above
- A **'statutory legacy'** of **£450,000** on the same terms as above
- One half of the residue *absolutely* (ie no life interest arises in this case)

The surviving parent(s) take the rest of the estate (in equal shares absolutely if they are both alive). If both parents have predeceased the intestate, the brothers and sisters of the whole blood take it on the **statutory trusts**.

As the brother and sister of the whole blood take on the statutory trusts, this means that if a brother or sister of the deceased has predeceased him leaving issue (ie nephews and nieces of the intestate), such issue take their deceased parent's share on the statutory trusts.

Examples

- Charlie dies intestate survived by his wife, Carla, and his parents, Leonard and Margaret. Charlie's residuary estate amount to £550,000, which includes personal chattels worth £10,000. Ignoring the incidence of debts, funeral and testamentary expenses, Carla receives the personal chattels, a statutory legacy of £450,000 and half the residue (£45,000) absolutely. The remaining £45,000 is divided equally between Leonard and Margaret.
- Petra dies intestate. Her residuary estate is worth £750,000, which includes personal chattels of £20,000. Her husband, Martin, her brother, Denver (33) and sister Minnie (38) survive her. Petra has no issue and both her parents died last year. Denver has two children, Sam (2) and Danny (3). Martin receives the personal chattels, a statutory legacy of £450,000 and £140,000 absolutely. The remaining £140,000 is divided between Denver and Minnie, who both have vested interests as they are both over 18. If Denver had died before Petra, his share (£70,000) would be held for his children, Sam and Danny, equally, contingently upon attaining the age of 18 (or earlier marriage/civil partnership).

As mentioned above, the right to require the PRs to appropriate the matrimonial home of the spouse/civil partner in full or partial satisfaction of that spouse's/civil partner's absolute entitlement applies equally here.

6.3 Spouse/civil partner and no issue, no parents or brothers or sisters

If the intestate dies with a surviving spouse/civil partner, but no issue, parents or brothers or sisters of the whole blood (or their issue), then the spouse/civil partner is entitled to the whole of the estate absolutely. All other relatives are irrelevant for the purpose of intestacy in this case.

7 Where there is no surviving spouse/civil partner

If the deceased has no surviving spouse/civil partner, the order of entitlement is as follows:

1 Issue on the statutory trusts, but if none

2 Parents and if both in equal shares, but if none

3 Brothers and sisters of the whole blood on the statutory trusts; but if none

4 Brothers and sisters of the half blood (different mother or father) on the statutory trusts, but if none

5 Grandparents and if both in equal shares, but if none

6 Uncles and aunts of the whole blood on the statutory trusts, but if none

7 Uncles and aunts of the half blood on the statutory trusts, but if none

8 The Crown (*bona vacantia*)

Each category, other than parents and grandparents, takes 'on the statutory trusts', which means that children under 18 take their interest contingently upon attaining 18 or earlier marriage. It also means that issue of any deceased relative (except parents and grandparents) may take that relative's share.

Examples

- Nina dies intestate survived only by her brother Edward (25). Her brother is entitled to her estate and his interest is vested as he is over 18.
- Horace dies intestate survived by his mother and sister. His mother is entitled to his estate outright.
- Jett dies intestate survived by his mother, daughter Sienna (32) and grandson, Harvey (12). Harvey is the son of Jett's daughter Mischa who died last year. Sienna is entitled to half the estate, vested. Harvey is entitled to his deceased mother's half-share, contingent on reaching the age of 18.
- Alma dies intestate survived only by her cousin Albert (80). Albert is entitled to her estate as the son of Alma's deceased aunt or uncle, as the case may be. Albert's interest is vested.
- Maria dies intestate survived by her brother (45) and her niece (13). Her niece is the daughter of Maria's sister who died several years ago. Her brother is entitled to half the estate, vested, and her niece is entitled to the other half, contingent on reaching 18.
- Fleur dies intestate survived by her son (21) and daughter (18). Her son and daughter are entitled in equal shares and their interests are vested.

---

8 Adopted children

Adopted children are deemed related to their adoptive parents and not to their natural parents for the purposes of intestacy. If an adopted person dies intestate, without a spouse/civil partner or children, his estate will be distributed between the closest relatives in his adoptive family.

An adopted child may also inherit on the intestacy of any member of his adoptive family.

9 Bona vacantia

In the case of property passing *bona vacantia*, the Crown has discretion to make provision for dependants of the intestate and for any other person for whom the deceased might reasonably have been expected to make provision.

In deciding whether to make a discretionary grant, the factors the Treasury Solicitor considers are similar to the considerations to which the court must have regard in exercising its discretion under IPFDA 1975 (see Chapter 26). However it is rare for estates to be *bona vacantia* as genealogists will normally be able to trace next of kin.

10 Change in entitlement

If a beneficiary of the intestate estate dies after the deceased, but before attaining a vested interest, the estate will be redistributed as if the deceased beneficiary had never existed.

Example

Dale dies intestate and is survived by his spouse, Cilla, his son, Zachary (aged 12) and his mother Betty. His estate amounts to £790,000 cash, plus personal chattels worth £10,000.
Cilla takes £10,000 personal chattels, a statutory legacy of £250,000 and a life interest in £270,000, subject to capitalisation.

Zachary takes half of the residue on the statutory trusts (ie contingent upon the attainment of 18 years or earlier marriage) and the other half of residue postponed to Cilla's life interest, on the statutory trusts, as above. Note that Zachary's entitlements are all *contingent*, not vested.

Zachary dies two years later, aged 14. This will cause Cilla's entitlement to increase as follows:

- Personal chattels – as before
- Statutory legacy increases from £250,000 to £450,000
- Life interest becomes an absolute interest in half of the residue.

The other half of the residue passes to Betty absolutely. The estate will be redistributed accordingly.

Had Zachary's interest been vested, his subsequent death would not have affected the beneficial entitlement to Dale's estate.

Summary

- Intestacy may be total or partial.
- If there is a partial intestacy the property not disposed of by will passes in accordance with the Intestacy Rules. There is no requirement for beneficiaries under the Intestacy Rules to bring into account assets or amounts they may have received under the will.
- Property that passes independently of any will also passes independently of the Intestacy Rules.
- Certain categories of beneficiary inherit on the 'statutory trusts'.
- Where there is a surviving spouse/civil partner, the entitlement depends upon whether there is also issue and, if not, whether there are surviving parents or siblings.
- A spouse/civil partner must survive by at least 28 days to inherit.
- A spouse/civil partner may elect to capitalise a life interest and/or to have the matrimonial home appropriated to them.
- Where there is no surviving spouse/civil partner, distribution of the intestate's estate is according to a prescribed order.
- The estate may have to be redistributed if a beneficiary dies after the deceased, but before attaining a vested interest.
- For intestacy purposes, adopted children are deemed related to their adoptive parents.

Self-test questions

1 When does a partial intestacy arise?

2 Maxine dies intestate survived by her husband Trey, and children Leona and Delroy. Maxine owns a house with Trey as beneficial joint tenants worth £250,000. She has taken out a life insurance policy for £100,000, which is written in trust for her children. She owns investments valued at £120,000. Explain what Trey, Leona and Delroy will receive from Maxine's estate.

3 Wayne dies intestate survived by his wife Coleen and his parents Roy and Tracey. The matrimonial home valued at £100,000 was held by Wayne and Coleen as beneficial joint tenants. Wayne had personal chattels worth £10,000 and investments of £650,000 in his sole name. Explain what Coleen, Roy and Tracey would receive under the Intestacy Rules when the estate is distributed 2 months later.

4 In the above question, what would be the position if Coleen died within 25 days of Wayne?

5 Your firm recently acted for Granville Robinson (aged 67) in connection with the sale of his successful building business, Ilkley Bricks Limited.

Granville is married to Christine (aged 40) and they have one son, Eric, (aged 12). Neither Granville, nor Christine has any other children.

Granville, Christine and Eric live at 7 Ripley Drive, Harrogate, which is owned in Granville's sole name.

Granville's estate is made up of the following assets, all of which are in his sole name:

Asset	*Current value* £
Proceeds of sale from Ilkley Bricks Limited – cash	800,000
Other bank and building society accounts	300,000
House (7 Ripley Drive), including contents	900,000
House in Otley, West Yorkshire	100,000
Personal items, including car	10,000

If Granville dies without having made a will, explain the beneficial entitlement to his estate and any rights Christine will have as a result.

Answers to self-test questions

1 A partial intestacy occurs when a person leaves a valid will but the will fails to dispose of all of that person's property. The Intestacy Rules apply to that part of the estate not left by will. A partial intestacy will occur when a non-residuary legacy fails and there is no residuary gift, or the residuary gift fails, in whole or in part, and there is no effective substitutional gift.

2 Trey receives Maxine's share of the house by survivorship.

The children receive the proceeds of the life policy under the terms of the trust.

The investments worth £120,000 pass under the Intestacy Rules to Trey.

3 The house passes to Coleen by survivorship. Under the Intestacy Rules she also receives the personal chattels and a statutory legacy of £450,000 and half the residue, £100,000 absolutely.

The remaining £100,000 is divided equally between Roy and Tracey.

4 Wayne's whole intestate estate would pass to Roy and Tracey under the Intestacy Rules. The matrimonial home would still pass to Coleen by survivorship immediately on Wayne's death and would form part of Coleen's estate.

5 Under the Intestacy Rules, Christine will be entitled to Granville's personal chattels outright, a statutory legacy of £250,000 outright and a life interest in half the remainder (with the interest on the remainder passing on her death to Eric on the statutory trusts). Eric will also be entitled to other half of the remaining estate on the statutory trusts – as he is 12 years old his interest is contingent upon him attaining the age of 18. Christine has right to capitalise her life interest within 12 months of the date of the grant. In addition, she can elect to have 7 Ripley Drive appropriated to her in satisfaction of her interest – she can make up any shortfall from her own funds.

24

Inheritance tax (IHT)

Topic List

Chapter overview

This Chapter will:

- Explain that IHT applies to lifetime transfers and transfer of value on death
- Describe the nature of the Nil Rate Band and the principles of cumulation
- Describe different types of lifetime transfer and the IHT consequences
- Explain how to calculate the IHT payable as a result of death
- Consider the application of tapering relief
- Explain the transferable Nil Rate Band between spouses and civil partners
- Discuss various administrative matters relating to IHT

1 Introduction

Inheritance tax (IHT) is primarily a tax which takes effect on death. When an individual dies, IHT is charged on the net value of his taxable estate (broadly his assets less liabilities), subject to various exemptions and reliefs.

However, as will be seen, IHT is also relevant when a person makes certain types of lifetime gift and, on death, certain lifetime gifts have to be taken into account when calculating the IHT payable as a result of death.

The *principles* are the same, regardless of whether a person has died testate, intestate or partially intestate, although, as will be seen, the exemptions which apply (if any) are determined by who inherits the estate on death, under the will or under the Intestacy Rules.

The rules set out in this Chapter apply if the deceased and beneficiaries are domiciled in England and Wales. We will assume that all deceased persons and beneficiaries are domiciled in England and Wales and that all assets are situated in England and Wales. Issues regarding domicile and *situs* of assets are outside the scope of this Study Manual.

The main IHT rules are set out in the **Inheritance Tax 1984**.

In 1- 8 below, we will ignore the potential impact of the 'new' transferable Nil Rate Band (see 9 below).

1.1 An introduction to IHT on death

When a person dies, broadly speaking, the IHT payable on the estate is calculated as follows:

(value of net taxable estate – current Nil Rate Band) × 40 %

The Nil Rate Band (NRB) is the IHT threshold and is currently £325,000 (for tax year 6 April 2009 to 5 April 2010). This means that if a person dies within tax year 09/10, the NRB applicable to their estate is £325,000.

It should be noted that the death rate of 40% is a *flat rate* of tax and does not change depending upon the value of a person's estate.

(The NRB is due to increase on 6 April 2010 and the NRB for tax year 10/11 will be relevant if death occurs between 6 April 2010 to 5 April 2011.)

Examples

- Ellis died on 10 December 2009, with a net taxable estate (taxable assets less liabilities, on the assumption that none of the assets qualify for any *reliefs*) of £300,000. He made a valid will in which he leaves everything to his daughter (transfers to children are not exempt from IHT). There is no IHT payable and his daughter receives the £300,000 intact (although there may be certain expenses that have to be paid before distribution to her).
- Carolyn died on 1 December 2009, with a net taxable estate of £525,000. She made a valid will in which she leaves everything to her son, Jason. The IHT on Carolyn's estate is calculated as follows:

  £525,000 – £325,000 (the NRB) = £200,000
  £200,000 × 40% = £80,000

  Jason receives £445,000

  (Again, there may be certain expenses that have to be paid before distribution to him.)

We will consider how to ascertain the value of a deceased's net taxable estate and consider the various exemptions and reliefs that may apply to the death estate later in this Chapter.

1.2 An introduction to IHT and lifetime gifts

If IHT were limited to a charge on death, one way to avoid tax would be to reduce the size of one's estate by making lifetime gifts.

IHT is therefore also charged on certain lifetime gifts (transfers) if the donor (transferor) dies within 7 years of making them. Such gifts are called **'potentially exempt transfers'** (PETS): at the time when the transfer is made, no IHT is chargeable; the transfer is 'potentially exempt'. If the transferor survives 7 years the transfer becomes exempt; if he dies within 7 years the transfer becomes chargeable.

It should also be noted that certain lifetime transfers are exempt from IHT.

In addition, certain lifetime transfers (notably those to most types of trust) are immediately chargeable to IHT when the transfer is made.

2 Lifetime transfers and transfers on death

2.1 General

The IHT legislation speaks of 'transfers of value', rather than 'gifts' (a gift being a transfer for no consideration). As will be seen, most gifts fall within the definition of 'transfer of value'.

IHT may apply both to **lifetime transfers of value** and **transfers of value on death**.

In both cases IHT is charged on **'the value transferred by a chargeable transfer'**. The expression **'chargeable transfer'** means **'a transfer of value made by an individual which is not exempt'**.

Therefore, putting this together we know that **IHT is charged on the value transferred by a transfer of value made by an individual in his lifetime or on his death which is not exempt**.

2.2 Lifetime transfers

In relation to **lifetime transfers**, transfer of value means any lifetime disposition made by a person which reduces the value of his estate. Therefore, most lifetime gifts fall within the definition of transfer of value. Certain lifetime transfers are exempt from IHT and some are potentially exempt; all other lifetime transfers are chargeable.

The transfer of 'excluded property' does not count as a transfer of value (eg property situated abroad if the beneficial owner is not domiciled in the UK) and certain disposals are not treated as transfers of value (eg transfers for family maintenance), but all gifts will be treated as transfers of value in this Study Manual.

2.3 Death transfers

On death, IHT is chargeable as if the deceased had, *immediately* before his death, made a transfer of value of an amount equal to the value of his taxable estate immediately before his death. The taxable estate means the aggregate of all property in which the deceased was 'beneficially entitled' and we will consider this in more detail later in this Chapter.

2.4 Life and death transfers

Over the course of a person's life, ending with their death, death is therefore the last transfer of value a person can make.

3 Rates of IHT

There are two rates of IHT:

- The 'death rate' is 40%.
- Chargeable lifetime transfers are charged at half the death rate (20%) at the time they are made, if IHT is payable. You have already seen that PETS are not chargeable when made and, by definition, neither are exempt transfers.

4 Cumulation and the NRB

Chargeable transfers within the 7 year period ending with the date of the chargeable transfer in question are cumulated (added together) for the purpose of calculating the IHT payable in respect of the chargeable transfer in question.

Where the cumulated chargeable transfers over a seven-year period including and preceding the chargeable transfer in question do not exceed the NRB, there is no IHT liability in relation to that chargeable transfer. As mentioned, the NRB can be expected to increase annually (on 6 April).

You do not know yet how to work out the value a person's taxable estate when they die, but nevertheless the following example may help you understand the principles we have so far considered.

Example

In order to consider the IHT position in *this* example, you need to be aware that the NRB for tax year April 2005/April 2006 (2005/06) was £275,000 and that for tax year April 2006/April 2007 (2006/07) it was £285,000. In this example we will ignore any lifetime exemptions which may otherwise be applicable.

Bert transfers £100,000 by way of a **lifetime chargeable transfer** in May 2005. He then transfers a further £75,000 in May 2006 by way of a **lifetime chargeable transfer**. He dies in January 2010 with a net taxable estate of £500,000. He has made no other chargeable transfers.

When Bert made the May 2005 transfer there was no IHT payable as, looking back over the previous 7 years from the date of *that* transfer, he had made no other chargeable transfers and therefore had a full NRB (£275,000) available.

Moving on to the chargeable transfer in May 2006, looking back over the previous 7 years from the date of *that* transfer we can see that £100,000 of the NRB for *that* 7 year period had been used up by the May 2005 transfer, but the 2006 transfer still does not take us above the NRB of £285,000 and so no IHT is payable.

Moving on to the death transfer, you should now be able to see that, looking back over the 7 year period before death, £175,000 of the current NRB (£325,000) has been used, which leaves only £150,000 left for the death estate. Assuming that there are no exemptions or reliefs available for the death estate (which we will cover later in this Chapter), the IHT on the death estate will be calculated as follows:

£150,000 @ 0% = NIL
£350,000 @ 40% = **£140,000**

We will now move on to consider life and death transfers in more detail, but if you are struggling with any of these ideas, it may help to come back and reconsider the principles covered here.

5 Lifetime transfers

5.1 General

IHT may apply both to chargeable lifetime transfers and transfers on death, which are not exempt. In both cases, IHT is charged on the value transferred by a transfer of value made by an individual which is not exempt.

Certain lifetime transfers are exempt from IHT, some are potentially exempt and all other lifetime transfers are chargeable.

Remember that, in relation to lifetime transfers, transfer of value means any lifetime disposition made by a person which reduces the value of his estate. Therefore, for our purposes, any lifetime gift falls within the definition of transfer of value.

It is important to distinguish between exempt transfers, PETs and chargeable transfers (often called immediately chargeable transfers or lifetime chargeable transfers). You need to understand the IHT effects of making such transfers and what constitutes such transfers.

5.2 Exempt transfers

An exempt transfer is exempt when made and remains exempt forever; it is not relevant whether or not the transferor dies within 7 years of making the transfer. Such a transfer is, in effect, IHT neutral.

When an exempt lifetime transfer is made, none of the available NRB for any 7 year period is used. Returning to the example in paragraph 4 above, had Bert made exempt transfers in 2005 and 2006, the IHT on his death estate would have been considerably less.

If a transfer falls within one of the following categories, it will be exempt:

- **Spouse exemption**

  Lifetime transfers between spouses/civil partners are exempt, provided the gift is outright.

  It will be seen later in this Chapter that gifts *on death* to a life interest trust for a spouse are exempt. *Lifetime* gifts to a life interest trust for a spouse are **not** exempt; they are chargeable.

- **The annual exemption**

  This exempts transfers of value in any one tax year to any person the extent they do not exceed in total **£3,000**, and if they do, only the excess is not exempt (ie potentially exempt or chargeable (see below)).

  The exemption is available in addition to other exemptions and if the full exemption is not used in full in any one tax year, the balance unused may be carried forward to the next tax year, but not further.

  As with all IHT exemptions and reliefs, each spouse/civil partner has his or her own annual exemption.

- **Small gift exemption**

  Outright gifts to any one donee (the donee does not have to be related to the donor) in any one tax year not exceeding **£250** are exempt. If this total is exceeded, the whole gift is either potentially exempt or chargeable (see below).

Example

Lucille has 10 grandchildren. She has used her annual exemption for this tax year and last tax year. She has made no other gifts. She can give £250 to each grandchild exempt from IHT. However, if she gives £500 to each of them, the gifts will not be exempt.

- **Normal expenditure out of income**

  A transfer of value is exempt to the extent that it is made as part of the normal expenditure of a transferor out of his income and provided that, after making the transfer, the transferor has sufficient income to maintain his usual standard of living.

  This exemption could be used to cover the payment of premiums on a life policy. (However, for IHT reasons, consideration should be given to writing the policy in trust for a non-exempt beneficiary (see below)).

- **Gifts in consideration of marriage**

  Such transfers are exempt to the extent that the value transferred by any one transferor in respect of any one marriage does not exceed **£5,000** in the case of a gift by a parent, **£2,500** in the case of gifts by remoter ancestors or **£1,000** in all other cases. Where the appropriate limit is exceeded, only the excess is not exempt.

  The gift must be outright to a party to the marriage or a trust for the benefit of the parties and their issue.

- **Gifts to charities**

  Gifts to charities are exempt.

5.3 Potentially exempt transfers (PETs)

A PET is a transfer of value by an individual to an individual (who can be, but need not be, related to the donor) which is not in one of the exempt categories listed above.

No IHT is charged when a PET is made (ie it is exempt when made) and it continues to be treated as exempt unless the transferor dies within 7 years, in which case it becomes chargeable at its value when made and as if it were chargeable at the time it was made. However, as will be seen, it is the NRB applicable at the date of *death*, which is used in the calculation. If the transferor survives for seven years after making the gift, the gift is exempt forever.

Examples

- Sunil gives £106,000 to his girlfriend. He has never made any other gifts. £6,000 is exempt (using this year's and last year's unused annual exemptions). The remaining £100,000 is potentially exempt. If Sunil lives for another 7 years, it will remain exempt forever. If he dies within 7 years, the PET will become a chargeable transfer and it will need to be reassessed for IHT purposes. Looking back 7 years from the date of the 'failed' PET you can see that there are no other chargeable transfers and so there is a full NRB (£325,000) available to the now chargeable PET and so no IHT is payable on it. However, it uses up part of the NRB for the 7 year period before death, leaving less for the death estate.

- Devlin gives £431,000 to his cousin. He has never made any other gifts. £6,000 is exempt (using this year's and last year's unused annual exemptions). The remaining £425,000 is potentially exempt. If he lives for another 7 years it will remain exempt forever. If he dies within 7 years it will turn the PET into a chargeable transfer. The 'failed PET' becomes chargeable as if it were chargeable at the date it were made and, as death has occurred, is chargeable at the death rate of 40%. Remember that, in doing the calculation, the NRB applicable at the date of death is used. If Devlin dies on 1 January 2010 (2 years after making the gift on 1 January 2008) the failed PET of £425,000 (£6,000 was exempt) has become chargeable and needs to be reassessed. Looking back 7 years from the date of the failed PET (1 January 2008), we can see that none of the NRB (using the NRB at the date of death) for *that* 7 year period has been used and so the full NRB is available for the now chargeable transfer. The IHT on the failed PET is calculated as follows:

£325,000 x 0% = NIL
£100,000 x 40% = £40,000

You should also note in this example that there will be no NRB available for the death estate.

5.4 Chargeable transfers

A chargeable transfer is a transfer of value by an individual which is not exempt, nor amounts to a PET. The main example is a transfer into a trust. Chargeable transfers are taxable when made at half the full death rate of tax (ie 20%) and, if the transferor dies within 7 years, IHT must be recalculated on the original value transferred at the full death rate of IHT, giving credit for tax already paid.

Examples (ignoring exemptions)

- Theo gives £325,000 to a trust. He has not made any other gifts. There is no IHT payable as it falls within his available NRB for *that* 7 year period, but if he dies within 7 years, there will not be a full NRB available to use against Theo's death estate.
- Honor gives £425,000 to a trust. She has never made any other gifts. The trust is going to bear the IHT payable.* The IHT payable in respect of the transfer is calculated as follows:

  £325,000 @ 0% = NIL
  £100,000 @ 20% = £20,000

  * As IHT is based on the loss in value to the donor's estate as a result of the chargeable transfer, then if the donor pays the IHT on the gift, that payment results in a further loss to his estate. The tax must therefore be taken into account in the transfer of value. The gift (net of IHT) must be 'grossed-up' to determine the actual transfer. This is a relatively complex exercise and for this reason in the above example it is more straightforward to assume that the trust will pay the tax.

---

6 Cumulation in more detail

As we have already seen, in order to calculate the IHT payable on a chargeable lifetime transfer or a chargeable transfer which occurs on death, it is necessary to cumulate it with chargeable transfers made within the preceding 7 years.

The following examples are intended to aid your understanding. In each of the examples, exemptions and reliefs will be ignored. We have discussed exemptions in relation to lifetime transfers and there are also exemptions which apply in relation to death transfers and reliefs which may be applicable on death (both of which are discussed later in this Chapter). You may ignore them for the purposes of these examples.

Example

Tom made a PET of £200,000 in June 2000. He made a further PET of £425,000 in June 2007. He dies in January 2010 with a taxable estate of £500,000, which he has left by will to a non-exempt beneficiary

To calculate the IHT payable *as a result of death* it is necessary to look back 7 years from the date of death. We can ignore the PET in June 2000 as 7 years have elapsed and so the PET remains exempt forever.

However, the PET in 2007 must be taken into account as it was made within 7 years of death and therefore turns chargeable as a result of death: it will need to be reassessed in itself and will impact upon the IHT payable on the death estate.

We first need to consider whether there is any IHT payable on the 2007 PET, which has turned chargeable. In order to do this we must look back 7 years from the date of the 2007 PET and see if there were any chargeable transfers, which used up the NRB (and we can use the NRB that is applicable at the date of death) for *that* 7 year period. There was a transfer in 2000 which is PET, but it is exempt as 7 years have now gone by so it does not need to be cumulated with the 2007 PET (which has turned chargeable) in order to calculate the IHT payable on the 2007 PET.

As the 2007 failed PET exceeds the current NRB (it is the current NRB that is used whenever you are calculating IHT *as a result of death*) there will be IHT payable on the failed PET at 40% of the balance.

The IHT payable as a result of Tom's death is calculated as follows:

2007 PET (now chargeable)

0 – £325,000 @ 0% = NIL
£325,000 – £425,000 @ 40% = **£40,000**

Death estate

Looking back 7 years from death, there is no NRB available for the death estate as it has all been used up by the 2007 failed PET.

£500,000 @ 40% = **£200,000**

The total IHT payable as a result of death is £240,000. Who is liable to pay it and the time limits applicable will be considered later in this Chapter.

Example

In July 2004 Penny makes a gift of £325,000 to her sister (a PET). In July 2008 she makes a payment into a trust (an immediately chargeable transfer) of £50,000. In January 2010 Penny dies with a taxable estate of £100,000, which she leaves by will to a non-exempt beneficiary.

In this example, we shall not only consider the IHT payable as a result of death, but **also** consider what the IHT position was when Penny made the lifetime transfers.

Penny's lifetime liability to IHT

The 2004 PET was exempt when made so no IHT was payable on it.

Although the transfer in 2008 was chargeable *when made*, no IHT will have been paid as it was within Penny's then NRB (the NRB for 2008/09 was £312,000) – there was no need to cumulate the PET made in 2004 as it was still exempt at that time ie Penny was alive.

IHT liability as a result of death

The 2004 PET becomes chargeable at death rates as Penny died within 7 years of making it, but no IHT is payable as it is within the NRB for that 7 year period (remember that you can now use the NRB at the date of death for the calculation as death has occurred).

0 – £325,000 @ 0% = NIL

The 2008 transfer must be reassessed. It cumulates with the former PET because it is within 7 years of the PET which has become chargeable as a result of death.

The NRB is exhausted by the 2004 failed PET (which has become chargeable). Thus the whole £50,000 is taxed @ 40% = £20,000 (payable by the trustees of the discretionary trust – see later). No credit is given for IHT paid at the time of the chargeable transfer in this example as no IHT was payable at the time of the transfer.

There is no NRB left to use against the death estate and therefore the IHT payable on the death estate is:

£100,000 @ 40% = £40,000

Example

Gay made gifts as follows: a chargeable transfer of £100,000 in 2001 and a PET of £425,000 in 2007. She died in December 2009 with a net taxable estate of £500,000 which passes to a non-exempt beneficiary. What is the IHT payable as a result of Gay's death?

There may have been IHT payable on the 2001 chargeable transfer, it depends what the NRB was at the time of the transfer. However, there is *no further tax* on the 2001 transfer because it was made more than 7 years prior to the date of Gay's death.

The 2007 PET must nevertheless be cumulated with the 2001 transfer as the 2001 transfer was actually chargeable at the time it was made and is within 7 years of the PET which has turned chargeable as a result of death.

The IHT on the failed PET is therefore calculated as follows:

NRB available for failed PET = £325,000 – £100,000 = £225,000

£225,000 x 0% = NIL
£200,000 (£425,000 – £225,000) x 40% = **£80,000**

The £500,000 death estate must be cumulated with the 2007 PET (but not the 2001 transfer) and therefore the IHT payable on the death estate is 40% of the full £500,000 as the PET in 2007 used up all the NRB for the 7 year period ending with Gay's death. The IHT payable on the death estate is therefore **£200,000**.

The total IHT payable as a result of Gay's death is therefore **£280,000**.

You should now understand why Her Majesty's Revenue & Customs (HMRC) requires personal representatives to record the deceased's lifetime chargeable transfers (failed PETS and chargeable transfers) for a period of 14 years prior to death (not merely 7 years).

7 Tapering relief

Tapering relief ensures that only a percentage of the full rate of IHT is charged where death occurs more than 3 years after the date of the chargeable transfer, whether it was an actual chargeable transfer or a PET which turned chargeable as a result of death.

IHT will be charged at the following percentage of the full rate of IHT:

- Transfers made 3 to 4 years before death – 80%
- Transfers made 4 to 5 years before death – 60%
- Transfers made 5 to 6 years before death – 40%
- Transfers made 6 to 7 years before death – 20%

It should be noted that tapering relief does *not* reduce the value of the transfer, but reduces the IHT payable on it as a result of death, if any.

Example

In September 2004 Chloe made a **PET of £425,000**. Chloe dies in January 2010.

The PET in 2004 (which is now chargeable as a result of Chloe's death) is liable to tax as follows:

£325,000 x 0% = NIL
£100,000 x 40% = £40,000

As Chloe died more than 3 years from the date of the PET tapering relief can be applied. She died more than 5, but less than 6 years after the PET, and therefore tapering relief applies. Only 40% of the tax is actually charged – 40% of £40,000 = £16,000.

In other words the effective tax rate is 16%.

If the September 2004 PET had been £325,000, tapering relief would not be applicable.

It should also be noted that tapering relief does not reduce the IHT payable on the death estate.

8 Transfers on death

8.1 General

As mentioned, on death, IHT is chargeable as if the deceased had, immediately before his death, made a transfer of value of an amount equal to the value of his taxable estate *immediately* before his death. The taxable estate means the aggregate of all property in which the deceased was beneficially entitled.

8.2 Calculating IHT on death

There are five stages involved in calculating IHT payable on death and they should be followed in the following order:

- Identify the deceased's taxable estate
- Value the estate
- Apply any available exemptions
- Apply any available reliefs
- Calculate the IHT payable (taking into account any chargeable transfers within the last 7 years)

Each of these stages will now be considered in turn.

8.3 Stage 1: Identify the deceased's taxable estate

A person's taxable estate is the aggregate (total) of all property to which that person was 'beneficially entitled' immediately before his death, with the exception of 'excluded property'.

Certain property, which would otherwise be included in the estate for IHT purposes, is defined in the inheritance tax legislation as 'excluded property'. 'Excluded property' is not part of the estate for IHT purposes. Excluded property includes property situated outside the UK and owned by a person domiciled outside the UK. This is not considered further.

If the deceased took out a life assurance policy which was written in trust for a named beneficiary, the proceeds do not form part of his estate for IHT purposes: he was not beneficially entitled to it immediately before his death. Similarly, a discretionary lump sum payment made from a pension fund to a third person is not part of the estate for IHT purposes.

Property to which that person was 'beneficially entitled' immediately before his death falls into three categories, set out at paragraphs 8.3.1 – 8.3.3 below.

8.3.1 Property which passes under the deceased's will or on intestacy

The deceased was 'beneficially entitled' to all such property before he died.

8.3.2 Property to which the deceased was 'beneficially entitled' immediately before his death but which does not pass under his will or on intestacy

This category includes the deceased's interest in any joint property passing on his death by survivorship.

Examples

- Higson owns a property as beneficial joint tenants with is brother. When Higson dies a notional 'half share' of the property (and its corresponding value – see below) is included within his estate for IHT purposes even though the property passes automatically by survivorship to his brother, regardless of the terms of Higson's will or the operation of the Intestacy Rules.
- Brian, Rachel and Shelly own a property as beneficial joint tenants. On the death of Brian, he is treated as owning a notional 'one-third' share of the property (and its corresponding value).
- Arnie and Greg have a joint bank account. If either of them dies then a 'half share' of the account will be included in their respective estates for IHT purposes despite the fact that the account passes automatically by survivorship to the other on the death of one of them.

8.3.3 Property included as a result of a special statutory provision

By statute, the deceased is treated as having been beneficially entitled to certain types of property which would otherwise fall outside the definition of 'beneficially entitled'.

These rules apply to certain trust property and to property given away by the deceased during his lifetime, but which is 'subject to a reservation' at the time of death.

- **Trust property included in the estate for IHT purposes**

  The IHT legislation provides that a life tenant of a life interest trust is to be treated as 'beneficially entitled' to the property in which the interest subsists.

  The types of life interest trust which are treated in this way are those created before 22 March 2006 and those created on death on or after that date. Life interest trusts created on or after that date by lifetime transfer are treated differently as a result of changes introduced by the Finance Act 2006 and they are outside the scope of this Study Manual.

  A person has a life interest in trust property if he is entitled to the income as it arises.

Example

In her will, Gillian left all her estate to her executors/trustees, Tim and Tina, on trust to pay the income to Gillian's son, Finlay, for life, with remainder to Daisy absolutely.

Tim and Tina must, as trustees, invest the property to produce income. Finlay is entitled to the income during his life. Tim and Tina must pay it to him. Therefore Finlay is the life tenant. When Finlay dies, his rights under the trust come to an end. Under the terms of the trust instrument (Gillian's will), Daisy is now entitled to the trust fund, and Tim and Tina must transfer all the trust property to her.

For IHT purposes, although Finlay was only entitled to the income from the trust property, and had no control over the disposition of the fund on his death, he is treated for tax purposes as 'beneficially entitled' to the underlying capital in the whole of the trust fund. The fund is taxed on his death as part of Finlay's estate. The tax attributable to the trust property will be paid from the trust fund.

- **Property subject to a reservation of benefit**

  There are anti-avoidance rules within the IHT legislation designed to prevent people from avoiding IHT by giving away property, whilst continuing to enjoy the benefits.

  If the property is subject to a reservation at the time of the donor's death, the donor is treated as being 'beneficially entitled' to the property.

  (If the donor released the reservation (ie the property ceased to be subject to a reservation) in the 7 years preceding the donor's death, then he is treated as having made a PET at the date when the property ceased to be subject to the reservation, at its then value.)

  Note. A gift with reservation of benefit can be avoided if the donor pays the donee a full market rent for the use of the assets in question.

Examples

- Claudia gives a valuable painting to Lionel (a PET), but continues to hang it in her house until her death. Claudia has reserved a benefit and the painting is considered as part of her taxable estate at its value **at the date of death**.
- In 1996 Archibald gave his holiday cottage to his son, Paul (a PET). Archibald continued to visit the holiday cottage regularly until his death in 2009. The property was subject to a reservation at the time of his death and he is, therefore, treated, for IHT purposes, as being beneficially entitled to the property at its market value at the date of his death.

8.4 Stage 2: Value the estate

8.4.1 Basic valuation principle

Assets in the estate are valued for IHT purposes at the price which the property might reasonably be expected to reach if sold on the open market immediately before death.

Some assets, such as bank and building society accounts and quoted shares, are easy to value. Others, such as land, may be more difficult.

The value of an asset for IHT purposes is known as the 'probate value'.

8.4.2 Particular assets

- **Bank and building society accounts**

  Their value for IHT purposes is the balance in the account including accrued interest up to the date of death. If the deceased owned a bank or building society account jointly with another person, they are treated as each owning a 'half share' and it is valued accordingly.

- **Quoted shares**

  The value of quoted shares is taken from the Stock Exchange Daily Official List at the date of death (or the nearest trading day). The list quotes two prices. To value the shares for IHT, take one quarter of the difference between the lower and higher price and add it to the lower price.

- **Unquoted shares**

  The value of unquoted shares is more difficult to ascertain, although the basic principle of open market value still applies. Information about the company and its record will be required. An accountant will usually be employed to value the shares.

- **Land**

  If the deceased owned an interest in land as beneficial joint tenants with another person, as mentioned, he is treated as owning a 'half' share in the asset. If the deceased owned land as tenants in common, his share is part of his estate IHT purposes and must be valued accordingly.

- **Debts owed to the deceased**

  If a debt is owed to the deceased, its value is part of his estate for IHT purposes. One of the duties of the PR is to ensure that the deceased's lifetime income tax and capital gains tax position has been settled. If the deceased has paid too much income tax or capital gains during his lifetime, the overpayment will be reclaimed from HMRC and will be included as part of his estate for IHT purposes.

8.4.3 Debts owed by the deceased and expenses

Liabilities owed by the deceased at the time of death are deductible for IHT purposes. Therefore, debts such as gas and telephone bills may be deducted. In addition, the deceased may owe income tax or capital gains tax at his death and this amount may also be deducted. Where the liability is an encumbrance on an estate asset (eg a mortgage on a property) it is treated as reducing the value of that property (rather than the estate generally).

In a calculation question, care must be taken to ascertain whether such an incumbrance attaches to property passing to an exempt beneficiary (see below) – if so the benefit of the liability is, in effect, lost.

Reasonable funeral expenses are also deductible.

8.5 Stage 3: Apply any available exemptions

Two potential exemptions apply on death, their application being subject to the identity of the beneficiary/beneficiaries.

8.5.1 Spouse exemption

Any property which is included in the estate for IHT purposes is exempt if it passes to the deceased's spouse/civil partner, regardless of whether this is by virtue of the terms of the will, under the Intestacy Rules or by survivorship (eg joint property).

Example

Daniel leaves all his estate by will to his wife, Ayesha. The spouse exemption applies and there is therefore no IHT payable on Daniel's death.

It should be noted that if property is left to a spouse in trust and the terms of that trust are that the spouse receives income only for their life from the trust assets (a life interest), then the spouse exemption will still apply because the IHT rules state that the spouse is treated for IHT purposes as if they have received the capital, even though on the spouse's eventual death the capital assets in the trust will in fact pass to the beneficiaries named in the trust.

8.5.2 Charity exemption

All property which passes to charity is exempt from IHT.

8.6 Stage 4: Apply any available reliefs

Both business and agricultural property reliefs may reduce the value of the property transferred.

8.6.1 Business property relief

The value transferred by a transfer of 'relevant business property' may be reduced by 100% or 50% according to the category of property concerned.

100% reduction is available for transfers of:

- A business or interest in a business
- Unquoted shares or securities.

50% reduction is available for transfers of:

- Land, building machinery or plant owned by the transferor but used immediately before the transfer for the purposes of a company controlled by the transferor or a partnership of which he was a member
- Shareholdings giving control of quoted companies.

Normally to qualify for the relief the transferor must have owned the relevant business property throughout the 2 years immediately before the transfer. It should be noted that investment businesses and shares in investment companies (including property investment) do not attract the relief.

8.6.2 Agricultural property relief

This relief is available in respect of agricultural property and takes the form of a percentage reduction in the agricultural value of the property. The percentage reduction in the agricultural value may be 100% of 50%.

100% reduction applies where the transferor had a right to vacant possession immediately before the transfer (eg the owner occupier).

50% reduction is available in other cases (eg where there is an owner and a tenant farmer).

To qualify, the property must have been either occupied by the transferor for agriculture throughout the 2 years immediately before the transfer, or owned by the transferor and occupied by someone for agricultural purposes throughout the 7 years immediately before the transfer.

8.7 Stage 5: Calculate the IHT payable

The IHT rate on death is a flat rate of **40%**.

However, as discussed earlier in this Chapter, lifetime gifts made within 7 years of death must be taken into account when calculating IHT payable on death.

Example

Alice dies with a taxable estate of £625,000. She made no non-exempt transfers during her life. In her will she leaves all her assets to her daughter. Her estate does not contain any business or agricultural property. The IHT payable on her death is calculated as follows:

0 – £325,000 x 0% = NIL
£325,000 – £625,000 x 40% = £120,000

Example

Evelyn died on 1 December 2009 having made a valid will in which she gives £10,000 to a registered charity and the residue to her brother Matthew.

Evelyn's assets and their respective probate values at her death were as follows:

Asset	*Value*
	£
House in Kidderminster – sole name, mortgage £40,000	340,000
Investment property 1 – in joint names with sister Barbara – joint tenants (value of entirety)	100,000
Investment property 2 – in joint names with Matthew – tenants in common in equal shares (value of entirety)	200,000
Bank accounts – sole name	100,000
Joint building society account with boyfriend Alistair (value of entirety)	60,000
Portfolio quoted stocks and shares – sole name	40,000
Personal possessions	20,000
Life insurance policy written in trust for Alistair	300,000

Evelyn made the following lifetime gifts:

- July 1999 – property in Wales to Matthew. Evelyn spent every summer and Christmas at the property. 1999 value – £80,000. Value at date of death – £335,000.
- May 2003 – gift to Alistair of £531,000

She made no other lifetime gifts. Evelyn was survived by Matthew and Alistair. Barbara died last year. Evelyn's outstanding liabilities in addition to the outstanding mortgage amount to £10,000 and her funeral costs were £5,000

The IHT payable as a result of Evelyn's death is calculated as follows:

Steps 1 and 2: Identify and value the taxable estate

Asset	*Value*	
	£	
House in Kidderminster	300,000	Reduce by value of outstanding mortgage
Investment property 1	100,000	Barbara predeceased Evelyn and therefore on her death property passed to Evelyn automatically by survivorship and therefore full value in her taxable estate
½ share in investment property 2	100,000	Owned with Matthew as tenants in common in equal shares, include value of half share
Bank accounts – sole name	100,000	
½ joint building society account with Alistair	30,000	Joint account, although will pass to Alistair by survivorship, still must include notional 'half share' in Evelyn's taxable estate
Portfolio quoted stocks and shares sole name	40,000	
Personal possessions	20,000	
Life insurance policy	–	Not included in taxable estate as written in trust for Alistair
Property in Wales	335,000	Include in taxable estate as reservation of benefit. Current market value is used
Gross value	1,025,000	

Deduct outstanding liabilities and funeral expenses:

Net taxable estate = £1,025,000 – £15,000 = £1,010,000.

Step 3: Apply exemptions

£10,000 passing to charity.

£1,010,000 – £10,000 = £1,000,000

Step 4: Apply reliefs

No BPR or APR (investment property does not attract BPR, nor do quoted shares, unless they give control of the company).

Step 5: calculate IHT

Gift of property in Wales

PET – over 7 years ago, therefore exempt for cumulation purposes, although of course we included it in the taxable estate.

May 2003 gift

Deduct two available annual exemptions (£6,000) – net gift of £525,000.

PET, turns chargeable due to death within 7 years. Current NRB is £325,000.

Balance of PET is £200,000 which is taxable at 40% – £200,000 x 40% = £80,000.

Tapering relief applies as over 3 years since death. 6-7 years since death therefore tax payable reduced to 20% = £16,000.

Alistair is liable to pay the IHT. However, if he does not pay within 12 months, the PR(s) will be liable (see later).

Death estate

Available NRB for previous 7 year period fully used up by 2003 failed PET and therefore no NRB left for death estate.

IHT on death estate therefore 40% of the full £1,000,000 = £400,000 – PR(s) liable to pay it.

---

9 The transferable Nil Rate Band

9.1 General

The Government announced in the pre-Budget Report on 9 October 2007, that, with immediate effect, ie from 9 October 2007, any unused NRB on a person's death will be transferable to the **surviving spouse** or **civil partner**.

Legislation was introduced in the **Finance Act 2008** to allow a claim to be made to transfer any unused NRB on a person's death to the estate of their surviving spouse or civil partner who dies **on or after 9 October 2007**. This will apply where the NRB of the first deceased spouse/civil partner was not fully used in calculating the IHT liability at their death.

As a result, the potentially available maximum married couple's/civil partners' allowance is **£650,000** for 2009–10.

The claim for the transferable NRB is made by the PR(s) of the surviving spouse/civil partner on HMRC form **IHT 402**.

9.2 The calculation

9.2.1 Mathematical proportion

Where a claim to transfer unused NRB is made, the NRB that is available when the surviving spouse or civil partner dies will be increased by the mathematical proportion of the NRB unused on the first death.

In the following examples, we will assume that there have been no lifetime gifts.

Examples

- John dies in November 2007 when the NRB was £300,000, survived by his wife Kathleen. On John's death the chargeable estate was £150,000. 50% of the then NRB was unused. If Kathleen dies when the NRB is, for example, £400,000, then that would be increased by 50% to £600,000.
- Henry dies in January 2010, survived by his civil partner Oliver. Oliver dies in March 2010. When Henry died he left all his estate to Oliver. 100% of his NRB was unused. When Oliver dies, he has an effective NRB of £650,000.
- Simone died in December 2007 (when the NRB was £300,000), leaving a legacy of £75,000 to her daughter, Rose, and the residue of her estate to her husband, Justin. Therefore, on Simone's death, three-quarters of the NRB was unused. Justin dies in March 2009, with assets valued at £668,750, which he leaves by will to Rose. The IHT on Justin's death is calculated as follows:

  NRB available on Justin's death = £325,000 + (3/4 x 325,000)
  = £568,750

  IHT on Justin's death:

  £568,750 x 0% = NIL
  £100,000 x 40% = £40,000

9.2.2 Unused proportion

The amount of the NRB that can be transferred does not depend on the value of the first spouse's or civil partner's estate, except for the purposes of calculating the percentage NRB unused. Whatever **proportion** of the NRB is unused on the first death (even if it could not have been used) is available for transfer to the survivor.

Example

Lauren died in January 2007, when the NRB was £300,000. All her assets were in her sole name and their aggregate value was £100,000. She left all her estate by will to her civil partner, Abigail. Abigail dies in March 2010, with assets (including those she inherited from Lauren) totalling £650,000 in value. Even though Lauren could not have use all her available NRB, the fact is that she did not. 100% is unused and can be claimed by Abigail's PRs on her death. As a result, there will be no IHT payable on Abigail's death.

Further examples

It does not matter whether the assets passed on the first death by will, under the Intestacy Rules or under their own rules (eg by survivorship).

- Chet died in September 2007, survived by his wife Polly. On Chet's death, all his assets passed by survivorship to Polly. Polly dies in March 2010, with assets valued at £650,000. There is no IHT payable on Polly's death.
- Rita died intestate in August 2007, survived by her husband Alf. Rita's assets at her death were valued at £100,000 and so all passed to Alf under the Intestacy Rules. Alf dies in February 2010, with assets valued at £750,000, which he has left by will to his daughter.

  The IHT payable on Alf's death is calculated as follows:

  £650,000 x 0% = NIL
  £100,000 x 40% = £40,000

---

10 Liability

10.1 General

The rules which follow concern the question of who is liable to account to HMRC for the payment of the tax due as a result of death. HMRC is concerned with obtaining payment of the tax, and not with the question of who bears the burden of the payment.

10.2 Lifetime gifts

Where extra tax is payable on a chargeable transfer because of the transferor's death within 7 years or where tax is payable on a PET which has become chargeable, the liability to pay falls upon the **transferee** (in other words, on the donee of the lifetime gift). However the PRs will be liable to the extent that the tax remains unpaid more than 12 months after the end of the month in which death occurred.

Property which the deceased gave away during his lifetime is treated as part of his estate on death if the donor reserved a benefit in the property which he continued to enjoy immediately before death. The donee of the gift is primarily liable to pay the tax attributable to the property. However, if the tax remains unpaid 12 months after the end of the month of death, the PRs become liable for the tax.

10.3 The death estate

With regard to the transfer on death, the PRs are generally liable and must pay the IHT before the estate is distributed to the residuary beneficiaries. In the case of IHT attributable to assets passing by survivorship, they are entitled to recover the respective IHT from the beneficiary to whom the assets have passed.

Note, however, that the trustees are liable to pay the IHT attributable to trust property which is treated as forming part of the estate.

11 Time for payment of IHT on death estate

11.1 Non-instalment option property

The IHT payable on the property in the estate which does not attract the instalment option is due for payment 6 months after the end of the month of death.

Interest is payable on tax which remains outstanding after that date.

The PRs must, on delivery of an account (see below and Chapter 25) to HMRC, pay all the IHT for which they are liable (other than IHT on property which attracts the instalment option).

11.2 Instalment option property

Where property in the estate qualifies for the instalment option, the PRs can elect to pay the tax on that property in 10 equal yearly instalments, the first instalment being payable 6 months after the end of the month of death.

The instalment option applies to the following assets:

- Land of any description
- A business or an interest in the business
- Shares (quoted or unquoted), which immediately before death gave control of the company to the deceased
- Unquoted shares, which do not give control if either:
  - The holding is sufficiently large (a holding of at least 10% of the value of the shares in the company and worth more than £20,000)
  - HMRC is satisfied that the tax cannot be paid in one sum without undue hardship
  - The IHT attributable to the shares and any other instalment option property in the estate amounts to at least 20% of the IHT payable on the estate

11.2.1 Interest

Where the instalment option is exercised in relation to tax on shares or any other business property, instalments carry interest only from the date on which each instalment is payable. Therefore, no interest is due on the outstanding tax, provided that each instalment is paid on the due date.

In the case of land, however, interest is payable with each instalment (apart from the first) on the amount of IHT, which was outstanding for the previous year.

If the instalment option property is sold, all outstanding IHT and interest becomes payable.

12 Accounts

On death, an HMRC account must be completed by the PRs containing details of all property forming part of the deceased's estate immediately before his death. There are two different accounts, one of which must be completed: **IHT 205** and **IHT 400**.

If IHT is payable as a result of death, IHT 400 is always completed.

If there is no IHT payable, normally IHT 205 is completed, although in some situations it will be necessary to complete the longer form IHT 400 even where no IHT is payable.

Summary

- IHT is applicable in relation to transfers on death and certain lifetime transfers.
- IHT is chronological and cumulative.
- Lifetime transfers of value will either be exempt, potentially exempt or chargeable.
- Exempt transfers are IHT neutral.
- PETs are lifetime transfers upon which no tax is payable at the time they are made, but which become chargeable if the donor dies within 7 years.
- IHT on the death estate is calculated using a 5-stage process.
- Before IHT is calculated on the death estate, lifetime gifts should be considered in order to determine how much of the NRB remains for the death estate.
- If the donor of a gift retains a benefit in the asset given away, he will be treated as owning that asset on his death because of the anti-avoidance provisions within the IHT legislation.
- Tapering relief applies to reduce IHT payable **not** the value of the gift itself.
- IHT is payable on certain types of assets by instalments.
- Legislation was introduced in 2008 to allow the mathematical proportion of the unused NRB band to be transferred to the surviving spouse/civil partner.

Self-test questions

1 Fred (divorced) died in December 2009 leaving a valid will, under which his entire estate passes to his son Edward, who survives him. He made a gift to Edward of £95,000 in May 2005. Fred had the following assets:

	£
House held as beneficial joint names with Edward	200,000
Bank a/c in joint names with Edward	14,000
Car	23,000
Life insurance policy payable to PRs	135,000
Unquoted shares	30,000
Building Society a/c	84,000

He had debts and funeral expenses of £8,000

Calculate the IHT payable on the estate and state who is liable to pay it.

2 Candice makes the following gifts to friends; on 1 May 2006 £106,000 to Rebecca and on 1 September 2007 £258,000 to Emma. Candice dies on 3 September 2009.

What IHT (if any) is payable on these lifetime gifts and who would be liable to pay it?

3 What is the difference between an exemption and a relief for IHT?

4 Which of the following gifts made by Samantha is a chargeable transfer? Assume that no annual exemptions may be applied.

(a) Samantha gives £80,000 to her son.

(b) Samantha gives £40,000 to the family trust.

(c) Samantha dies leaving her whole estate worth £260,000 to her favourite animal charity.

5 Mark died in August 2009, survived by his wife and daughter. At his death, his assets amounted to £400,000 and he left his entire estate by will to his daughter. He made no lifetime gifts. Which of the following statements is correct?

(a) If Mark's wife dies in March 2010 she will have an NRB of £650,000
(b) If Mark's wife dies in March 2010 she will have an NRB of £325,000
(c) If Mark's wife dies in March 2010 she will have an NRB of £245,000

Answers to self-test questions

1 **Value of estate**

	£
Life insurance policy	135,000
Unquoted shares	30,000
Building Society a/c	84,000
Car	23,000
Interest in House – notional ½ share	100,000
Interest in bank a/c – notional ½ share	7,000
	379,000

Less debts and funeral expenses = £371,000

Apply exemptions: here there are none as Fred had no spouse/civil partner and left no property to charity.

Apply reliefs – the unquoted shares qualify for business property relief at 100%

100% of £30,000 = £30,000
£371,000 – £30,000 = £341,000

The gift to Edward was a PET. The value of the gift £95,000 less two annual exemptions (3,000 x 2) =£89,000. This falls within Fred's NRB so no tax payable on the failed PET. However Fred's NRB reduced to £325,000 – £89,000 = £236,000

Of £341,000 value of the estate the IHT is calculated as follows:

On £236,000 at 0% = NIL
On £105,000 at 40% = £42,000
The PRs are liable for £42,000.

2 Assuming that no previous transfers have been made, the gift on 1 May 2006 is a PET which has become chargeable.

£106,000 less 2 annual exemptions (06/07 & 05/06) = value transferred of £100,000

This falls within Candice's NRB so no IHT is payable.

On transfer of 1 September 2007 value transferred is £258,000 less 1 annual exemption (07/08) = £255,000

Cumulate this with the value of any transfers made in the previous 7 years ie £100,000

IHT payable

On £225,000 at 0% = NIL
On £30,000 at 40 % = £12,000

£12,000 payable by Emma. If the tax remains outstanding 12 months after the end of the month of Candice's death then the PRs will have to pay.

3 If a transfer is exempt it is not a chargeable transfer. If relief is available, the transfer is chargeable but the value transferred may be reduced or the tax reduced depending on the nature of the relief.

4 (b)

5 (b)

25

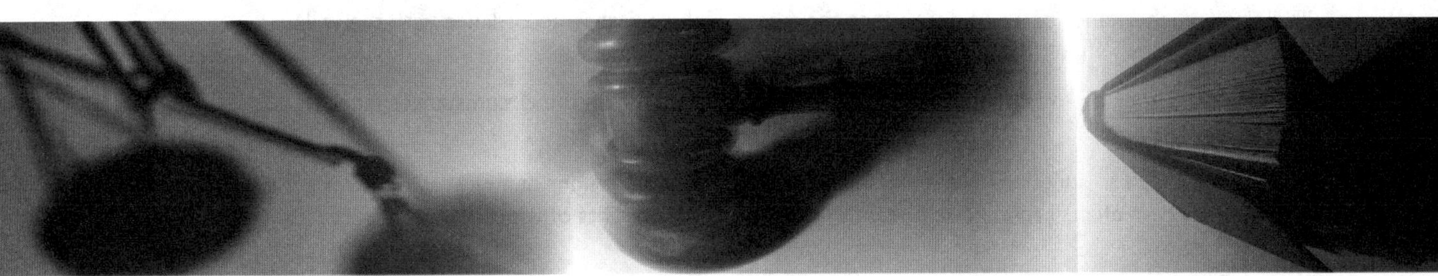

Administration of estates

Topic List

Chapter overview

This Chapter will:

- Outline the extent of a solicitor's duties in the administration of an estate
- Explain the steps involved in administering an estate
- Describe the main types of grant of representation
- Indicate the persons entitled to apply for each type of grant
- Explain the concepts of renunciation and power reserved
- Describe the documentation to be submitted to obtain a grant
- Explain how IHT is dealt with and the IHT forms that need to be completed
- Describe how the PRs administer an estate
- Consider the protection available to PRs in carrying out their duties

1 Introduction

In this Chapter we consider the steps that need to be taken after in order to administer the deceased person's estate. This is often referred to generically as 'probate', although, is more correctly the 'administration of estates', as 'probate' is only relevant when the deceased appointed executors in a valid testamentary document.

1.1 Personal representatives

The personal representatives (PRs) are responsible for managing the deceased's affairs after his death, which broadly involves collecting in the deceased's assets, paying his debts and other liabilities (eg inheritance tax) and distributing the assets of the estate in accordance with the will (if any) or Intestacy Rules (or a combination of the two).

The PRs will either be **executors** or **administrators**, depending on the circumstances (see later in this Chapter).

A minor or a person suffering from a mental incapacity such as to render him incapable of managing his own affairs cannot take a grant of representation. Grants of representation are discussed below.

1.2 The Probate Service

The Probate Service forms part of the **Family Division of the High Court**. It deals with non-contentious probate business (where there is no dispute about the validity of a will or entitlement to take a grant of representation) and issues grants of representation.

The Probate Service is currently made up of:

- The Principal Registry in London
- 11 District Probate Registries
- 18 Probate Sub-Registries situated throughout England and Wales

There are also a number of Probate 'offices' (usually a room in a court or local authority building) which staff attend, as necessary, to interview personal applicants.

An application for a grant of representation is usually made to one of the District Probate Registries.

1.3 Grant of representation

A grant of representation is a document issued by the court which enables the person(s) named in it to deal with the estate of the deceased. It will be needed to collect assets and sell or transfer them to beneficiaries.

A grant of representation is required to deal with most, but not all, assets in the estate.

1.4 The solicitor's role

A solicitor will be involved either because he has been instructed by the PRs of the estate to deal with the administration of the estate, or because the solicitor is appointed as executor in the will. In either case the procedure will be broadly the same. Where a solicitor receives instructions to administer the estate of a deceased person, he owes duties to the PRs and they are his clients.

A solicitor has a duty to:

- Advise on IHT and deal with IHT payable on the estate.
- Advise on succession/beneficial entitlement.

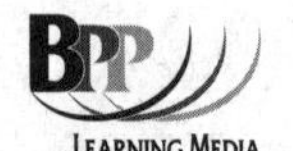

- Apply for the grant of representation.
- Administer the estate, which involves collecting in the assets, paying liabilities and testamentary expenses and distributing the estate.
- Prepare estate accounts.

2 Initial steps

2.1 Obtain the will and any codicil(s) to it

The deceased's original will (if there is one) and any codicil(s) must be obtained and the solicitor should make sure that all the PRs have a copy.

The will should be studied carefully at an early stage in order to check:

- That it is valid.
- Whether any of the beneficiaries (or their spouse/civil partner) has witnessed the will.
- Whether executors have been appointed and if they are willing and able to act.
- The beneficial entitlement under the will.
- Whether any affidavits are likely to be required by the Probate Registry (eg an affidavit of due execution).

2.2 Disposal of the body

The disposal of the body will need to be arranged and regard should be had to any wishes the deceased may have expressed.

This is usually organised by the family members and frequently the deceased's bank will agree to pay the funeral bill directly from the deceased's funds before the grant is issued.

2.3 Secure the assets of the estate

Any property should be locked and insured. Title documents to any assets should be located and safeguarded.

Although a grant of representation is theoretically needed to deal with the deceased's personal chattels, they are often distributed at this stage (to the beneficiary or beneficiaries entitled).

2.4 Death certificate

Official copies of the death certificate should be obtained. The family will usually do this when they register the death. You will see that they will be needed during the administration of the estate.

2.5 Assets and liabilities

2.5.1 Assets

The solicitor should obtain full details of the assets of the estate and their respective values at the date of death. This will involve writing to all institutions holding assets, requesting whatever details they possess about the assets ie the value of the asset at the date of death, including interest accrued but not yet paid. Other assets may need to be valued, for example property, shares etc.

2.5.2 Liabilities

The solicitor should also ascertain details of any liabilities of the estate, for example loans, unpaid utility bills, unpaid tax, mortgages etc.

2.5.3 Statement of assets and liabilities

Once this information has been received, the solicitor should prepare a statement of the deceased's assets and liabilities. This list should be continuously updated during the administration of the estate including details of what steps are being taken with regard to them.

2.6 Beneficiaries

The identity and details of the beneficiaries of the estate should be ascertained at an early stage and their beneficial entitlement established.

2.7 Assets for which a grant is not required

As noted above, a grant of representation is not required for all assets.

2.7.1 Administration of Estates (Small Payments) Act 1965

Certain assets (worth no more than £5,000) can be paid to someone who appears to be beneficially entitled to those assets without the requirement for a grant of representation (which may take some time to obtain). This is a discretion to be exercised by whoever holds the assets and the PRs cannot demand payment.

These assets include:

- Unpaid salaries of public sector employees.
- National Savings bank accounts, certificates and premium bonds.
- Building society and Friendly Society accounts.

2.7.2 Life insurance policy held on trust

An official copy of the death certificate is needed to gain access to the proceeds of the policy and the proceeds are paid to whomever was assigned the benefit of the policy. The same principle applies to nominated death in service payments.

2.7.3 Property held as beneficial joint tenants

Production of an official copy of the death certificate establishes a joint tenant's right to take through survivorship.

In the case of real property, it is common for the Property Register not to be updated at this stage and only updated on a subsequent dealing with the property, for example on sale.

In the case of joint bank and building society accounts, on production of an official copy of the death certificate to the bank or building society, they will update their records to show the surviving account holders(s) as the account holders.

2.7.4 Chattels

As mentioned, although a grant of representation is theoretically needed to deal with chattels, in practice they are often distributed before the grant has been applied for, otherwise the PRs will need to arrange for them to be secured.

3 Applying for the grant of representation

3.1 General

A grant of representation is necessary to administer the deceased's estate; the PRs will need to be able to prove that they have authority to collect, sell and transfer assets.

A grant of representation is conclusive evidence of the PRs' title to estate assets and asset holders will accept production of an official copy of the grant in order to release the assets.

3.2 Types of grant of representation

There are three main types of grant:

- Grant of probate
- Grant of Letters of administration with the will annexed
- Grant of Letters of administration

3.2.1 Grant of probate

A grant of probate is applied for where there is an **executor appointed in a valid** will who is willing and able to act. This might be the case even if the estate passes under the Intestacy Rules.

An executor may abandon the right to probate by **'renouncing'** probate. The renouncing executor simply signs a document relinquishing the title to the grant which must be witnessed by an independent person.

It is not possible through a renunciation to confer right to a grant of probate on any other person.

It should be noted that an appointed executor can only renounce probate if he has not 'intermeddled' in the deceased's estate, which means that he must not have actively administered the estate. Anything other than arranging the funeral constitutes 'intermeddling'.

3.2.2 Grant of letters of administration with the will annexed

A grant of letters of administration is applied for when there is a **will**, but:

- No executor(s) has/have been appointed
- The executor(s) appointed cannot act for some reason (eg death);
- The executor(s) appointed is/are unwilling to act and has/have renounced probate

The persons entitled to such a grant are listed in Rule 20, **Non-Contentious Probate Rules 1987 (**NCPR) and are known as 'administrators with the will annexed'.

The order of entitlement under Rule 20 is:

- Any residuary legatee holding in trust for any other person (ie trustees of residue).
- Any other residuary beneficiary; a vested interest takes priority over a contingent interest.
- A PR of any residuary beneficiary (who survived the testator) or the PR of any person entitled under the Intestacy Rules (who survived the testator).
- Any other non-residuary beneficiary (vested interests are preferred to contingent interests) or any creditor
- A PR of any non-residuary beneficiary (who survived the testator) or creditor.

An applicant for a grant under NCPR Rule 20 must swear or affirm why those with priority are unable or unwilling to apply for the grant and this is known as **'clearing off'**.

Where there are a number of persons entitled in the same degree, a grant may be made to any of them without notice to others entitled. Any dispute can be settled by application to the court.

3.2.3 Grant of letters of administration

This grant is made where there is a **total intestacy** ie there is no will capable of being admitted to probate or annexed to a grant of letters of administration. Here the PRs are known as 'administrators'.

The order of entitlement to the grant is governed by Rule 22 NCPR and the following order of priority applies:

- Surviving spouse
- Children and any issue of any child who has predeceased the intestate
- Parents
- Brothers and sisters of the whole blood and issue of any who predeceased
- Brothers and sisters of the half blood and issue of any who have predeceased
- Grandparents
- Uncles and aunts of the whole blood and issue of any who have predeceased
- Uncles and aunts of the half blood and issue of any who have predeceased
- The Treasury Solicitor on behalf of the Crown
- Any creditor of the deceased

An applicant for a grant under NCPR Rule 22 must swear or affirm why those with priority are unable or unwilling to apply for the grant ('clearing off').

Where there are a number of persons entitled in the same degree, a grant may be made to any person without notice to others entitled. Any dispute can be settled by application to the court.

3.2.4 Other types of grant

There are other types of grant that may be appropriate depending on the circumstances (for example, a 'double grant of probate' – see below).

3.3 Renunciation and 'power reserved'

As discussed, an executor may renounce probate provided that he has not intermeddled in the estate.

If an executor does not wish to act for the time being, but does not wish to go as far as renouncing probate, provided that there is another executor(s) willing and able to act, a request can be made by the executor who does not wish to act for the time being that power be reserved to him.

The executors who apply for the grant must give notice to the executor to whom power is being reserved. The executor to whom power is being reserved has the option of applying for a grant at a later stage (known as a **'double grant of probate'**) and becoming involved at a later stage if they wish. However, unless and until this happens, after the grant of probate is made to the other executor(s) he or they may administer the estate without consultation with the executor to whom power is being reserved.

3.4 Number of executors and administrators

3.4.1 Executors

Up to four executors may apply for a grant. Power could be reserved if there are more than four.

3.4.2 Administrators (with or without the will annexed)

Up to four administrators may apply for a grant. At least two are required if there is minority interest or life interest, although the court has power to permit one administrator.

3.5 Procedure

Application is usually made to a District Probate Registry.

The following items will need to be sent:

- An official copy of the death certificate.
- An oath - there are different types of oath depending on which type of grant is being applied for. (This is dealt with in more detail below.)
- The original will and any codicil(s) to it – this will obviously not be appropriate in the case of an application for a grant of letters of administration.
- IHT205 or receipted IHT421. (This is dealt with in more detail below.)
- Affidavits, if required. For example, an affidavit of due execution if there is no attestation clause in the will.

The grant is usually issued within 5 to 10 days. It is usual to request a number of 'office copies' of the grant, to facilitate the administration of the estate. These will be accepted as evidence of title.

3.6 The Oath

3.6.1 General

Every application for a grant must be supported by a relevant oath, sworn or affirmed by the applicants for the grant (the PR(s)). The oath must be sworn or affirmed before a Commissioner for Oaths or an independent solicitor.

The oath should be completed and adapted to fit the requirements of each case. There are three types of oath:

- Oath for executors
- Oath for administrators with the will annexed
- Oath for administrators

If there is a will, the original will and any codicil(s) to it will be attached to the oath as an exhibit and marked (signed) on the front page by the executors.

3.6.2 Information needed in all cases

The following information is to be included in the oath:

- Details of the solicitor's firm lodging the oath.
- The deceased's name and any other alias should be given, with reasons for that alias.
- The deceased's date of death and age at the date of death.
- The deceased's last address and the address of the deceased when he made the will, if different.
- The gross and net value of the estate and whether it is an 'excepted estate' for IHT purposes (see below).

3.6.3 Additional information needed when preparing an oath for executors

- Whether power has been reserved and, if so, to whom.
- If an executor has renounced probate, the renunciation should be attached to the oath.

3.6.4 Additional information needed when preparing an oath for administrators with the will annexed

- Details of the applicant's right to apply for a grant under NCPR Rule 20 and an explanation of why an executor is not applying, for example renunciation.
- If an executor has renounced probate, the renunciation should be attached to the oath.
- Reasons, if applicable, why those with priority are unable or unwilling to apply for the grant (clearing off).
- Details of whether a minority interest or life interest arises, in which case two administrators are required.

3.6.5 Additional information needed when preparing an oath for administrators

- Details of the applicant's right to apply for a grant under NCPR Rule 22.
- Reasons, if applicable, why those with priority are unable or unwilling to apply for the grant (clearing off).
- Details of whether a minority interest or life interest arises, in which case two administrators are required.

4 Dealing with IHT

4.1 General

It is not possible to obtain a grant before the IHT position of the estate has been dealt with.

In every estate, an IHT account must be completed, giving details of all the deceased's assets and liabilities, even if no IHT is payable. The level of detail required is determined by which account is appropriate.

The two main forms of account are:

- IHT205 (a relatively short form used for **'excepted estates'**)
- IHT400 (a long and detailed form).

IHT402 will also need to be submitted to HMRC if a claim is being made in respect of the transferable NRB (see Chapter 24)

4.2 Excepted estates

4.2.1 General

Most estates are excepted estates. This means they have no IHT to pay. However, not all estates with no IHT to pay are excepted estates. Notably, the transferable NRB does not affect the excepted estate limit.

An excepted estate is an estate where no IHT is due and a full IHT account (IHT400) is not required. Instead, IHT205 is completed.

There are three types of excepted estate:

- Low Value Estates
- Exempt Estates
- Foreign Domiciliaries (We will not consider this type of excepted estate.)

4.2.2 Low value estates

These are estates where there can be no liability to IHT because the gross value of the estate does not exceed the NRB.

The conditions for these include:

- **The deceased died domiciled in the United Kingdom**
- **The gross value of the estate does not exceed the excepted estate limit**

  If the death was between 6 August and 5 April in any one tax year, you should use the NRB (this being the excepted estate limit) that applied at the date of death.

  If the deceased died after 5 April but before 6 August in any one tax year and the grant of representation is applied for before 6 August of that year, the threshold which applies for an excepted estate is the one from the tax year before that in which the deceased died.
- **If the estate includes any assets in trust, they are held in a single trust and the gross value does not exceed £150,000**
- **If the estate includes foreign assets, their gross value does not exceed £100,000**
- **If there are any 'specified transfers', their chargeable value does not exceed £150,000**

  Specified transfers are gifts of cash, chattels, quoted shares or securities, or outright gifts of land or buildings to individuals, not gifts into trust. For an estate to qualify as an excepted estate, specified transfers made within 7 years of death cannot exceed £150,000.
- **The deceased had not made a gift with reservation of benefit**

4.2.3 Exempt estates

These are estates where there is no liability to IHT because one or both of the following exemptions apply:

- Spouse exemption
- Charity exemption

and the gross value of the estate does not exceed £1 million.

The conditions for these estates include:

- **The deceased died domiciled in the UK**
- **The gross value of the estate, does not exceed £1,000,000**
- **The net chargeable value of the estate after deduction of liabilities and spouse or civil partner exemption and/or charity exemption only does not exceed the IHT threshold**

  As above, if the death was between 6 August and 5 April in any one tax year, the applicable rate of NRB is that which applied at the date of death. If the deceased died after 5 April but before 6 August in any one tax year and the grant of representation is applied for before 6 August of that year, the threshold which applies for an excepted estate is the one from the tax year before that in which the deceased died.
- **If the estate includes any assets in trust, they are held in a single trust and the gross value does not exceed £150,000 (unless it is a life interest trust for the spouse, in which case this condition does not apply)**
- **If the estate includes foreign assets, their gross value does not exceed £100,000**
- **If there are any specified transfers, their chargeable value does not exceed £150,000**
- **The deceased had not made a gift with reservation of benefit**

4.2.4 What to do with completed IHT205

Completed IHT205 should be sent the District Probate Registry, together with the other items required for the application for the grant of representation. It is not sent to HMRC.

4.3 IHT400 estates

4.3.1 General

If there is IHT payable, or if the estate is not an excepted estate, IHT400 must be completed, although where no IHT is payable a *reduced* IHT400 can be completed.

The main form to complete is IHT400 and there may be supplementary pages which are required, depending on the facts of the case.

Form IHT421 (Probate Summary) will also need to be completed. This is a summary form and will be receipted and returned by HMRC once the IHT due has been paid or, if there is no IHT due, HMRC have agreed the position. Receipted IHT421 is sent to the Probate Registry with the application for the grant.

An IHT reference number and payslip will also need to be requested if there is IHT to pay. This can be done online or by post.

IHT400 and IHT421 should be sent to HMRC, with a payment of the IHT due, if there is IHT due.

IHT400 and related forms must be submitted to HMRC no later than 12 months after the end of the month in which the deceased died. However, IHT due must be paid no later than 6 months after the end of the month in which the deceased died (see Chapter 24 in relation to assets which qualify for the instalment option). If any IHT is due, IHT 400 and related forms should be completed and submitted with payment no later than 6 months after the end of the month in which the deceased died. Interest is charged on any IHT that has not been paid by the due date.

4.3.2 Payment of IHT

IHT can be paid in a number of different ways, for example by post or online. The fact that the IHT due has to be paid before the grant is obtained and that assets cannot be collected before the grant is obtained can present a problem in terms of the payment of IHT!

However the deceased's bank may agree to pay the IHT directly to HMRC (the direct payment scheme) if there are sufficient funds in the account(s), otherwise a bridging loan may have to be taken out for a short period of time. Alternatively a beneficiary may be prepared to lend the money to the estate.

5 Administering the estate

This stage commences once the grant has been issued and received by the PR(s).

Broadly speaking, administration of the deceased's estate involves the following:

- Collecting the assets
- Paying debts, funeral and testamentary expenses
- Paying/transferring non-residuary gifts under a will
- Obtaining an IHT discharge, if applicable.
- Ascertaining and distributing residue

5.1 Collecting the assets

The PRs should write to the institutions holding assets, enclosing an official copy of the grant and requesting the assets be transferred to the PRs.

If PRs wish to sell an asset, they should check the terms of the will (if any) and any codicil(s) to it, to make sure the asset in question has not been given to a beneficiary by will.

5.2 Paying debts, funeral and testamentary expenses

In a solvent estate the assets are sufficient to cover the debts, funeral and testamentary expenses and to satisfy all non-residuary gifts. (Insolvent estates are outside the scope of this Study Manual.) The PRs should pay the debts and funeral costs (if not already paid). They will have obtained these details before applying for the grant. The IHT should already have been paid and other testamentary expenses (eg legal fees) are paid before the residue is distributed.

See below in relation to unknown creditors.

5.3 Paying/transferring non-residuary legacies and devises under a will

When the PRs have paid all debts, funeral and testamentary expenses and they are satisfied that estate assets are not required for the purposes of administration, the PRs will give effect to the non-residuary gifts made by the testator.

The methods for transferring assets include:

- **Cash**
  A cheque is drawn on the PR(s)' account and sent to the beneficiary.
- **Chattels**
  There is no need for any formal document, although it is preferable for the PRs to prepare a written transfer document know as an 'assent'.
- **Shares**
  A stock transfer form is used.
- **Land**
  A written assent is signed by the PRs. HM Land Registry has its own form of assent which can be used. The beneficiary can then apply to register the property in his name on production of the assent and an official copy of the grant.

When paying/transferring such legacies and devises, the PRs are entitled to a discharge from liability. Such a discharge is usually given by means of a signed receipt from the beneficiary.

In the case of infants who, in the absence of an infant receipt clause, are unable to give a good receipt, the PRs should hold the gifted property until the infant attains the age of 18.

5.4 Ascertaining and distributing residue

5.4.1 Tax

The IHT position should be finalised, if necessary. If any changes to the assets/liabilities of the estate have been discovered, the PRs can complete a corrective account and send it to HMRC. The result may be that more IHT is payable or a refund is due to the estate and this will need to be dealt with before the estate is finalised.

If a variation or disclaimer has altered the IHT position of the estate this should also be reported to HMRC and a payment of additional IHT made or a refund requested.

Variations and disclaimers are dealt with in more detail in Chapter 26.

Once the PRs are satisfied that no further adjustment to the IHT is necessary and any outstanding IHT has been paid, they should apply to HMRC for a **'clearance certificate'** by completing and signing application form IHT30, in duplicate.

Provided all the IHT for which the PRs are liable has been paid, one copy of the form will be returned duly signed on behalf of HMRC certifying that (in the absence of fraud or non-disclosure of any material facts) the applicant is discharged from any further claim to IHT on the property concerned.

If an election has been made to pay by instalments and any instalment remains outstanding, an application can still be made for a clearance certificate. When returning the duplicate duly signed, HMRC will simply qualify it to indicate that it does not apply to the instalment option property.

In the case of an excepted estate, the PRs are automatically discharged from any claim for IHT on the deceased's death unless, within 35 days of the grant, HMRC calls for an account of the property in the estate. This automatic discharge will not apply, however, where further property is later shown to form part of the estate.

The PRs will also ensure that the income tax and capital gains tax position of the estate has been dealt with. Note that for each tax year of the administration, the PRs must submit tax returns on behalf of the estate.

5.4.2 Distributing residue

Once the professional fees have been finalised, estate accounts should then be prepared and produced for the residuary beneficiaries showing the balance available for distribution.

These accounts should be presented to the residuary beneficiaries and a discharge obtained for the PRs. The residuary beneficiary/beneficiaries should be asked to sign an appropriate endorsement which signifies their approval of the accounts and releases the PRs from any further liability in connection with the administration. The residuary estate can then be distributed and receipt(s) obtained.

6 Protection of PRs

6.1 Unknown creditors and beneficiaries

PRs who have distributed the assets remain personally liable to unknown creditors and beneficiaries even where the PRs did not know of their existence at the time of distribution.

S.27 TA 1925 protects PRs from such claims provided they make the appropriate **statutory advertisements**.

PRs are protected under s.27 if they give notice of their intention to distribute and require any person interested to send particulars of their claim to the PRs within a period of not more than 2 months from the date of the notice.

The notice is given by:

- Advertisement in London Gazette
- Advertisement in a newspaper circulating in the district in which any land owned by the deceased is situated (eg in a local newspaper)

PRs should also make the necessary searches to reveal any charges which exist over land held in the estate. It is also advisable to carry out a bankruptcy search against the deceased.

PRs should give such notices as early as possible in the course of administration, although administrators must wait until a grant has been issued. Provided the PRs wait for the period specified in the notice to elapse, they may distribute the estate having regard only to claims of which they then have notice. PRs will not be personally liable to any claimant who subsequently appears, provided they have no knowledge of him. Creditors and beneficiaries may nevertheless pursue assets into the hands of the beneficiaries. However, note that s.27 TA 1925 does not protect PRs where they are aware of a creditor's or beneficiary's rights, but cannot trace him (see below).

6.2 Lost beneficiaries

Where the PRs are aware that a beneficiary may exist but cannot be found, they are personally liable to that beneficiary if they distribute assets to his prejudice.

The PRs may protect themselves from personal liability in the following ways:

Benjamin Order	This court order provides that the PRs may distribute the estate upon the basis of an assumed state of affairs, eg that a beneficiary who cannot be found has predeceased the deceased without leaving issue. The court would normally require that advertisements under s.27 TA 1925 be made and that the PRs advertise for information in newspapers circulating in the locality where the beneficiary was last known. The court may direct further advertisements or enquires to be made if necessary in the circumstances. If the PRs distribute the estate assets in accordance with the Benjamin Order, they will be personally protected from liability should the beneficiary subsequently appear. Note that a Benjamin Order does not affect proprietary rights and therefore a beneficiary who is prejudiced can seek remedies against those to whom the estate has been distributed.
Insurance	Alternatively, the PRs may try to obtain insurance cover against the risk of such a beneficiary appearing. The cost of this option should be considered carefully. Where the risk is not great - because the sums involved are small - this is likely to be less expensive than applying for a Benjamin Order. Insurers may be unwilling to take on the risk unless the estate has first employed a genealogist.
Indemnity	The PRs could take an indemnity from known beneficiaries to whom they distribute the estate assets. However, an indemnity is only as good as the person giving it and this course of action involves considerable risks for the PRs.
Reserve fund	The PRs could set aside a reserve fund to meet the possible liability and distribute the remainder of the estate, but the question arises as to how long such a fund be kept in existence.

6.3 Inheritance (Provision for Family and Dependants) Act 1975

IPFDA 1975 is covered in more detail in Chapter 26.

A PR who distributes after the expiry of six months from the date of the grant cannot be held personally liable if a successful application is subsequently made. This protection is without prejudice to the right of a successful applicant to recover the property from beneficiaries.

Summary

- The administration period commences with the death of the deceased and ends when the PRs distribute the residuary estate.
- The PRs will generally need to apply for a grant, which confers authority on them to deal with the assets of the estate, although a grant is not needed for all assets.
- Where an executor has been appointed and is able and willing to act in the administration, a grant of probate will be applied for.
- In other cases, a grant of letters of administration will be appropriate: either a grant of letters of administration with the will annexed or a simple grant of letters of administration.
- An executor can renounce probate provided that he has not intermeddled in the estate.
- Power can be reserved to an executor who does not wish to act, but does not wish to renounce.
- The persons entitled to obtain letters of administration (with or without the will annexed) are set out in NCPR Rule 20 and Rule 22.
- IHT must be dealt with before a grant will be issued.
- An IHT account must be completed even if there is no IHT payable on the estate; there are two main forms of IHT account: IHT205 and IHT400.
- The PRs will need to swear or affirm an appropriate form of oath and submit this with their application for the grant.
- PRs should make statutory advertisements and searches to protect against liability to unknown claimants and beneficiaries.
- PRs should consider other forms of protection in respect of lost beneficiaries that might be appropriate and adequate.
- Once the grant has been issued, the PRs collect the assets of the estate, pay the debts, funeral expenses (unless already paid) and testamentary expenses, deal with the non-residuary gifts, deal with any outstanding tax matters (and apply for IHT clearance if applicable), prepare estate accounts and then ascertain and distribute the residue.
- The PRs should wait 6 months from the date of the grant before they distribute assets in order to protect themselves personally from a claim under IPFDA 1975.

Self-test questions

1 Name the three different types of PR.

2 Name the three main types of grant of representation.

3 Name the three different types of oath.

4 In 3. above, in which case(s) (if any) will a copy will be submitted to the probate registry with the application for the grant?

5 What is an excepted estate?

6 Joel died without a valid will and assets amounting to £2,000,000. He made no lifetime gifts. What items will be sent to the Probate Registry to obtain the grant and which grant will be applied for?

7 Zoe's executors obtained a grant of probate three months ago and now wish to pay some legacies. How would you advise them?

8 Sarah's will appoints Jez as an executor. On Sarah's death there is a lapsed share of residue giving rise to a partial intestacy. What type of grant is required?

9 You have been instructed by Louise Tamworth (aged 52). Her husband, Dean, died on 17 December 2008, aged 51. Louise is the sole executor and beneficiary of Dean's will, dated 9 May 2007. The value of Dean's assets at the date of his death was £1.8 million. This includes his half-share in the family house, which Dean and Louise owned as beneficial tenants in common in equal shares (value of whole at date of death: £600,000). The remaining assets comprise various bank and building society accounts in Dean's sole name. Dean had no liabilities at the date of his death. Identify which IHT account must be completed and submitted by Louise in respect of Dean's estate.

10 Can a s.27 Notice be used to protect the PRs against personal liability in the following cases?

(a) Missing beneficiaries
(b) A claimant under IPFDA 1975

Answers to self-test questions

1 Executor, administrator with the will annexed and administrator.

2 Grant of probate, grant of letters of administration with the will annexed, grant of letters of administration.

3 Oath for executors, oath for administrators with will annexed, oath for administrators.

4 None. It is the *original* will which is sent and only in the case of the oath for executors and oath for administrators with will annexed; it is exhibited to the oath.

5 An excepted estate is an estate where no IHT is due and a full IHT account (IHT400) is not required.

6 Official copy of death certificate, oath for administrators, receipted IHT421, and probate fee.

7 The executors should wait 6 months from the grant before distributing in case of a claim under the IPFDA 1975. Failure to do so may render the executors personally liable to a successful applicant. Have the executors made statutory advertisements under s.27 TA 1925? If so, has the period of two months elapsed from the date of notice? If not, the executors will be personally liable to unpaid beneficiaries and creditors, even if they did not know of their claims at the date of distribution.

8 Jez can obtain a grant of probate for the whole estate including that part which passes under the Intestacy Rules.

9 IHT400, although a reduced version can be completed as no IHT is payable.

10 (a) No.

(b) No. A s.27 Notice only provides protection against personal liability in the case of *unknown* creditors and beneficiaries.

26

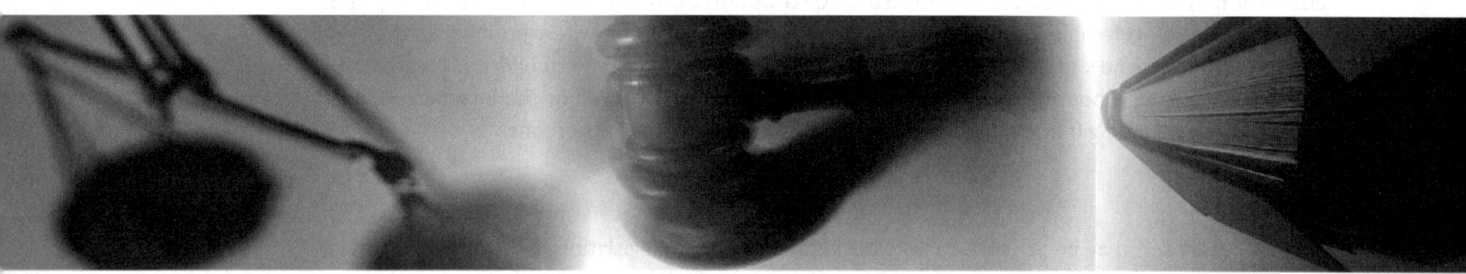

Post-death changes

Topic List

Chapter overview

This Chapter will:

- Explain how disclaimers and variations can be used to enable an alternative distribution of the deceased person's estate
- Consider the IHT and CGT consequences of disclaimers and variations
- Consider the IHT consequences of a spouse who capitalises her life interest under the Intestacy Rules
- Explain how claims can be made and orders granted under the Inheritance (Provision for Family and Dependants) Act 1975

1 Post-death disclaimers and variations

1.1 General

1.1.1 Disclaimers

Not all beneficiaries wish to accept their inheritance under a will or under the Intestacy Rules. A **disclaimer** is a refusal to accept an entitlement under a will or the Intestacy Rules.

1.1.2 Variations

A beneficiary may wish to give his inheritance (under a will or the Intestacy Rules) to someone else or it may be considered that an alternative distribution of the deceased's estate among the family would be preferable for some reason. For example, a surviving wife who inherits the whole of her husband's estate may wish to make some provision for their children. A variation, unlike a disclaimer, is not merely a refusal to accept property under a will or the Intestacy Rules, but in effect a lifetime gift from the beneficiary to a particular person or persons.

1.1.3 Tax

For tax reasons, it may be possible to take advantage of certain legislation in making disclaimers and variations. In fact, it is often the case that variations are solely tax-driven.

1.2 Disclaimers

1.2.1 General

A disclaimer is a refusal to accept an entitlement under a will or the Intestacy Rules.

There are no formalities required for a disclaimer to be effective, although the disclaiming beneficiary must indicate his intention to disclaim to the deceased's PRs in order for the disclaimer to be effective: in writing would be preferable.

It is not always possible for a beneficiary to disclaim property. It will be too late to disclaim if the beneficiary has gained some benefit from the property, for example, once the beneficiary has received a dividend from shares given to him specifically by will.

In addition, the beneficiary cannot disclaim part of the property given to him: he must disclaim the entire gift. If, however, the beneficiary receives two gifts under a will, he may disclaim one and retain the other.

The effect of a disclaimer is that the property will pass as if the disclaiming beneficiary had predeceased the deceased. In the case of a non-residuary gift in a will, therefore, on disclaimer it normally falls into residue. In the case of a residuary gift, the subject matter may pass under the Intestacy Rules.

A disclaimer differs from a variation in that the beneficiary has no control over the destination of the disclaimed property. For this reason, disclaimers are not commonly encountered in practice.

Example

Under her will, Tamsin, leaves her residuary estate to her cousin, Jemma, her only living relative. If Jemma disclaims the gift, the property will pass as though Tamsin had died intestate and Jemma will, therefore, inherit under the Intestacy Rules, although she could also disclaim this entitlement.

1.2.2 Inheritance tax

A disclaimer is treated as a transfer of value by the beneficiary who disclaims. Usually this will be a PET and, therefore, if the beneficiary dies within 7 years of the disclaimer, tax may be payable (subject to any exemptions etc).

However, under **s.142 IHTA 1984**, if the disclaimer is made in writing within two years of death and is not made for consideration (in money or money's worth) the effect for IHT purposes will be that the disclaimer will be treated as if the deceased had left the property directly to the person entitled by reason of the disclaimer. There is no requirement to elect for s.142 to apply by including a statement in the disclaimer to this effect.

If the person disclaiming is an exempt beneficiary (eg a spouse) and the person now entitled is non-exempt, this may increase the amount of IHT payable on the deceased's estate.

There is no requirement for the PRs to consent to the disclaimer, even where more IHT is payable.

If the original beneficiary is non-exempt and the person now entitled is exempt, then less IHT will be payable.

1.2.3 Capital gains tax

A disclaimer is a disposal for capital gains tax (CGT) purposes. However, under **s.62 Taxation of Chargeable Gains Act 1992** ('TCGA 1992'), if the disclaimer is made in writing within two years of death and is not made for consideration (in money or money's worth), the effect for CGT purposes will be as if the deceased had made the gift directly to the person now entitled. In other words, as no CGT arises on death (death is not a disposal for CGT purposes), there will be no charge to CGT if the disclaimer satisfies the conditions. An election must be made in the instrument effecting the disclaimer if s.62 TCGA 1992 is to apply.

1.3 Variations

A variation, unlike a disclaimer, is not merely a refusal to accept property under a will or the Intestacy Rules, but, in effect, a lifetime gift from the beneficiary to a particular person or persons.

The original beneficiary therefore controls the ultimate destination of the property.

It is possible for a beneficiary to vary part of the gift . In addition, a variation is possible if a benefit has been enjoyed from the property, for example, by receiving an income from it.

1.3.1 Inheritance tax

A variation is treated as a transfer of value by the beneficiary who varies. Usually this will be a PET and, therefore, if the beneficiary dies within 7 years of the variation, tax may be payable (subject to any exemptions etc.)

However, under s.142 IHTA 1984, if the variation is made in writing within two years of death and is not made for consideration (in money or money's worth) the effect for IHT purposes will be that the variation will be treated as if the deceased had left the property directly to the person entitled by reason of the variation. However, it should be noted that in order to take advantage of the 'reading back' provisions in s.142, the variation must contain a statement that s.142 is intended to apply.

If the person varying is an exempt beneficiary (eg a spouse) and the person now entitled is non-exempt, this may increase the amount of IHT payable on the deceased's estate.

There is no requirement for the PRs to consent to the variation, unless additional IHT is payable as a result of the variation, in which case their consent will be needed.

If the original beneficiary is non-exempt and the person now entitled is exempt, then less IHT will be payable.

Example

Under her will, Lucy leaves the residue of her estate (£500,000) to her brother, Jonathan, absolutely. Jonathan is wealthy and has no need for the money. He wishes to pass it to his two children outright. If he enters into a variation of the gift, and the various conditions are met, the liability in Lucy's estate will be unaltered as one chargeable beneficiary (Jonathan) is to be substituted by two. However, the gift will not be treated as PET by Jonathan and so it will not matter if he dies within 7 years of making the variation.

1.3.2 Capital gains tax

A variation is a disposal for capital gains tax purposes. However, under s.62 TCGA 1992, if the variation is made in writing within two years of death and is not made for consideration (in money or money's worth), the effect for CGT purposes will be as if the deceased had made the gift directly to the person now entitled. In other words, as no CGT arises on death, there will be no charge to CGT if the variation satisfies the conditions. As with s.142, an election must be made in the instrument effecting the variation if s.62 is to apply.

1.3.3 Other points to note

A disclaimer or variation can be entered into before or after the grant of representation has been issued.

If the disclaimer/variation is effected before application for the grant and alters the IHT position of the estate, a copy should be sent to HMRC, with IHT400 and IHT paid taking into account the effect of the disclaimer/variation.

If the disclaimer/variation is effected after application for the grant and alters the IHT position of the estate, a copy should be sent to HMRC, with a corrective account if more IHT is payable or an application for a refund if, as a result of the variation/disclaimer, less IHT is payable on the estate.

There is no need to elect in the same way for both taxes.

As variations are usually IHT driven, an election for IHT would normally be made.

As far as CGT is concerned, the election will normally be made as no CGT arises on death, however, the following points should be considered if:

- A loss has arisen since the date of death, the original beneficiary may wish to set off those losses against his own gains and so may choose not to elect.
- The property has increased in value it may nevertheless be worth considering not making the election if the gain falls within the annual exemption since the donee can then take the benefit of the increased acquisition cost.

2 Capitalisation of a surviving spouse's life interest under the Intestacy Rules

Under the Intestacy Rules, a spouse/civil partner who survives the intestate together with issue is entitled, among other things, to a life interest in half of the residue.

The spouse/civil partner may elect to redeem the life interest for a capital sum.

IHT on the death of the intestate will be calculated on the basis that the surviving spouse/civil partner had been entitled to the capital sum on death. The election will usually mean less property passes spouse-exempt on the death of the intestate, causing a recalculation of IHT liability (ie more will be payable).

However, this election is not treated as a transfer of value from the spouse/civil partner for IHT purposes.

3 Inheritance (Provision for Family and Dependants) Act 1975

3.1 Purpose

It is a fundamental principle of English law that a person may give away his assets, whether during his lifetime, or on death, to whomever he wishes. IPFDA 1975 does not alter this principle.

However, it allows people who are aggrieved because they have been left out of a will, or are not inheriting on intestacy (or who have inherited, but don't believe that they have received enough) to apply to the Family or Chancery Division of the High Court for an order for a benefit from a deceased person's estate.

If the court grants the application, the property will devolve to the applicant according to the terms of the order and not to the beneficiary otherwise entitled under the will or Intestacy Rules.

3.2 Lifetime gifts

IPFDA 1975 does not apply to lifetime gifts (unless, as will be explained later, they have been made with the intention of defeating a post-death claim under IPFDA 1975).

A claim cannot be made under IPFDA 1975 until death has occurred.

3.3 When can a claim be made?

Under IPFDA 1975, a claim can only be made on the ground that the disposition of the deceased's estate effected by his will, or the law of intestacy, or a combination of his will and the law of intestacy, is not such as to make **reasonable financial provision** for the applicant.

A claim under IPFDA 1975 can only be made if the:

- Deceased died domiciled in England and Wales
- Applicant is eligible to apply under the provisions of IPFDA 1975
- Applicant makes the claim within the time limit prescribed by IPFDA 1975, which is *six months* from the date of the grant of representation

3.4 Categories of applicant

IPFDA 1975 lists the different categories of person who are eligible to apply to court for financial provision from the estate of the deceased on the ground that the disposition of the deceased's estate effected by his will or the law relating to intestacy, or a combination of his will and that law, is not such as to make reasonable financial provision for the applicant under IPFDA 1975.

The categories of person are:

- The spouse or civil partner of the deceased
- The former spouse or civil partner of the deceased who has not formed a subsequent marriage or civil partnership
- A cohabitant of the deceased, whether in a same sex or different sex relationship
- A child of the deceased

- Any person (not being a child of the deceased) who, in the case of any marriage or civil partnership to which the deceased was at any time a party, was treated by the deceased as a child of the family in relation to that marriage or civil partnership
- Any person who, immediately before the death of the deceased, was being maintained, either wholly or partly, by the deceased

These categories are further explained below.

3.4.1 Spouse or civil partner

In order to fall within the category of spouse or civil partner of the deceased, the applicant must have been married to, or have been in a civil partnership with, the deceased at the time of death.

If the applicant remarries or registers a new civil partnership before the hearing, whilst not a bar to a successful claim, the court may take this into account in deciding whether or not to make an order.

3.4.2 Former spouse or civil partner

A former spouse or civil partner is a person who has been married to (or in a civil partnership with) the deceased, but whose marriage or civil partnership was terminated before the death occurred.

The category is limited to a former spouse or civil partner who has not remarried or formed another civil partnership at the time of the hearing.

Before a solicitor advises a former spouse or civil partner to make an application under IPFDA 1975, he should check the terms of the final divorce/dissolution order to ensure that there is nothing in it preventing the potential applicant from bringing a claim. If there is, a claim will not be entertained by the court.

3.4.3 Cohabitant

The category of cohabitant includes any person who lived as the spouse or civil partner of the deceased and in the same household as the deceased during the whole period of two years immediately before death.

3.4.4 Child of deceased

A child of the deceased can make an application, whether they are legitimate, illegitimate, adopted or *en ventre sa mere* at the date of the parent's death. There is no age restriction and marriage is not a bar to a claim.

Also note that an adopted child is treated as the child of the adoptive parents, not the natural parents.

3.4.5 Person treated as child of deceased

This category includes any person (not being a child of the deceased) who, in the case of any marriage or civil partnership to which the deceased was at any time a party, was treated by the deceased as a child of the family in relation to that marriage or civil partnership (for example a stepchild).

The applicant must show that the deceased took on a parental role, which is more than showing affection and kindness.

An adult may apply even if he was over 18 when the deceased married his parent.

3.4.6 Person who is being maintained by the deceased

An application can also be made by a person who was being maintained by the deceased immediately before his death. The maintenance must have continued up to death and only ceased as a result of the death.

To be maintained, the deceased must have been making 'a substantial contribution' in money or money's worth towards the reasonable needs of the applicant otherwise than for full valuable consideration.

The provision of rent free accommodation has been held by the Court of Appeal to be a 'substantial contribution'.

3.5 Time limit

IPFDA 1975 states that a claim shall not, except with the permission of the court, be made after the end of the period of **6 months** from the date on which the grant of representation is issued.

It is therefore essential that the solicitor is aware of the date from which the commencement of the 6 month period is calculated. PRs are protected from personal liability provided that they wait 6 months from the date of the grant of representation before distribution.

To ensure that a potential applicant brings a claim in time, a standing search can be made at the Probate Registry. This will reveal whether a grant of representation to the estate in question has been issued during the preceding 12 months. If a grant has not yet been issued, the search will ensure that the searcher is notified if a grant is issued in the following 6 months. The Probate Registry will send a copy of the grant to the searcher, which will mean the applicant can ascertain the names and addresses of the PRs and any solicitor acting. In addition, they will be able to calculate the date by which they must make their claim. A standing search can be renewed.

Under IPFDA 1975, an applicant may apply to court for leave to apply out of time. However, the court's power to grant or refuse an application for leave to apply out of time is discretionary. The court will only exercise this discretion in exceptional circumstances.

3.6 Reasonable financial provision

IPFDA 1975 sets out two standards for determining what is **reasonable financial provision**, namely the:

- **Surviving spouse or surviving civil partner standard**. This is such financial provision as would be reasonable in all the circumstances of the case for a spouse or civil partner to receive, *whether or not* that provision is required for his or her maintenance
- **Ordinary standard**, which applies to all other categories of applicant. This is such financial provision as would be reasonable in all the circumstances of the case for the applicant to receive for his maintenance

3.7 Common guidelines

IPFDA 1975 sets out guidelines to assist the court in deciding whether or not reasonable financial provision has been made. These matters should be considered for every applicant and are sometimes referred to as the *common guidelines.*

The common guidelines are:

- The financial resources and needs of the applicant, other applicants and beneficiaries of the estate, both now and in the foreseeable future
- The deceased's moral obligations towards any applicant or beneficiary
- The size and nature of the estate
- The physical or mental disability of any applicant or beneficiary
- Anything else which may be relevant, including the applicant's conduct and lifetime provision by the deceased

In applying these standards, the court will take into account the facts as at the date of the hearing rather than at the date of death and the court will consider statements by the deceased in reaching its decision, eg a written statement by the deceased kept with his will. However, little weight is generally attached to a testator's reasons for excluding an applicant .

3.8 Special guidelines

There are also *special guidelines* that the court will consider for each particular category of applicant.

Spouse or civil partner	The spouse standard of reasonable financial provision applies. In addition to the common guidelines, the court will consider the age of the applicant and the duration of the marriage or civil partnership. Hence the longer the marriage or civil partnership, the stronger the claim. In addition, the court will look at the contribution the applicant has made to the welfare of the family, including looking after the home. Additionally, the court will consider what the applicant might have received if the marriage had ended on divorce, rather than on death.
Former spouse or civil partner	The ordinary standard of reasonable financial provision applies. In addition to the common guidelines, the court considers the age of the applicant and the duration of the marriage or civil partnership. The court will also consider the contribution made by the applicant to the welfare of the family, including looking after the home. In reality, claims by a former spouse or civil partner are probably only likely to succeed if the deceased was paying maintenance prior to his death.
Cohabitant	The ordinary standard of reasonable financial provision applies. In addition to the common guidelines, the court will consider the age of the applicant and the length of the cohabitation. The court will also look at the contribution made by the applicant to the welfare of the family including looking after the home and caring for the family.
Child of deceased	The ordinary standard of reasonable financial provision applies. In addition to the common guidelines, the court considers the manner in which the applicant was being, or might expect to be, educated or trained.
Person treated as child of deceased	The ordinary standard of reasonable financial provision applies. In addition to the common guidelines, the court will consider the manner in which the applicant was being, or might expect to be, educated or trained, the extent to which the deceased assumed responsibility for the child and whether or not the deceased knew the child was not his own. The court will also consider whether anyone else is legally responsible for the applicant's maintenance.
Person who is being maintained by the deceased	The ordinary standard of reasonable financial provision applies. In addition to the common guidelines, the court will consider the extent to which, and the basis upon which, the deceased assumed responsibility for the maintenance of the applicant and the duration of the maintenance prior to death.

3.9 The court's power to make orders

IPFDA 1975 sets out the orders the court can make, which include:

- Periodical payments, for any period of time.
- A lump sum payment.
- The transfer of property.
- The acquisition of property for transfer.

Additionally, the court can make an order against the deceased's 'share' of any property to which he or she was beneficially entitled as a joint tenant immediately before his death, but only if the application has been brought within six months of the issue of the grant of representation.

3.10 The effect of an order

Once made, the orders are deemed effective from the date of death.

An order may result in other beneficiaries receiving less under the will or Intestacy Rules.

The burden of an order can be placed on any part of the estate, not just on residue.

3.11 Anti-avoidance provisions

IPFDA 1975 contains anti-avoidance provisions, which are intended to prevent the provisions of IPFDA 1975 being defeated by the deceased giving away his property during his lifetime.

As a result of the provisions, the court can make an order in favour of an applicant against any property that the deceased has given away within 6 years of his death with the intention of defeating a claim under IPFDA 1975.

3.12 Practice points

The following practice points should be kept in mind:

- When advising a client who is making a will, IPFDA 1975 should be discussed and it should be ascertained whether there are any potential applicants. If there are, appropriate advice should be given.

- If a solicitor is advising PRs, he should advise them not to distribute the estate until six months have elapsed from the date the grant of representation was issued. If they distribute before this time and an applicant brings a successful claim, the PRs will be personally liable to satisfy the claim if there are insufficient assets in the estate to do so.

- If a solicitor is acting for an applicant, any claim must be brought within six months of the issue of the grant of representation.

- Beware of conflicts of interest. A solicitor should not act for an applicant if he is already acting for the PRs.

Summary

- Changes to the disposition of an estate are often made for tax advantages and can be achieved by way of a post-death variation or, less commonly, a disclaimer.
- A beneficiary who disclaims has no control over the destination of the disclaimed property.
- With a variation, the original beneficiary controls the ultimate destination of the property.
- Part of a gift cannot be disclaimed and a gift must be disclaimed before the beneficiary has received a benefit from it.
- It is possible for a beneficiary to vary part of the gift . In addition, a variation is possible if a benefit has been enjoyed from the property.
- A disclaimer is treated as a transfer of value for IHT purposes (usually as a PET by the beneficiary making the variation) unless certain conditions are met and a disposal for CGT purposes, unless certain conditions are met.
- A variation is treated as a transfer of value for IHT purposes (usually as a PET by the beneficiary making the variation) unless certain conditions are met and a disposal for CGT purposes, unless certain conditions are met.
- A life interest can be capitalised and this will not be treated as a transfer of value by the spouse/civil partner for IHT purposes.
- If the spouse capitalises the life interest, the IHT on the death of the intestate will be re-calculated on the basis that the surviving spouse/civil partner had been entitled to the capital sum on death.
- IPFDA 1975 enables certain persons who are aggrieved because they have been left out of a will, or are not inheriting on intestacy, or are dissatisfied with the amount of their inheritance, to make a claim for a benefit from the estate.
- Only certain categories of applicant are eligible to make a claim under IPFDA 1975.
- The time limit for a claim is six months from the *grant of representation*.
- The only ground for a claim is that the deceased did not make *reasonable financial provision* for the applicant and there are two standards by which this is judged.
- The court will consider the common guidelines in each case and the special guidelines in relation to each specific category of applicant when considering whether reasonable financial provision has been made.
- The court can make a number of orders which are deemed effective from the date of death.
- A solicitor needs to consider the provisions of IPFDA 1975 when advising a client on the making of a will and when advising the PRs in the administration of the estate.

Self-test questions

1 Why are disclaimers less common than variations?

2 Which of the following statements is true:

(a) A post-death variation of varies the terms of the deceased's will.
(b) A post-death variation does not vary the terms of the deceased's will.

3 Which of the following statements is correct?

(a) A variation must be made within two years of the grant of representation if the s.142 IHTA 1984 reading back effect is desired.

(b) If a varying beneficiary elects for the variation to be treated as a transfer from the deceased, they cannot elect in a similar way for CGT.

(c) A variation must be made within two years of death if the s.62 TCGA 1992 reading back effect is desired.

4 What are the grounds for making a claim under IPFDA 1975?

5 Which of the following people can make a claim against the estate of a deceased?

(a) Mother
(b) Brother
(c) 30 year old daughter
(d) Ex-wife

6 What is the time limit for making a claim under IPFDA 1975?

7 Which of the following statements is correct in relation to IPFDA 1975?

(a) In order to be eligible to apply as a cohabitee, the applicant must be able to demonstrate that he lived with the deceased for a two year period at any time before death.

(b) Civil partners can only make a claim if they can show that they were being maintained by the deceased immediately before death.

(c) In order to be successful in a claim, a child must prove that such financial provision has not been made for him as is reasonable in all the circumstances.

Answers to self-test questions

1. In the event of a disclaimer, the disclaiming beneficiary has no control over the destination of the disclaimed property.
2. (b)
3. (c)
4. There is only one ground: that the deceased did not make reasonable financial provision for the applicant.
5. (a) Only she is eligible to apply as a person being maintained by the deceased immediately before death.

   (b) Only he is eligible to apply as a person being maintained by the deceased immediately before death.

   (c) Eligible.

   (d) Eligible, although she will not be able to claim if she has remarried or is barred from claiming under the terms of the final divorce order.
6. Six months from the date of the grant, although the court has a discretionary power to extend this time limit in exceptional circumstances.
7. None of them are correct.

Example Test and Outline Solution

Example Test

Part A – Land Law & Conveyancing

Candidates **must** answer Question 1 **and** Question 2.

Question 1

You are instructed by Victoria and David Lingard in connection with their purchase of 2 Corn Road, Clifton, Bristol BS8 2PG. The purchase price is £590,000, and your clients will be funding their purchase with the assistance of a mortgage of £250,000 from Gloucester Bank plc, for whom you are also acting. Your firm holds the balance of the purchase price following the sale of Mr and Mrs Lingard's previous house in London.

You have received from the Seller's solicitor the Official Copies of the Register (**Document 1**). They have omitted to send the filed plan, but have assured you it will be sent in time for your meeting with the Buyers tomorrow, so that you can check it accords with your clients' understanding of what they are buying. You are not required to comment on this. You have also received a draft Contract, which incorporates the Standard Conditions of Sale (4th Edition) (without amendments). The draft Contract is not reproduced for the purpose of this Question.

Victoria telephoned you yesterday to arrange the meeting tomorrow. She has already sent you a copy of the estate agent's details (**Document 2**). She mentioned that she is very excited about this house as it has a studio which would be an ideal area in which she could continue her business making and selling contemporary jewellery, specialising in tension set engagement rings.

The house is currently vacant. Lewis Montgomery died last month in a boating accident and his personal representative, Gemma Groves, is selling the property.

(a) From your consideration of the Official Copies of the Register and the estate agent's details, explain what problems arise and what steps you would take on behalf of your clients to resolve those issues. **(18 marks)**

(b) Outline the steps that you will take in order to effect exchange of Contracts on behalf of your clients by telephone. Assume that each solicitor will hold their own client's/clients' part of the Contract. **(6 marks)**

(c) Following completion of the purchase, list the steps that you must take in order to perfect your clients' title to the property, the time limits within which each step must be taken, the documentation required for each step, and the consequences of failing to take such steps. **(11 marks)**

Total 35 marks

Document 1

OFFICIAL COPY OF REGISTER ENTRIES

This office copy shows the entries subsisting on the register on **1 January 2009 at 10.22.05.**

This date **must be quoted as the 'search from date' in any official search** application based on this copy.

Under s.67 of the Land Registration Act 2002 this copy is admissible in evidence to the same extent as the original.

Issued on 1 January 2009 by the Land Registry. This title is administered Gloucester District Land Registry

Land Registry

Title Number: EGL895301

Edition Date: 8 June 1994

A: Property Register

Containing the description of the registered land and the estate comprised in the Title.

COUNTY	**DISTRICT**
CITY OF BRISTOL	BRISTOL

(8 June 1994) The **Freehold** land shown and edged red on the plan of the above title filed at the Registry being 2 Corn Road, Clifton, Bristol (BS8 2PG)

B: Proprietorship Register

Stating the nature of the title, name and address of the proprietor of the land and any entries affecting the right of disposal.

Title Absolute

(8 June 1994) **Proprietor**: Lewis Montgomery of 2 Corn Road, Clifton, Bristol BS8 2PG

NOTE: The transfer to the proprietor contains a covenant to observe and perform the covenants referred to in the Charges Register and an indemnity in respect thereof.

C: Charges Register

Containing charges, incumbrances etc adversely affecting the land.

(8 June 1994) A conveyance of the land in this title dated 22 July 1941 made between (1) Arthur Kenlee Builders Limited (Vendor) and (2) George Sproston (Purchaser) contains the following covenants:

"The Purchaser with intent and so as to bind the property hereby conveyed and to benefit and protect the retained parts of the Vendor's adjoining land hereby covenants with the Vendor that he and his successors in title:

1. Will not extend the property without the consent of the Vendor.
2. Will forthwith erect and thereafter maintain a fence along the eastern boundary of the property."

****END OF REGISTER****

NOTE: A date at the beginning of an entry is the date on which the entry was made in the Register.

Document 2

FISHERWICK ESTATE AGENTS

80 Queens Road, Clifton, Bristol BS8 1QU

AWAITING PHOTO

As the Vendor's sole agents, we have pleasure in offering for sale this large detached house in a much sought-after area of Clifton.

This beautiful property comprises three large double bedrooms, three reception rooms and a stunning kitchen.

This spacious property is a very short walk away from the bars and restaurants of Clifton and very close to St. Peter's Church, which is 700 years old and steeped in local history.

Benefits include gas central heating, two bathrooms and a large rear garden, with mature shrubs and decked area.

This property is in immaculate condition throughout having been extended last year to include a large ground and first floor extension, with integral garage and studio.

Early viewing is highly recommended.

Question 2

You are acting on behalf of Shellani Sampson in connection with her proposed purchase of 4 Hill View Terrace, Swettenham Village, Cheshire CW12 6YH from Harold Goss. You have just received the Epitome of Title (**see attached**) from the solicitors acting on behalf of the Seller, together with copies of **Documents 1 and 2** referred to in the Epitome. The copy death certificate is not reproduced for the purpose of this Question.

(a) The Seller's solicitor has not sent copies of the Land Charges Search results with the Epitome of Title and you have asked him to forward these to you. List each name and the relevant periods against which you would expect the Land Charges Searches to be undertaken. **(6 marks)**

(b) Against whose name(s) will you carry out a Land Charges Search after exchange of Contracts and explain when it should be carried out. **(3 marks)**

(c) What action will you need to take in order in ensure that your client obtains a good legal and beneficial title from Harold Goss? You can assume that the 1989 Conveyance is a good root of title and that the 1952 Conveyance contains and adequate description of the property. **(6 marks)**

Total 15 marks

Document 1

Epitome of Title

relating to freehold property known as

4 Hill View Terrace, Swettenham Village, Cheshire CW12 6YH

No	EVIDENCE	DATE	DOCUMENT OR EVENT	PARTIES	MARK IF ORIGINAL TO BE HANDED OVER ON COMPLETION
1	Photocopy	07.06.1962	Conveyance	Edward Brampton (1) James McGovern (2)	Yes
2	Photocopy	05.09.1989	Conveyance	James McGovern (1) Harold Goss & Margaret Goss (2)	Yes
3	Photocopy	02.01.1995	Death Certificate	Margaret Goss	Yes

Document 1

THIS CONVEYANCE is made the *7th* day of *June* One thousand nine hundred and sixty two **BETWEEN** EDWARD BRAMPTON of 4 Hill View Terrace, Swettenham Village, Cheshire CW12 6YH (hereinafter referred to as 'the Vendor') of the one part and JAMES McGOVERN of 1 Station Road, Congleton, Cheshire CW1 7GH (hereinafter referred to as 'the Purchaser') of the other part.

WHEREAS the Vendor is seised of the property hereinafter described for an estate in fee simple absolute in possession free from incumbrances and has agreed to sell the same to the Purchaser for the sum of Fourteen Thousand pounds.

NOW THIS DEED WITNESSETH as follows:

In pursuance of the said agreement and in consideration of the sum of Fourteen thousand pounds (£14,000) paid by the Purchaser to the Vendor (the receipt of which sum the Vendor hereby acknowledges) the Vendor as beneficial owner **HEREBY CONVEYS UNTO** the Purchaser **ALL THAT** piece or parcel of land situate at 4 Hill View Terrace, Swettenham Village, Cheshire CW12 6YH together with the buildings erected thereon as the same is shown more particularly delineated edged in red on the plan annexed to a conveyance made on the 11th June 1952 between George Brownfield as seller of the one part and Mary Louise Butterworth as buyer of the other part **TO HOLD** the same **UNTO** the Purchaser in fee simple.

IT IS HEREBY CERTIFIED that the transaction hereby effected does not form part of a larger transaction or series of transactions in respect of which the amount or value or aggregate amount or value of the consideration exceeds £15,000.

IN WITNESS whereof the Vendor has set his hand and seal the day and year first before written.

SIGNED SEALED AND DELIVERED as
a deed by **EDWARD BRAMPTON**

Document 2

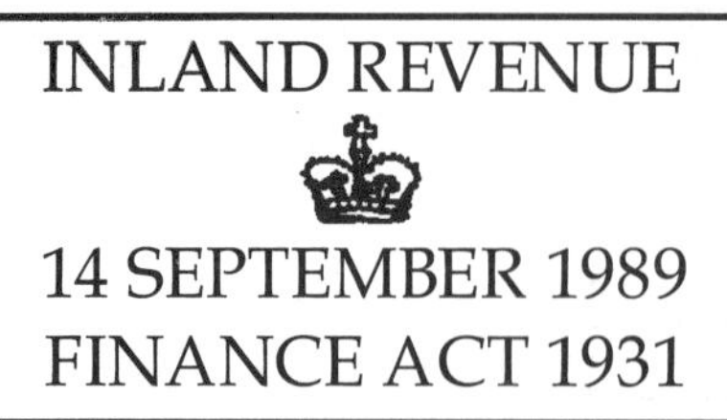

THIS DEED OF CONVEYANCE is made the *5th* day of *September* One thousand nine hundred and eighty nine **BETWEEN** (1) JAMES McGOVERN of 4 Hill View Terrace, Swettenham Village, Cheshire CW12 6YH (hereinafter referred to as 'the Vendor') and (2) HAROLD GOSS and MARGARET GOSS both of 5 Bank Street, Nottingham NG1 3DF (hereinafter referred to as 'the Purchasers')

WHEREAS

(a) The Vendor is seised of the property hereinafter described for an estate in fee simple in possession.

(b) The Vendor has agreed with the Purchasers for the sale to them of the same for Twenty Four Thousand Pounds.

NOW THIS DEED WITNESSETH AS FOLLOWS:

IN pursuance of the said agreement and in consideration of the sum of Twenty Four Thousand Pounds (£24,000) paid by the Purchasers to the Vendor (the receipt whereof the Vendor hereby acknowledges) the Vendor as beneficial owner **HEREBY CONVEY UNTO** the Purchasers **ALL THAT** piece or parcel of land situate at 4 Hill View Terrace, Swettenham Village, Cheshire CW12 6YH together with the buildings erected thereon as the same is shown more particularly delineated edged in red on the plan annexed to a conveyance made on 11th June 1952 between George Brownfield as seller of the one part and Mary Louise Butterworth as buyer of the other part **TO HOLD** the same **UNTO** the Purchasers in fee simple as beneficial tenants in common in equal shares.

IN WITNESS whereof the parties hereto have hereunto executed this Deed the day and year first written.

SIGNED SEALED AND DELIVERED
as a deed by said JAMES McGOVERN

SIGNED SEALED AND DELIVERED
as a deed by said HAROLD GOSS

SIGNED SEALED AND DELIVERED
as a deed by said MARGARET GOSS

Part B – Wills, Probate & Administration

Candidates **must** answer Question 3 **and** Question 4.

Question 3

You have been instructed by Richard Farley and Stephen Antrobus, accountants at the firm of Farley & Co, Church Street, Brighton BN2 8HT. They have both been appointed as executors and trustees under the Will of Rose Burns, who died on 1 December 2009, aged 72.

A copy of Rose's Will dated 2 August 2006 is attached.

Rose's assets at the date of death were as follows:

Assets	*Value at date of death*
	£
House – 13 Whitechapel Street, Brighton BN13 8UB	300,000
Bank and building society accounts	400,000
Personal chattels (including two William IV mahogany library chairs, which are clearly identifiable)	50,000
Portfolio of shares	20,000
Cottage in Dorset, which was owned jointly with her son Rupert as beneficial joint tenants	250,000

All assets were held her sole name except for the cottage in Dorset.

Rose was divorced in 1981 and did not remarry. Her son, Rupert Burns, died three weeks before Rose, aged 46. He left a widow, Amelia, and two daughters, Martha (aged 7) and Mia (aged 8). Amelia is 7 months pregnant. Rupert was a successful actor, living in London. Amelia's father died in 2004, leaving all his estate in trust for Martha and Mia.

One of Rose's daughters, Hannah Wentworth (aged 49), a history lecturer, lives in North Yorkshire with her husband, Jack, and her son William Wentworth (aged 19), from her previous marriage to Dylan Wentworth, who died in March 2007. Rose's other daughter, Grace (aged 50), is a doctor living in France. Rose had not had any contact with Grace for ten years before her death.

On 8 May 2003 Rose gave £351,000 to Hannah. Rose made no other lifetime gifts.

Rose Burn's Will

THIS IS THE LAST WILL of me ROSE BURNS of 13 Whitechapel Street Brighton BN13 8UB dated 2 August 2006 by which I REVOKE all former Wills and testamentary dispositions

1. I APPOINT my son RUPERT BURNS of The Lodge, Mayfair Mews, London W1 OX2 RICHARD FARLEY of Farley & Co, Church Street, Brighton BN2 8HT and STEPHEN ANTROBUS also of Farley & Co, Church Street, Brighton BN2 8HT to be the executors and trustees of this my Will
2. I GIVE the sum of £20,000 to my said son RUPERT BURNS
3. I GIVE the sum of £20,000 to my daughter HANNAH WENTWORTH
4. I GIVE my two William IV mahogany library chairs to my daughter Hannah's husband
5. SUBJECT TO the payment of my debts funeral and testamentary expenses I GIVE the residue of my estate to my grandson William Wentworth if he attains the age of 25

Signed by the testatrix in our joint presence)
and then by us in hers:) Rose Burns

Witnesses:

Martin Davidson

Martin Davidson
9 Bank Road
Brighton

Stella Rimmer

Stella Rimmer
14 Church Lane
Brighton

(a) Explain who is entitled to apply for the grant of representation to Rose's estate and which type of grant of representation will be applied for. **(2 marks)**

(b) Explain the beneficial entitlement to Rose's estate. **(13 marks)**

(c) Grace believes she should benefit from her mother's estate. Explain to what extent, if any, Grace could make a claim against her mother's estate. **(4 marks)**

(d) If William were to die one month after Rose, explain how this would affect the beneficial entitlement to Rose's estate, if at all. **(6 marks)**

(e) Calculate, with explanation, the inheritance tax payable as a result of Rose's death, if any, in respect of the lifetime gift that Rose made to Hannah. Please note that the Nil Rate Band for tax year 08/09 is £312, 000. **(10 marks)**

Total 35 marks

Question 4

Jessica Squires has instructed you in connection with the estate of her late husband, Quentin Squires, who died last month. Quentin had never made a Will.

Quentin's only surviving relatives are Jessica and his nieces, Allegra and Summer, both aged 17. Allegra and Summer are the daughters of his sister, Verity, who died last year.

Jessica tells you that Quentin had assets in his sole name at the date of his death amounting to approximately £1,000,000. They also owned their house as beneficial joint tenants.

Explain who is beneficially entitled to Quentin's estate. *Candidates do not need to calculate the actual amount each beneficiary will receive.*

(15 marks)

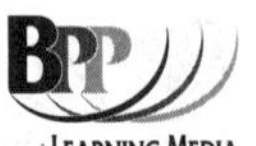

Outline Solution to Example Test

Question 1

(a) **18 marks**

Proprietorship Register

(i) Lewis Montgomery is shown as the Registered Proprietor.

(ii) He has died and Gemma Groves is selling the property in her capacity as PR.

(iii) We need to ask the Seller's solicitors to send an official copy of the grant of representation appointing Gemma Groves as PR, to prove that she has authority to sell.

(iv) This will also be needed in order to register the Transfer to our clients.

Charges Register

Restrictive covenant

(i) The Charges Register shows a restrictive covenant not to extend without consent.

(ii) Under the rule in *Tulk v Moxhay 1848*, it is likely that our clients will be bound in equity by the burden of the restrictive covenant as it is negative in substance, they have notice of it (it is registered), it benefits the dominant tenement and it is deemed that it was intended to run with the land.

(iii) The property has been extended, according to the estate agent's particulars, to include a large ground and first floor extension, with integral garage and studio.

(iv) Will need to check whether consent for the extension was obtained from the person with benefit of the covenant.

(v) If consent was not obtained, there will have been a breach. Ask the Seller to obtain restrictive covenant indemnity insurance in event of claim by the person with the benefit of the covenant – this is the best option.

(vi) Alternatively, to seek retrospective consent from person with the benefit of the covenant or, as a last resort, to make an application to the Lands Tribunal for discharge, if insurance not available and retrospective consent cannot be obtained.

Positive covenant

(i) There is also a positive covenant noted in the Charges Register to erect and thereafter maintain a fence along the eastern boundary of the property.

(ii) The burden of positive covenants does not run with the land, in law or in equity.

(iii) However, it is clear from the Proprietorship Register that Lewis Montgomery gave an indemnity covenant in respect of the covenants noted in the Charges Register.

(iv) The Buyers would normally be required to give an indemnity on transfer to them, according to SCS 4.6.4.

(v) However, as the Registered Proprietor has died, SCS 4.6.4 unlikely to apply as chain of indemnity covenants breaks with death.

Other

Extension

(i) Lewis Montgomery may have needed planning permission for building works as they fall within the meaning of 'development'.

(ii) It is unlikely that the extension falls within the scope of the GPDO 1995 (within 15% of the original volume of the property), as it is described as 'large' in the estate agents particulars, but if it does planning permission will not have been needed.

(iii) Check whether planning permission was obtained. If not this will need to be remedied by the Seller.

(iv) Lewis Montgomery will have needed building regulations consent for the works; ask the Seller for the building regulations certificate.

Victoria's business

May need planning permission for change of use for Victoria's business making and selling jewellery. Advise clients accordingly.

St Peter's Church

The Property is close to a church. The owner might have a liability to contribute towards the cost of chancel repairs, particularly as this is an old church. Any such liability attaches to the land and is, at present, an overriding interest. Consider carrying out a ChancelCheck search or obtaining insurance against the risk of liability of repairs.

(b) **6 marks**

(i) Formula B will be used.

(ii) Both solicitors confirm that they hold their client's/clients' signed contracts.

(iii) The Buyers' solicitor confirms they hold the deposit.

(iv) A completion date is agreed and inserted in the Contract.

(v) The Contract is dated.

(vi) Each solicitor undertakes to send their Contract (and deposit in the case of the Buyers) that day.

(c) **11 marks**

(i) Pay SDLT – submit Land Transaction Return (SDLT1) within 30 days of completion, with payment.

(ii) Failure to do so may result in a penalty/interest.

(iii) Obtain certificate of payment of SDLT: SDLT 5.

(iv) Make application for registration to the Land Registry using form AP1

(v) Within priority period of OS1 search result (30 working days), which was carried out before completion.

(vi) Include Transfer (TR1), Buyers' executed mortgage deed, SDLT 5, official copy grant of representation, form D1 disclosing interests known to override (e.g. chancel repair liability if applicable), Land Registry fee.

(vii) Failure to do so: legal title will not pass to Buyers/priority will be lost if not registered within priority period given by OS1 search.

Question 2

(a) **6 marks**

George Brownfield	1926 – 1952
Mary Louise Butterworth	1952 – 1962
Edward Brampton	1952 – 1962
James McGovern	1962 – 1989
Harold Goss	1989 – 2009
Margaret Goss	1989 – 1995

(b) **3 marks**

(i) Against the name of the current seller: Harold Goss.

(ii) A clear search is conclusive in favour of the Buyer and gives 15 working days' protection.

(iii) If Shellani completes within this period she takes free from any entries made after the date of the certificate and so the K15 search should be done shortly before completion is expected to take place.

(c) **6 marks**

(i) Legal title held by Harold and Margaret Goss (co-owners) as joint tenants and so passes by survivorship.

(ii) Need to see official copy of the death certificate of Margaret Goss to prove that she is dead and that the legal title has passed; this will also be required on an application for first registration on behalf on the Buyer.

(iii) Beneficial title held as tenants in common.

(iv) As evidenced in the 1989 Conveyance.

(v) Survivorship did not therefore apply to Margaret's beneficial interest on her death.

(vi) Insist second trustee is appointed to take receipt of purchase monies and overreach beneficial interests.

Question 3

(a) **2 marks**

As Rupert predeceased Rose the appointment of him as executor failed; Richard Farley and Stephen Antrobus are entitled to apply for a grant of probate, as they are validly appointed as executors in the Will.

(b) **13 marks**

(i) Rose's Will dated 12 August 2006 appears to be valid, as executed in accordance with s.9 WA 1837 and nothing to suggest lack of capacity or intention or undue influence etc.

(ii) All her property passes under her Will and nothing passes outside the Will. This includes the cottage in Dorset which passed to Rose by survivorship on Rupert's death as it was owned by them as beneficial joint tenants. The Dorset cottage therefore forms past of the residue of Rose's estate.

(iii) **Clause 2**

Rupert has predeceased Rose. This pecuniary legacy to him is saved from lapse by s.33 WA 1837 and therefore the sum of £20,000 passes to Martha, Mia and the unborn child in equal shares, vested, although they will not be able to give receipt for the monies until they are 18 (there is no infant receipt clause in the will) and so the monies will be held by the trustees until such time.

(iv) **Clause 3**

This is a pecuniary legacy to Hannah and, as she is alive, she receives £20,000, vested.

(v) **Clause 4**

This is a specific legacy and the subject matter is sufficiently certain and forms part of the estate at death. However, the gift is construed as a gift to Hannah's husband at the date of the will. This was Dylan and, as he predeceased Rose, the gift lapses and the chairs will pass in accordance with the gift of residue. Jack does not receive the chairs.

(vi) **Clause 5**

As William is 19, the residue of Rose's estate (including the chairs and the Dorset cottage), after the payment of debts, funeral and testamentary expenses, will be held by the trustees pending William reaching the age of 25 – William has a contingent interest, which means that he does not receive the assets until he reaches 25, at which time the assets will vest in, and be transferred to, him.

(c) **4 marks**

Grace is eligible to make a claim under IPFDA 1975 as a child of the deceased. Claim must be made within six months of the grant of probate. Grace must be able to show that reasonable financial provision has not been made for her. The ordinary standard applies i.e. what is reasonable for her to receive for her maintenance. Need to consider the guidelines as to what constitutes reasonable provision, which includes, amongst other things, how the applicant might expect to be educated or trained. Given Madeleine's age and the fact that she is a doctor, it is unlikely that her claim would succeed.

(d) **6 marks**

William's interest is contingent upon him reaching the age of 25. If he dies one moth after Rose, he will not have attained the contingency and, as there is no substitution provision in the Will, the residuary gift lapses and the residue passes in accordance with the intestacy rules – there will be a partial intestacy of Rose's estate. S.46 AEA 1935 lists the categories entitled in order of priority. Rose has no surviving spouse. Rose's issue are therefore entitled on the statutory trusts. This means that Hannah and Grace each receive one-third, vested as they are aged over 18. Rupert's children (including the unborn child) receive his one-third share (eg a one-ninth share each), contingently upon reaching the age of 18.

(e) **10 marks**

May 2003 gift

(i) Rose had two unused annual exemptions (2 x £3,000) from tax years 2002/3 and 2003/4 to set against the gift. The net gift is therefore £345,000.

(ii) This is a PET.

(iii) There was no IHT payable when the PET was made, but it has become chargeable as a result of Rose's death within 7 years of making it.

(iv) NRB at the date of death was £325,000.

(v) Therefore first £325,000 of PET, which has become chargeable, is taxed at 0%.

(vi) Balance of £20,000 is taxed at 40% = £8,000.

(vii) As death occurs more than 3 years after transfer, tapering relief applies.

(viii) Death occurred between 6 and 7 years after the date of the PET.

(ix) Therefore the IHT payable is reduced by 80%

(x) IHT payable = £1,600.

Question 4

15 marks

- The house passes to Jessica automatically by survivorship, independently of the Intestacy Rules
- As it was owned by them as beneficial joint tenants.
- No Will therefore devolution of all other assets governed by the Intestacy Rules, as set out in s.46 AEA 1925.
- Quentin was survived by spouse, no issue, but issue of his deceased sister.
- Therefore, Jessica, as surviving spouse, receives:
- All Quentin's personal chattels outright.
- A statutory legacy of £450,000 outright.
- Half of the residue outright (ascertained after payment of above and debts, funeral and testamentary expenses)
- Because of application of statutory trusts
- Allegra and Summer inherit the other half of residue in equal shares.
- As surviving issue of Quentin's deceased sister, Verity, who would have been entitled if alive
- Which means they each receive ¼ of residue of estate.
- Contingently upon reaching the age of 18, as they are 17.

Indexes

B

C

LEARNING MEDIA

R

S

B

C